Second Edition

Arguments
and
Arguing

Second Edition

Arguments
and
Arguing

The Products and Process
of Human Decision Making

Thomas A. Hollihan
University of Southern California

Kevin T. Baaske
California State University, Los Angeles

WAVELAND

PRESS, INC.

Long Grove, Illinois

For information about this book, contact:
Waveland Press, Inc.
4180 IL Route 83, Suite 101
Long Grove, IL 60047-9580
(847) 634-0081
info@waveland.com
www.waveland.com

Credit, p. 89, "A Model for Systems Analysis," from pages 3–4 of *Public Policy Decision-Making: Systems Analysis and Comparative Advantage Debate* by Bernard L. Brock. Copyright © 1973 by Harper & Row Publishers, Inc. Reprinted by permission of HarperCollins Publishers, Inc.

ISBN 1-57766-362-4

Printed in the United States of America

7 6 5 4 3 2

CONTENTS

9   Refuting Arguments   **159**

PART II
ARGUMENTATION IN SPECIALIZED FIELDS   179

10   Academic Debate: Overview   **181**

11   Academic Debate: Additional Insights   **203**

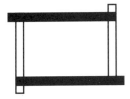

PREFACE

Arguments and Arguing: The Products and Process of Human Decision Making, Second Edition, is intended to meet the needs of students enrolled in undergraduate courses in argumentation. Because the text also introduces students to rhetorical theory, and to several of the most important theorists, the book may also be suitable for courses in rhetoric. The book offers chapters on arguing in specialized fields and contexts, including academic debate, courts of law, politics, business and organizations, and interpersonal communication. Thus it may also be of interest to those seeking materials for courses in these areas.

WHY THIS BOOK AT THIS TIME?

As is the case with many textbooks, the first edition of this book was written because we both taught argumentation at the undergraduate and graduate levels and we were frustrated that the books available to us did not suit the approach that we took in our classes. We attempted to create a book that drew from recent developments in argumentation theory and research, and especially the narrative paradigm. The first edition of the book found a loyal following. Although authors such as John Gresham and Dan Brown never had to move over to make room for us on the *New York Times* best-seller list, we often ran into colleagues at academic conferences who told us that they had discovered the book and that their students liked it. As the years passed, however, these colleagues became increasingly surly with us because we had not yet produced a second edition.

Argumentation texts work best if the examples are current and relevant to the experiences of students. In the case of our book, some of the examples no longer seemed relevant to readers who could claim firsthand familiarity only with the social and political issues that had surfaced during the past decade. There are, of course, exceptions. In the first edition we wrote about President Bush and the war in Iraq. In this edition we continue to write about *a* President Bush and *a* war in Iraq. In the first book we proclaimed the Los Angeles Lakers as the best team in basketball over the past decade. Now, another decade later, perhaps that claim still fits too. Nonetheless, we have attempted to update our examples so that they will appeal to today's students.

THE ORGANIZATIONAL PLAN

The primary focus of the book is left unchanged. The second edition, like the first, is organized into two parts. Part I discusses the general principles and theories of argumentation. It introduces the narrative approach to argumentation and draws heavily on Walter Fisher's narrative paradigm. We also introduce Kenneth Burke's dramatistic theory of communication and especially his discussions of the importance of symbols as instruments for communication. To establish the claim that arguments are a naturally occurring dimension of communication we cite the work of Wayne Brockriede. To support the notion that argumentation fundamentally concerns human values, we draw upon the work of Milton Rokeach. To introduce the principles of audience expectations we include a brief discussion of Chaim Perelman and Lucie Olbrechts-Tyteca. To provide a theoretical foundation for an approach to argumentation that stresses the importance of attending to the different characteristics of argumentation across a wide range of discursive communities and fields we include a discussion of the writings of Stephen Toulmin. The remaining chapters in part I look at how arguments are actually researched, structured, and developed. We examine alternative techniques for analysis, different types of arguments, and the grounds for establishing arguments. Finally, we offer suggestions both for creating, organizing, and refuting arguments.

In part II we introduce the different characteristics and requirements for creating arguments in specialized field contexts. One chapter familiarizes students with some of the basic principles of academic debate; a second offers students additional information about some of the more advanced theories and practices of debate for those who will engage in tournament-type debating. The remaining chapters discuss the unique requirements for arguing in politics and political campaigns, the courtroom, business or organizations, and interpersonal conversations.

ACKNOWLEDGEMENTS

This book has been influenced by many people including those who taught us about arguments, our colleagues (with whom we have argued!), and our many students whom we have taught how to argue. We are reluctant to begin naming people individually because we will surely omit someone, but there are some friends whom we must explicitly thank: Jim Klumpp, Walt Fisher, Geoff Cowan, Stephen O'Leary, Randy Lake, Gordon Stables, David Damus, and Tom Goodnight have served as terrific colleagues who give meaning to the term "collegiality." We are grateful for the helpful comments of the reviewers on the first edition: Jeffrey Bineham, Pat Ganer, Steven Goldzwig, Dale Herbeck, Jack Kay, and Robert Powell. In addition, our thanks go to Neil and Carol Rowe and Jeni Ogilvie at Waveland Press for their roles in producing the second edition.

We would also like to thank our families for their patience and support and for the excellent argumentation practices that they have enabled us to "live" and to observe. Patti Riley, Alexandra and Sean Hollihan, Nancy and Megan Baaske, these are people who have really learned how to hold their own in arguments with us, and we love and respect them for it.

T.A.H.
K.T.B.
Los Angeles, California

Part I

Principles
of Argumentation

Our goal in this book is to demonstrate the important role that arguments play in helping you understand complex issues, form opinions, shape decisions, and resolve disagreements. We therefore present argumentation as an essential dimension of the human communication process. Part I of the book introduces you to argumentation theory and principles and part II considers the unique characteristics of argumentation in specialized fields or contexts.

In chapter 1 we discuss human reliance on symbols to create and share meanings. Because humans create different meanings and hold different opinions, the urge to argue is natural. This chapter focuses on the different meanings of the term *argument*, the importance of argumentation in decision making, and the role that our values play in the arguments we develop. Finally, chapter 1 discusses the importance of ethics in argumentation.

Chapter 2 examines the stories people use to structure and create their arguments. These stories help people understand and evaluate arguments, and they provide an important means for using arguments to explore complex issues.

Chapter 3 makes the case that because arguments are typically generated to influence someone's opinions or actions and are shaped by human values, arguers should consider the beliefs or values of their audience when creating their claims.

In chapter 4 we focus on the language that gives life to arguments. Specifically, this chapter looks at the use of linguistic devices in the creation and evaluation of stories.

In chapter 5 we consider the role that argumentation plays in the development of critical thinking skills. This chapter discusses different strategies used in argumentation analysis and offers recommendations that will sharpen your analytical skills.

Chapter 6 discusses different types of arguments and focuses on the differences between inductive and deductive claims. This chapter also introduces the syllogism and offers insights into how arguments can be diagrammed.

In chapter 7 we turn our attention to the grounds for argument. We include here a discussion of how arguments are discovered and how they are evaluated. This chapter considers the different types of grounds available to arguers and also contains a brief discussion of the unique challenge that the use of statistical support poses to advocates.

Chapters 8 and 9 are companion chapters. In chapter 8 we focus on the process of building arguments. The chapter discusses the importance of research, offers recommendations for how to most effectively conduct research, suggests strategies for note taking, and gives advice on how to organize your findings into arguments. Chapter 9 then focuses on how to refute arguments, or the process of undermining the argumentation claims that have been advanced by others. This chapter also discusses some very common fallacies (arguments that are logically flawed) and provides advice on how fallacies can be identified.

By the time you have finished part I of *Arguments and Arguing* you should have a well-formed understanding of the component parts and principles of argumentation. This groundwork should prepare you for the discussion of the unique traits of argumentation in specialized settings offered in part II.

ARGUMENTATION AS A
HUMAN SYMBOLIC ACTIVITY

The feature that most distinguishes humans from other creatures is their capacity for using *symbols*. Suzanne Langer declared, "[Language is] . . . that great systematic symbolism . . . that sets men apart from their zoological brethren. The line between animals and men is, I think, precisely the language line."[1] Symbols can be defined as special types of signs. As the name implies, "signs call attention to significances: they relate to what has been perceived; they point to, indicate, or denote something other than themselves."[2] Symbols are the primary building blocks of our language system; they allow us to name objects, emotions, and actions, and to share our thoughts and feelings with others. The ability to share in a symbol system permits us to build social communities and to solve problems jointly in order to improve the quality of our lives. This symbolic capacity also puts us in touch with the past. Through the sharing of significant symbols (both orally in the form of stories and through personal journals, books, manuscripts, and even films), we learn of the events, values, and experiences of those who lived before us. Thus, humans have the complex and sophisticated ability to symbolically experience the past and to anticipate the future.

As symbol users we are constantly seeking ways to improve the quality of our lives. No matter how satisfying our current situation, we are apt to imagine ways in which our lives, our society, and our world can be improved. Much of our symbolic "tinkering" is designed to achieve such improvements. We inevitably will also encounter problems that demand resolution as we find ourselves

3

interacting and negotiating our experiences and our needs with members of our family, friends, teachers, coworkers, and employers. The complex web of inter-personal and professional relationships that we must create and sustain poses new problems and issues that must be resolved if we are to enjoy harmonious and productive lives.

Many of the problems that we encounter are not only ours personally—they are also shared social problems that we understand and relate to because of our intrinsic capacity to use symbols. For example, in the course of our life we encounter illnesses and diseases that cause us pain and suffering. We also observe how illnesses and diseases diminish the quality of, and even end, the lives of loved ones, neighbors, friends, and colleagues. Experiencing such suffer-ing motivates us to search for cures and to symbolize about the importance of healthy lifestyles. Likewise, we see and hear about problems in our schools and are motivated to search for strategies to improve the quality of our educational system. We observe the personal and social destruction caused by drug abuse; as a result, we come together individually and socially to discuss alternative solu-tions. We see damage to our environment, and we look for ways to conserve and better manage our resources. Our attention is captured and our fears are aroused by terrorist acts, and we are thus motivated to find ways to better pro-tect ourselves so that we may lead safer lives. In all of these activities, we use symbols to name the problems that we face, to develop common understand-ings, and to propose and evaluate solutions.

Because humans are fundamentally social beings, we derive satisfaction from our interactions with others. Throughout history humans have improved their condition in life by pooling their knowledge and sharing their discoveries with each other. Despite this instinctive pull to interact with other people and to build social communities, we often pursue objectives that seem fundamentally incompatible with those that are pursued by others. In personal and public lives, in relationships between friends and lovers, and in relationships between nations and cultures, the problems that we confront sometimes seem so great as to be insolvable and beyond our ability to find a suitable compromise or to reach an amicable accommodation.

From personal experience as well as from the accumulated understanding of history, we have learned that when communication fails and people cannot reach accommodation with each other, the potential for conflict and even war increases dramatically. We have also learned, however, that the situations that spark conflict will never disappear. Learning how to identify, analyze, name, reach understanding about, and then solve the problems that we individually and collectively face is essential if we wish to live in harmony.

This book provides the communication skills required for human problem solving and decision making and for the maintenance of effective and harmoni-ous social relations. This book is about *arguments*—the claims that people make when they are asserting their opinions and supporting their beliefs—and *argu-ing*—the process of resolving differences of opinion through communication.

SENSES OF THE TERM *ARGUMENT*

Two different, but equally important, senses of the term *argument*[3] corre-spond to two of the most important objectives for the use of arguments: effective decision making and the desire to achieve social harmony. The first, which can be called *argument1*, refers to the claims that people make. As we have mentioned, when people encounter problems, they seek solutions. To find solutions they must consider the causes of the problems, and they must weigh the costs and benefits of different solutions. Advances in all aspects of human intellectual life evidence the creativity and the reasoning capacity of humans as they reach deci-sions. Our intense desire to understand our world and to improve our condition in it combined with our ability to reason and to evaluate opinions through argu-ment prompt us to assert our knowledge claims about the world that we inhabit. Then, we continually find ourselves testing and challenging these knowledge claims as they are subjected to new events, new information, new problems, and new interactions with others who may see the world differently than we do.

We know that people respond to problems in a variety of ways. As a result of differences in their experience, culture, education, values, interests, objec-tives, economic circumstances, and so forth, people will isolate and assign prior-ity to different problems and will propose different solutions. The problems that are of greatest concern to well-clothed, well-fed, and well-housed Americans might seem trivial to impoverished citizens from Africa, who may be struggling to find access to clean drinking water.

Even within the same culture and/or political community, profound differ-ences can be found. Political liberals and conservatives have deep differences of opinion both about the problems that they believe are most important in society and about the possible solutions to those problems. Likewise, those who adhere to fundamentalist Christian doctrine often hold markedly different theological beliefs than do those who follow more liberal or reformed religious doctrines. Some of these differences of opinion may be highly technical in nature, as is the case, for example, when scientists argue about alternative approaches to the con-duct of their research or when literary or visual arts critics comment on the value and/or meaning of a particular artistic creation. We are thus exposed to myriad alternative arguments and symbolically expressed claims each day of our lives.

In a robust, pluralistic, and democratic society these different claims and opinions compete for our attention and acceptance. We sort through them all and manage to form our own beliefs and to determine our own course of action because we come to understand that not all opinions or claims are deemed to be equal. We grant some opinions and some arguments more credibility than we do others. Our differences cause us to identify and form opinions in unique ways, and those differences also cause us to evaluate arguments differently.

The "marketplace" of ideas is thus a marketplace of competing arguments, where "sellers"—arguers hawking their worldviews—seek to find "buyers" who will accept their claims. The argumentative marketplace, much like the eco-nomic marketplace of modern capitalism, is not always a place of free and fair competition. Not all arguments are given an equal opportunity to be aired or considered, and some arguments are much more likely to receive a favorable hearing than are others. Particular argumentative positions may be more likely to be presumed as true because, for example, they are advocated by persons perceived to have greater competence or credibility, because many people already believe them, or because they have been accepted as probably true for a long period of time. Some arguments are not given a "fair" hearing, perhaps because they represent distinctly minority viewpoints, because they are not accepted by the perceived experts, or because they counter accepted historical understandings. Even though the argumentative marketplace may be less than perfect, arguments *do* compete against each other. Some arguments will win support and perhaps gain wide public agreement, while other arguments will fall by the wayside and eventually be forgotten. Why some arguments win support while others fail is among the primary issues discussed in this book.

The second sense of the term argument, which can be called *argument2*, refers not to the statements and claims that people make, but rather to the type of interactions in which these claims are developed. This sense of the term *argument* refers to an interaction characterized by disagreement. To argue is to have a dispute with someone. From this perspective, an argument does not exist until some person perceives what is happening as an argument.[4] Most textbooks in argumentation emphasize the first sense of the term argument and not the second sense. These books primarily want to help people learn how to become better arguers—meaning more insightful or analytical arguers. While this is also one of our primary goals, we believe that the second sense of the term argument is also important. The ability to conduct a civilized and polite argument with someone—the ability to argue and disagree with others while also managing to protect your relationship with them—is one of the most important things that people must learn.

The two senses of the term argument are:

Argument1: Claims that people make.
Example: Pharmaceutical companies have a moral obligation to make anti-AIDS drug therapies available to the citizens of poor African nations at an affordable price.

Argument2: Types of interactions in which people engage.
Example: The dispute that would occur when someone disagreed with the above stated claim. For instance, someone could respond to the claim offered above by arguing that pharmaceutical companies are profit-seeking enterprises that would not have an incentive to engage in expensive research on new drug therapies if they could not sell their products for a profit. Or, they might argue that it is unfair for some people (e.g., those suffering from AIDS in developed countries) to have to pay more for their prescription drugs in order to subsidize the drug companies so that they could sell their products more inexpensively in poor nations.

It is possible to make arguments (argument1) without engaging in disputes or disagreements (argument2). If we agreed on the need to assure access to affordable anti-AIDS drugs in Africa, for example, there would be no argument2. However, it is not possible to have disputes (argument2) without making knowledge claims (argument1). Disagreements are therefore expressed through argument1.

The distinction offered here between argument1 and argument2 is important because it illustrates that argumentation is not merely a problem-solving capability. Argumentation is a very basic social and communication skill, and it has profound importance for the quality and character of our interactions with others.

Many people have been taught and have come to believe that arguments are unhealthy, destructive of human relationships, and thus should be avoided. Indeed, to describe someone as "argumentative" is generally not considered flattering. Those who are too quick to argue, too intense or passionate in their arguments, or too unwilling to surrender their positions when confronted by superior arguments are often viewed as disagreeable or even as unpleasant people.[5] Although the U.S. culture is certainly more argumentative and more confrontational than some other cultures (e.g., most Asian cultures), even among people living in the United States there seems to be a strong presumption that arguments are not good for human relationships. The linguist, Deborah Tannen, laments that an "argument culture" causes people to "approach the world—and the people in it—in an adversarial frame of mind."[6] Tannen protests that this human tendency toward argument accentuates differences, discourages compromise, falsely polarizes opinions, and encourages aggressive behavior. Although Tannen does not mention it, we cannot help but note the irony that exists when she offers such forceful arguments to make her case about the dangers and negative consequences of this argument culture. Given the nature of our book, readers will not be surprised to learn that we disagree with most of the arguments that Tannen advances.

While Tannen worries that humans are too quick to argue, we believe that our language system actually conditions us for analysis and gives us the tools to reach agreement. We believe that arguing can be—and often is—healthy both for relationships and for societies. People argue to negotiate their social perspectives with others and to enhance their understanding of complex problems. They argue to resolve their disagreements and problems and to make tough decisions about how to move forward. The problem, as we see it, is not that arguments per se are unhealthy; rather, too many people have never learned how to argue in a constructive and socially beneficial fashion. Our goal for this book is thus to help students learn some strategies and techniques that will enable them to improve their argumentation skills and to argue constructively. Constructive arguments permit disagreements to surface so that people can examine alternative ways of viewing problems, identify different solutions, and select from the competing positions those that are most compelling.

ARGUMENTATION AND INDIVIDUAL DECISION MAKING

We are challenged every day to make decisions in our personal lives. Some of these decisions are small and relatively insignificant; others are major and will end up shaping our lives. Should I go out with my friends or stay home and study? What college should I attend? What should be my major? Should I buy a car? Do I have the money to take the vacation that I have planned? For whom should I vote? Should I accept the job offer that will require me to move across the country and away from my friends and family? All of these decisions, and thousands like them that we make every day, test our analytical and argumentative abilities. Whenever we are compelled to carefully consider alternative choices and to make decisions, we make use of arguments. Thus, as a problem-solving activity, argumentation may involve decisions and choices that are distinctly personal in nature, many of which we might not even bother to disclose to our friends or families.

Often, however, we are called upon to discuss and even to account for our decisions. In such discussions we explain our actions to those people whose opinions matter to us. We want them to understand why we made the choices that we made, and often we seek their approval and respect for our decisions and our reasoning processes. We make our choices based on our understanding of the unique problems that we face, our knowledge and view of the world, and our goals and values. We strive to be rational, and we want others to validate our rationality and to confirm that our choices were, in fact, the right ones. Depending on the nature of the decision, we may be accountable to a wide range of different people. For example, most of us are accountable to our parents because even after we are adults, we are driven by the desire to please them and to make them proud of us. We are also accountable to our lovers and spouses, to other family members, to friends, to teachers, to coworkers, and to our employers. Thus, even intensely personal decisions may be argued or reasoned out with an assumed audience in mind.

ARGUMENTATION AND DEMOCRATIC DECISION MAKING

The ability to argue is a fundamental survival skill for life in a democracy. The mastery of subject matter knowledge, the ability to reason and articulate our opinions, and the ability to defend them when others may disagree with us become important to the empowerment of us as deliberating citizens. Democratic political systems assume that citizens have the knowledge and the ability to decide complex issues and to evaluate competing arguments involving both values and public policy. The continued health and vitality of any democratic government depend on the respect that citizens have for each other and for a democratic process that permits people to express their opinions, register their disagreements, evaluate the alternatives available to them, and then select a policy and move forward. A democratic political system requires an informed, capable, and interested citizenry that will deliberate about their political choices.

The preservation of democracy also demands that people meet certain accepted standards of civility and decorum in their public lives. Positive models of deliberative civic discourse are needed to help citizens learn techniques for appropriate and productive argumentation and to help people make well-reasoned decisions. It is unfortunate that so many of our contemporary political candidates spend so much of their time and energy on negative attacks and scurrilous charges; such tactics do not foster productive political deliberations. While it may be funny to watch baseball managers kick sand onto the umpire's pants and gesture wildly while protesting a decision, these same tactics would alarm us if they occurred, for example, in the halls of Congress.

As citizens of a democratic nation we surrender certain powers to elected officials. We acknowledge the right of these officials to set limits on how fast we may drive, to assess taxes, to determine what chemicals we may freely ingest, and so forth. The elected officials must, however, convince us that they are acting in our best interests. If a majority of our citizenry (or even a substantial, well-organized, vocal minority) decided not to accept the legitimacy of the established political order or the correctness, fairness, and justice of the laws, our society would quickly disintegrate.

Given that people do not always agree and that there are always differences of opinion about what the government should do, argumentation is the primary means for shaping the course of public policy. As citizens, we participate in public debates, express our opinions, and listen to and evaluate the arguments made by competing politicians. Ultimately, we pledge our support to one candidate or another and to one political position or another by the way that we cast our vote. Lively public arguments occur around almost all of the complex policy issues that shape our daily lives. Issues such as abortion, gun control, or capital punishment, for example, are sure to spark spirited debates. Political candidates seek to create arguments that will attract public support and win elections. They must listen to public arguments in order to understand and to best carry out the will of their constituents. Public policies are formed, deliberated upon, and ultimately passed or rejected by decision makers engaged in the creation and evaluation of arguments in legislative hearings and in debates on the floor of Congress, in state legislatures, or in city council chambers.

Argumentation skills are important for our political life because they enable us to express our opinions in a coherent manner, to make ourselves understood, and to convince others that they should share our beliefs. These same skills also help us as consumers and critics of public arguments. People who understand argumentation principles are more careful and critical audiences for arguments. We are exposed to myriad different arguments on a daily basis. Advertisers, political leaders, newspaper reporters, and so forth, all attempt to influence our opinions. Knowledge of argumentation theory should make you a more skeptical listener who is better able to analyze the merits of the arguments that you hear. Obviously such knowledge will make for an informed electorate—one that is less susceptible to the deceptive or exaggerated claims made by political demagogues.

ARGUMENTATION AND VALUES

As we have mentioned, people are continually trying to make sense of their worlds by naming and structuring their experiences. Kenneth Burke, a noted rhetorical theorist and literary critic, observed:

One constructs his [sic] notion of the universe or history, and shapes attitudes in keeping. Be he poet or scientist, one defines the "human situation" as amply as his imagination permits; then, with this ample definition in mind, he singles out certain functions or relationships as either friendly or unfriendly. If they are deemed friendly, he prepares himself to welcome them; if they are deemed unfriendly, he weighs objective resistances against his own resources, to decide how far he can effectively go in combating them. . . . Our philosophers, poets and scientists act in the code of names by which they simplify or interpret reality. These names shape our relations with our fellows. They prepare us for some functions and against others, for or against the persons representing these functions. The names go further: they suggest how you shall be for or against. Call a man a villain, and you have the choice of either attacking or cringing. Call him mistaken, and you invite yourself to attempt setting him right. [7]

The very act of naming—the choice of one symbolic referent over another—helps to form our attitudes and *values.* It thus should come as no surprise that all arguments, to some extent, concern human values.

Certainly some arguments concern more important or substantive values than do others. For example, an argument about who makes the best pizza in town may center on the value of thin versus thick crust. Perhaps to the true pizza aficionado this is a value of great significance, but most of us can enjoy both thick- and thin-crusted pizzas. On the other hand, an argument about abortion will involve assessments of such competing values as a woman's right to control her own body and to privacy versus the need to protect the life of the unborn. These are certainly more significant and complex value questions.

Arguments can become even more "sticky" and difficult to resolve when the symbols themselves provoke intense feelings or emotions. An example would be the public debate over "late term" abortions. Such abortions have for many years been allowed by law when they were deemed medically necessary, either due to the discovery of a severe fetal abnormality or to protect the health of the mother. When opponents of abortion chose to label these procedures "partial-birth" abortions, however, they sparked an even more intense public debate. This debate further polarized public deliberations about the legality and morality of abortion. What was perhaps obfuscated by the intensity of this public debate, however, was that these "late term" abortions, though long accepted as an appropriate or medically necessary treatment in some cases, were very rarely undertaken.

The declaration that all arguments concern human values does not suggest that all values are equally significant. Still, issues of value underlie virtually all concerns about which people are inspired to argue. This also means that some issues will prove especially difficult to resolve, because they reveal fundamental differences in the ways in which people conceive of themselves. Milton Rokeach defined "values" as "abstract ideals, positive or negative, not tied to any specific attitude, object or situation, representing a person's beliefs about ideal modes of conduct and ideal terminal goals."[8]

Although persons hold many different attitudes and beliefs, Rokeach argued that they include only a few, perhaps a dozen, core values.[9] Our values are formed very early in our lives. While they may be changed by our education and experience, they are for the most part stable touchstones from which we can draw lessons and create meanings for our experiences.[10] We learn values from our parents, our schools, religious instruction, and the mass media. We also learn them by experiencing day-to-day life in our culture. Thus, to grow up in the United States is to be influenced by the U.S. value system.

However, there is not just one U.S. value system; rather, there are many different and often competing conceptions of values that exist and even thrive in different communities.[11] For example, the values that guide daily life in the rural Midwest may be quite unlike those operating in a city on the East Coast or in the suburbs of a city on the West Coast. There also may be important differences in values that are reflected in particular socioeconomic experiences, ethnic communities, subgroups, or families. Furthermore, people acquire their political beliefs and values as they acquire a vocabulary of symbols that carry ideological meaning. A citizen who has acquired the values that are deemed appropriate to their culture has also learned how to function as an effective, although not necessarily compliant, member of that society.[12]

Values dramatically shape the arguments that people make and the arguments that they will find convincing. We argue in accordance with those truths that we accept.[13] These values are also influenced by how people conceive of their own self-interests. Because our values are shaped by the situations in which we find ourselves, our objective both in making and evaluating arguments will be to improve our place in the world and to reinforce our conceptions of ourselves. It makes intuitive sense, therefore, that young, single women may be more inclined to favor a pro-choice position on abortion, and that middle-aged and older men may be more inclined to oppose the right of a woman to choose abortion to end an unwanted pregnancy. It is reasonable to assume that poor citizens may be inclined to support increased government spending on social programs to help provide for human needs, while affluent citizens may be motivated to cut such programs in order to keep their taxes as low as possible. People are influenced by values, and their values are in part shaped by the particular problems and needs that they face as they attempt to create a more perfect and satisfying life for themselves and for their loved ones.

Acknowledging the role of human values in argumentation also helps make us aware that while arguments may be designed to reach the truth, there may be more than one "truth." Our opinion regarding what constitutes a truth is given shape by our values and experiences. Thus, complex value questions are often complex precisely because there is no single true answer. Reasonable people can and do differ on issues such as abortion, capital punishment, euthanasia, and access to pornography. Arguers who chooses to participate in the public dialogue on these issues should recognize the role of their values in shaping their arguments. Arguers debating such controversies should also be aware that the persons with whom they are arguing might see the world through very different value structures.

The values that people hold also shape what claims they see as worthy of argument. The claim that the government should not concern itself with regulating the safety of food or prescription drugs might not spark much controversy at a convention of the American Libertarian Party, but it would probably seem preposterous to most of the delegates at a Democratic Party convention. Democratic delegates would probably not take this idea seriously, and thus might not even deem it worth arguing. As another example, Democrats might actively support legislation to set aside more wilderness areas in the West to protect them from future development, while Republicans might support selling land that the government already holds so that it can be developed. The values that people hold function as lenses through which they view their world, and the way in which one views the world largely determines what one accepts as true and what one believes must be contested. Our values are shaped by our awareness of our position in society and our position in an economic and social hierarchy. Because we experience new events and day-to-day uncertainties, our values are subjected to new challenges. We may evaluate and change our values when we encounter new information, live new experiences, confront new realities, and acquire new perspectives.

Values also play a dramatic role in determining argumentative sufficiency. It should be easier to convince a farmer that the government should set minimum price supports for agricultural products than to convince the urban consumer who would have to pay the resulting higher prices. The farmer presumably would value most the financial security for producers that the government price supports provide, while the consumer presumably would value most the competitive free market in which products are sold at the lowest possible prices. When people have fundamentally different values there will be more conflict, and it will be far more difficult to reach agreement. Likewise, arguers facing audiences that hold fundamentally different values from their own will find it especially challenging to persuade those audiences to support the positions that they are defending.

We often hear it claimed that when values come into conflict we might as well forget about arguments—that people cannot, or will not, reason about issues of value. Although arguing about values is not easy, there is no satisfactory alternative.[14] We know from many experiences that value disagreements cannot be ignored. If the underlying differences in values are substantial, they may eventually lead to armed conflict. The situation in the Middle East provides an example. The Israelis and their Arab neighbors have been in or near a state of war for almost sixty years as a result of unresolved conflicts concerning religious beliefs, cultural traditions, political autonomy, economic equality, and history. Young Arabs and Israelis have been raised in a climate of fear and distrust. The creation and maintenance of an effective argumentative dialogue given the magnitude of such long-standing problems, although enormously difficult, is clearly better than the alternative: terrorist assaults, the bulldozing of homes, and other acts of violence that could potentially escalate to a full-scale war that might kill thousands of people.

The fact that all arguments are to some extent shaped by human values suggests that people must learn how to reason about issues, even when those issues are characterized by profound differences in values.[15] (We will discuss propositions of value in chapter 5.) When we use reason, we attempt to discover and account for value differences, to accommodate people who hold values different from our own, and to preserve a sense of civility and respect—acts that make for a far more hospitable and even safer world.

ETHICS AND ARGUMENTATION

We have already made several references to the importance of maintaining a climate of civility and decorum when you are engaging in an argument. Decorum and civility are foundations for the conduct of ethical argumentation, and we believe the issue of *ethics* is of vital concern for any student of argumentation theory and practice. Ethics can be understood as a philosophy of human action, as a set of rules for appropriate conduct, and as a way of being and relating to others.[16] Examining ethics in argumentation generally means considering the motives and means used by an arguer.

Wayne Brockriede, a distinguished argumentation theorist, suggests that the images that arguers have of each other are particularly important in shaping the nature of argumentative exchanges. Brockriede proposes a metaphor to express this relationship.[17] He declares that some arguers are like rapists. These arguers see those with whom they are arguing as objects or as inferior human beings, and their intent is to manipulate or violate these objects. Brockriede's use of the rape metaphor is consistent with the view that rape is not a crime of sexual attraction; it is instead a crime of power and violence. Rapists seek to dominate their victims and to demonstrate their control over them. Brockriede says that arguers who use coercive argument strategies likewise seek to gain or to maintain a position of superiority over those with whom they are arguing. They may focus so much on prevailing in the argument, on getting their desired outcome, and on humiliating their opponent that they lose sight of all other objectives.

Brockriede described a second type of arguer as a seducer. Whereas rapists conquer by the force of coercive argument, seducers operate through charm or deceit. The intent of seducers is to beguile others and thereby have their way with them. Seducers seek their own personal gratification without regard for the desires, feelings, wishes, needs, or emotional consequences that the act of seduction might have for other people. Seductive arguers pursue their personal objectives even if doing so harms others.

A third type of arguer is the lover. Lovers differ from rapists and seducers because they see other people as human and not as objects and because they want power parity rather than a power advantage. Whereas rapists and seducers want immediate personal gratification, lovers want to develop continuing, bilateral relationships. Because they have respect for those with whom they argue, lovers acknowledge that those persons have the intellect, ability, and wisdom to decide for themselves what they wish to believe after being exposed to all of the competing arguments. Arguers as lovers also have self-respect. Those who argue from this perspective are willing to put themselves on the line for the positions that they believe in, and they argue with a sense of genuineness and conviction that demonstrates argumentative integrity. The arguers also come to understand that they could lose the argument and thus have to confront the fact that their beliefs and/or long-standing opinions might be in error.

Brockriede's metaphor of these different argument styles is persuasive. All of us would prefer to engage in arguments with people who value and respect us rather than seeing us as objects only to be used. How can you create such a climate for argumentative encounters? We suggest a principle much akin to the "golden rule" that you learned about in childhood: "Do unto others as you would have them do unto you," or "if you want a friend, be one." Although some manipulative and unethical arguers will always exist, we think the best way to overcome them is to be certain that you do not resort to the same tactics. Imposing high standards of ethical conduct on yourself will act as a positive encouragement to others to do the same. If enough people embrace this philosophy there will be fewer unethical, deceptive, and coercive arguers in our society, and the contrast between those who conduct themselves in an ethical fashion and those who do not will create strong social pressure to interact honorably.

Ethical arguers are honest arguers. They seek to discover and to investigate the relevant facts carefully. They do not misrepresent those facts; they do not conceal information that would cause people to interpret their arguments differently; and they do not attempt to persuade others to embrace positions or viewpoints that they themselves know are not true. Ethical arguers do not try to get people to do things that work against their best interests, or, at a minimum, they freely acknowledge the possibility that if certain actions are taken they could prove incompatible with those interests. Walter Fisher argues that our ethical standards are "intersubjectively created and maintained through symbolic transactions over time. They are neither irrational nor rational; they are historically, and culturally created 'goods' we acquire through socialization, the stuff of the stories we tell, hear, read and enact everyday."[18]

Ethical arguers enter the argumentative marketplace with the assumption that others who are selling their own ideas are persons of integrity and good will, persons who will be open to other ideas. They acknowledge that force and coercion do not lead to effective decisions and that people will make the best decisions if given the opportunity to consider the issues on both sides of a question carefully and systematically.

Learning how to argue effectively means learning how to argue in an ethical and positive manner. We believe that if you set high standards for yourself as an arguer and treat others with respect and dignity, they will be more likely to treat you in the same way. In the process, the argumentative marketplace will become a more civilized and valuable place for the free exchange of ideas and for the pursuit of policies and programs that will improve all our lives.

SUMMARY

The ability to argue is necessary if people are to solve problems, resolve conflicts, and evaluate alternative courses of action. While many people are taught that arguing is a counterproductive activity and that arguments should be avoided, we believe that arguing is an essential and fundamental human activity. Learning how to argue effectively entails learning not just the strategies and principles of analysis and logical reasoning but also the importance of arguing in a positive and socially constructive fashion.

Key Terms

arguing   symbols
arguments   values
ethics

Activities

1. Keep a log for a day. Pay careful attention to and take notes on those occasions when you were exposed to advocacy.
   a. How many times were you exposed to advocacy?
   b. What was the form of the advocacy? Was it written, oral, or nonverbal?
   c. What individual decisions were you called upon to make?
   d. What decisions were you called upon to make as a member of a democratic society?
2. Recall a recent situation in which you engaged in argumentation2 (an interaction characterized by disagreement).
   a. What was the point of the disagreement?
   b. What values were reflected in your viewpoint? What values were reflected in the views of the other individual?
   c. How did you resolve the disagreement?
   d. Were you satisfied with the outcome of the interaction?
3. Consult the opinion pages of today's newspaper. Analyze the arguments that are offered in one of the editorials. What value assumptions has the author made? What values might someone have who holds an opposite view?
4. Make a list of the five values you hold most dear. Now order them in the priority that you see appropriate. Ask a friend, classmate, sibling, parent, or significant other to make a similar list. Then compare the two lists.
   a. How many values appear on both lists?
   b. How similar were your rankings?
   c. What accounts for the similarities?
   d. What accounts for the dissimilarities?

Recommended Readings

Aristotle. *The Nichomachean Ethics*. Translated by W. David Ross. London: Oxford University Press, 1998.

Aristotle. *On Rhetoric: A Theory of Civil Discourse*. Translated by George A. Kennedy. London: Oxford University Press, 1991.

Bok, Sissela. *Common Values*. Columbia: University of Missouri Press, 1995.

Brockriede, Wayne. "Characteristics of Arguments and Arguing." *Journal of the American Forensic Association* 13 (1977): 129–132.

Cox, J. Robert, and Charles Arthur Willard, eds. *Advances in Argumentation Theory and Research*. Carbondale: Southern Illinois University Press, 1982.

Ehninger, Douglas. "Argument as Method: Its Nature, Its Limitations and Its Uses." *Speech Monographs* 37 (1970): 101–110.

Goodnight, G. Thomas. "Toward a Social Theory of Argument." *Argumentation and Advocacy* 26 (1989): 60–70.

Hanssen, Beatrice, Rebecca Walkawitz, and Marjorie Garber, eds. *The Turn to Ethics*. New York: Routledge, 2000.

Lunsford, Andrea A., John J. Ruskiewicz, and Keith Walters. *Everything's an Argument: With Readings*. Boston: Bedford, 2004.

MacIntyre, Alasdair. *Whose Justice? Which Rationality?* Notre Dame, IN: Notre Dame University Press, 1988.

Trapp, Robert, and Janice Schuetz, eds. *Perspectives on Argumentation: Essays in Honor of Wayne Brockriede*. Prospect Heights, IL: Waveland Press, 1990.

Willard, Charles Arthur. *A Theory of Argumentation*. Tuscaloosa: Alabama University Press, 1989.

Notes

1 Cited in Joyce O. Hertzler, *A Sociology of Language* (New York: Random House, 1965), 21. See also: Kenneth Burke, *Language as Symbolic Action* (Berkeley: University of California Press, 1966), 3.

2 Hertzler, 28.

3 For a more complete discussion of this concept, see Daniel J. O'Keefe, "Two Concepts of Argument," *Journal of the American Forensic Association* 13 (1976): 121–128.

4 Wayne Brockriede, "Where Is Argument?" *Journal of the American Forensic Association* 11 (1975): 179.

5 Sally Jackson and Scott Jacobs, "Structure of Conversational Argument: Pragmatic Bases for the Enthymeme," *Quarterly Journal of Speech* 66 (1980): 251–65.

6 Deborah Tannen, *The Argument Culture: Stopping America's War of Words* (New York: Ballantine Books,1998), 3.

7 Kenneth Burke, *Attitudes Toward History* (Boston: Beacon Press, 1937; rpt. 1961), 3–4.

8 Milton Rokeach, *Beliefs, Attitudes, and Values* (San Francisco: Jossey-Bass, 1968), 124.

9 Ibid., 124.

10 Ibid., 123–126.

11 Joseph W. Wenzel, "Toward a Rationale for Value-centered Argument," *Journal of the American Forensic Association* 13 (1977): 150–158.

12 A. K. Sherman & A. Kolker, *The Social Bases of Politics* (Belmont, CA: Wadsworth, 1987).

13 Malcolm O. Sillars & Patricia Ganer, "Values and Beliefs: A Systematic Basis for Argumentation," in *Advances in Argumentation Theory and Research*, ed. J. Robert Cox and Charles Arthur Willard, 184–201 (Carbondale: Southern Illinois University Press, 1982).

14 For a very useful and complete discussion of the role of values in human argumentation see Chaim Perelman and L. Olbrechts-Tyteca, *The New Rhetoric: A Treatise on Argument* (Notre Dame,

IN: The Notre Dame University Press, 1969). The book explains how arguers can learn how to develop their argument skills so that they can improve the quality and criticism of arguments in value disputes. See especially: pp. 54–114.

[15] Nicholas Rescher, "The Study of Value Change," in *Value Theory in Philosophy and Social Science*, ed. E. Lazlo and J. B. Wilbur, 14–16 (New York: Gordon & Breach, 1973).

[16] Walter R. Fisher, "The Ethic(s) of Argument and Practical Wisdom," in *Argument at Century's End: Reflecting on the Past and Envisioning the Future*, ed. T. A. Hollihan, 1–15 (Annandale, VA: National Communication Association, 2000).

[17] Wayne Brockriede, "Arguers as Lovers," *Philosophy and Rhetoric* 5 (1972): 1–11.

[18] Fisher, 4.

THE FOUNDATIONS
OF ARGUMENT

People make arguments when they express, justify, or explain their opinions. These arguments both reflect and have implications for the values that people hold. Arguments have value implications because they reveal how people have constructed their views of the world and how they have interpreted and assigned meaning to their experiences. Consequently, an examination and analysis of arguments tells us a great deal about the people who created them, those who accept them as convincing, and the societies and/or cultures in which those people live.

People are continually challenged by new experiences and situations that they must interpret and make sense of in order to make their way in the world. Events acquire meaning for us as we think about them, interpret them, and most important, as we talk about them with others. It is through discussing our experiences that human culture is created, shared, and thereby re-created. Human values develop as they do, largely because those who came before us have witnessed and learned the utility of living their lives in accordance with certain principles. Some of these principles are revealed through the teachings of religious prophets, priests, and other clergy. We also learn values from the proverbs, fables, and historical lessons that we are taught. Still other values are taught by our parents, our teachers, and by civic and community leaders. Finally, our values are shaped and influenced by our experiences and our interactions with our friends. That people's values differ reflects how their experiences and cultures differ.

This chapter considers how values influence how people select and evaluate arguments and the formation of the argumentative marketplace. We believe that people come to understand their world and their values in **narrative** (or **storytelling**) form. Throughout our lives we both hear and tell stories. Some **stories** we believe, enjoy, and find useful; because we find them appealing, we repeat them. Other stories we find unbelievable; we discredit and discard these stories. Through storytelling we give form to the world around us. The stories that we tell are not simply reflections of what we regard as significant, they become our reality.

Some stories are simple and straightforward, such as those learned in childhood. These stories often contain simple moral lessons that are intended to guide us in our life decisions. For example, all of us can probably recall the story of the three little pigs. The first pig built a house of straw, a second pig built his house of sticks, and the third pig labored long and hard to build a sturdy structure of bricks and mortar. Only the pig that took the time and effort to build the secure brick home had shelter when the wolf with the immense blowing ability came by. Obviously, the point of the story goes far beyond the relative merits of alternative porcine dwellings. The intended moral is that hard work will be rewarded, one should anticipate the possibility of adverse conditions and circumstances (perhaps not just wolves but nasty winds!), and that people, like pigs, need to exert the energy to prepare for their future. From such stories, children learn important lessons that should help them later in life, and they learn them in ways that are easily apprehended and remembered.

It is in narrative form that we learn about several core values that should guide our lives. For example, from childhood fables most of us learned the importance of doing good deeds for others (e.g., the child who removes the thorn from the paw of the angry and wounded lion is not only spared injury, he makes a friend), about what happens to those who would raise a false cry of danger (e.g., the boy who always cries wolf discovers that no one takes him seriously when he really needs assistance); about the importance of telling the truth (e.g., the story of George Washington admitting to his father that he chopped down the cherry tree, and as a result of his honesty he is not punished). The exposure to so many different stories teaches us how to craft and tell our own stories as well has how to reason in narrative form. As our intellects develop and as the problems that we face become more complicated, so too our stories become more complex, requiring a greater degree of nuance in order to account for situations that are morally ambiguous. They almost certainly entail more sophisticated language, storytelling techniques, and plot devices. Despite these developments, however, the nature of the narrative reasoning process remains fundamentally the same.

An interesting example of the power of a compelling story can be drawn from President George Bush's (the elder's) arguments to justify his decision to send U.S. troops to the Middle East in the "Desert Storm" war against Iraq. President Bush argued that the troops were necessary because the United States had an obligation to counter the Iraqi aggression against Kuwait. If we did not intervene, President Bush argued, Iraqi leader Saddam Hussein would eventually try to capture Saudi Arabia and the other nations of the region. Hussein's goal, according to this story, was to capture all of the oil reserves in the region so that he could hold the United States and other oil-dependent countries hostage. Furthermore, he sought to oppress the people in the region. President Bush claimed that Hussein was utterly ruthless and had no respect for the sanctity of human life. Hussein was said to have seized power by force, to have silenced all of his critics, and to have used chemical weapons against the Kurdish citizens of his own nation.

However, there had been countless other brutal dictators in the world that the U.S. government not only tolerated but befriended and claimed as allies. For example, men such as August Pinochet of Chile, Ferdinand Marcos of the Philippines, and Chiang Kai-shek of China (eventually he was forced to flee the mainland for Taiwan) were also capable of great cruelties and/or corruption, yet all received vast amounts of military and economic assistance from the United States. Indeed, in previous years Saddam Hussein had been depicted as a U.S. ally, no doubt in part because his opposition to Iran was seen as furthering U.S. strategic interests. Yet, suddenly he was being depicted as a cruel villain. How were the apparent inconsistencies between President Bush's characterization and intentions toward Hussein and these other stories reconciled?

The decision to send troops was justified in large part on the basis of arguments that likened the Iraqi ruler to Adolf Hitler. Hitler is perhaps the most notorious figure in history, embodying deliberate evil in its most horrific form. The claim that Hussein was another Hitler gained its power by encouraging the American people to recall the lessons of World War II. These lessons were relived in the stories of that great conflict. World War II stories almost always begin with accounts of how the British Prime Minister Neville Chamberlain sought to appease Hitler and to negotiate with him in order to prevent a broader conflict. Ultimately, of course, Hitler could not be appeased and a total and complete state of war was necessary to unseat the German dictator and to thwart his deadly territorial ambitions. Surely, the lessons of history tell us, it would have been better had Great Britain, France, and the United States responded more aggressively to Hitler much earlier, before he had acquired so much power. A columnist in the *London Daily Telegraph* drew the following conclusion: "A pre-emptive strike against Hitler at the time of Munich would have meant an immediate war, as opposed to the one that came later. Later was much worse."[1] Thus, if we were to extend the comparison between Hitler and Hussein, it would seem desirable to respond to Hussein's aggression before he managed to further consolidate his power and strengthen his control over captured Kuwait and the other nations in the region.*

The power of the "Hussein as Hitler" narrative is obvious and recurred when George W. Bush argued for invading Iraq in 2003. Hitler, the most heinous of modern villains, was capable of outrageous acts of genocide, and was com-

---

* The Hitler–Hussein analogy had a particular appeal to President George Herbert Walker Bush, who served as a Navy pilot and was actually shot down in combat during World War II. An excellent discussion of the power of the comparison between Adolf Hitler and Saddam Hussein as a rhetorical and argumentative strategy is provided by James Gerstenzang, "World War II Lessons Helped Form Bush Strategy," *Los Angeles Times*, January 14, 1991.

pletely beyond the reach of any rational argument. He was willing to destroy his own people and his own nation in the pursuit of his own delusional, grandiose plans. Hitler was stopped only by extreme force. If Hussein is akin to Hitler, then he is also an evil force who must be dealt with quickly and definitively. As James Fallows argues: "Nazi and Holocaust analogies have a trumping power in many arguments, and their effect in Washington was to make doubters seem weak— [the] Neville Chamberlains versus the Winston Churchills who were ready to face the truth."[2] Fallows further argues, however, that

> the Nazi analogy paralyzed the debate about Iraq rather than clarifying it. Like any other episode in history, today's situation is both familiar and new. In the ruthlessness of the adversary it resembles dealing with Adolf Hitler. But Iraq, unlike Germany, has no industrial base and no military allies nearby. It is split by regional, religious, and ethnic differences that are much more complicated than Nazi Germany's simple mobilization of "Aryans" against Jews.[3]

Yet, as was demonstrated as the crisis unfolded, arguments that asserted that Hussein was in reality not a mad Hitler clone, or that Iraq was no Nazi Germany, seemed less persuasive because they lacked the narrative appeal of the Hitler analogy.

As the Hitler-Hussein examples demonstrate, people naturally seek to understand current world events by comparing them to events from history. As we apply the lessons of history, the historical stories that we swap become the lens through which we view our current situation. Those historical stories that have acquired meaning in our life provide the patterns for our reasoning and problem-solving deliberations. It is in this sense that people can be said to reason through narrative structures.

A related example of an attempt to explain a contemporary event by searching for an appropriate historical narrative is provided by the terrorist attacks on the World Trade Center in New York and on the Pentagon in Washington, D.C., on September 11, 2001. The events of that day, now widely known in the public lexicon as 9/11, were so dramatic and terrifying that ordinary citizens, media spokespersons, and elected officials alike searched for the appropriate historical narratives to explain them. Many storytellers likened these terrorist attacks to the Japanese attacks on the U.S. Navy base at Pearl Harbor on December 7, 1941, which began World War II. As a result, many of these storytellers declared that the United States should respond to the 9/11 attacks with a declaration of war and a strategy of total military conflict. These storytellers noted that the events were similar because both attacks represented an assault on U.S. soil and because they occurred without warning and without specific provocation.

What these storytellers seemed to miss in making the analogies between the two events, however, was that the recent attacks were not made by a nation or by the airplanes and personnel of a standing army. Instead, they were undertaken by a loosely structured terrorist network. Consequently, a declaration and pursuit of war might not be either as appropriate or as effective as it was in World War II.

The terrorist network that created the contemporary attacks operated in a number of different nations in the Middle East, Asia, Africa, and even Europe. Was the United States military to engage the terrorists in open and declared warfare in all of these locations? There was convincing evidence of collusion between the terrorists and the ruling Taliban government in Afghanistan that made that nation a logical primary target for a military response. But what about those nations where the evidence of official cooperation with the terrorists was present but less overwhelming? What should the United States' response be in these cases? Indeed, it soon became clear that many of the terrorists who hijacked the airplanes that were used to crash into the World Trade Center and the Pentagon were citizens of Saudi Arabia, a nation that the United States had long considered a close ally. What was the appropriate response in a situation such as this? The point is that although stories can serve as powerful resources in the construction of narrative understandings of events, storytellers also need to recognize that the selection of a particular narrative may lock people into worldviews and resulting policy actions that might be ill-suited to those events if they are seen from the perspective of an alternative narrative.

Stories also serve an important formative purpose both for the people who choose to tell them and believe them and ultimately for the cultures that come to accept them. For example, as U.S. citizens, many of us have developed an understanding of our identity as a nation on the basis of stories about our founding fathers and, though far too infrequently, stories about our founding mothers. In elementary school we were taught to respect George Washington's honesty, Benjamin Franklin's inventiveness and ingenuity, Thomas Jefferson's concern for equality, and Abraham Lincoln's humility. Our teachers did not dwell on the facts that George Washington padded his expense accounts; that Benjamin Franklin and Thomas Jefferson were philanderers; or that Abraham Lincoln was a successful corporate attorney (representing the railroads, the most powerful corporations of the day). These aspects of our founding fathers' life stories are not recounted as frequently because they serve our contemporary needs less well. In short, the stories that are retold time and again are those that fulfill contemporary needs.

The telling and retelling of the stories of our birth as a nation and the accounts of the personal lives and achievements of our founding fathers invites collective identification among U.S. citizens with their government. It also helps citizens identify the morally correct course of action. It is fully consistent with our self-image that freedom-loving Americans—a people descended from the patriotic and selfless Washington, Franklin, Jefferson, and Lincoln—will unite to help eliminate evil in the world. Whether the evildoer is Osama Bin Laden, Saddam Hussein, Slobodan Milosevic, or any other terrorist or dictator intent on killing innocent people and thwarting the free will of people, the United States has a duty to use its moral authority, and perhaps its diplomatic and military might, to help end oppression.

The confidence that we, as U.S. citizens, have in the moral certainty of our actions is thus a result of our own narrative experience—we have created our world to fit our stories, as much as we have created the stories to fit our world. The purpose of this discussion is not to discredit the stories that make up U.S. history, nor do we see the process as a negative one. All humans reason through narratives, which helps to explain why the citizens of Iraq, and apparently of many other Middle East nations, believed in the legitimacy of Iraq's takeover of Kuwait, admired the courage of Saddam Hussein, and advocated that the sanctions against Iraq be ended. How can these other nations, many of which are also our allies, maintain a sympathetic view of a man whom we depict as the modern Hitler? Why is it that young people in the streets of Pakistan's largest cities burned George W. Bush in effigy while holding posters that proclaimed Osama Bin Laden to be a hero? How is it that terrorist actions such as those that occurred on September 11, 2001, are seen as clearly reprehensible in one society yet deemed fair, just, and appropriate to another? How can international diplomacy be conducted and reasoned arguments occur when people tell such completely different stories—and as a result construct their reality in such incompatible ways?

One lesson that quickly becomes apparent from an attempt to answer the above questions is that those patriotic stories that on the surface seem so positive to the formation of values of a political culture may have negative consequences. For example, the stories about Washington, Franklin, Jefferson, and Lincoln previously discussed may have led many Americans to have an unquestioning faith in the legitimacy of the American experience. Such stories may cause Americans to be either unwilling or unable to see the faults in our nation. This in turn may cause many Americans to believe that what is good for the United States' interests is also good for everyone else's interests. Americans may be too inclined to believe that the American way is the best way, if not the only way to solve problems. This argument is sometimes referred to as "American exceptionalism."[4] Can Americans who largely live lives of prosperity and privilege in a nation that cherishes pluralism and democratic values really anticipate that they will tell the same stories, live the same experiences, and share the same worldviews as do those who live in repressive, undemocratic, tribal, or impoverished nations?

Before you surrender to the belief that all attempts at reasoned discourse are futile, however, it is important to recognize that it is quite possible for people to critique and evaluate the quality of the stories they hear and tell. When comparing the rival stories that compete for acceptance as people seek to explain themselves and express their convictions, one can gain insight into the underlying differences in cultures, values, political conditions, and experiences that shape human life. Narrative arguments are rational arguments, and we can learn a great deal about how people reason through stories. Knowing more about the narrative reasoning process will help us to learn how to tell better— that is, more convincing, credible, and compassionate—stories.

THE NARRATIVE PARADIGM

We are exposed to literally hundreds of different stories in any given week. We hear stories in conversations with friends and family members, we hear them on the news, we watch them unfold in television programs, and we read them in books, newspapers, and magazines.

How do we determine which are true and should guide our lives and which are not true and should be dismissed? One criterion that we can apply is to determine whether or not the stories were intended as fictions. However, the line between real and fictional accounts often becomes blurred. Some fictions come to be accepted as truths and are especially useful in shaping our lives and helping us make sense of our experiences. Perhaps one of the best-known examples of a work of fiction that was taken as truth was Harriet Beecher Stowe's classic novel *Uncle Tom's Cabin*, a story about the experiences of slavery told through the eyes of a slave family. This book had a tremendous impact on public attitudes toward slavery and came to be accepted as fact, despite its fictional characters. Indeed, the book was sometimes credited with having so inflamed abolitionist attitudes that it may have sparked the Civil War. Upon meeting Harriet Beecher Stowe, President Lincoln is purported to have said: "So this is the little lady who made this great war."*

People will accept stories as true if these stories speak to them and account for their experiences. Walter R. Fisher has argued that people reason through narratives. He referred to this mode of reasoning as the narrative paradigm, which he summarized as follows:

> (1) Humans are . . . storytellers. (2) The paradigmatic mode of human deci-
> sion making and communication is "good reasons," which vary in form
> among situations, genres, and media of communication. (3) The production
> and practice of good reasons are ruled by matters of history, biography, cul-
> ture and character. . . (4) Rationality is determined by the nature of persons
> as narrative beings—their inherent awareness of narrative probability, what
> constitutes a coherent story, and constant habit of testing narrative fidelity,
> whether or not the stories they experience ring true with the stories they
> know to be true in their lives. . . . (5) The world as we know it is a set of sto-
> ries that must be chosen among in order for us to live life in a process of con-
> tinual re-creation.[5]

Fisher claims that human reasoning need not be bound to argumentative prose, or to clear-cut inferential or implicative structures, because it is typically achieved through the stories that people tell. Viewed from this perspective, virtually all arguments can be understood and evaluated as stories. One of the most noteworthy aspects of this theory of argument is its assumption that ordinary people who are untrained in argumentation techniques are capable of resolving complex problems because they reason through narrative structures. For purposes of clarification, we will look at both the tests of arguments, and the criteria for evaluating "good reasons" that Fisher mentions.

People first assess arguments by evaluating their **narrative probability.** This concept refers to whether a story seems coherent. Is the argumentative structure of the story satisfying and complete? Does the chronology of events seem credi-

---

* There is no evidence that Abraham Lincoln ever read *Uncle Tom's Cabin,* or that he ever saw the play focused on the book. Lincoln was, however, very much aware of the impact the book had on the American public. For a discussion of his conversation with the author Harriet Beecher Stowe, see Thomas F. Gossett, *Uncle Tom's Cabin and American Culture* (Dallas: Southern Methodist University Press, 1985), 314–315.

ble and convincing? Does the story seem to account for the material facts of the situation in a satisfying manner? How do the primary characters in the story acquire their dramatic motivation? Do the heroes behave in ways that are appropriately heroic? Do the villains behave as villains are expected to behave? Are the actions of the characters reliable? Do their actions seem to follow from the plot that has been developed in the narrative structure? Do their behaviors seem consistent with the values that the plot attributes to them?

In our earlier discussion about Iraqi leader Saddam Hussein, for example, we noted that both presidents named Bush cast Hussein as a notorious villain. Using the test of narrative probability would encourage arguers to question whether or not Hussein indeed lives up to our expectations for a villain. Is he the "Beast of Baghdad"? Or is he a patriotic and heroic Iraqi strongman who has earned the admiration of his own citizens and of others in the region by standing up to the developed Western powers? Did the United States fight to secure the freedom and self-determination of the people of Kuwait? Or did we merely try to secure our access to cheap oil? Did the diplomatic sanctions that we placed on the government of Iraq serve as an appropriate response given the continued aggressive ambitions of Saddam Hussein? Or did the sanctions unfairly punish the people of Iraq, for example, denying them access to pharmaceutical products that could reduce diseases and save lives? Was the decision to intervene in Iraq and depose Hussein's regime moral and legitimate? Or did the George W. Bush administration exaggerate the danger that Iraq posed to the world? What are people to make of the fact that the "weapons of mass destruction" that we were told that Hussein possessed were never found?

People seek stories that do not leave loose ends untied. We prefer stories that offer resolution and satisfy our need to understand rapidly developing and complex issues and events. For example, have you ever watched a film that left you dissatisfied because the plot did not hang together very well? Although audiences enjoy films with surprise endings, the best of such films are carefully planned so that when they are finished the audience can look back and discover the clues that were available all along. Our interest in compelling and satisfying stories is no less intense outside of books or films. Most Americans did not wish to fight a war in the Middle East until they were convinced that the conflict was unavoidable, the objectives were moral and justified, and the probability of victory was high.

The second test of stories, **narrative fidelity**, concerns whether or not a story represents accurate assertions about social reality.[6] This dimension of narrative reasoning is firmly rooted in the human capacity for making judgments about issues of value. Fisher argued that people seek to make their decisions in accordance with the values that they hold. They also seek to determine if the "facts" revealed to them in the stories they encounter are indeed facts, if they are reliable and relevant, and whether or not they have been taken out of context.

People thus consider the degree to which any new story seems consistent with the stories that they have heard before and have already accepted as true—stories they have used to explain their past experiences. The "Hussein as Hitler" story, for example, fares well in a test of narrative fidelity for many Americans.

This is not a story, however, without some fairly obvious flaws. First, Iraq is not Nazi Germany. While President Bush pointed out that Iraq fielded one of the world's largest armies, the Iraqi forces lacked the discipline, training, or weapons systems to put up much of a fight against U.S. and allied forces. Second, Nazi Germany was a nation with a strong industrial base and very well educated scientists, engineers, and other professionals. It also boasted a very well trained industrial workforce. Third, for all of his flaws, there is little evidence to suggest that Saddam Hussein was the driven megalomaniac dictator that Hitler was. Still, many Americans no doubt came to believe that a negotiated settlement with Iraq was as doomed to failure as were attempts to make peace with Hitler. In addition, Hussein's willingness to bomb clearly civilian targets in Israel, his killing of innocent women and children in his own nation, and his policies against any who opposed his regime, suggested that he may have harbored the same blind hatreds and hostilities that Hitler did.[7]

As we have already mentioned, Fisher argued that the capacity for narrative argument is present in all humans, because all of us are socialized and taught through stories. The power of this form of argument is often illustrated in the courtroom. Lance Bennett and Martha Feldman, in their analysis of courtroom arguments, observed that jurors were able to make sense of complicated and sophisticated legal arguments when they evaluated these arguments as stories.[8] A prosecutor, for example, must fashion a structurally complete and internally consistent story that takes into account all the evidence in the case.[9] A defense attorney can succeed if he or she can find a way to reveal flaws in the prosecutor's story. These flaws might involve such issues as evidentiary inconsistencies, locating new evidence that is important to the case yet fundamentally incompatible with the prosecutor's story, or the construction of a rival story that seems equally or more probable.

Human nature causes people to accept stories that fit their own needs or further their own interests. For example, a political candidate's story containing promises to fund increases in social programs while also decreasing taxes may appeal to voters because it promises benefits without pain. A rival story that says that these benefits will require an increase in taxes may be less appealing to many voters. Only when the first political story is refuted by material evidence in the form of data that will convince people that the story cannot account for the observed facts will people be inclined to reject it. As we have already argued, stories must meet the tests of narrative probability and fidelity, but sometimes it seems that people will work harder to convince themselves that a story that seems to serve their interests is true while one that does not is inaccurate.

The appeal of some stories, and the lack of appeal of other stories, is closely connected to the values and life experiences of people and of the cultures in which they live. Those stories that people tell and come to believe as probably true give form to their lives and thus help to shape their values and their self-conceptions. Fisher argued that people seek out stories that confirm their sense of themselves. Those stories that justify people's behaviors and motives, and make them feel important and worthwhile, have an easier time gaining public acceptance than do those stories that negate their self-image. People are more readily compelled to action on the basis of stories that make such action and their own conduct seem appropriate and just. Skilled storytellers understand that people seek stories that affirm their self-concept. For example, when political candidates go before groups like the American Legion or the Veterans of Foreign Wars, they appeal to the veterans' sense of pride in their patriotism, their love of country, and their feelings of camaraderie with fellow veterans.

A politician who wants to refute a story that we can increase spending on social programs and also lower taxes might stress the fact that the numbers have been "cooked" and that the result would be an increase in the budget deficit. Then this arguer could claim that the budget deficit might make it more costly for the government to borrow money and to service the new debts that are incurred. The arguer could then suggest that our decision to live beyond our means today shifts our burdens onto the backs of our children. This appeal to the obligation that today's citizens have to future generations is persuasive because it addresses our desire to nurture and protect our offspring. The concern for the well-being of children is a natural human emotion, and thus a form of argument that will appeal to audiences across a wide span of time and a wide range of specific issues. As a result, it is also a recurring theme for stories. More than 2,500 years ago, Aristotle wrote that happiness, justice, courage, fear, praise, sympathy, and empathy (among others) are common issues that are capable of influencing the opinions formed by listeners to public arguments.[10] Listeners might thus be motivated to accept certain stories as more probably true than others, simply because these stories appeal to their values, emotions, sense of virtue, or instincts.

If all humans possess an almost instinctive ability to engage in narrative arguments—to tell stories, and to evaluate and choose between the stories that they are told—what need is there for a course in argumentation? The answer, we believe, lies in the fact that although all people are capable of arguing through stories, some people are better storytellers than others. Although everyone can tell a story, not everyone can write a poem, a novel, or even a short story. The assumption we make is that by learning certain argumentative principles people can hone their storytelling skills and learn how to become better storytellers (advocates) and better critics of the stories that they are exposed to on a daily basis. The next section is devoted to the benefits of learning argumentation theory.

THE LIMITS OF ARGUMENT

One clear measure of a competent arguer is the ability to recognize when to argue and when to remain silent. Another measure is the ability to recognize a superior argument. A competent arguer knows when an adversary has presented arguments that are superior to his or her own. Learning when to argue and when not to argue will not only make you a more convincing advocate for the positions that you espouse, it may also help you to preserve your friendships. Although we will discuss the relationship between argumentation style and interpersonal relationships in greater detail in the last chapter, at least brief attention is devoted to this issue now, because it is so important to developing the skills of effective argumentation.

Often we find ourselves in conversations where someone makes a statement that we disagree with, but our disagreement is so trivial that we need to decide whether the relational tension that might result from a public disagreement is warranted. Sometimes arguments are not worth the effort because the issue about which we differ is not very significant. It may not seem worthwhile, for example, to argue that the color of a couch that you admired in a furniture store was turquoise, if your friend insists that it was teal. Obviously both turquoise and teal come in many different shades, and our ability to distinguish between them may be limited, as may be our ability to recall what we saw. Breaking into a full-fledged dispute over precisely what the color was may simply not be worth the effort.

The decision to argue (to engage in argument2) over every trivial difference of opinion will obviously impair your relationships with others. None of us choose as friends, lovers, or even close colleagues, people with whom we find ourselves in constant disagreements over trivial issues. The tension level that results from such disputes can begin to undermine even otherwise healthy relationships.

Still other arguments are not worth having because they do not concern questions that can be readily resolved through disputation, regardless of the relative skills of the competing arguers. For example, an argument over which college football team has gone to the Rose Bowl more often, the University of Southern California or Ohio State University, is not a dispute that can be resolved through arguments (although such arguments have certainly occupied the time of many a sports fan!). This is an empirical question that can be answered simply by consulting a sports almanac. If, however, the argument concerned which school had established the better football tradition, it would be resolvable only through argument. Empirical evidence to support your position would certainly be helpful to resolve such a dispute, but the nature of the question would also require the evaluation of argumentative claims. For example, in answering this question, evidence of Rose Bowl participation would be relevant, but not sufficient to prove one football program superior to another. One might also be motivated to make and evaluate arguments about the appearance in other bowl games over the years, the respective strength of the conference and nonconference schedules, the quality of the coaches, consistency over a wide span of years, recent performance on the gridiron, etc. All of these arguments and the empirical evidence that supported them might provide grounds for making claims about the relative merits of the two football powers.

Still another type of argument that might not be worth making is an argument directed toward changing the mind of a genuinely and firmly committed ideologue. Some people hold beliefs so strongly that they are not open to critical reflection. Many arguments over the merits of particular religious philosophies are of this type. Someone who is, for example, a committed Roman Catholic, and who faithfully adheres to the teachings and philosophies of that faith, is not likely to be very open to arguments about its flaws or errors. Such arguments would be especially difficult to accept if they came from someone outside of the faith, since one might question both the arguer's knowledge of the religious teachings of Catholicism and his or her motives for seeking to discredit the faith.

Similarly, arguments between intensely committed political conservatives and equally committed political liberals are often not worth spending the time and energy on, because so little of their disagreement can be resolved through dispute and reasoning. For an effective argumentative exchange to occur, both parties must be open to arguments. They need not have suspended their beliefs and become what is known as *tabula rasa* or "blank slates," but they must be willing to confront the possibility that the beliefs that they hold could indeed be demonstrated to be wrong. For this reason, all arguments entail risk for those who engage in them.[11]

Our goal is not to discourage you from forming strong opinions or from engaging in arguments with others who also hold such opinions. Instead, our point is that some assessment of the nature of the argumentative climate is important. Arguers need to make conscious decisions concerning whether or not participation in any given argument will serve their interests. They should ask themselves: will having this argument damage my relationship with this person? And, will the arguments that we make really resolve the dispute? It is, of course, often difficult to predict the outcome of a disagreement or to determine in advance how it will affect our relationships. Nevertheless, sometimes we can predict quite accurately if we take the time to weigh the potential consequences of our words carefully and deliberately before we speak or write them. We believe that arguers should choose their arguments carefully, based on their own sense of where each is likely to lead, and not permit themselves to be ruled only by their tempers. We believe that this selectivity, along with equally careful selection of the situations in which they will argue and the habit of keeping an eye on argumentative strategy, are all traits of effective arguers.

THE STUDY OF ARGUMENTATION

The study of argumentation we undertake in this book will help you to further develop your arguing and critical analytic skills. In the remaining chapters we will consider the following topics:

- What issues are worth arguing over and what issues are beyond argument?
- How can arguers adjust their arguments to suit their audiences?
- What is the relationship between argumentation and critical thinking?
- What are the various forms of argument?
- What role does evidence play in argumentation?
- How do I best refute the arguments offered by others?
- How do the forms and types of arguments that occur differ by context or situation?

The techniques for argument do, of course, vary from situation to situation. We have taken the position that most arguers reason primarily from a narrative perspective and that most arguments are presented as stories. However, not all argumentative contexts or situations demand the same kind of stories. In fact, certain argument situations, and certain communities of arguers, have created their own standards for arguing. Thus, the arguments that are developed in the courtroom are substantially different from those developed in a legislative hearing, an academic debate, a classroom, a business meeting, a religious conference, or a discussion between friends or family members. Learning the techniques for effective arguing therefore means developing one's sensitivity to the demands of a wide variety of different argumentative contexts.

One of the primary objectives of this text is to help you to explore resources that may be useful to you as you are called upon to develop arguments in a variety of contexts. We will consider how one finds, selects, and develops appropriate evidence; how this evidence is used to support the analysis and reasoning that strengthens claims; and how these arguments are best organized. We will also be focusing on techniques that will enable you to refute the arguments offered by others and to defend and rebuild your own arguments after they have been refuted. Finally, we will offer suggestions that will help you to analyze your audience, enabling you to make the strongest possible case in support of your position. By adapting your arguments to your audience you can present a case that is not only well reasoned, well evidenced, and well organized, but also well suited to the interests, values, and experiences of those who are evaluating your arguments.

SUMMARY

We believe that all people have the capacity to argue and to evaluate arguments, because people are by nature rational beings. The primary mode for the creation and evaluation of arguments is through storytelling, and our stories are tested through an evaluation of their narrative probability and narrative fidelity. Despite the fact that we all have the capacity for arguing, we can improve our argumentation skills by learning conventions and norms for arguing effectively in particular contexts—and by recognizing that some arguments will not result in agreement, may erode relationships, and hence should be avoided.

Key Terms

narrative
narrative fidelity
narrative probability

stories
storytelling

Activities

1. Watch a Saturday morning cartoon, then analyze the characters and elements of the story.

a. Who is the hero of the cartoon? Is the hero male or female? What ethnicity is the hero? What are the personality characteristics of the hero?

b. Who is the villain of the cartoon? Is the villain male or female? What ethnicity is the villain? What are the personality characteristics of the villain?

c. What do the depictions of the hero and villain say about these types of individuals?

d. What is the moral of the cartoon?

e. What values does the moral of the cartoon teach?

2. Make a list of what you think are the traditional values of U.S. culture. Now select a different culture or subculture. Make a list of the values of that culture. If you are not familiar with another culture, ask someone who is to make the list instead.

a. Are there differences in the values of the two cultures?

b. How are these differences manifested in behavior?

c. Can you identify similarities in the values of the two cultures?

d. Are these similarities manifested in similar behaviors?

3. Think about the last movie you saw.

a. Were there points in the plot of the movie that did not seem to fit together?

b. Were there subplots that where left unresolved?

c. Did the characters act the way you think characters in real situations would behave?

d. How do these aspects of the story reflect Fisher's concepts of narrative probability and fidelity?

4. Pick a public issue from the headlines of the local newspaper. Discuss the issue with a classmate or friend. Then analyze your discussion.

a. Were there points on which you disagreed with your partner?

b. Did you voice all such disagreements or did you keep some of them to yourself?

c. If you voiced all of your disagreements, what effect did this have on the discussion?

d. If you kept some points of disagreement to yourself, why did you do this?

Recommended Readings

Fisher, Walter R. "Clarifying the Narrative Paradigm." *Communication Monographs* 56 (1989): 55–58.

Fisher, Walter R. "Rationality and the Logic of Good Reasons." *Philosophy and Rhetoric* 13 (1980): 121–130.

Fisher, Walter R. "Toward a Logic of Good Reasons." *Quarterly Journal of Speech* 64 (1978): 376–384.

Ging-Pemble, Lisa M. "'Are We Now Going to Govern by Anecdote?': Rhetorical Constructions of Welfare Recipients in Congressional Hearings, Debates, and Legislation, 1992–1996." *Quarterly Journal of Speech* 87 (2001): 341–365.

Rokeach, Milton. *Beliefs, Attitudes and Values.* San Francisco: Jossey-Bass, 1970.

Rowland, Robert C. "Narrative: Mode of Discourse or Paradigm?" *Communication Monographs* 54 (1987): 264–275.

Rowland, Robert C. "On Limiting the Narrative Paradigm: Three Case Studies." *Communication Monographs* 56 (1989): 39–54.

Stroud, Scott. "Multivariant Narratives: Extending the Narrative Paradigm with Insights from Ancient Philosophical Thought." *Western Journal of Communication* 66 (2002): 369–393.

Stutts, Nancy B., and Randolph T. Barker. "The Use of Narrative Paradigm Theory in Assessing Audience Value Conflict in Image Advertising." *Management Communication Quarterly* 13 (1999): 209–245.

Turpin, Paul. "Reconsidering the Narrative Paradigm: The Implications of Ethos." In *Argument in a Time of Chance: Definitions, Frameworks, and Critiques*, ed. James F. Klumpp, 75–79. Annandale, VA: National Communication Association, 1998.

Wallace, Karl C. "The Substance of Rhetoric: Good Reasons." *Quarterly Journal of Speech* 49 (1963): 239–249.

Warnick, Barbara. "The Narrative Paradigm: Another Story." *Quarterly Journal of Speech* 73 (1987): 172–182.

Wenzel, Joseph W. "Toward a Rationale for Value-Centered Argument." *Journal of the American Forensic Association* 13 (1977): 150–158.

Notes

[1] Cited by James Fallows, "The Fifty-First State?" *Atlantic Monthly*, November 2002, 53.

[2] Ibid., 53.

[3] Ibid., 54.

[4] The argument for "American exceptionalism" is nicely developed by Robert J. McMahon, "By Helping Others We Help Ourselves," in *Critical Reflections on the Cold War: Linking Rhetoric and History*, ed. Martin J. Medhurst and H. W. Brands, 233–246 (College Station: Texas A & M University Press, 2000).

[5] Walter R. Fisher, *Human Communication as Narration* (Columbia: University of South Carolina Press, 1987), 5.

[6] Ibid., 105.

[7] For a discussion of these similarities and their argumentative power see: Gerald F. Seib and Walter S. Mossberg, "Iraqi Missiles Hit Israel and U.S. Presses Air Attacks," *Wall Street Journal*, January 18, 1991.

[8] W. Lance Bennett and Martha S. Feldman, *Reconstructing Reality in the Courtroom* (New Brunswick, NJ: Rutgers University Press), 5.

[9] Ibid., 97.

[10] *Rhetoric and Poetics of Aristotle,* trans. W. Rhys Roberts (New York: The Modern Library, 1954), see *Rhetoric*, Book 1.

[11] Wayne Brockriede, "Where Is Argument?" *Journal of the American Forensic Association* 9 (1975): 181.

3

AUDIENCES AND FIELDS OF ARGUMENT

Arguments are created for many different reasons, including to change an opinion, to influence someone's behavior, or to justify one's own beliefs or actions. All arguments, however, regardless of their purpose, should be developed with an audience in mind. This is not to suggest that arguers are always aware of their audiences. The exchange of arguments, like many other human activities, sometimes becomes so reflexive that we do not take the time to think carefully through our argument strategies. One of the goals for this book is to help you to become more strategic in the arguments that you choose to develop. To achieve this goal and to enhance the effectiveness of your arguments you need to think about the people who compose the audiences you want to influence with your arguments.

We have already established that people reason by assessing the quality of the competing claims that they hear in rival stories. Some stories hold together better than others. Their plots are more compelling, their characters are given clear and distinctive roles to play, and they play them in accordance with our expectations. These stories are judged to have met the test of narrative probability. Likewise, some stories are especially believable and credible to us because they seem to confirm and explain the experiences that we have had in our lives. These stories ring true to us, and because they correspond with our prior experiences they lend a sense of predictability to our lives. When confronted with such a story we know how to respond, because we have seen how such stories can be expected to turn out. These stories are judged to have narrative fidelity.

While we believe that all people reason by testing the quality of the stories they encounter in their daily lives, we also know that alternative stories appeal to different people. An arguer who seeks to prove that a story is credible must find a way to appeal to the values, experiences, and beliefs of his or her audience. Arguers should seek to construct stories that are coherent, complete, and satisfying. They should also attempt to tell stories that are similar in both content and form to other stories that the people whom they are trying to convince have already heard and experienced. Stories are much more likely to be accepted as believable if they seem somewhat familiar to us. Arguers should also attempt to find ways to tell their stories so that these narratives affirm the self-concept and self-interest of the person(s) whom they are trying to convince.

KNOWING YOUR AUDIENCE

One of the first challenges that you face as an arguer is to identify the *audience* for your arguments. Sometimes this is easy. If, for example, you are having an argument with a close friend about how the two of you should spend your evening together, the target for your arguments is obvious. In other argument situations, however, identifying your audience is much more difficult. A salesman who is showing a new car to a married couple, for example, might direct his arguments about the car's features primarily to the husband on the assumption that men may be more knowledgeable about and interested in automotive features. If the car is going to be driven primarily by the wife and she is going to be responsible for making the decision about what type of car is purchased, however, it might be a big mistake for the salesman to focus on persuading the husband of the car's benefits. Not only might the salesman not be fully responsive to the wife's questions or concerns about the car, but his misdirected arguments, and of course, the sexist attitudes that they reveal, could alienate the couple and result in a lost sale.

In complex argument situations, even identifying the appropriate audience for your arguments can be more difficult. In a political campaign candidates conduct expensive, complicated, and time-consuming public opinion polls in order to identify the values, beliefs, and interests of potential voters. Candidates must address the issues that voters believe are most important. Yet, there may be times in a campaign when a candidate's personal political convictions and ideology might prompt him/her to advance arguments that do not seem to resonate very well with potential voters. For example, during the 2000 presidential campaign, Governor George W. Bush frequently emphasized his proposal for a huge $1.6 trillion tax cut. Public opinion polls consistently revealed, however, that the voters, especially moderates, were not particularly motivated by the tax cut issue. They were much more interested in focusing on issues such as educational policy and health care.

Another challenge that political candidates often face is that they must simultaneously address arguments to political partisans who already share their ideology as well as to undecided voters who may not share these opinions. To win the nomination of a political party, for instance, candidates seek to appeal to voters who are highly partisan and already committed to the values that shape the agenda of their particular party. Such voters tend to make up their minds fairly early in a campaign season. Once having made their decision about which candidate they will vote for they tend not to be very open to appeals from other candidates. In most closely contested general elections, however, candidates also attempt to appeal to voters who are far less committed to a particular viewpoint or to a particular candidate. These undecided, independent, and crossover voters actually determine the outcome of most closely contested elections. These voters tend not be very partisan, are often not very interested in politics and do not pay very much attention to the campaigns or issues, and tend to make their decisions about how they will vote, or even if they will vote, very late in a campaign. A vital part of the campaign process for a candidate then is identifying precisely who these undecided voters are and what issues are most likely to provoke them to vote for him or her (or to discourage them from voting for the opponent).

The techniques of modern public opinion polling permit political candidates to target their appeals toward very unique and specific clusters of potential voters. A candidate seeking to win the votes of suburbanites working in white-collar jobs will want to make very different arguments than a candidate seeking to win support from blue-collar residents of big cities. Candidates sometimes develop such sophisticated knowledge about their audiences that they construct appeals that are explicitly targeted toward very narrow audience segments. In local elections, for example, candidates may focus on winning the votes of teachers or public employees. Even if such voters might represent only a small portion of the total electorate, their votes can swing an election. Candidates will also emphasize issues that cut across economic or social class issues to reach out to voters who might share certain views or concerns. For example, a candidate might emphasize child-care issues because he or she understands that a substantial number of potential voters are single parents who must worry daily about balancing their responsibilities as wage earners with their responsibility to provide care for their children.

ASSESSING YOUR AUDIENCE

Although you will not likely know as much about the values and opinions of the audience that you are trying to convince with your arguments as will a politician who has consulted with a public opinion researcher, you should try to understand your audience as well as you can. One way to begin assessing your audience is by considering its demographic characteristics. Demographic characteristics are, of course, far from reliable predictors of the attitudes and values that people hold. Indeed, these attributes may sometimes even serve to mislead arguers. Nonetheless, this is at least an appropriate place to start thinking about the characteristics of your likely audience. Knowing demographic characteristics—age, social affiliations, gender, education and knowledge, background and experience, and culture—can be potentially useful for assessing your audience.

Age

In his book, *The Rhetoric,* written in the fourth century B.C.E., Aristotle discussed the differences between trying to persuade the young, the elderly, and those in the prime of life. Aristotle observed that young people were more likely to have volatile tempers, and they were also more concerned with pursuing victory and with proving their superiority over others. In contrast, he noted that old people were far less likely to have the emotional volatility of youth, but they were far more likely to be stubborn and set in their ways. Persons of middle age, however, those whom Aristotle described as being in their prime, typically did not have the extreme characteristics of those either younger or older than themselves.[1] One can surmise that Aristotle probably made these statements while he was himself in the prime of life! While Aristotle's notions of how the attitudes and values of people may change as they age might seem a bit simplistic and stereotypical today, his comments continue to have some validity.

Common wisdom suggests that age might have significant influence on the values that people hold and on how open they are to arguments suggesting alternative views. An audience composed of older persons may, for example, be more likely to hold conservative views on social issues than might an audience composed of younger persons. Also, because audiences are most likely to be concerned about issues that directly affect them, young persons might be especially concerned with issues such as a military draft or the availability of federal funds to help them finance their education. Middle-aged persons might be especially concerned with issues such as access to quality day-care programs for their children or the condition of local parks and recreational facilities. Older persons might be more concerned about issues such as the cost of medical care, the sufficiency of their pensions or Social Security checks, and the level of their property taxes.

An especially interesting example of an issue that has different impacts on people depending upon their age is interest rates. The young are delighted when interest rates are low. Lower rates make borrowing money to attend college, buy a car, or purchase or furnish a home much easier. Older people are less likely to be negotiating new loans to buy property. Indeed, many retired citizens seek to live off the income from their investments. Extended periods of time with low interest rates means that elderly investors will get a much smaller return on their investments. Thus, economic conditions that greatly benefit one age group can pose serious problems for another.

American political candidates seem to spend significantly more time discussing issues that are of concern to elderly and middle-aged voters than they do to issues of concern to young people. This is because these politicians have learned that young people are far less likely to vote than older citizens. Yet many studies have suggested that the avoidance of issues that might interest, concern, and motivate young voters has the effect of further discouraging their political participation, diminishing their interest in politics, and decreasing their sense of political empowerment.[2] Neglecting any segment of your audience when advancing arguments can thus have consequences that may go beyond your likelihood of achieving a successful outcome in any single situation. It may leave behind a residue of attitudes and opinions that inhibit your ability to be effective in future situations.

Social Affiliations

People belong to a variety of groups, and these memberships may give you some insight into their attitudes and values. People select their affiliations because they are interested in certain topics, issues, and problems; because they enjoy certain types of interactions or recreational activities; because the group reflects their cultural or occupational interests; and so forth. Most people are socialized to acquire many of the values, attitudes, and beliefs of those with whom they spend our time and engage in conversations; people often become more like those with whom they interact.

Obviously, you can learn something about people if you determine what political party they belong to; if they are religious or not; what church they might attend; and what civic, occupational, or recreational groups they belong to. A member of the National Rifle Association probably would have very different values than would a member of the Sierra Club, even though both groups may have an interest in the preservation of wetlands. People who belong to the Reverend Jerry Falwell's group known as the Moral Majority and people who belong to the gay rights group ACT UP probably have little in common. People who are drawn to membership in the Jaycees or the local Chamber of Commerce will likely acquire attitudes about their communities, about the importance of civic identity, and about the political issues that concern these associations.

Knowledge about the specific group affiliations of your audience will help you to construct your arguments to be maximally effective. Such knowledge might also reveal that you are attempting to appeal to an audience who either already agrees with you or is beyond persuasion, regardless of the best arguments that you can muster.

Gender

While it might be difficult to ascertain people's values on the basis of their gender, gender often influences our values and attitudes and the degree to which certain arguments appeal to us. For example, an audience composed primarily of men might be more receptive to football examples than might an audience composed of women. On the other hand, an audience of women might be expected to be more interested in arguments focused on women's rights.

Women are more likely than men to have experienced gender discrimination, and consequently we can expect that they would be more sensitive to it. While male attitudes on issues such as acquaintance rape, sexual harassment, and domestic spousal abuse are no doubt changing, it is likely that these issues will still be more compelling for an audience of women than for an audience of men. This was certainly revealed by the public responses to the 1991 confirmation hearings of Supreme Court Justice Clarence Thomas. While the Senate was conducting hearings to determine whether or not Justice Thomas should be confirmed, Anita Hill, a law professor from the University of Oklahoma and a former law clerk for Justice Thomas, came forward and charged him with sexual harassment. The charge was investigated by the Senate Judiciary Committee, which at the time was composed entirely of men. Ultimately the committee held televised public hearings where Hill was called to testify. Others were then called to testify both to buttress and to refute her statements. Thomas, who like Hill is an African American, appeared before the committee and sought to frame the episode as an expression of American racism. He protested that the charges made against him were tantamount to a "high-tech lynching." Many women, especially feminist activists, expressed outrage that the committee seemed to turn on the alleged victim rather than the accused perpetrator. After Thomas was confirmed and sworn into office the issue was kept alive in public arguments that lambasted the Senate as a "boys club" and declared that women could not expect a fair and impartial hearing by such a group of men.

Further evidence that substantial differences in how arguments and/or positions on issues may appeal to men and women was also revealed by the so-called "gender gap" that has persisted in American politics over the past decade. Public opinion polls have revealed with some consistency that women are more concerned with social issues such as education, health, retirement security, the environment, and public welfare. Men, on the other hand, are more likely to be concerned about the state of the economy, crime, and foreign policy. Likewise, in recent years women have been more inclined to favor moderate and/or liberal candidates while men have more likely favored conservative candidates. Indeed, the victories by the Democrats in 1992 and 1996 were frequently cited as resulting from the strong "gender gap" that advantaged Bill Clinton over both George Herbert Walker Bush and Robert Dole. Even though the Republicans captured the White House in 2000, the Bush-Cheney ticket lost the popular vote in large part because the significant "gender gap" persisted.[3]

Education and Knowledge

Arguers must seek to adapt their arguments to the educational and intellectual level of their audiences. Not only might persons of different educational backgrounds harbor different attitudes and values, they may process arguments differently. The more sophisticated and educated an audience is, the more likely that they will be able to follow and to evaluate complex argument forms. In fact, more sophisticated and educated audiences are more likely to demand such arguments and are less likely to be swayed by emotional appeals.

Those who share knowledge about a subject also share the ability to communicate in the jargon of that discipline. Thus, an audience composed of physicians will argue about alternative treatments for patients with AIDS using more sophisticated terms than the general public would use. Arguers should also recognize the fact that certain educational experiences might predispose people toward certain beliefs. An audience composed of scientists, for example, would be more inclined to place their faith in science as a means to solve social problems than might an audience composed of musicians. Even a shared appreciation of the scientific method might not be sufficient to facilitate shared understanding, however. For example, an audience of nuclear engineers is more likely to favor the continued development of nuclear power than would be an audience composed of biologists.

Background and Experience

The background and experience of audience members will have tremendous influence on their attitudes and values. An audience member who has had a friend or family member killed by a drunk driver, for example, may have far stronger opinions about the need to tighten controls on those who drink and drive than might someone else. Likewise, a parent who is raising a rebellious teenager might be more sympathetic to the parents of a gang member than might the parents of a docile and well-adjusted teenager.

People screen the arguments and the stories that they hear through their own experiences, and the more knowledge you have about the experiences of your audience members the more effective you can be in adjusting your ideas to them. People seem naturally to favor stories that elevate their own personal sense of importance and worth. We have a natural resistance to stories that make us personally responsible for negative consequences or outcomes if we can find a story that credibly affixes the responsibility on others or on external factors beyond our control. In a previous research study for example, Hollihan and Riley discovered that the parents of delinquent children were resistant to arguments that blamed their own parenting practices or personal failings (e.g., their alcoholism or failed marriages) for the behavior of their children. They were, on the other hand, quite willing to blame their children's delinquency on the inadequacy of the public schools, on their children's friends, on the images of youth conveyed by the mass media, on the police, or even on their own children's intrinsically evil nature.[4] Therefore, in addition to knowing about the experiences of audience members you need to consider how they see themselves as actors in their own life stories.

Culture

One especially important factor that influences how people evaluate arguments is their culture. People are socialized into their culture in myriad different ways, and their cultures can unknowingly influence their opinions, values, and actions. For instance, people raised in the U.S. culture generally have very different values, attitudes, and opinions than those raised in the Middle East, Asia, or even Europe. We often see the effects of cultural differences when immigrants come to the United States. People from different cultures may clash with their neighbors over such issues as child-rearing, religious practices, style of dress, and so forth. Sometimes there are also tensions between generations. Parents who have come to the United States from abroad bring their cultural traditions with them. However, their children, who are exposed to U.S. culture at school, through interactions with peers, and through the media, see the world very differently than they do. Given the tremendous differences in their native environments, religious beliefs, forms of government, family traditions, and political systems, it should come as no surprise that people from these different cultures experience and evaluate arguments differently.

Research has suggested, for example, that Chinese arguers use very different strategies and argumentation styles than do Westerners. Chinese arguers are more likely to mask their emotions; they are more likely to use silences to punctuate their differences; and they are far less likely to display their disagreements or negative feelings.[5] Westerners frequently misunderstand what Chinese arguers are actually communicating. Westerners assume that the absence of direct disagreement or the lengthy silences mean the Chinese arguers agree with them, when in fact they may not.

Arguers should be aware that in our world people from different cultures are more and more frequently coming into contact with each other. The great cities of the world—for instance, London, Paris, Amsterdam, Rome, Hong Kong, New York, and Los Angeles—are becoming increasingly diverse. In addition, new global economic forces are changing the way nations and their citizens must conduct business. People can no longer live in isolation. The management of our social and political life and the public policies that must be designed to maintain social harmony increasingly demand that arguers be sensitive to differences in culture.

PEOPLE EVALUATE ARGUMENTS DIFFERENTLY

We have already asserted our claim that people evaluate arguments in accordance with the principles of storytelling. It is understandable that people evaluate these stories based upon their own unique backgrounds, experiences, age, interests, affiliations, and culture. If arguments must appeal to such a wide range of viewpoints, what is an arguer to do? How can you ever learn enough about your audience to be able to tailor your arguments to suit them? Furthermore, how can you avoid alienating some people in the effort to appeal to others? The Belgian philosopher and legal theorist, Chaim Perelman and his colleague L. Olbrechts-Tyteca, observe:

> Argumentation aimed exclusively at a particular audience has the drawback that the speaker, by the very fact of adapting to the values of his [sic] listeners, might rely on arguments that are foreign or even directly opposed to what is acceptable to persons other than those he is presently addressing.[6]

Perelman and Olbrechts-Tyteca suggest that arguers direct their appeals to a **universal audience**. This universal audience is not an actual, existing one but is instead created in the mind of the arguer. They believe that by using this abstract audience as a reference point for evaluating arguments, one can better tailor arguments to a broad range of potential audience members. Perelman and Olbrechts-Tyteca stress that "argumentation addressed to a universal audience must convince the reader that the reasons adduced are of a compelling character, that they are self-evident, and possess an absolute and timeless validity, independent of local or historical contingencies."[7] To create arguments for this universal audience, one should seek to create claims that will appeal to all reasoning persons. Although not an easy task, this is an appropriate goal for arguers to pursue. So how should an arguer proceed?

Perelman and Olbrechts-Tyteca stress that one should seek to develop arguments that make use of *objective facts* that are knowable and uncontested. Such objective facts can then be used to assert *obvious truths*, generalizations that are commonly shared and understood. Perelman and Olbrechts-Tyteca acknowledge the difficulty in finding such readily agreed upon "facts" and "truths" when they observe that there are significant differences among people in this regard. They argue, "Everyone constitutes the universal audience from what he [sic] knows of his fellow men, in such a way as to transcend the few oppositions he is aware of. Each individual, each culture, has thus its own conception of the universal audience."[8] The universal audience is thus a construction of the arguer—a self-conscious test that the arguer should submit any argument to in order to make it as strong as possible. Perelman and Olbrechts-Tyteca also recognize that, on rare occasions, there might be audience members who do not recognize the "objective facts" or "obvious truths" present in the arguments that you create. To some extent they feel that it would be legitimate to dismiss these recalcitrant few as stupid or abnormal. The danger in this is that you may find yourself making arguments designed to persuade fewer and fewer people, because you have castigated as stupid all those who do not agree with you and see the world as you see it.

Although the conception of the universal audience does not eliminate all challenges in adapting arguments to different viewpoints, it does lead to the creation of arguments that appeal to the largest number of people. Arguers should therefore be aware of the need to create arguments that will convince the broader universal audience in addition to the unique interests, concerns, and beliefs of their particular audiences. Arguers need to search continually for objective facts and obvious truths, because the very process of argumentative investigation can strengthen arguments and help create stronger cases.

THE PRINCIPLE OF *PRESENCE*

Perelman and Olbrechts-Tyteca also propose that arguers consider the notion of *presence*. In using this term, they stress how arguers should take steps in order that the arguments they create will be seen as especially important to their audience. Perelman and Olbrechts-Tyteca suggest that the simplest way to given an argument presence is through repetition. If a particular argument is important to your overall case it should be stated repeatedly, either in the same speech or essay or in several speeches or essays. For example, President George W. Bush in the first one hundred days of his term of office emphasized his desire to enact a significant income tax cut in virtually every speech he gave. The tax cut had been the primary plank in his platform during the campaign and it was declared to be his most pressing priority once he was inaugurated. By trying to sell his tax cut to the public at every opportunity he sought to create such a groundswell of support that he could overwhelm all opposition in Congress.

Perelman and Olbrechts-Tyteca also observe that an arguer can further accentuate important arguments or passages in oral presentations by the tone of voice that is used, by increasing one's volume, or by pausing just before uttering them.[9] Successful speakers often find that they can increase the presence that a particular argument may have by the use of gestures, facial expressions, and other nonverbal cues.

Even if you have created your arguments with the notion of a universal audience in mind, it is helpful if you can find a way to make your arguments uniquely appealing to the particular audience that you are addressing. We have already detailed the ways in which different people might be expected to have different responses to the arguments that they encounter. How then do you accomplish this task? How do you create arguments that have universal appeal but that also elicit your particular audience's attention to and concern for the issues you are presenting?

To a certain extent, the notion of presence suggests concern for the stylistic dimensions of creating and communicating your arguments. It is typically help-ful to try to communicate with your audience, rather than to adopt a preachy or highly judgmental tone. You should also be sensitive to the feedback your audi-ence is providing by watching for signs of confusion or misunderstanding, nods of agreement, head shakes, frowns, or others responses that might signal a fail-ure in communicating your message.

Arguers should also seek to pique the interests of their audiences, to pro-voke their sympathy or their feelings of empathy, to construct arguments so that audiences really feel them. Perelman and Olbrechts-Tyteca illustrate the concept of presence with a Chinese proverb: "A king sees an ox on its way to sacrifice. He is moved to pity for it and orders that a sheep be used in its place. He confesses he did so because he could see the ox, but not the sheep."[10]

One of the rescue missions that provide assistance to the homeless in Los Angeles sends out mailings to potential donors to raise funds to support their efforts. Even though most of the recipients of the aid, and indeed most homeless people in Los Angeles, are men who abuse and have become dependent on alco-hol or drugs, the mission's solicitations often emphasize the plight of homeless children. In this way, the mission creates greater presence as to the problem of homelessness in the city and probably gains more donations. It is much easier to provoke concern for the plight of the homeless when the emphasis is on victims who did not make choices that led to their own suffering.*

As an arguer, your goal should be to develop arguments and a style of pre-sentation that will make the issues that you raise seem uniquely important to your audience so that they will choose to devote their attention to them. During the 2000 presidential campaign, for example, Vice President Al Gore sought to convince voters that the strong economy and low rates of unemployment and

---

* We are not suggesting that there are not significant numbers of homeless children and families in Los Angeles, or in any other large U.S. city. Nor are we suggesting that the homeless missions in Los Angeles do not provide assistance to such families. We also are not arguing that their appeals for donations are in any way deceptive. Instead, we see these appeals as conscious decisions to try to capitalize on the public's understandable sympathies and concern for disadvantaged children.

inflation achieved during the eight years of the Clinton–Gore administration were so significant that he should be elected president. In essence, Gore was arguing that he should be elected to the third term that President Clinton was prohibited from earning. Republican candidate Governor George W. Bush, on the other hand, argued that the moral failings of the Clinton administration were the real legacy of this era. Bush argued that these problems represented such a stain on the Clinton and Gore administration that they were alone sufficient reason to deny Gore the White House. Unfortunately for the vice president, he discovered that the economic achievements of the past eight years did not seem to have sufficient presence for voters to assure his election. Although it is difficult to say precisely what issue or issues may have tipped the balance toward the Republican candidate, an argument can be made that many voters were upset about the Clinton scandals, and Governor Bush was able to win a narrow majority of the votes in the Electoral College.

Identifying which arguments will have presence for your audience, and finding ways to present your arguments in a style that maximizes their importance, requires knowledge of your audience and of the techniques for presenting arguments. In contemporary election campaigns candidates will make extensive use of public opinion polls to learn more about their audiences. In addition, they will then frequently test their argument strategies through the use of focus groups. Although such discovery strategies are not likely available to most arguers, they demonstrate the importance of adjusting ideas and arguments to listeners.

ARGUMENT FIELDS

Philosopher Stephen Toulmin developed another view of how people construct and evaluate arguments. Trained as a logician, Toulmin became increasingly frustrated with the limitations of formal logic. He felt that the principles of formal logic were useful but did not reflect how people actually reasoned when making everyday decisions. Toulmin's colleagues believed that logical models were the most appropriate means for rationally arriving at conclusions and that the requirements for a rational argument did not change from one context to another. Toulmin argued, however, that different situations or contexts—which he came to refer to, as *fields*—demanded different standards for arguments. As Toulmin and his coauthors Richard Rieke and Alan Janik declared:

> The trains of reasoning that it is appropriate to use vary from situation to situation. As we move from the lunch counter to the executive conference table, from the science laboratory to the law courts, the "forum" of discussion changes profoundly. The kind of involvement that the participants have with the outcome of the reasoning is entirely different in the different situations and so also will be the ways in which possible outcomes of the argument are tested and judged.[11]

Arguments can be considered to be in the same field when the data and conclusions are of essentially the same logical type. They will be in different fields when the data and conclusions are markedly different or in a case where the same data leads to different conclusions.[12]

To understand Toulmin's view of argumentation theory it is important to determine what he meant by "*fields*." Toulmin viewed the term *fields* and the term *disciplines* as roughly synonymous. His claim was that physicists argue similarly because they share training in physics. Likewise, attorneys argue in a similar fashion, members of the clergy share an argument style, as do historians, physicians, engineers, and so on. These disciplinary boundaries are not always formal or predictive. For example, physicists might be expected to argue in a similar fashion to engineers, biologists, chemists, and perhaps even physicians, because the scientific method underlies their shared fields.

Still other complications can occur because people are often members of several different argument fields simultaneously. Someone may be, for example, both a fundamentalist Christian and a scientist. As a Christian, this person might accept the biblical account of the creation of the universe as outlined in the Book of Genesis. As a scientist, on the other hand, this person might be inclined to accept Charles Darwin's theory of evolution. In such a situation the person who belongs to the incompatible fields is continually forced to reconcile the tensions that may occur between them, and also to decide from situation to situation which field's argument standards to apply.

Other argumentation theorists have suggested that it would be useful to consider argument fields from a broader perspective than that of disciplines. Charles Arthur Willard has suggested that fields should be seen as sociological entities. Willard says that fields encompass terms such as "groups," "organizations," "frameworks," and "relationships," particularly when these entities come to share a "constellation of practices."[13]

Willard claims that the practices of any field are consensually developed as its members come to agreements regarding how their day-to-day work proceeds. Thus, chemists forge appropriate techniques for resolving disputes in the field of chemistry as they conduct their daily work. Likewise, accountants discuss their daily challenges and responsibilities, and then they propose appropriate means for addressing the problems that they share, so that they continually hone the standards and practices of their profession. There may be times as well when there are arguments within a field and even across fields about what should be the appropriate standards of a field.

One illustration of such a confrontation of conflicting standards might be the recent controversy involving the Enron Corporation and its accounting practices. Arthur Anderson, the accounting firm whose accountants conducted the audit of Enron, argued that it was "normal accounting practice" to destroy the records of the audit and to shred documents. The attorneys, representing both the government and private investors, argued that the destruction of the audit records were tantamount to the destruction of evidence in a court action and therefore constituted a criminal act. The dispute that resulted concerned whether or not the destruction of such records did indeed constitute accepted practice within the field of accounting (an intrafield dispute); then, assuming that it did, the dispute would focus on whether or not the practices of the legal field should be given primary consideration over those of accounting once a court action had been filed (an interfield dispute).

Willard acknowledges that although some fields may simply take a body of knowledge for granted, most fields actively attempt to perfect and improve the knowledge in the field.[14] Thus for example, chefs argue about the best way to prepare a soufflé, orthopedic surgeons about the best way to treat a ruptured disc, hairdressers about the best way to color hair so that it looks natural, accountants about the best ways to conduct audits, and so forth. Willard also stresses that even the decision to participate in a particular field (which may on some occasions be an unconscious choice) may end up constraining the participant's ways of thinking about and approaching problems. To participate in the discussions within a field usually entails surrendering a certain amount of personal freedom, because one will now begin to see the world from the perspective of that field. Consequently, the attorney is always seeing problems from the perspective of questions of law, the scientist from the perspective of scientific inquiry, and the artist from an aesthetic perspective.[15]

Just as their audiences are composed of persons who represent fields or perspectives, arguers themselves represent particular fields or perspectives. Awareness of the implications of field theory should help you to become more aware of the degree to which your own experiences, beliefs, training, and membership in certain groups or organizations influences your argumentative techniques.

A few arguments may be so compelling that they meet the requirements for argumentative proof in all fields. Toulmin calls these arguments *field-invariant*.[16] For example, most of us would accept as true the claim that parents who love their children naturally want to protect them from harm. This claim could be called field-invariant. Even a claim that seems as clear-cut as this one, however, may not indeed always be true. As an illustration, let us recall the religious cult called the Branch Davidians.

In 1993, members of the Branch Davidians, including many parents and children ranging in age from infants to teenagers, holed up in a compound outside of Waco, Texas. When agents of the Bureau of Alcohol, Tobacco and Firearms tried to serve a search warrant on them to investigate claims that the group was dealing in illegal guns, the cultists opened fire on the federal agents, killing several of them. The FBI then surrounded the compound and for fifty-one days sought to convince the cultists to surrender, or at least to send the children out of the compound so that they would not be hurt. Finally, the government decided to fire tear gas into the compound to try to force the occupants to leave. Suddenly the building burst into flames. It is still under dispute whether the federal agents somehow inadvertently sparked the fire, or if the people inside deliberately set fire to the compound. What is known, however, is that the flames consumed almost one hundred persons, including twenty-four children, seventeen of whom were under the age of ten.[17]

It was extremely difficult for the rest of the world to understand how parents could intentionally put their children at such risk, or perhaps even cause their deaths, especially in such a terrible manner. Those of us who do not share these parents' beliefs and who did not participate in the Branch Davidians' field, may feel that these parents did not love their children enough to try to save them.[18] To members of this religious community, however, the decision to perish in the fire may have seemed very rational, and the taking of their children's lives might have been an expression of their love for them. In their minds, the fiery end to this siege may have confirmed a biblical prophecy that fire would consume the earth and that the true believers of Christ would find their way to heaven.[19] Thus, for the Branch Davidians, fiery Armageddon represented not the end of their children's lives, but the promise of a new beginning in heaven. Even the argument that parents who love their children want to protect them, which seems to be field-invariant, is thus found to be *field-dependent*.[20]

Arguers should try to be sensitive to the requirements for establishing claims in the argument field in which they are participating and create arguments that will satisfy the audience by appealing to their identification with a particular field. When dealing with people from different argument fields, or when it is difficult to determine what field's standards should be applied, it is desirable to create arguments that will appeal to people in as many different fields as possible. In a sense, this is the pursuit of arguments that appeal to the universal audience.

Another task that arguers sometimes face is the need to translate arguments from one field to another. Frequently this process means creating stories that appeal to people from different fields. As an illustration of this process we might cite the case of a scientist who is attempting to find scientific explanations for biblical stories. For example, an astronomer might speculate on any events in the heavens on the night Christ was born that could explain the story about the three wise men following the path of a star to find the newborn baby.

SUMMARY

If possible, arguers should carefully consider the values and attitudes of their audiences in forming their arguments. The audience's demographic factors may provide insight into their interests, needs, and experiences. Arguers should also attempt to emphasize and give greater presence to those aspects of their arguments that are most likely to appeal to their listeners. In addition, arguers should recognize that people respond differently to arguments and often use different standards for evaluating arguments based on the fields to which they belong. Although it may be impossible to convince all your listeners, your goal should be the creation of arguments that will appeal to a universal audience of reasoning persons.

Key Terms

audience
field-dependent
field-invariant
fields

objective facts
obvious truths
presence
universal audience

Activities

1. To practice analyzing an audience, conduct a demographic analysis of your class.

   a. What is the age span of your class? What is the average age of your class?

   b. What are the social affiliations of the class members?

   c. What is the educational background of the class?

   d. What are the cultural perspectives of your classmates?

2. Select a recent public controversy. Based on the information gleaned above, assume that your classmates compose your audience for arguments that you would make about this controversy. How will your classmates view the controversy? Answer the following questions:

   a. Would your classmates' views change if they were older? Were their views different when they were younger?

   b. Would your classmates' views change if they had different social affiliations?

   c. Would your classmates' views change if they were better educated? Would their views be different if they were less well educated?

   d. Would your classmates' views change if they were part of a different culture?

3. Take a position on the public controversy identified in the preceding exercise. Now imagine supporting your position with two different audiences. If the only difference you knew about the two audiences was that they differed in age, how might you adapt your argument to gain the adherence of each of these two audiences? Repeat this for each of the audience variables identified in this chapter.

4. Listen to an argument interaction by, for instance, listening to a radio talk show, watching a talk show on television, attending a public meeting of local or student government, or observing your friends engaging in argument. Now analyze the interaction.

   a. List the objective facts (those facts that are knowable and uncontested by the disputants).

   b. List the obvious truths (those generalizations that are commonly shared and understood).

   c. What facts and truths were contested? Were these points of disagreement resolved? If so how were they resolved? If not, how might they have been resolved?

5. To learn more about the nature of argument fields, attend a meeting of your local city council and observe a criminal trial proceeding.

   a. What are the differences, if any, in what constitutes acceptable evidence in the two fields of argument?

b. How do the participants introduce facts?

c. How do the participants challenge the facts introduced by another participant?

d. Are there controls on who may speak or on what they can say?

Recommended Readings

Crosswhite, James. "Universality in Rhetoric: Perelman's Universal Audience." *Philosophy & Rhetoric* 22 (1989): 157–172.

Dean, Farmer J. "Scholarly Communities and the Discipline of the Communication Discipline." *Southern Communication Journal* 63 (1998): 169–173.

Dearen, Ray D. "Perelman's Concept of Quasi-logical Argument: A Critical Elaboration." In *Advances in Argumentation Theory and Research*, ed. J. Robert Cox and Charles Arthur Willard, 78–94. Carbondale: Southern Illinois University Press, 1982.

Farrell, Thomas B. "Validity and Rationality: The Rhetorical Constituents of Argumentative Form." *Journal of the American Forensic Association* 13 (1977): 142–149.

Gross, Alan. "A Theory of the Rhetorical Audience: Reflections on Chaim Perelman." *Quarterly Journal of Speech* 85 (1999): 203–211.

McKerrow, Ray E. "Rhetorical Validity: An Analysis of Three Perspectives on the Justification of Rhetorical Argument." *Journal of the American Forensic Association* 13 (1977): 133–141.

Murphy, John J. "Presence, Analogy, and Earth in the Balance." *Argumentation and Advocacy* 31 (1994): 1–16.

Prosise, Theodore O., and Greg R. Miller. "Argument Fields as Arenas of Discursive Struggle." *Argumentation & Advocacy* 32 (1996): 111–129.

Rieke, Richard D., and Malcolm O. Sillars. *Argumentation and Critical Decision Making*, 4th ed. New York: Longman, 1997.

Scult, Allen. "A Note on the Range and Utility of the Universal Audience." *Journal of the American Forensic Association* 22 (1985): 83–87.

Toulmin, Stephen E. *Human Understanding.* Princeton: Princeton University Press, 1972.

Toulmin, Stephen E., Richard Rieke, and Allan Janik. *An Introduction to Reasoning.* New York: MacMillan, 1979.

Tucker, Robert E. "Figure, Ground and Presence: A Phenomenology of Meaning in Rhetoric." *Quarterly Journal of Speech* 87 (2001): 396–414.

Notes

[1] *Rhetoric and Poetics of Aristotle*, trans. W. Rhys Roberts (New York: The Modern Library, 1954), 121–126.

[2] Thomas A. Hollihan, *Uncivil Wars: Political Campaigns in a Media Age* (New York: Bedford/St. Martin's Press, 2001).

[3] "Big Gender Gap Distinguishes Election 2000," http://www.gallup.com (Accessed 2/22/02).

[4] Thomas A. Hollihan and Patricia Riley, "The Rhetorical Power of a Compelling Story: A Critique of a 'Toughlove' Parental Support Group," *Communication Quarterly* 35 (1987): 13–25.

[5] Michael J. Cody, Wen-Shu Lee, and Edward Yi Chao, "Telling Lies: Correlates of Deception Among Chinese," in *Recent Advances in Social Psychology: An International Perspective*, ed. J. P. Forgans and J. M. Innes, 359–368 (North-Holland: Elsevier Science Publishers, 1989).

[6] Chaim Perelman and L. Olbrechts-Tyteca, *The New Rhetoric* (Notre Dame: The University of Notre Dame Press, 1969), 31.

[7] Ibid., 32.

[8] Ibid., 33.

[9] Ibid., 144.

[10] Ibid., 116.

[11] Stephen E. Toulmin, Richard Rieke, and Alan Janik, *An Introduction to Reasoning* (New York: MacMillan, 1979), 7.

[12] Stephen E. Toulmin, *The Uses of Argument* (Cambridge: Cambridge University Press, 1958), 14.

[13] Charles Arthur Willard, "Argument Fields," in *Advances in Argumentation Theory and Research*, ed. J. Robert Cox and Charles Arthur Willard, 30 (Carbondale: Southern Illinois University Press, 1982).

[14] Ibid., 30.

[15] Ibid., 38.

[16] Toulmin, 36.

[17] For a discussion of the siege and its fiery conclusion, see J. Michael Kennedy, "Waco Cultists Perish in Blaze," *Los Angeles Times*, April 20, 1993.

[18] For a discussion of public reactions to the tragedy in Waco, see J. Michael Kennedy and Lianne Hart, "In the Eye of the Cult Firestorm," *Los Angeles Times*, April 20, 1993.

[19] Ibid.

[20] Toulmin, 38.

THE LANGUAGE
OF ARGUMENT

Israel has been subjected to repeated attacks by suicide bombers: Ordinary public spaces, including restaurants, bars, billiards parlors, markets, buses, and a university student center, have been rocked by explosions. Hundreds of persons, including men, women, and children, have been killed or injured. The rhythms of daily life have been destroyed as even the most mundane tasks now expose people to risk. Such wanton and unpredictable acts of violence create palpable feelings of anxiety, damaging people's psyches as well as devastating the economy.

The suicide bombers, almost all of whom have been Palestinians, have ranged in age from their early teens to their forties and have included both men and women. Most of these bombers have come from conditions of dire poverty, and many have spent their entire lives in teeming refugee camp ghettoes. In a few cases, however, the bombers have come from educated and middle-class families. Some of these bombers have been highly religious; others are said to have been more secular in their beliefs. Some of the bombers have been married or engaged to be married, a few had children, and almost all of them left behind parents and/or siblings. In many instances, close friends and family members actually assisted them by helping them to build the bombs or by strapping the bombs to their loved ones' bodies. How does one make sense of such a situation? What would motivate people to strap bombs onto their bodies so that they simultaneously end their own lives and those of strangers? Why would families and/or friends help their loved ones in such a gruesome and deadly task?

To Israelis, and probably to most people in the world, these suicide bombers are vile terrorists and their actions represent a core capacity for unthinkable evil. No political objectives and no experienced injustices could warrant such inhumane and despicable actions as the slaughter of innocent civilian lives. Yet to many Palestinians, and to a significant number of others who also feel that they have experienced poverty and oppression, these suicide bombers are considered heroic freedom fighters and martyrs to a cause whose significance and purpose justifies such sacrifice. From this perspective, the victims in these killings are not innocent civilians, but they are instead representatives of the unjust Israeli state that has denied Palestinians their aspirations for their own nation. Although such killings are unfortunate, they are justified for many because they represent the only means of attack available to a people who lack the resources for conventional war.

Terrorist or freedom fighter, murderer or martyr, wanton slaughter of innocents or justified military action, what then is in a name? Everything. Think for a moment of the different images that these symbols conjure up. Embedded within each of these terms are all kinds of baggage that guide people in the formation of attitudes about the acts themselves and about the motives of those who are responsible for them. The particular symbols that people select to describe the suicide bombings give insight into the experiences, attitudes, values, and ideological positions of those who have selected one term over another. Likewise, the exposure to the different terms in the accounts of the experiences in the aftermath of the violent acts colors the response of those exposed to such conversations.

The televised images of these tragedies are remarkably similar and consistent from one news report to the next. We see images of the site of the explosion, for example the smoking hulk of the now almost unrecognizable city bus; we see pictures of bleeding victims and hear the piercing screams of those around them lamenting their losses; we hear the wail and see the images of the speeding ambulances or see the images of victims in their hospital beds; and we often see contrasting images of the families and friends of those who died—mourning and tears by the families of the victims and joyous celebrations for the heroic acts of the suicide bombers. Despite the similarities in the images that are broadcast on different television networks, the language they use to describe the events and the names given to the bombers and their victims may significantly differ. Each network supplies text to account for and explain the facts illustrated in the visual images, but how those facts are given presence (made especially important to an audience), how those facts are interpreted, and how those facts are given meaning and context change as a result of the language used to describe them. Thus the voice-over texts that accompany the images on CNN will be substantially different from those of Al Jazeerah, the Middle Eastern network.

In the previous chapter we discussed how strategic arguers analyze their audience and the argument context so that they may adapt their arguments and increase their effectiveness. In this chapter, our goal is to demonstrate how language enhances your ability to create arguments that audiences find compelling. We begin by discussing the importance of language in argumentation, move on to consider how language influences the components of a good story, and then conclude by examining a special type of argument: metaphor.

UNDERSTANDING LANGUAGE

The symbols we use to make sense of our experiences are rich with meaning. They reflect our thoughts and values, and they direct us how to act. A label, or more appropriately, language, is a template that constrains what we think and what we know.

Language Defined

Language is a shared symbol system. This rather simple statement has profound implications for the study of argument. First, language is symbolic. In chapter 1 we defined *symbols* as special types of signs that call attention to significances: they relate to what has been perceived; they point to, indicate, or denote something other than themselves. Because symbols relate to what has been perceived, they are, as Kenneth Burke argues, a partial reflection of reality. Furthermore, because we choose which words will represent the thing perceived, our choices reflect our values. Therefore, symbols are also a deflection of reality.[1] By this Burke means that language intervenes between the thing (also known as the subject) and the arguer, and this intervention is not benign. Rather, language has an **epistemic function**; that is, the language we learn and employ shapes and constrains our understanding of what constitutes reality. What is real to us is what we express linguistically, and the language we possess influences how we make sense and what we choose to make sense of in our daily lives.[2]

Meanings do not, of course, inhere in language. We may agree that the object that speakers stand behind when delivering a speech is referred to as a podium, but we also know that many other speakers using our same shared English language might refer to it as a lectern. We also know that if this same podium were found in a church it might be called by still another name, a pulpit. This makes possible linguistically rich understandings of the use of particular terms. For example, if a reporter declares that President George W. Bush used his presidency as a pulpit when delivering a speech about the need to pursue the expulsion of President Saddam Hussein from power in Iraq, he might be referring to a speech that Bush delivered in a church, but he more likely meant that the president spoke from a conventional podium but in a style exhorting us to action in the same way a preacher might in church.

Although such linguistic choices then give texture, complexity, and added power to our rhetorical and argumentative interactions, the fact is that all of the terms themselves are arbitrary. We could have called the podium a *smerl* and the pulpit a *worquel*. The words have meaning only to the extent that everyone using the shared symbols of the language system have agreed to give them the same meaning. The groups agreeing to a meaning may be as large as a culture or as small as a clique that creates its own lingo: surfers, bikers, rockers, skateboarders, heads, and the like.

A culture's agreed upon word meanings are usually detailed in a dictionary, but of course, most of us have never read the entire dictionary. When one does consult a dictionary, one often sees multiple definitions for a single world. Multiple definitions frequently result in misunderstandings about precisely what a word means, what a speaker intended, or what a listener heard being said.

Consider for a moment the word *stump*. According to the *American Heritage Dictionary*,[3] *stump* can refer to a "part of a tree trunk left protruding from the ground after a tree has fallen or been felled"; "any part of a branch, tree, limb, or tooth remaining after the main part has been cut away"; "an artificial leg"; a "short or thick-set person"; a "platform or space used for political oratory"; "to stub a toe"; or "to leave someone in a quandary." Thus if we use the term *stump* in a sentence, and you do not know which usage we intended, we have *stumped* you!

How then do we make sense of the words that others use? One answer is that the symbols we share are governed by the *system* of language, or what is often referred to as the grammar. The rules of language use help us to ascertain which of the various meanings of a word is intended. This principle of linguistic context permits a single word to be used in a multitude of ways. In fact, as I. A. Richards wrote, "Most words, as they pass from context to context, change their meanings; and in many different ways. It is their duty and their service to do so."[4] Understanding the rules of grammar enables us to make sense of the context and assign meanings to the words. Thus if a reporter declared on the evening news that "President Bush traveled up and down the State of California *stumping* for another tax cut," you would presume that he was urging voters to agree with his proposed policy alternative and not that he was deliberately moving about the state seeking to leave voters in a quandary about his intentions with regard to economic policy.

Understanding the definition of a word is only part of the game; dictionaries provide only the **denotative meaning**, that is, the content level of the word. Dictionaries do not always convey the value judgments that are often embedded in words. Nor do they relate how an individual feels about a word. These are considered the **connotative meanings** of the word.

Think for a moment about the term *mother*. The *American Heritage Dictionary*[5] defines mother as "a female that has borne an offspring." But the dictionary also acknowledges a mother as "a female who has adopted a child or otherwise established a maternal relationship"; as "a woman having some of the responsibilities of a mother"; and even as "qualities attributed to a mother, such as the capacity to love." Which sense of the term did you think of initially? None of these dictionary definitions may reflect how you as an individual may think of this term. Were your experiences with your own mother positive? If so, then the word *mother* probably evokes a warm sense of security, fond memories, and love. But for another individual, who may have had an unhappy relationship with his or her mother, perhaps a mother who was neglectful, abusive, or overly controlling, the word *mother* may awaken ambivalent or even negative feelings. In exhorting his people to prepare for the first Gulf War, Saddam Hussein declared that the coming conflict would be "the *mother* of all battles." He was probably not promising a "loving" war. He may or may not have been revealing something about his feelings for his own mother. More likely, however, he was referring to a confrontation that would be so fierce and intense that it would be the equivalent of the primal or first war that defines the very essence of the human experience in conflict. Certainly, as we have shown, words may have different connotative meanings even for those who generally agree on the denotative meaning of the word.

Abstraction

That a speaker and a listener might speak the same language does not mean that arguers and audiences always understand each other. One reason for the failure to achieve shared understanding arises from the principle of **abstraction**. The word *pen* is more specific and concrete than *writing instrument*. The more abstract the term, the more meanings it conveys, and the more opportunity for confusion or obfuscation. Sometimes though, we must recognize that it is the specific and concrete term that has the rhetorical and argumentative power and not the more abstract term. Thus, for example, the declaration: "the *pen* is mightier than the sword" may communicate a greater sense of power than the declaration: "the *writing instrument* is mightier than the sword." It may also have a much greater impact than the more contemporary declaration: "the *word processor* is mightier than the sword."

Confusion can arise when someone who is developing arguments to advocate a position uses language that is more abstract than necessary. This lack of precision can lead an audience to believe they understand an advocate when they do not. Unscrupulous advocates sometimes take advantage of imprecise language to purposely mislead audiences. Political scientist W. Lance Bennett argues that many political candidates ritualistically use highly abstract language.[6] One example of such language would be President George W. Bush's declaration that he is a "compassionate conservative." Individual voters, responding to this message are invited to assign whatever meanings they see as appropriate to each of these terms. They are also free to determine which of these terms that they believe should receive the greatest emphasis, *compassionate* or *conservative*. Candidates often use broadly based appeals, Bennett argues, so that different constituencies can take the candidate's message to mean whatever they want to hear. When a candidate calls for eliminating waste in government, for example, the broad language invites audience members to fill in the specific details themselves. Voters can interpret the targeted wasteful programs as those that benefit others, while presuming that programs beneficial to themselves will be recognized by policy makers as truly essential and will thus be preserved.

Understanding the possibility of ambiguity, the skilled advocate chooses words carefully. If the advocate wants the audience to have a more precise understanding, the advocate uses more precise language. If the opposite is desired, then more abstract language is employed. In that our goal is to emphasize the use of arguments that will enable people to make informed, deliberate, and rational choices, we would strongly urge you to use language that is precise, not misleading or deceptive.

Advocates who wish to enhance understanding should not only select more concrete language, they should also build in argument strategies that include the use of redundancy, repetition of key claims, and the restatement of positions in alternative ways. Listeners often do not hear what is being said the first time and benefit from having arguments repeated. When repeating arguments, it is more effective not to keep repeating the exact same words; this can be annoying and can even cause people to disregard or in extreme cases even mock your arguments. As an example, during the 2000 presidential campaign Vice President Gore kept reasserting that he intended to put social security payments into a "lock box" that could not be raided for any alternative uses. This phrase was repeated so frequently that late-night comedians began to mimic his words and trivialize the importance of his argument.

Since the meanings that we assign to phenomena vary depending on the language used, then the way we depict the characters, scenes, and events can be crucial to how audiences come to understand them. How audiences come to understand arguments, in turn, influences whether or not they will grant adherence to the claims advanced. We will consider how audiences come to evaluate arguments in the next section.

LANGUAGE AND GOOD STORIES

One of the foundational assumptions of the narrative orientation that we employ in this text is that all arguments are conveyed through the use of stories. There are three central elements to any story—characters, scenes, and events. We will now consider how language influences each in turn.

Depicting the Characters in Stories

Central to the narrative perspective is the belief that all humans are social actors. As such, they assume roles; they create images and act in accordance with the impressions that they wish to sustain. They are **characters** in the stories of social life. Dan Nimmo explains: "The dramatistic viewpoint regards all social relationships as dramatic action. A person in a social drama . . . performs in accordance with the image he [sic] wants to leave on his audience."[7] There are two components to the characters in stories: roles and character types.

A **role** is a set of assumptions about how an individual should act based on his or her position, occupation, behavior, and status. We don't expect teachers and students, doctors and patients, parents and children to behave the same way. What behavior we do expect of them is influenced, to an extent, by the roles the individuals are playing. We also judge people's effectiveness at least in large part by how well they seem to fulfill our expectations for the role they are in. Your professor, for example, should be friendly with you but will probably not become your best friend, because to do so might undermine his or her effectiveness as an educator. A "too close" relationship between a student and a professor may diminish the student's respect for the professor and make it awkward for the professor to provide honest and necessary feedback about the student's academic progress. Such a relationship between a student and a professor can also create problems because other students come to perceive that students who are too close to their professors may get special treatment or better grades than they merit.

As another example of our expectations for how people fulfill roles, we could cite the role of judges. We expect that judges will exude confidence, knowledge of the law, and a fair and impartial temperament. We would not feel comfortable having our legal dispute resolved by a judge who seemed tentative, uncertain, uninformed about legal issues, or who seemed to have already made up his or her mind against us before hearing all the facts in the case. Indeed, judges who are unable to fulfill our expectations for their role because they make too many judicial errors, are reversed too often on appeal, or openly express their prejudices from the bench may not only be removed from office but could even, in highly unusual cases, find themselves disbarred.

Another constraint upon how characters fulfill their role in dramas is their *character type*. In his analysis of American literature, Orrin Klapp concluded that there are three major American social types: heroes, villains, and fools.[8] Klapp argued that Americans are guided by the desire to emulate positive social types and to avoid negative ones. Thus, these social types serve as models for how we should behave. Although Klapp's focus was on the unique American character models, we would contend that other cultures probably pursue these same social types, although there will almost certainly be culture-specific expectations for particular roles. For example, Japanese cultural traditions have formed expectations about the personal and social style of a hero that differ from those in the West. In Japan individuals are encouraged not to stand out from the group, whereas in the West individuality is valued as a heroic construct.

One important way to understand the role of characters in stories is to think about different character types as "an organized set of actional tendencies."[9] Because certain character types tend to act in characteristic ways, we develop expectations of how these characters are supposed to act. If they do not behave as we expect them to, we may question whether their presentation is accurate. Kenneth Burke described this phenomenon as satisfying our desire for the fulfillment of "form." He described form as "creation of an appetite in the mind of the auditor and the adequate satisfying of that appetite."[10]

Consider for the moment the character types heroes, villains, and victims. As we observe or even create a story or dramatic plot we can envision actors in each of these roles. Within each character type we can also imagine alternative ways in which the role might be enacted. For example, heroes can be willing or reluctant. They can demonstrate their heroism through the power of their intellect, their raw courage, their moral character, or their physical strength. Heroes can be glib or taciturn. Think for a moment about two heroes from classic American films. In the 1939 film *Mr. Smith Goes to Washington*, Jimmy Stewart plays a shy individual upon whom the role of hero is thrust. He is sent to Congress to represent his state and his simple and straightforward values. He is immediately uncomfortable in this role, and he is depicted as so much the outsider in a capital dominated by cynical professional politicians and highly paid lobbyists that he is the subject of mockery. Yet his naive genius and fundamental moral character are attributes that contribute to the role of the bashful American hero. His greatness stems from his simplicity, and through his honesty, determination, and his willingness to adhere to his own moral compass he is able to bring the forces of corruption to their knees. As the audience watches Mr. Smith confront these evil forces they come to identify with his simple values and thus are enabled to feel just a bit heroic themselves.

Another interesting example of a naive film hero is the role that Tom Hanks plays in the film *Forrest Gump*. Forrest is allowed to emerge as a hero even though he is depicted as mentally challenged and is not especially courageous or physically strong (although he does excel in table tennis). Forrest's heroism emerges through a combination of good fortune and moral innocence. Indeed, his greatest appeal is that he is not corrupted by the dominant values of an era that might have tainted the judgments and the essential "goodness" of contemporaries. Forrest therefore grows up in the racist South, but evidences no bigotry. He loves his childhood sweetheart with a love that is so pure that he immediately forgives her for her own failings or inadequacies. As audiences witness the results of these events they are given reason to reconsider their own values and attitudes.

Compare these heroic characters with the roles played by Arnold Schwarzenegger in his many films. Schwarzenegger's heroism does not emanate from his intellect or even from his naive wisdom. His strength is almost purely physical. With violence, instead of words, Schwarzenegger rights the wrongs of the world and thereby brings evil to its knees. As a protagonist, Schwarzenegger does not give audiences much reason for introspection or self-evaluation. His focus is on action, not wisdom, and on quick reactions, not careful reflection. One might not naturally assume that these heroic traits will help him govern the State of California.

Just as a heroic character may take alternative forms, so too villains will likely come in different types and forms. Klapp differentiates, for example, between villains who symbolize a threat to social order and those who use that order to accomplish their evil deeds. The desperado, outlaw, or gangster may use violence to cause harm and is typically antithetical to social order. When the outlaws ride into town all kinds of terrible things can happen. If all humans acted this way there would be no social order, only anarchy.

The authoritarian dictator, or the manipulator, on the other hand, may adhere to an established social order, but it may be an order that has been manipulated to meet the character's need for power. Such a dictator can achieve control of the military by rewarding generals and key troops and can then use the military to exert control over others who might be inclined to challenge the power of the state. Soon the police, judges, and key business leaders can all be a part of a corrupt state machine that seeks to identify strategies to maintain and expand upon power. The result may be a denial of fundamental human freedoms and democracy, or even the elimination of those persons deemed to be the enemies of the state. Through all the suffering, however, the order of the state is preserved.

Finally, victims may be of various sorts. Some are innocent and unsuspecting, while others are willing martyrs. Still others bring ruin upon themselves because they are unwary, ignorant, or uninvolved. People might be expected to feel greater sympathy for victims who are depicted as innocent and naive and as unexpecting of the damage inflicted on them. Likewise, we have greater sympathy for victims with whom we can identify because they are like us in some discernible ways.

Successful arguers understand the importance of character types and depict the actors in the social dramas they describe accordingly. President Ronald Reagan, for example, almost completely reframed the public discussion about the civil war in Nicaragua in the early 1980s when he began to call the guerrilla soldiers—who had previously been referred to as the "contras"—"freedom fighters." This renaming helped to transform the American public's negative images of these warriors into something more favorable. Americans had been very reluctant to involve themselves in the Nicaraguan conflict up until that time, probably due to the painful memories of the Vietnam War. President Reagan's rhetoric softened up this opposition to American involvement, however, and as a result the United States began to more actively support the contra warriors.

If the contras were truly freedom fighters, we had no real choice but to support their efforts. To abandon freedom fighters would be to abandon freedom itself. Freedom fighters, much like our own founding fathers, are heroic personae, and heroes require and merit our support, especially if they are fighting a common enemy. In this case Reagan declared they were waging war against the forces of global communism. Despite Reagan's successful efforts to reframe the dispute, his administration had difficulty in sustaining public support for American intervention in the war. Evidence emerged that the contra "freedom fighters" illegally mined the harbors, blew up schools and roads, trafficked in illegal drugs, and plotted assassinations, including the assassinations of leftist clerics. Such actions failed to live up to the expectations we would have for heroes, and this had the effect of diminishing the appeal of Reagan's story and support for his efforts to intervene in the conflict.*

As we discussed in chapter 2, both presidents named George Bush declared Iraq's strongman ruler Saddam Hussein as a despicable desperado-villain in their speeches, calling for military intervention against Iraq. Indeed, President George W. Bush declared that destroying Hussein's weapons of mass destruction would be insufficient to counter the danger that Iraq posed for the free world. Bush repeatedly argued that nothing short of a regime change could be depended upon to reduce the risk of war. The ever-present photographs of Saddam Hussein in schools, office buildings, and on public billboards may have served to increase his hold on power inside Iraq, but to anxious public audiences outside his own country these same photos seemed to serve only to increase the perception that his was the face of evil in the world.

---

* Because President Reagan was unsuccessful in convincing the American public and the Congress to support his efforts to direct military assistance to the contras, he permitted members of his administration to devise a clandestine strategy to provide such aid. For example, Colonel Oliver North solicited support from U.S. allies around the world, but especially in the Middle East, to donate weapons and ammunition directly to the rebels. He also arranged the sale of weapons donated by these allies to Iran, and then diverted the profits to Nicaraguan rebels. This was in violation of U.S. law, and resulted in criminal indictments against North, Secretary of Defense Caspar Weinberger, and others. President Reagan himself was damaged by the disclosure of these violations of law, which were the subject of extensive congressional hearings and lengthy court proceedings. For an excellent discussion see: *United States v. Oliver L. North*, U.S. Criminal Case # 88–0080–02 GAG.

Depicting the Scene in Stories

In addition to presenting the actors in terms of the character types they play in the story, arguers also construct images of the *scene*. Scene refers to what is transpiring on the stage. In public argumentative dramas this notion of scene may include the immediate context surrounding events, a larger international scene, and even a broad sweep of history. An arguer selects what elements of the scene to give presence and how to present them.

In justifying the United States' October 2001 invasion of Afghanistan, for example, President Bush emphasized the scene in Afghanistan under the ruling Taliban. Although there was no claim that the Taliban's leadership was directly involved in the actual planning of the specific terrorist attacks against the United States that took place on September 11, 2001, President Bush's rhetoric depicted Afghanistan as a lawless place in which the Al Qaeda terrorists had been given free rein to plot their attacks against the West. The terrorist cells were permitted to recruit in many other nations and then bring the recruits to Afghanistan without any restrictions to train. They were able to maintain full-scale military-style training camps, practice with guns and other explosive devices, move capital in an out to finance their operations, and finally send their trained and armed cadres out to do their dirty deeds.

Afghanistan under the Taliban was also described as a scene of wanton physical violence and political oppression. Persons who violated strict Islamic laws were subjected to beatings, the amputation of limbs, and even to public executions in a soccer stadium. Women were prevented from going to school or work and were forced to wear *burkas*—garments that concealed their faces and identities. Women were also denied access to medical care from male physicians, and as a result, many women whose lives might have been saved were instead permitted to die due to the inadequate medical care. Young males were rounded up and conscripted for military service and in many cases shipped out to the front lines without training, sufficient clothing or provisions, or even weapons. These troops were thrown into battle against elements of the Afghan resistance and were sacrificed without regard to their safety or their value as human beings. This barbaric regime was depicted as a remnant of the dark ages; certainly the violence, injustice, inhumanity, and brutality of the scene justified American military intervention.

Notice how important it is that the nature of the scene warranted the type of action that was called for by the Bush administration. If the violations of human rights and the risk to life were not so significant, then perhaps some course of action short of military invasion would have been appropriate. Perhaps the United States could have relied upon diplomatic efforts, foreign aid, and gentle persuasion to bring the Taliban government into the global diplomatic community of nations. But given the horrific nature of the scene that was described, this government was cast as beyond reason and beyond persuasion, and the threat to global peace was described as so significant that only immediate military action could be depended upon to restore peace and harmony to the region and to expel the terrorists.

The decision to depict the scene in Afghanistan as one where a government had been manipulated by and even captured by a global terrorist network was also consistent with the way in which Osama Bin Laden, the purported head of the terrorist network, was cast as an actor. If bin Laden were merely a minor warlord or thug the act of war might not seem appropriate. Because he was cast as a clever and evil criminal mastermind in command of a vast network of well-trained followers, the most serious and dramatic of military responses were demanded, even at the risk of the inevitable loss of civilian casualties in Afghanistan.

Depicting the Events in Stories

The third element of a story is the *events*, or the actions engaged in by the various characters. As with the first two components of a good story, the language one uses in this aspect of the argument is important. Change the important terms and you change the argument. For example, the Korean War was originally labeled a *police action*. Why? Perhaps because the connotations of this term are generally more limiting and seem to entail significantly less risk than the use of the term *war*. To a nation tired of war (remember, World War II had ended only a few years earlier), a call to military action was no doubt very unsettling. Furthermore, in that the Korean conflict began as a dispute between two halves of a nation, the police action metaphor might seem appropriate. This was a dispute between those who held power and those who would foment disorder and challenge that power. As a domestic dispute then, a police action might create an appropriate argumentative response. Once the vast armies of the People's Republic of China were drawn into the conflict, however, this police action metaphor no longer seemed appropriate as a description of the events. The arguments used to describe and justify military intervention by the United States (through the auspices of the United Nations) eventually shifted to include more straightforward defenses of the appropriateness of military action.

Still another interesting example of the power of stories in the construction of events was provided by the attempt to impeach and remove President Bill Clinton from office. On February 11, 1994, Paula Jones, a low-level former employee of the state government of Arkansas, held a news conference and declared that the chief officer of the state, then Governor Clinton, had summoned her to his hotel room in Little Rock. She claimed that the governor then lowered his trousers to demand oral sex. Clinton immediately denied the story and Jones filed suit for sexual harassment. Settlement talks between attorneys for both parties were undertaken, but the talks broke down when Clinton refused to admit responsibility. Nonetheless, the parties were reported not to be very far apart and the prospects for a settlement were promising. Jones became upset, however, when she learned that Clinton's attorneys were making disparaging statements about her to the press. She decided to fire her attorney and then retained as counsel a firm with a long record of involvement in conservative causes. This firm pursued the matter aggressively and filed a subpoena demanding that the president submit to providing testimony on the alleged incident. Although Clinton sought to postpone his testimony until after he left the presidency, the Supreme Court ultimately denied this request and demanded that he testify in a civil deposition. Jones's attorneys were permitted to ask the president, under oath, whether he had engaged in sexual relations with other women whose careers he could influence. Clinton testified, under oath, that he had not. One of the women whose name arose in the questioning was that of a young White House intern, Monica Lewinsky.[11]

Lewinsky had confided in a friend, Linda Tripp, another White House employee who had been hired originally by the previous Bush administration but retained by the Clinton administration, that she and President Clinton had been sexually intimate. Tripp notified the office of Kenneth Starr, a special prosecutor who had been brought into office to investigate allegations of financial improprieties that the president and Mrs. Clinton may have committed in Arkansas. Starr summoned Lewinsky to a meeting to determine whether or not he could prove that the president had perjured himself during his testimony in the Jones case. Lewinsky refused to wear a wire, as the special prosecutor wished, but she did ultimately come to cooperate with the investigation in order to escape prosecution for perjury herself. Clinton's problems worsened when Lewinsky reported that she still had in her possession a blue dress that she claimed was stained with Clinton's semen. Starr secured the dress, and then requested a blood sample from Clinton for DNA testing. The DNA tests confirmed that the semen stain was the president's, and Clinton's denials under oath of sexual intimacies with staff members were proven to be lies.[12]

Special Prosecutor Starr referred this new evidence to the Judiciary Committee of the House of Representatives. On a partisan vote with the Republicans supporting the resolution, and Democrats opposing it, the committee recommended that President Clinton be impeached and removed from office for perjury. The full House of Representatives, again voting largely along party lines, agreed and passed two articles of impeachment, which were then forwarded to the Senate for trial. Public opinion polls consistently revealed that the American people did not support the attempts to remove the president from office, however, and the articles of impeachment failed when the Republicans could not convince more than 55 senators (67 were needed to convict) to vote for either of the impeachment resolutions.[13]

To many conservative Americans, President Clinton was a morally loathsome and contemptible figure who was completely unfit to serve in the office of the presidency. These people saw the original complaint by Paula Jones as evidence of his immorality and personal corruption. Their distrust and dislike for the president were fueled by the additional stories that he had engaged in sleazy sexual contact with Monica Lewinsky, a girl who was the age of his daughter. These sordid events were more than ample justification to turn the president out of office.

Many other Americans, however, saw President Clinton as much as a victim as a perpetrator in this sorry episode. Many of these people found Jones's story unconvincing and the events she described as unlikely to have occurred. Furthermore, they thought Lewinsky and her friend Tripp were the true villains in this episode: Lewinsky, because she seemed to have intentionally sought to seduce the president, and Tripp, because she was such a poor friend and breached her pledge of confidence when she told the office of the special prosecutor. As for the impeachment process, many Americans believed that these unpleasant events, Clinton's poor judgment, and his infidelity to his wife were not grounds for impeachment or removal from office.

These events were thus given very different meanings in the competing stories that played out in the press. To some storytellers these events revealed Clinton's deep moral failing and his lack of respect for the law and for the office of the presidency; thus they justified his immediate removal from office. Other storytellers conceded that the president had erred, but they argued that these events in no way justified his impeachment and that almost everyone lies about sex. That these events were criminalized and blown out of proportion as they were, they believed, was due to the political ambitions and blind hatred of the conservatives for the Clintons. Public opinion polls revealed that the actions of Kenneth Starr, the special prosecutor, were especially condemned by many citizens as having more to do with his own political goals than with the pursuit of justice. As has already been observed, ultimately the public opinion polls revealed that most Americans did not support the removal of the president from office, and the impeachment effort failed.[14]

Even though polls showed that the public did not support President Clinton's removal from office, it is noteworthy that many analysts and experts who evaluated the results of the 2000 presidential election suggested that the question of Bill Clinton's character mattered a great deal to the voters and that negative perceptions of Clinton damaged Vice President Gore. As we have previously indicated, audiences make sense out of the world by actively evaluating discourse as a story. George W. Bush understood this and directed voters' sense making along the lines of good judgment and moral behavior to enhance the effectiveness of his own advocacy. Vice President Gore was aware that suspicions about President Clinton's morality might damage his own campaign, and he sought to distance himself from the Clinton presidency and Clinton's moral failings. As an example, when accepting the nomination of his party at the Los Angeles Democratic Convention, Gore made headlines with his long, drawn out, and deeply passionate kiss with his wife Tipper. Certainly this was not the kiss of a philandering husband! Gore even distanced himself from Clinton by refusing to ask the president to appear with him or to promote Gore's candidacy on extensive speaking tours. However, as noted above, Gore's strategies failed to make a difference in the voters' impressions, and as we all know, he failed to win the election. For example, one poll suggested that nearly half (44 percent) of those who voted said that the Clinton scandal was very or somewhat important in determining their vote, and three quarters of them voted for George W. Bush.[15]

METAPHOR

Savvy arguers have also learned that there are special forms of argument that can enhance the appeal of a claim. One illustration is the use of *metaphor*. You probably learned all about metaphors, similes, and other figures of speech in English classes. They are often referred to as ornaments of language. Saying a classmate "roars like a lion" (simile) and is "bullheaded" (metaphor) communicates information about that classmate in a manner that is more creative than merely saying the classmate is very loud and strong-willed. (Of course these examples are trite clichés that you should probably avoid!) Metaphor is, however, a very useful and highly influential form of argumentation, and thus it has value beyond being ornamental language.

An *ornamental metaphor* asks audiences to see that phenomenon A has some characteristic that resembles phenomenon B. If we say, "Peter is as strong as an ox," we are only comparing one aspect of Peter—his strength—with one aspect of the ox—its strength. No one would surmise that Peter walks on four legs, pulls carts behind him, and has a tail suitable for making soup. And the point of the comparison is figurative only—Peter certainly does not have the actual equivalent strength of an ox. Some metaphors are intended to be taken literally, however. As an example, when former President Reagan urged Americans to see the Soviet Union as "the evil empire," he meant the comparison between the communist superpower and the villains from the film *Star Wars* to be taken literally. An *argumentative metaphor* contends that phenomenon A should be seen *as* phenomenon B. An argumentative metaphor is a powerful tool for influencing how we make sense of our world.

A metaphor thus acts as a template for interpreting new information. Viewing A as B limits, shapes, and constrains our understanding of A. We come to "know" A (in this case the Soviet Union) with respect to what we "know" about B (an evil empire), and the values embodied in B are transferred to A through this sense-making process. Those who accepted President Reagan's argument in the early 1980s that the Soviet Union was an "evil empire" would have been invited to interpret the actions of the Soviet state and of the United States within a narrative frame of evil versus good. Such a dramatic structure would also demand that these nations act accordingly. Armed with this perspective Americans would be invited to evaluate Soviet actions in order to confirm their examples of evil intent. Even those occasions where the Soviets acted charitably or morally would likely be viewed with suspicion and with a skeptical questioning of their genuine motives, because all storytellers understand that evil people cannot be trusted and must have ulterior motives.

Another illustration of the sense-making power of a metaphor was provided in a study that sought to understand how children learn to use metaphors and engage in storytelling. In this study a child's father died. Despite the mother's best efforts at explaining what the death really meant, the young child seemed not to really understand the finality of this loss. Only when the child lost a helium-filled balloon did the child comprehend, metaphorically, the finality of death.[16]

Steven Perry provides an example of rhetoric that successfully incorporated an argumentative metaphor. Perry argues that the writings and speeches of Adolf Hitler were permeated with a view of the Jewish people as an infestation. Although we find the rhetoric repugnant, we agree with Perry's claim that understanding the power of the metaphor is essential to understanding the structure of Hitler's argument:

These figurations are more than stylistic devices: Hitler's critique of the Jew's status as a cultural being, for example, is not illustrated by the metaphor of parasitism, it is constituted by this metaphor and the figurative entitlements it carries. The Jew's cultural inferiority, that is, is never argumentatively demonstrated in prepositional fashion by reference to real events or rational principles, but is rather only there to be inferred from Hitler's use and elaboration of parasitism imagery. The figurative language employed by Hitler is not supplementary or subordinate to some argumentative or discursive structure; it is itself Hitler's argument.[17]

The power of a metaphor lies in its completeness. If an audience accepted this abhorrent depiction, the response and the desired course of action are implicit in the metaphor. Infestations, as negatively valued entities, call for containment and eradication.

Another example of a metaphor that achieved great persuasive power is a statement that was supposedly made by former Chinese Communist leader Deng Xiaoping: "It doesn't matter whether it's a black cat or a white cat; as long as it can catch mice, it's a good cat." This metaphor was especially important because in China, absolute loyalty to Communist Party orthodoxy had always been demanded of all party leaders. Deng's metaphor stressed that faithful adherence to Marxist (or Maoist) principles were less important to solving China's political and economic problems than the pursuit of pragmatic policies that would invigorate the Chinese economy, attract foreign investment, and raise the standard of living of the Chinese people.

The power of this metaphor cannot be fully appreciated unless one understands a bit more about his life and his political struggles. Deng studied Marxist theory in Paris during the 1920s and became involved with a French branch of the Chinese Communist Party when he was only twenty years old. He helped organize a Communist military base and guerrilla movement among Chinese peasants in Guanxi Province, and in 1934–35 he participated in the "Long March" and became a key ally of Mao Zedong. He was elected to the Central Committee of the Communist Party in 1945, where he served until 1966 when he was removed from office during the Cultural Revolution because he was viewed as not being sufficiently "pure" in his adherence to Mao's teachings. Deng's intellectual gifts and leadership abilities were sorely missed, however, and he was returned to power and named the vice primer of China in 1973, only to be purged again in 1976 following the death of another of his key political allies, Zhou Enlai. In 1977, Deng gained control of the Chinese government after the death of Mao and the arrest of the members of the "Gang of Four" who had led the Cultural Revolution. Deng's return to power for the second time signaled that the Chinese Communist Party was finally ready to recognize the need for real economic reforms.

Deng's metaphor had been cited as a reason for purging him during the Cultural Revolution but it was also a reason to resurrect him as others in the party came to understand the need to modernize China's economic system. The metaphor continues to play an important role in Chinese politics today, even though Deng died in 1997, as other political leaders seek to define his legacy and to argue for still more reforms in China to respond to the now widening gaps between urban and coastal Chinese who are acquiring new sources of wealth and power and the rural Chinese peasants who are lagging farther and farther behind. Finally, Deng's metaphor, and his legacy, are also a resource for arguments by Chinese activities who are demanding political as well as economic reforms. His metaphor reduces the objectives of governmental economic planning to very simple and easily understood pragmatic goals that, because of their simplicity, are much more difficult to refute. Furthermore, his metaphor clearly appeals to an accepted form of storytelling that strongly resonates within the Chinese culture. Even though some today express doubts that he made the statement in this exact way, the statement persists as a very powerful argumentative metaphor.

Unlike the figurative or ornamental metaphor, in which only one characteristic of A is seen in terms of B, the argumentative metaphor views all of A as B. This gives the metaphor a *generative capability*. That is, if we know some of the characteristics of A in terms of B, we can infer (or generate) other characteristics. This makes the metaphor a powerful argumentative tool, for it enables us to evoke in an audience a deep, intense response, simply by noting a superficial connection between A and B. As an example, Lakoff and Johnson wrote that Americans conceive of argument as war.[19] This can be seen in the language that is commonly used to describe arguments:

"Your claims are indefensible."

"He attacked my argument point by point."

"I demolished his argument."

"I have never won an argument with her."

"She preempted my arguments."

This can also be seen in how we prepare for and actually engage in arguments, as well as in the personal stake we sometimes feel in the arguments that we advance. If our position is defeated, we might feel personally lessened. These are some of the consequences of seeing arguments in terms of war. If you can come up with other similarities between how we argue and how we wage war, then you've proven the generative capability of the argumentative metaphor.

Argumentative metaphors and analogies, which we discuss more fully in chapter 6, are not the same. Both entail comparisons and both have generative functions, but the literal analogy compares cases of phenomena that are materially similar. Metaphor, like the figurative analogy, compares cases that are materially dissimilar.

When citizens express their fears that a war with Iraq might become another Vietnam, they are arguing analogically. Both are cases of American military intervention in a foreign nation. Respondents may counter such arguments by claiming that the analogy is false because military objectives are more clearly definable in the case of Iraq, or because the desert landscape is very different from the dense jungles of Vietnam. On the other hand, if someone argues that homelessness is a plague that is sweeping the nation, they are not literally arguing that homelessness is a contagious disease, only that it is useful to conceive of one in terms of the significance of the other.

SUMMARY

In this chapter we viewed argument from the perspective of the advocate. We considered the ways that advocates can use alternative language strategies to increase the effectiveness of their arguments. Language shapes understanding, and therefore, advocates should judiciously and wisely select the language that will best communicate their intended argumentative positions. We have discussed the qualities of language, looked at how good stories utilize language, and considered a specific type of argument tool, the metaphor.

Key Terms

abstraction
character type
characters
events
language
    epistemic function of
meaning
    connotative
    denotative

metaphor
    argumentative
    generative capability of
    ornamental
role
scene

Activities

1. In this chapter we discussed language and indicated that each culture or subculture creates its own characteristic way of talking about the things it considers important. For example, think about the kind of music you like to listen to. How do you describe it? What label do you use for music you consider good? How do you label music you consider bad? Now, select a subculture with which you are familiar. List some of the unique language that culture employs and provide a definition of these terms. If you are unfamiliar with the language of a subculture, you may need to interview someone to complete this exercise.

2. Provide your own definition for each of the following terms and indicate whether the term evokes positive feelings for you or negative ones. Now ask a friend or classmate to do the same. Are there differences? Discuss the source of the similarities and differences.

freedom   marriage

government   children

welfare   charity

retirement   religion

3. Select and read an editorial or opinion piece from your local newspaper. Then answer the following questions about its narrative form:

   a. Who does the advocate think are the heroes?

   b. Who does the advocate think are the villains?

   c. Who does the advocate think are the victims?

   d. What qualities does the advocate assign to these characters in their representative roles?

   e. What are the acts that each of these sets of actors engage in?

   f. How does the advocate describe the scene?

4. Throughout the day, you enact many roles. Think about your day and list the roles you fill (for instance, student, parent, child, worker, sibling). Now select two of these roles and consider how they influence your behavior.

   a. Are some behaviors acceptable in one role but not in the other?

   b. Are their differences in the amount of power you have in the two roles?

   c. Are their differences in whether or how you express your feelings in the two roles?

   d. Do others respond differently to you when you enact the different roles? For example, are you more likely to be listened to in one role than in the other?

5. Try to discover the influence of metaphors in your life. For example, if you work, think about your place of employment and how your boss talks about it. Does your boss talk about the workers as part of a team? Then perhaps a sports metaphor is being invoked. If your boss uses military terminology, then perhaps your boss wants the work environment to function like the military. List examples of the metaphors your employer uses. Try to understand what else these metaphors reveal about how your boss wants the workers to act. If you have the good fortune of not having to work, or if you are the boss, then try to analyze the metaphors in a different environment. Perhaps you belong to a fraternity or sorority, or even a church or a club with leaders who employ metaphors. How are they used?

Recommended Readings

Anderson, Karrin Vasby. "Hillary Rodham Clinton as 'Madonna': The Role of Metaphor and Oxymoron in Image Restoration." *Women's Studies in Communication* 25 (2002): 1–24.

Boyd, Josh. "A Quest for Cinergy: The War Metaphor and the Construction of Identity." *Communication Studies* 54 (2003): 249–265.

Carpenter, Ronald H. "America's Tragic Metaphor: Our Twentieth-Century Combatants as Frontiersmen." *Quarterly Journal of Speech* 76 (1990): 1–22.

Dobkin, Bethami A. "Paper Tigers and Video Postcards: The Rhetorical Dimensions of Narrative Form in ABC News Coverage of Terrorism." *Western Journal of Communication* 56 (1992): 143–160.

Hollihan, Thomas A., and Patricia Riley. "The Rhetorical Power of a Compelling Story: A Critique of a 'Toughlove' Parental Support Group." *Communication Quarterly* 35 (1987): 13–25.

Johnson, Mark, ed. *Philosophical Perspectives on Metaphor.* Minneapolis: University of Minnesota Press, 1981.

Kent, Michael. "Managerial Rhetoric as the Metaphor for the World Wide Web." *Critical Studies in Media Communication* 18 (2001): 359–376.

Kovecses, Zoltan. *Metaphor: A Practical Introduction.* London: Oxford University Press, 2002.

Lakoff, George, and Mark Johnson. *Metaphors We Live By.* Chicago: University of Chicago Press, 1980.

Longinus. *On the Sublime.* Translated by A. O. Prickard. London: Oxford University Press, 1907.

McGee, Jennifer J. "A Pilgrim's Progress: Metaphor in the Rhetoric of Mary Fisher, AIDS Activist." *Women's Studies in Communication* 26 (2003): 191–214.

Nafus, Dawn. "The Aesthetics of the Internet in St. Petersburg: Why Metaphor Matters." *Communication Review* 6 (2003): 185–212.

Ortoney, Andrew, ed. *Metaphor and Thought.* London: Cambridge University Press, 1993.

Osborne, Michael. "Archetypal Metaphor in Rhetoric: The Light-Dark Family." *Quarterly Journal of Speech* 53 (1967): 121–131.

Patterson, Robert, and Ronald Lee. "The Environmental Rhetoric of 'Balance': A Case Study of Regulatory Discourse and the Colonization of the Public." *Technical Communication Quarterly* 6 (1997): 25–41.

Stearney, Lynn M. "Feminism, Ecofeminism, and the Maternal Archetype: Motherhood as a Feminine Universal." *Communication Quarterly* 42 (1994): 145–160.

Notes

1. Kenneth Burke, *Language as Symbolic Action: Essays on Life, Literature, and Method* (Berkeley: University of California Press, 1966), 45.
2. See for example, Suzanne K. Langer, *Philosophy in a New Key: A Study in the Symbolism of Reason, Rite, and Art* (Cambridge: Harvard University Press, 1942). An excellent investigation of the epistemic function of rhetoric was offered by Richard A. Cherwitz and James W. Hikins, *Communication and Knowledge: An Investigation in Rhetorical Epistemology* (Columbia: University of South Carolina Press, 1986).
3. *American Heritage Dictionary* (Boston: American Heritage Publishing, 1973).
4. I. A. Richards, *The Philosophy of Rhetoric* (London: Oxford University Press, 1936/1981), 11.
5. *American Heritage Dictionary.*
6. W. Lance Bennett, "The Ritualistic and Pragmatic Bases of Political Campaign Discourse," *Quarterly Journal of Speech* 63 (October 1977): 219–238.
7. Daniel Nimmo, "The Drama, Illusion and Reality of Political Images," in *Drama in Life: The Uses of Communication in Society,* ed. James E. Combs and Michael W. Mansfield (New York: Hastings, 1976), 261.
8. Orrin E. Klapp, *Heroes, Villains, and Fools: The Changing American Character* (Englewood Cliffs, NJ: Prentice-Hall, 1962).
9. Walter R. Fisher, *Human Communication as Narration: Toward a Philosophy of Reason, Value, and Action* (Columbia: University of South Carolina Press, 1987), 47.
10. Kenneth Burke, *Counter-statement* (Berkeley: University of California Press, 1931, rpt. 1968), 31.
11. "Pathway to Peril," *Los Angeles Times,* January 31, 1999.

[12] "An Affair of State," *Time*, September 21, 1998.

[13] R. A. Serrano and M. Lacey, "Clinton Acquitted: Votes Fall Far Short of Conviction," *Los Angeles Times*, February 13, 1999.

[14] For an account of the arguments and the political dimensions of this episode see: Thomas A. Hollihan, *Uncivil Wars: Political Campaigns in a Media Age* (New York: Bedford/St. Martin's Press, 2001), 236–251. See also: William J. Bennett, *The Death of Outrage: Bill Clinton and the Assault on American Ideals* (New York: Simon and Shuster, 1998).

[15] Jill Lawrence, "Country vs. City, Spelled in Red, Blue." *USA Today*, November 9, 2000, 19A.

[16] B. Moore, "A Young Child's Use of a Physical-Psychological Metaphor," *Metaphor and Symbolic Activity*, 3 (1988): 223–232.

[17] Steven Perry, "Rhetorical Functions of the Infestation Metaphor in Hitler's Rhetoric," *Central States Speech Journal* 34 (1983): 230.

[18] *Los Angeles Times*, October 12, 1991, A1.

[19] George Lakoff and Mark Johnson, *Metaphors We Live By* (Chicago: University of Chicago Press, 1980).

ARGUMENTATION AND CRITICAL THINKING

In the preceding chapters we focused on argumentation as a form of story-telling. We have emphasized that people are natural storytellers and that they are able to create and test competing stories. Although this is true of all people, some people are more gifted arguers than others. Just as in most other human endeavors, people do have different argumentation talents. Some are more articulate than others, some use more vivid examples than others, some have better vocabularies, some have better memories, some think on their feet more quickly, and some have a better capacity for refuting the claims made by others.

You can enhance your arguing skills if you understand some of the techniques for creating reasoned arguments. Different argument fields often demand different argumentation styles, strategies, and techniques. In addition, several different analytical techniques are available to you to help you improve the quality of your claims and assure a more systematic analysis of the arguments that you encounter. Our objective in this chapter is to enhance your critical thinking skills—to sharpen your analytical abilities—so that you create better arguments, evaluate others' arguments more carefully, and, ultimately, make better decisions. This chapter will explore alternative principles for the evaluation of propositions, suggest how arguers can make strategic decisions regarding how they can best express their own arguments and their disagreement with others' arguments, and discuss some alternative methods for the analysis of arguments.

Argumentation theory, like theory in any other discipline, can be formally taught and learned. Our focus now—on the examination of argumentation as a set of principles that can be learned, rather than as a naturally occurring human activity—does not contradict our earlier claims about argumentation. We continue to believe that humans are by nature storytellers and that arguments are primarily created and understood through stories. In fact, the theories that we will now discuss can be understood as a unique style of storytelling that is especially appropriate for evaluating argumentative propositions.

Although people do not require specialized training to engage in arguments in conversational settings, for instance with friends or family members, such training will help them become more effective arguers in meetings, when writing papers or reports, in formal debates, or at rare but important occasions such as a visit to traffic court or small-claims court.

PROPOSITIONS

A natural starting point for the consideration of any argumentative interaction is with an investigation of the proposition under dispute. A *proposition* is a statement that expresses the subject of the dispute. The degree of formality in the actual wording of a proposition will vary in accordance with the formality of the setting.

In a casual conversational setting, for example, the proposition might be stated very simply and informally: "I think we should go to the movies," or the rival proposition: "We always end up at the movies; I think we should go hear some live music." As the setting becomes more formal, however, there will be a more careful statement of the proposition. For example, in a curriculum committee meeting, which is likely to follow parliamentary procedure, a participant would probably be required to state the proposition as a formal motion: "I move that all students be required to complete a course in argumentation." In a court of law the proposition would most likely be stated even more formally: "The State contends that the accused, Michael Smith, did, on April 17, 2004, commit a second-degree sexual assault, which is a felony according to Section 364A of criminal statute." In an academic debate the proposition would also be stated formally: "Resolved: That the federal government should provide a comprehensive program of medical care for all persons in the United States."

There are several benefits to formally stating or expressing a proposition for argument, even in an informal interaction. First, a formally stated proposition clearly establishes the issues that are in dispute. In casual interactions arguments may rage even when the participants lack a clear understanding of precisely what they are disputing. For example, in the informal argument cited above, one person is arguing that they should go to a movie while the other is arguing that they should go to hear live music. The dispute, however, may have less to do with the specific entertainment planned for the evening than with the underlying tensions in the relationship. Thus the claim, "We always end up at the movies, I think we should go hear some live music," might really be a disguised version of a different proposition: "You always get to decide what we will do when we go out, I think that I should have the opportunity to decide this time." If the disputants were to clearly state their actual propositions, they might discover the precise cause for their disagreement and thus reach a resolution sooner.

Second, a formally stated proposition divides the ground between the disputants. The advocate of the required course in argumentation (no doubt a faculty member from the Speech or Communication Department), for example, might well be pitted against someone who believes that if students are taught how to argue more effectively they might become more disagreeable. Or, the opponent might believe that students should not be saddled with specific requirements but instead should have a high degree of freedom to design their own programs of study. Someone who favors increasing the foreign language requirement by adding another language course might oppose the argumentation requirement on the grounds that it would overload the curriculum and therefore diminish the likelihood that a foreign language requirement would be made more rigorous. In any case, the explicit statement of the proposition helps the participants to gain a clear understanding of the specific motion at hand before moving on to the consideration of alternative motions.

Third, explicitly stated propositions help disputants to see what might result from the completion of an argument. For example, if the legal proposition mentioned earlier is proven true, and Mr. Smith is found guilty of the charge of sexual assault, he can expect to face the state's penalty for this crime. If, on the other hand, his defense attorney is able to establish that Smith could not have committed the alleged act or that the act Smith did commit was of a very different character than that which the prosecution alleged—namely that it did not fit the requirements of the state's charge of second-degree sexual assault—Smith will be acquitted.

Finally, a formally stated proposition helps to facilitate a clear argumentative *clash*, or sharply focused disagreement between rival positions. The proposition lays out the issues that are disputed, directs the advocates in how to develop their arguments, and reveals the issues likely to be used to support the opposing cases.

TYPES OF PROPOSITIONS

There are three different types of propositions, each appropriate to the particular types of issues that may be in dispute.

Propositions of Fact

Whenever there are disagreements about factual statements, a ***proposition of fact*** is in dispute. For example, two friends who are having an argument about the hottest place in the United States are disputing a proposition of fact. Thus the statement, "Death Valley is the hottest place in the country," is a proposition of fact. The rival proposition, "Corpus Christi is the hottest place in the country," is also a proposition of fact. While propositions of this type readily lend themselves to argument, they are also typically resolvable through the appropriate empirical evidence. In this case, the National Weather Service keeps records of the average temperatures of reporting stations around the United States. However, even when this data is introduced, their might still be room for interpretation and disagreement. For example, one might contend that the appropriate data is the year-long temperature in Corpus Christi. The other might argue that only decade-long averages can be used. Still another might maintain that the hottest single days on record, or the use of "comfort indexes" that include such factors as humidity or average wind speed would be more appropriate.

As anyone who has ever engaged in such an argument knows, the possibilities for avoiding resolution are as unlimited as are the creative energies of the arguers. Before such disputes can be proved or disproved by the access to appropriate factual evidence, the parties must agree on the meaning of the key terms. Only after the advocates agree on the definition of "the hottest place in the country" can the dispute be resolved by consulting the appropriate reference.

Legal disputes are typically stated as propositions of fact, and almost all focus on issues that have already occurred (except for those cases in which people seek court injunctions to prevent something from occurring). The jury called upon to decide defendant Smith's guilt or innocence in the sexual assault case would seek to determine whether or not the offense had occurred and, if it had, would then consider whether it met the legal definition for the charge and whether Smith perpetrated the attack.

Arguers sometimes differ over propositions of future fact, although such arguments are always speculative in nature and therefore do not lend themselves to tidy resolution. We could assert, for example, that at some point during your lifetime you will see the election of the first woman or the first African American president of the United States. This claim of future fact is certainly arguable. The resolution of such an argument, however, rests on the arguer's prognostications about the changing political landscape in the United States and its future consequences and not on verifiable material evidence.

Propositions of Value

Closely related to propositions of fact are **_propositions of value_**. The primary difference between the two types of propositions is factual propositions hinge upon verifiable evidence, but value propositions can be resolved only on the basis of the opinions and beliefs of the arguers and their audiences. For example, the claim that "the Los Angeles Lakers were the most successful NBA team from 1994 to 2004" is a proposition of fact. It may be proven either true or false by consulting an almanac listing the win-loss record of all the NBA teams. On the other hand, the proposition, "The Los Angeles Lakers are the best team in the NBA" is a proposition of value. The proposition can only be decided based on the arguers' conception of what the term "best" means. A team's win-loss record could certainly be one consideration, but so might several other factors:

the record in the playoffs, the number of championship titles, the quality of the other teams in the division in which they competed, the quality of key players or of the bench, the quality of the coach, and—perhaps most important—whether the arguers reside in Los Angeles, Chicago, Boston, or Detroit.

Because propositions of value focus on subjective beliefs and judgments they seem impossible to resolve through reasoned argument, and we feel we have no alternative but to fight over them. We are often eager to avoid engaging in value disputes for this very reason. Disputes have raged for generations over such value propositions as: "abortion is morally wrong," "capital punishment is morally justified," and "our obligation to protect the first amendment outweighs our concerns about pornography." In any complex, multicultural, and diverse society we can expect that values will be hotly contested in the fabric of civic discourse.

In an attempt to effectively argue value propositions, it is helpful to analyze value propositions by asking yourself the following questions:

1. What are the foundations for the value under dispute? Is the value expressed in civil, religious, or natural law? If so, is it consistently expressed across these contexts?

2. How closely is the value adhered to, and by how many persons? What sorts of people ascribe to this value? Have they particular expertise in the subject under dispute.

3. How important is this value in the hierarchy of values? People are influenced by many values, how central is this particular value?

4. Is the value absolute? Are there situations in which this value is set aside? For example, most of us believe that killing is morally wrong, yet the Supreme Court has repeatedly upheld each state's right to execute convicted murderers when certain criteria are met. What criteria, if any, must be met for this particular value to be suspended?

5. How might an advocate go about establishing that certain criteria have been met to uphold a proposition that goes against a widely held value? Are these criteria formally established (as in the case of legal burdens that must be met), or are they informally agreed upon?[1]

Even when these questions are systematically asked and answered, however, some value differences are so fundamental that they cannot be easily minimized or overcome. The outcome of many human value disputes therefore is that those engaged in such arguments simply must agree to disagree.

Propositions of Policy

A *proposition of policy* is a statement outlining a course of action that the advocate believes should be taken. Such a statement can range from the informal: "We should go to the movies tonight," to the complex, "Resolved: That the federal government should provide a system of comprehensive medical care for all United States citizens." Propositions of policy imply such value judgments as movies are a worthwhile way to spend one's time, and medical care is a right that government should guarantee to all its citizenry. These propositions may also imply factual judgments—that we have no previous commitments, so we have free time to see a movie, or not all citizens currently receive medical care, for instance.

Propositions of policy always concern the future, and they typically state that a certain policy change should occur. The best-formulated propositions of policy are those that specify the precise change that should occur and also the agent of that change. The following are examples of well-formulated policy propositions.

Resolved: That the State of Indiana should legalize casino gambling.

Resolved: That the NCAA should permit student athletes to receive a payment for their services, such payment to be generated from the revenues produced by their respective sports.

Resolved: That the federal government should legalize the cultivation, sale, and possession of marijuana by any person over the age the age of 21.

If our goal is to produce the fairest and best argumentation on an issue, then we should strive to create explicitly and carefully worded propositions. A precisely worded proposition is easier for arguers to dispute. In order to best facilitate clash on an issue, a proposition should be worded so that it leaves ground on both sides. A very narrowly worded proposition might not make for very effective clash and might also fail to result in successful or effective public policy:

Resolved: That the federal government should fund a program to provide polio vaccines for all Hopi Indian children residing in Arizona.

There are two problems with this proposition. First, it is difficult to justify limiting the program to only Indian children, let alone the children of only one tribe that resides in only one Western state. An advocate who opposed this proposition could make the case that all children need protection from the polio virus. If that advocate were able to show that other children also failed to receive polio vaccines, this would be an effective argument against the adoption of this particular proposition or at the very least an argument for rewriting and expanding the scope of the proposition.

Second, this proposition severely limits its advocates' ground. Why fund a program to vaccinate children for only one disease rather than a program to vaccinate children for many childhood diseases? Children who are not receiving polio vaccinations may also not be receiving the necessary vaccinations to prevent a wide variety of other diseases as well, such as measles, diphtheria, and tetanus. Would it not be more efficient and productive to fund a program that would systematically vaccinate children against many of these diseases at the same time? Thus, the proposition might make more sense if it were worded:

Resolved: That the United States government should fund a program to provide immunizations against contagious diseases for all children living in poverty.

This wording does a better job of dividing ground to enhance clash on the issue. It focuses on the problem in such a way that makes it easier for the advocates to find materials to support their arguments, and it would probably lead to more effective and responsible health management policies. While there may be times when a narrowly worded proposition is warranted—for example, when advocates already have extensive expertise and knowledge on the subject or when a preliminary investigation has already narrowed the range of policy alternatives—in most cases a broader proposition facilitates better clash on the issues.

THE TECHNIQUES FOR ANALYZING PROPOSITIONS

Once the proposition to be disputed has been created or discovered, it is time to begin the process of *analysis.* It is through analysis that arguments in support of or against a proposition are created. This process is the most interesting and creative dimension of the argumentative enterprise. In his theory of rhetoric Aristotle referred to this process as invention, meaning the invention of arguments to support the position that you want your listeners to accept. As you are aware, both weak and strong arguments can be advanced in support of almost any proposition. Your task as an advocate is to create the best arguments that you can and to create arguments that will appeal to your audience. In short, you must invent arguments that cast your claims into stories that your audience finds appealing and believable given their experiences and values.

Defining Key Terms

The first step in the analysis of a proposition is to define the key terms. For the purposes of illustration, we will go back to the proposition that we just created.

Resolved: That the United States government should fund a program to provide immunizations against contagious diseases for all children living in poverty.

There are several important terms that must be defined for this proposition to be understood. For instance:

- "United States government": the federal government—not state or local governments and not private industry or insurance companies
- "fund": to create the monetary support for, but not necessarily to administer or operate
- "a program": an ongoing effort, as opposed to a one-time only event
- "immunizations against contagious diseases": prophylactic injections to prevent people from becoming infected with a wide range of diseases, including polio, tuberculosis, diphtheria, influenza, measles, tetanus, chicken pox
- "children living in poverty": children under the age of 18 from families whose incomes fall below the existing federal poverty standard

The foregoing examples are suggested only to illustrate reasonable interpretations of the key terms in this proposition. Different disputants would almost certainly choose to define some of these terms differently in order to stake out the ground they wish to argue. For example, an advocate could use a very narrow definition of "children living in poverty" to try to limit the discussion only to the medical problems routinely faced by children in rural America. The advocate's opponent, however, would then be entitled to argue that it is unreasonable to focus only on rural children and to exclude urban children. Another advocate could attempt to use a more expansive definition. Thus, for example, this advocate could seek to provide access to vaccines to children who may not be actually below the poverty line, but who may not have current access to private health insurance or to other governmental medical assistance programs. Such a strategy might serve to expand the benefits of the program to cover more recipients and thus prevent more diseases. It would also increase the cost of the program, which could lay the groundwork for reasons that such a program would be undesirable.

Another strategy an advocate might use to narrow the proposition "immunizations against contagious diseases" would be to focus the arguments on the need for children to receive measles vaccinations. An opponent then might argue that it is unreasonable to limit the discussion to only one disease when the explicit wording in the proposition is "diseases."

In most argument situations, arguers do not formally define their terms. Instead, they rely on their own notions of what the terms mean, usually by recalling the contexts or stories in which they have previously heard such terms used. Definitions are, in other words, shaped by popular usage. Terms acquire their meanings from their use in conversation, and these accepted usages give us our commonsense notions of what terms mean. In some cases, however, arguers may need to define their terms more systematically and can consult a number of different sources in order to do this. They can consult a dictionary, although dictionaries typically offer several alternative definitions in descending order of commonality, and many of these will not be equally acceptable to all audiences. Arguers can also consult specialized sources in the relevant literature of the field. On a topic about medical care, for example, they can consult the journals and periodicals of the medical profession; on issues of law they can consult a legal dictionary or legal periodicals; on an issue pertaining to education policy they can consult journals in the field of education; and so forth.

Definitions may themselves frequently become the subject for further argument. If during the course of an argument your adversary challenges your definitions of the key terms of a proposition, it is helpful to cite the source for your definitions and to argue their reasonableness and appropriateness by providing examples drawn from relevant literatures.

Establishing the Point of Clash

Once you have defined the key terms in the proposition, you need to decide what issues you wish to advance—where you will choose to draw your point of clash. This is known as establishing your point of *stasis*, or the place where you choose to differ with the arguments developed by your opponent.

Turning again to our example about immunization policy, an advocate for a federal program to provide immunization for poor children might stress the severity of the debilitating effects of childhood illnesses, including the number of lives lost to diseases that could have been prevented. The advocate would also want to argue that many children now go without vaccinations because their parents lack the financial means to provide adequate medical care. This would be a logical and appropriate point of stasis. Those who wished to oppose the proposition might contend that almost all children who need vaccinations currently receive them either through existing public assistance programs at the state and local level or through private insurance. They might also argue that a large and unwieldy federal program might only increase the governmental bureaucracy and not be the best way to help these children.

As an arguer, one of your greatest challenges is to decide how to attack your opponent's argument. This decision should be based on your research and your knowledge of the proposition, your understanding of effective argumentation tactics, and your awareness of the attitudes and beliefs of the audience whom you are hoping to convince with your arguments. The key, of course, is to attack arguments at their most vulnerable point.

Hermagoras—a Greek philosopher, rhetorical theorist, and teacher of rhetoric who lived during the second century B.C.—developed a checklist for determining where to draw stasis.[2] He suggested that there were four different levels for considering claims:

1. **Conjecturing about a fact.** At this level the arguer seeks to establish or dispute a material claim. The advocate arguing for or against the claim that "significant numbers of poor children are not vaccinated and suffer diseases because their parents cannot pay for required medical care" is conjecturing about a fact.

2. **Definition.** At this level the arguer contends that while a material fact may be true, it is not described or defined precisely as it should be. For example, an advocate might admit that significant numbers of poor children are not vaccinated, but argue that this is not because there are no programs available to provide the vaccinations. Instead, the advocate might assert that children fail to receive vaccinations because their parents do not take advantage of the existing programs, perhaps because they lack awareness of their availability, because they do not understand their importance, because of other barriers such as inadequate transportation, because they have religious or cultural objections to modern medicines, or because they fear that the vaccines themselves might make their children ill.

3. **Quality.** At this level the arguer asserts that although the material facts might be true, and although the material evidence is correct, other aspects influencing the material quality of the claims might lead to different interpretations. An advocate arguing from quality might admit that poor children are not vaccinated, and that there are inadequate programs to provide for vaccinations, but contend that the failure to vaccinate is not a significant factor in the children's health. Instead, he or she might argue that poverty itself leads to poor health by detailing the con-

sequences of poverty that can affect health: poor diet, substandard housing, low birth-weight babies, drug or alcohol addicted parents, and so on.

4. **Objection.** This is a decision to draw stasis at the level of interpretation. An advocate who draws stasis here might concede that poor children are not vaccinated and suffer disease as a result, that the problem results from a lack of government programs to provide health care, and that the failure to vaccinate is responsible for a significant number of deaths of these children. The advocate might contend, however, that the health statistics are not reliable, and many of these children may have actually died from other diseases for which no immunizations were available.

As should be clear from the examples that we have provided, these levels of stasis are presented in descending order of their strength or power. Consequently, it is better to be able to argue at the level of fact than it is to be compelled to argue at the level of definition. Both are stronger arguments than those directed at the issue of quality, and the weakest type of argument is one that relies on objection. Because Hermagoras was fundamentally concerned with inventing arguments he focused almost exclusively on the quality of the logical claims that the arguers made, and he stressed that appropriate logical techniques could be learned and taught to others.

Whether you argue in support of a proposition or in opposition to it, you must decide where and how to draw our point of stasis. The decision is an important one, for once you have developed the primary argument strategy that defines your case—your central story—it is difficult to change your mind later and dart off into some different direction. There is no substitute for careful planning and preparation when developing your arguments.

Stock Issues

One approach that has been developed to assist arguers in the analysis of policy propositions is the use of *stock issues*. The stock issues are those that readily lend themselves to consideration and focus in policy disputes. They are issues that recur throughout history, and as such, they are issues that seem to consistently draw the attention of arguers and of those who constitute the audiences for arguments.

Many argumentation theorists adhere to the perspective, originally developed by John Dewey in 1910, that thinking, and thus decision making, follows five logically distinct steps: (1) recognition of a felt difficulty, (2) location and definition of the difficulty, (3) suggestion of a possible solution, (4) development by reasoning of the bearings of the suggestion, (5) further observation and experiment leading to its acceptance or rejection.[3] Dewey's claim that policy changes most often occur in response to the location of a felt difficulty, or the identification of a problem in existing policy, led to the formulation of the stock issues perspective.

Based on Dewey's reflective thinking model, Lee Hultzen further developed and added a clear explanatory framework for the stock issues perspective.[4] The stock issues involve a consideration of the ill, the blame, the cure, and the cost. We will discuss each in turn.

Ill

The stock issue of an ***ill*** challenges the advocate to analyze the proposition by considering the inadequacies or problems in the existing system. Turning again to our earlier example, when the advocate demonstrates that poor children are contracting infectious diseases, especially when these diseases might have been prevented by vaccination, he or she is demonstrating the existence of an ill, or a flaw, in current health-care policy.

The identified ill must also be shown to be significant. An advocate can demonstrate two different types of significance. One type is quantitative significance—that large numbers of children are affected. The other type of significance is qualitative significance—that those affected are harmed in a serious way: perhaps they suffer grievously; perhaps are permanently disabled; or they may even die. To develop a strong case in justifying the seriousness of a flaw in an existing policy system, an advocate would want to demonstrate both quantitative and qualitative significance, because to do so would enhance the impact and power of his or her arguments. Meanwhile, it is the task of an opposing advocate to attempt to undercut the impact of this significance; that is, to demonstrate that few people suffer from the supposed ill and/or that those who do suffer may suffer only minimally.

Blame

When considering the stock issue of ***blame***, the advocate attempts to assign responsibility for the existence of an ill. In a policy dispute an arguer claims that an established policy should be changed to address and eliminate a currently existing harm or ill or to prevent an impending harm or ill. To succeed, the advocate must prove that current policy (that which is reflected in the ***status quo***—the way things now stand) is inadequate and fails to achieve its stated purpose. In most cases the arguer seeks to identify a problem that is inherent in the present system. The notion of ***inherency*** suggests that the problem will certainly repeat itself unless the current policy is changed. This is a powerful suggestion, since, normally, policy makers would not concern themselves with ills that would probably repair themselves if left alone.

There are three types of inherent ills. The first is called *structural inherency*. A program may be said to have structural inherency if its inadequacy results from the very design or lack of an established policy. The ill of our lacking an immunization program for children living in poverty might be shown to have structural inherency if the advocate points out that there is currently no single government agency responsible for providing medical services to poor children. Instead, an advocate may choose to argue, we have a patchwork of medical programs operating at the federal, state, and local levels, supplemented by inadequate private charities and private health insurance. As a result, many poor children may slip through the cracks and not receive the necessary immunizations that might protect them against devastating diseases.

A second type of inherency is *attitudinal inherency*. An ill may be said to result from attitudinal inherency if an advocate can demonstrate that while there may be a policy in place to correct the ill, that policy is undermined by the attitudes or values either of the people who administer it or perhaps even of the people who it is intended to serve. As a result, even if a program to provide immunizations to poor children were to exist, it might fail to provide the necessary vaccinations. In the case of vaccinations, for example, an advocate might argue that although we have programs intended to provide medical care for the poor, these programs are flawed because they have a crisis orientation: children receive medical care when they are grievously ill, often in an overcrowded emergency room at a public hospital, but they do not always receive the preventive care that might have decreased or even eliminated the risk of the disease. The inconvenience created by the scarcity of facilities available to serve the poor—perhaps the long distances that must be traversed or the long wait times required before one is seen by a health-care provider—all serve to prevent people from seeking care except in the most dire of emergencies. It is noteworthy to remember that the advocate can point to attitudes on the part of the patients themselves (e.g., fear of needles), their parents (e.g., anxiety about modern medical practices or techniques), the health-care providers (e.g., a lack of caring or compassion for their patients), or program administrators (e.g., a focus on providing crisis care), as possible attitudes that might serve to prevent current policies from being effective.

Structural inherency is typically more compelling than attitudinal inherency, because it supports the claim that a policy change is needed to remedy the structural deficiencies that lead to the existence of the ills. Essentially, governmental actors *cannot* solve a problem if there is structural inherency. If attitudinal inherency is claimed, current governmental actors could solve the problem but they *will not*. It is better if the advocate can demonstrate that these attitudes result from characteristics of the existing policy that are themselves caused by structures. If the attitudes are caused by the structures, then amending the structures might in and of itself lead to a change in attitudes. If the attitudes are not a result of the structures, however, and merely reside in the people, it is more difficult for an advocate to demonstrate that these attitudes can be changed and thus that the underlying problem can be resolved through policy change.

Considering the examples from the earlier paragraph for instance, it is unlikely that an advocate can easily overcome children's fear of needles. To the extent that children do not receive vaccines today because they fear needles, it is not likely that a new comprehensive federal program will overcome this fear. On the other hand, if the primary attitudinal barrier argued is the crisis orientation of program administrators, it might be easier to repair this problem. The crisis orientation more than likely results from a shortage of funds and a lack of emphasis on preventive care. A new federal mandate to provide such preventive care, and new funding to meet the cost of such a program, would likely be able to change these attitudes.

The third type of inherency exists when the current policy makers have not yet considered or addressed the problem, and the advocate of change argues that they should. In 2001 at the height of the post–9/11 terrorism scare, some advocates contended that the United States should begin a smallpox immunization program for adults. The Bush administration decided that only select health-care workers would be immunized, so that in the case of a smallpox out-break these individuals could assist the sick without risk of contracting the disease. The potential ill resulted from a deficiency in the status quo, but there was no policy that caused the problem and no attitude that prevented the ill from being addressed; rather the problem was new and had not been considered before. Thus, the inherency existed at the existential level.

The primary purpose for analyzing a policy proposition from the perspective of the stock issue of blame is to focus attention on the specific deficiencies in existing policy that might be remedied through the adoption of new policies—policies that are outlined in the wording of the proposition that is being argued.

Cure

Once the advocate has identified an ill and placed the blame for its existence on the deficiencies of current policies, it is time to propose a **cure**. The cure is the new policy that the advocate believes will remedy the ill. The proposed cure should be developed to address the specific ill that has been outlined and to overcome the inherent factors blamed for the creation of the ill.

If the inherency is structural, the cure should include the creation of a new structure that replaces, remedies, or modifies the structures that are now in place. In the case of the inoculation program for children in poverty, the cure might be a program funded by the federal government that requires all children to receive vaccinations. A bureaucracy to staff and administer the program might be established and a means to locate and treat the children created. This policy would address the structural indictments made—such as that no program currently exists that makes vaccinations against communicable diseases its primary mission—and would reshape the health-care bureaucracy.

If the identified inherency is attitudinal, the proposed cure must correct the blighted attitudes blamed for the existence of the problem. For instance, if the inherency is that parents do not take advantage of existing medical assistance programs and do not seek vaccinations for their children, then the advocate must propose a policy that will either change or circumvent those attitudes. For example, he or she might propose that in addition to the program outlined above to locate and treat the children, a health education and awareness program be created to reach the parents in maternity wards, through welfare and social workers, at schools, and in the workplace in order to educate and convince them of the importance of vaccinations and other preventive health measures.

The greatest challenge to the advocate who proposes a new policy is to argue in a convincing manner that this new policy will remedy the specific ills cited, and that it will also overcome the inherency barriers claimed as flaws in existing policy. There is no merit in changing policies if doing so will not remedy the problems plaguing the current policies.

Cost

The final stock issue is **cost**. While the previous stock issues were discussed from the perspective of the advocate who favored a policy change (although it is important to remember that the issues that surfaced also served to guide the selection of arguments by advocates opposing a policy change), the stock issue of cost is approached from the perspective of the arguer who seeks to refute the need for policy change. This stock issue asks the arguer to consider what the likely costs of the proposed policy change might be. The issue of cost can concern the purely monetary costs of the proposed policy: How much would it cost to undertake the new health initiatives that are outlined above? Certainly comprehensive national health insurance has long been favored by many policy makers, but it has never been created at least in part due to its daunting costs. Given the size of our current national budget deficit, the many other pressing social problems that our society faces (homelessness, declining educational systems, deteriorating highways, rampant crime, homeland security fears) and the reluctance of many people to pay increased taxes, is this proposal the best way to spend scarce public money? An advocate should not simply ask this question, of course, but should argue that this either is, or is not the way to spend public funds, and that a program to provide vaccinations for children either will or will not produce sufficient benefits to justify these costs.

Another way to think about the costs is to consider the disadvantages that might result from the adoption of a new policy. An arguer could assert, for example, that there is actually a certain amount of danger from inoculations and that some people might actually contract diseases or suffer illness as a result of adverse reactions to the vaccines. These are difficult arguments to make given this proposition, because the research is quite conclusive that vaccinations save lives, but they might serve to diminish some of the opposing advocate's significance about the numbers of lives saved through the prevention of the diseases by the new policy by demonstrating that indeed some lives would be lost to the vaccinations themselves.

When considering the issue of the costs of new policies advocates should allow their creative energies to direct them, and they should consider a wide range of potential outcomes from a change in policy. The fact that a program such as the one proposed might be costly, for example, might allow an advocate to develop arguments about the implications of these costs: The government is so short of money that money spent for one program will almost certainly mean less to go around and available to fund other programs—spending more money on health might prevent increased spending on education and that without improvements in education these children will be locked into a life of poverty.

An advocate might also argue that there are too few laboratories to produce the needed vaccines, and encouraging pharmaceutical companies to gear up to produce more vaccines would divert their attention and resources from producing other medicines that are even more badly needed. For example, one might argue that the focus on vaccinating for currently known diseases might prevent the development of a vaccine for a truly deadly new disease such as SARS (severe acute respiratory syndrome). Indeed, an advocate could also argue that the long-term health of the world's citizenry would be far better served by a program that focused on the prevention of infectious diseases perhaps as yet unknown but likely to develop. Such an example is in south China where many very poor people live "cheek by jowl and in close proximity to pigs and poultry," and where deadly cross-species viral mutations have been known to occur.[5]

Decision Calculus

Arguers who use stock issues as starting points for the analysis of propositions should be mindful of the *decision calculus* that will be applied to the arguments that they develop. Decision calculus can best be summarized as:

Ill (significance of harm)
> Mitigated by: Cure (degree to which new policy reduces ill)
>> Less: Cost (problems or disadvantages of new policy)
>>> Equal: Benefits of Policy Change

The stock issues perspective is a tool that guides arguers in the application of cost benefit analysis to a study of policy issues. Like all other tools of analysis, however, it works only as well as the person who is using it permits it to work. The advocate who is thorough, creative, and thoughtful in the application of the stock issues perspective will create better arguments than will the advocate who is sloppy, indifferent, or uncreative. Another consideration is that this approach strongly values the quantification of argument claims. The very notion of costs and benefits suggests the importance of empirical verifications of arguments.

Nevertheless, certain intangible dimensions of arguments that go beyond their empirical significance might have a dramatic effect on listeners, and advocates need to keep this in mind. In the example about vaccinations, an advocate would want to keep in mind that we have been arguing about children—children who are exposed to serious and preventable diseases; children who may suffer and die from these diseases. Cold calculations about the costs of policy change may not sufficiently account for the personal loss suffered when a family loses a child who might have been saved had he or she received the appropriate vaccination. Arguers need to always keep in mind the moral, ethical, and philosophical values that are often bound up with policy deliberations but that sometimes do not lend themselves to objective measures.

An arguer who chooses to utilize cost-benefit analysis should also remember that arguments must still be adapted to their audiences, and listeners respond to arguments by evaluating them as stories. The stories of suffering children can be very compelling indeed, even when the best case for the high costs of a program of prevention and treatment has been presented.

Systems Analysis

An alternative approach for the analysis of propositions, especially propositions of policy, is provided by general systems theory and the method that is known as *systems analysis*. A system may be defined as "an assembly of objects all of which are related to one another by some form of regular interaction or interdependence so that the assembly can be viewed as an organic or organized whole."[6] When applying the principles of systems theory in propositional analysis, the advocate attempts to identify, study, and evaluate the constituent parts of the system in order to determine their effectiveness.

There are several important underlying assumptions that must be understood before systems theory can be applied. First, systems theory presumes that the constituent parts (often called components) of a system are interdependent of one another. Thus if one component is changed, one might expect that the other components of a system will also be influenced.

Second, systems are characterized by an ordered sequence of events. Because systems (both naturally occurring ones, such as the human body, and created ones, such as a university) are designed to achieve some purpose, their component parts must all function in accordance with their established purpose. When one or more components fail to carry out their assigned functions, the entire system may begin to falter. A problem with your liver, for example, might lower your resistance to disease and place your life in jeopardy. Similarly, a university might have a very strong faculty and outstanding students, but if the curriculum is poorly conceived or poorly designed students might not be taught the courses and subject material that is essential to their educational foundation.

Third, a system's components are connected to and controlled by each other. Because systems are often extremely complex, they must contain procedures for communication and control that keep the system operating an in a state of balance. Thus a system might begin to fail either because a component is not performing its assigned function or because the networks of communication and control intended to link the components to each other are failing.

Fourth, systems entail both a structure and a set of processes.[7] The processes that the system must carry out determine the structure of a system, and likewise, the processes of the different components in a system are determined by the structures that are present. Thus, if the structures are inadequate for the processes that need to be performed, those structures must be changed, or if the processes underway do not reflect the maximum utilization of the characteristics of the structures, the processes must be changed. An illustration might be the changes in systems that must occur as organizations become larger and/or more complex. Small businesses may, for example, operate in a very effective manner with somewhat informal accounting and administrative procedures that have been permitted to develop via practices established over time. At some point, however, a larger business organization might demand a new, more rigorous, and more consistent set of procedures better suited to the opportunities and challenges of the new business environment.

Systems theory is applied to describe the operations of an existing system; it can also be utilized to evaluate the effectiveness of that system and to compare it with possible alternative systems. Because systems theory is a tool of analysis, it benefits an advocate only if it is artfully and creatively applied to the study of a proposition.

A Systems Analysis of a Policy Proposition

An advocate who chooses to use systems theory to analyze a policy proposition should first describe the components of the existing system and their relationship to each other and then evaluate them in terms of their effectiveness in meeting their goals. To illustrate the process we will suggest steps for analyzing the following proposition:

> Resolved: That the federal government should establish a program to promote sex education, birth control information, and access to contraceptives in clinics in all public secondary schools in the United States.

A Model for Systems Analysis[8]

Function	Terms	Definitions
Description	Components	the discrete, unique, or constituent parts that compose the system
	Relationships	the identity that exists between two or more components; the action of a system, that is, the nature or characteristics of the activity between two or more things taken together
Evaluation	Goals	the stated or operational objectives, designs, aims, or intentions of the people interacting with their environment; the critical decision-making process is designed to achieve these goals
	Effects	the assessment, fulfillment, accomplishment, impression, or outcome of a system as a result of certain components interacting in relationships toward certain goals; an evaluation of the elements of the system as measured against the goals of the system

The advocate should first seek to detail the components of a system that currently provides sex education and contraceptives to teenagers. This advocate would likely find that many different organizations, with very different objectives provide information and services. The components of such a system may include:

Existing clinics in public schools. A few schools might have precisely the type of clinics that the advocate would like to see developed at other schools throughout the nation. Advocates can frequently research and locate such "demonstration" projects and argue for the expansion of a network of such programs. In the case of this topic, such clinics might provide teenagers with information on preventing pregnancies, avoiding sexually transmitted diseases, and might even provide staff capable of conducting medical examinations for students who may not have access to suitable health care. These clinics could serve as pilot projects to illustrate the benefits of school-based programs. Currently, however, these programs would likely be limited in number and able to serve only a small fraction of the total number of teens in the United States.

Sex education classes in public schools. More schools might have classes that provide information about contraceptives, the prevention of sexually transmitted diseases, and even information about dating, child-rearing, and parental responsibility, but they would not be able to provide students with contraceptives or with physical examinations. Although such classes might produce some of the benefits the advocate might seek, they would not likely exist in all schools and would thus not be available for all students. They also, of course, would not assure actual access to the contraceptives or to the desirable level of medical services.

Planned Parenthood and/or other nongovernmental organizations. In many communities, schools do not provide sex education, family planning or contraceptive information, or information about sexually transmitted diseases to children. Often organizations like Planned Parenthood are available to fill in the gaps. Many such organizations even offer free or low-cost medical examinations for students who cannot access such services through other means. The challenge, of course, is in making students aware of the existence of such services and also in helping them to overcome barriers, such as lack of transportation to get them to such programs. It may be awkward, for many young women, for example, to announce to their mom that they need to be driven to the local Planned Parenthood office so that they can get a prescription for oral contraceptives. Thus having potential access to such services through a community organization is not necessarily equivalent to access to such services through one's public school

Churches and religious groups. Many communities have sex education programs sponsored by churches, religious denominations, or religious support groups. Such programs may provide very useful information to teens but will often focus on trying to prevent them from becoming sexually active, rather than explicitly dealing with such issues as preventing pregnancies or recognizing or preventing sexually transmitted diseases. Such programs may also close off certain kinds of choices for the teens who utilize them. For example, programs that attempt to persuade teens that terminating pregnancy is a sin and therefore should never be considered may then fail to address many associated problems or issues that teens might face.

Parents, friends, and others. For some teenagers there may be no access to information about sex from organized and professional external sources. These students may, as a result, get their information from parents or other relatives, their friends, or even from comparative strangers. Since many parents feel uncomfortable discussing sex with their children, and may not want to believe that their children are sexually active, they may put off the discussion until it is too late to prevent the pregnancy or the sexually transmitted disease. Furthermore, such sources may provide teenagers with incomplete or even inaccurate information.

The media. Many teenagers will today turn to the media for information about their sexual health. For the few who actively seek such information they may find very useful material in books, magazines, or on the Internet. For many others, however, their information will be gleaned largely from entertainment media, which may mislead rather than inform them about their sexuality.

Once the advocate has identified the different components of the system that exists to provide sexual information and services to teenagers, he or she can begin to assess how these different components function in relationship to each other. One will likely find, for instance, that only a small number of teenagers has access to the kind of comprehensive education and services that school-based clinics can provide. Perhaps sex education programs are in existence at some schools, but they are not in all schools. Urban teens may have access to nongovernmental organizations, such as Planned Parenthood, but these organizations may not be available to teens living in rural areas. Others will not know about the availability of such services or will have transportation problems or other barriers that prevent them from accessing the programs. Consequently, the advocate might learn that most teenagers get most of their information about sex from their parents, or their friends, and they must utilize their own initiatives to get contraceptives.

An analysis of the goals of the present system would also help inform the advocate. For example, the goal of many current sex education programs, and the focus of much of the instruction provided to teenagers, is to prevent them from becoming sexually active. Many parents and religious groups, for example, do not tell children much about sex beyond preaching the merits of abstinence. The advocate can critique the system, however, by observing that many teenagers do become sexually active despite this instruction, and thus they badly need information that will help them prevent both pregnancy and disease. The advocate might find that the very goals of the present system might limit its effectiveness in solving the problems society faces. A teenager who is getting a strong dose of preaching about the importance of sexual abstinence from his or her parents and church may not turn to these same sources of information with a question about the most effective means of preventing a pregnancy or about how to recognize the symptoms of an STD. Yet, for many students, there may be few alternative sources of information available.

Through an analysis of the effects of the current system, the advocate can identify the problems left unresolved by the existing policies of sex education. Current policy leaves the design, implementation, and administration of sex education programs to individual communities, school districts, and parents. We have soaring rates of teenage pregnancy; sexually transmitted diseases have reached epidemic levels; and the specter of AIDS looms over the entire globe. It may well be time to propose a more comprehensive program to address such problems.

The final task for the advocate is to utilize systems theory in designing an alternative to the current system. In this step the advocate seeks to enact the resolution to achieve a solution to the problems identified in the current system through the creation of a new system. The school-based clinics mentioned earlier might be seen as the most effective way to provide information and health services because they are easily accessible to students and meet them on their own turf.

Those who seek to defend the current system can also utilize systems theory. Often advocates can argue that the system either functions well as currently designed or that only minor alterations in the existing system would effectively address the problems. For example, they could argue that the current programs could be expanded, the mass media could be used more fully to get information out to teens who do not receive information in school or from other programs or sources. Finally, these advocates might argue that a change in the system might actually prove to be counterproductive and could worsen the problems. For example, one could argue that an attempt to create a federal program to provide sex education in public schools could result in a public backlash. Conservative or very religious parents could voice such strong objections to a government mandate creating high school clinics or a standardized sex education curriculum in public schools that they would withdraw their children and enroll them in private or religious schools. Such a backlash might result in less sex education for many students and consequently more teenage pregnancies or STDS. Or, an advocate might argue that access to contraceptives and information about sex might lower the students' resistance to peer pressures to become sexually active. Consequently, these advocates might argue, the new program would increase the likelihood that children will engage in sexual relations at a younger age. Then, there is the argument that no contraceptive is 100 percent effective, some risk of pregnancy or disease would exist, and that sexual activity at a younger age can create other emotional or physical problems for children, resulting in their making other unwise decisions, such as to consume drugs or alcohol.

The Benefits to Applying Systems Theory

While the traditional theory of stock issues presumes that change occurs only when there is some recognizable need, "felt difficulty," or ill, systems theory suggests that change is always occurring and must be managed in the best way possible. It presumes that minor policy corrections are inevitable and desirable. Consequently, some have argued that systems theory is a more desirable way to evaluate policy arguments in contemporary society.[9]

Another benefit of systems theory is that it more accurately reflects the increasing complexity of modern life. We have so many layers of government involved in decision making today, with state and local governments, regulatory agencies, the federal government, and even multinational and/or nongovernmental organizations (e.g., the World Trade Organization, the International Monetary Fund, etc.) all making decisions that can affect our lives, that it is useful to employ a tool of analysis that reflects this complexity and the characteristics of contemporary decision-making structures.

Both systems theory and the stock issues theory are best understood as tools of analysis. They are useful because they guide both advocates and critics in the careful and thoughtful consideration of arguments.

SUMMARY

This chapter considered the different types of propositions that may be argued: propositions of fact, propositions of value, and propositions of policy. It also discussed the importance of defining the key terms of any proposition, and the process of analysis. The chapter offered suggestions for how advocates should select the point of stasis (or the point of clash) in an argument, and it discussed two systems for propositional analysis: the stock issues perspective and the systems theory perspective.

Key Terms

analysis   stasis
clash   status quo
decision calculus   stock issues
inherency   ill
proposition   blame
  of fact   cure
  of policy   cost
  of value   systems analysis

Activities

1. As practice in writing propositions, select controversies from your local or student newspaper. Try to locate the main point of stasis for each controversy. Phrase these differences as propositions of fact, value, or policy, depending on the nature of the disagreement.

2. Recall the last time you and a significant other got into an argument. Looking back, what was the issue that caused the dispute? Try to phrase it as a proposition (fact, value or policy).

3. Examine the following propositions, identifying whether each is a proposition of fact, value, or policy:

   a. The weather today is nice.

   b. The high temperature today was 46 degrees.

   c. If you do not wear a jacket today you will be cold.

   d. You should wear a jacket today.

   e. Parents should require their children to bring jackets to school on chilly days.

   f. Failing to wear a jacket when it is cold can cause illness.

   g. Protective outerwear keeps a person warm.

4. Select a public controversy and analyze how the key terms in the controversy might be defined. Note the differences, if any, in the alternative definitions and consider how the differences may influence the argument process. Consult each of the following as appropriate:

   a. your own personal definition

   b. a popular dictionary definition

   c. a specialized dictionary definition from the appropriate field (for example, from a legal, medical, scientific, or technical dictionary)

   d. how advocates who are engaged in the controversy defined the key terms

5. Select an article in which an advocate is calling for a change (for example an editorial or opinion essay). Then examine the way the advocate identifies the ill, places the blame, and proposes a cure. Were all three of the stock issues presented? Did the advocate also refute the potential arguments about costs?

Recommended Readings

Benoit, William I., Steve R. Wilson, and Vincent F. Follert. "The Decision Rules for the Policy Metaphor." *Journal of the American Forensics Association* 22 (1986): 135–146.

Kline, Susan L. "Toward a Contemporary Linguistic Interpretation of the Concepts of Stasis." *Journal of the American Forensic Association* 16 (1979): 95–103.

Klumpp, James F., Bernard L. Brock, James W. Chesebro, and John F. Cragan. "Implications of a Systems Model of Analysis on Argumentation Theory." *Journal of the American Forensic Association* 11 (1974): 1–7.

Langsdorf, Lenore. "Argument as Inquiry in a Postmodern Context." *Argumentation* 11 (1997): 315–328.

Lichtman, Allan J. "Competing Models of the Debate Process." *Journal of the American Forensic Association* 22 (1986): 147–151.

Lichtman, Allan J., and Daniel M. Rohrer. "The Logic of Policy Dispute." *Journal of the American Forensic Association* 16 (1980): 236–247.

Mader, Thomas F. "The Inherent Need to Analyze Stasis." *Journal of the American Forensics Association* 4 (1967): 13–20.

Pfau, Michael. "The Present System Revisited Part One: Incremental Change." *Journal of the American Forensics Association* 17 (1980): 80–84.

Thompson, Wayne N. "Stasis in Aristotle's Rhetoric." *Quarterly Journal of Speech* 58 (1972): 134–142.

Notes

[1] For a more complete discussion of criteria for the evaluation of value propositions, see Thomas A. Hollihan, "An Analysis of Value Argumentation in Contemporary Debate," *Debate Issues* 14 (1980): 7–10.

[2] For a discussion of the principle of stasis see Ray Nadeau, "Some Aristotelian and Stoic Influences on the Theory of Stasis," *Speech Monographs* 26 (1959), 248. See also, George Kennedy, *The Art of Persuasion in Greece* (Princeton: Princeton University Press, 1963), 303–309.

[3] John Dewey, *How We Think* (Boston: Heath, 1910).

[4] Lee S. Hultzen, "Status in Deliberative Analysis," in *The Rhetorical Idiom*, ed. Donald C. Bryant, 97–123 (New York: Cornell University Press, 1958).

[5] "China's Chernobyl?" *The Economist*, April 26–May 2, 2003, 9–10.

[6] Bernard L. Brock, James W. Chesebro, John F. Cragan and James F. Klumpp, *Public Policy Decision Making: Systems Analysis and Comparative Advantages Debate* (New York: Harper and Row, 1973), 27.

[7] Ibid., 27–29.

[8] Ibid., 50.

[9] Ibid., 1–22.

6

TYPES OF ARGUMENTS

Humans are natural arguers—we have an affinity for making, using, and evaluating arguments. Despite this natural proclivity for arguing, however, learning the basic components of arguments can enable decision makers to more systematically dissect and evaluate argumentative claims. Learning argumentation principles will also enable arguers to construct stronger arguments. In this chapter we discuss the reasoning process and consider arguments as complete logical claims.

From a logical perspective, arguments are considered rational when they correspond with accepted standards of reasoning. The reasoning process involves three separate elements. First, you must identify the data or grounds that will be used to develop your claim. Second, you must reason from that data through logical induction or deduction. Third, you must offer a claim or conclusion that builds upon the data and that constitutes a new and original insight. This chapter focuses primarily on the second step, the inductive and deductive reasoning process.

Inductive reasoning might be described as arguing from specific cases to more general conclusions. *Deductive reasoning* is essentially the opposite process, and entails moving from overall theories or generally accepted principles to conclusions about specific cases. Both inductive and deductive arguments occur frequently and naturally, because they are typically embedded in the stories that people tell to make decisions, resolve disputes, or identify solutions to their problems. Both forms of reasoning can be equally compelling and persuasive, and neither form is preferred over the other. Instead, arguers create inductive or deductive arguments in response to the problems they face and for the purposes most suited to the arguments they are creating.

INDUCTIVE ARGUMENTS

When you are faced with a situation where you have knowledge or information about a number of specific cases, but you lack an understanding of the factors that might unite those cases into a general theory or principle, you can utilize the inductive reasoning process to seek conclusions. There are three types of arguments that you may utilize to reason inductively.

Argument by Example

An *argument by example* examines one or more cases within a specific class and reasons that if these cases have certain common features, then other, as yet unknown cases in that class will also have these features. All arguments by example are based on generalizations from these known cases to unknown ones. Here are some examples:

- Susan Jones, Ann Harper, and Liz Kent are members of the Delta Delta Delta sorority, and they are all on the dean's list. Tri-Delts are good students.

- My friends Bill, Dianne, and Lynn were communication majors and they got into really good law schools. Communication must be a good pre-law major.

- The last time I tried to get help from the Advising Office I got passed around from one person to another. No one knew the answers to my questions. That department is incompetent.

- When the standards for the disposal of hazardous waste in the United States become more stringent, or when the government increases the regulations to improve worker safety, American companies will ship the hazardous waste overseas or build their manufacturing plants in places that are not so well regulated. American corporations don't care about worker safety or the environment.

As is illustrated in the examples above, the process of arguing on the basis of examples is familiar and common. Not all arguments from example are strong or convincing, however, and several tests of these arguments can and should be applied.

First, are there a significant number of examples offered to support the claim? Obviously there is a great danger in arguing from a very limited number of examples to a more general conclusion. All of the arguments offered above might be challenged on the basis of the sufficiency of the examples cited. The arguer who reasons from only a limited number of cases always risks making judgments about those cases that may not be true for other unknown cases. For example, there may be seventy young women in the Delta Delta Delta sorority. Knowing that three of them are very good students may not give you too much confidence that the other sixty-seven are equally successful in the classroom.

Second, are the examples cited typical of the category of class that the arguer is trying to generalize to? Because one individual asked questions that the staff members of the Advising Office were unable to answer does not necessarily suggest that this office is typically unable to answer students' questions.

Perhaps these questions were truly extraordinary and rare; they might have been questions that the staff had never encountered before, for example, about transfer units from an unknown university. Or, it is conceivable that the specific advisors to whom this student spoke were new to their positions and not yet sufficiently well trained to answer such questions. Perhaps other advisors, who might have been busy assisting other students, would have been able to answer the student's questions. In order to determine if this experience is typical you might consider your own personal experiences with the staff in this office. You might also consider the previous stories you have heard recounted about this office from other students.

Third, are negative examples or rival stories sufficiently accounted for in the argument? For example, Bill, Dianne, and Lynn may have had great success in qualifying for admission to very competitive law schools, yet there are certainly many other communication majors who probably failed to gain admission to any law schools during that same admission cycle. Should you not also consider these cases? Also, of course, students majoring in other academic disciplines were also applying for admission to law school. How well did they fare on gaining admission to law school? Certainly, this might also be useful information in any evaluation of the relative merits of different undergraduate majors with regard to law school admissions.

Fourth, are the cited examples relevant to the claim being advanced? Many factors might, for example, influence a company's decision to shift their operations overseas. Increased environmental safety or worker safety legislation might indeed be a factor in this decision, but companies might also be seeking to benefit from lower wage rates, transportation variables, ready access to foreign suppliers, or access to foreign markets to sell their products, among other reasons.

Arguments from examples to a generalization that move too quickly or without sufficient rationale may be labeled a *__hasty generalization__*. A hasty generalization is a logical *fallacy*. A fallacy is a flaw in the reasoning process. An advocate who commits a hasty generalization has potentially reasoned fallaciously and the generalization, that is the claim, should be examined more closely.

Arguments by Analogy

An *argument by analogy* seeks to identify similarities between cases that might on the surface seem to be quite dissimilar, in order to permit an inference to be drawn. Analogies are typically literary and creative devices that appeal to the listeners' experiences and beliefs, and they are often used to embellish our stories. There are two types of analogies: literal and figurative.

A *literal analogy* is a statement drawing a direct comparison between two or more cases. The following are examples of literal analogies:

- In business circles there is a new awareness of customer service. It is time for professors to begin thinking of students as the customers of the university.

- Students who want an education only to prepare them for careers are like apprentices attaching themselves to a carpenter. That is not what a liberal education should seek to achieve.

- Gorbachev, Yeltsin, and Putin, the leaders who have tried to create democratic institutions in Russia, faced the same kinds of problems that Thomas Jefferson, Benjamin Franklin, and our other forefathers faced more than two centuries ago.

A *figurative analogy* is a statement that makes comparisons between classes that are materially dissimilar from each other but that are nonetheless suggestive of each other in some characteristic or manner. The following are examples of figurative analogies:

- The builders and developers have attacked the undeveloped hillsides of the city like hungry locusts.
- Many senators responded angrily to the bill limiting their income from outside sources. They are like drug addicts demanding their daily fix.
- The Iowa presidential caucuses are like a beauty contest for all the candidates who want to gain their party's nomination.

Both literal and figurative analogies are especially compelling types of arguments in that they correspond to people's ability to create stories and to test those stories when they argue. There is an important dramatic element to an effective analogy, for it creates a vivid picture in the minds of the audience. Consequently, analogies readily lend themselves to the tests of narrative probability and fidelity that we have already discussed in great detail.

In addition to these narrative tests, however, asking two questions can also test analogies. First, are the compared cases alike in some meaningful way? Is it really useful, for example, to think of students as customers? Customers are typically passive consumers who expect the businesses they patronize to wait on them. Students, on the other hand, should be active participants in the learning process. Education is not something that can be done for you; it is something that students must largely do for themselves. Thus, while this analogy might appeal to students, it is not likely to appeal to many other listeners, and especially not to the professors to whom it may be directed!

Second, are the compared characteristics accurately described? For example, the candidates who march through Iowa campaigning for support in the Iowa presidential caucuses are expected to meet thousands of voters in gatherings large and small, to give countless "stump" speeches and media interviews, and to lay out their political agenda and qualifications for the presidency. Although these processes may strongly advantage candidates who can raise large amounts of campaign contributions as well as those who may already be well known to the voters, and although these caucuses may not constitute an idealized form of deliberative democracy, the claim that they are merely a beauty pageant for contenders seems unfair and less than persuasive.

An advocate who compares apples with oranges may be said to have committed a logical fallacy called *false reasoning by analogy.* If you encounter such advocacy you should demand more information before granting adherence to such an argument.

Arguments from Causal Correlation

An even more sophisticated form of inductive reasoning is the **argument from causal correlation**. This type of argument examines specific cases, classes of cases, or both, in order to identify an actual relationship or correlation between them. Most research in the scientific tradition adheres to the principles of the inductive causal correlation argument, or its deductive cousin, the causal generalization, which we shall discuss in the next section.

The following examples might help you identify arguments from causal correlation:

- Children, who are exposed to excess levels of lead, either from eating paint chips or from air pollution, often suffer serious brain deficiencies and learning disabilities as a result.

- Excessive exposure to violence on television or in video games leads to a willingness to accept violence as appropriate behavior and decreases people's sense of revulsion toward violence in real life.

- People today are given so many different antibiotics to combat infections that they are increasingly becoming inured to them. All too often the result is the development of resistant strains of diseases that are much more difficult to cure.

There are several tests of causal correlation that enable an arguer to assess this type of argument. First, is the association proposed between the cause and the effect consistent? For example, do all, or even most people who watch violent television shows or who play violent video games become more accepting of violence? Do people who are more inclined toward pacifism watch a lesser amount of television violence? These questions are designed as tests of causal correlation such as those that were first proposed by John Stuart Mill, an English philosopher and logician. Mill claimed that causal correlations could be tested on the basis of three canons that assessed the strength of the associations being claimed. The questions posed above all assess what Mill described as concomitant variation.[1] This test says that if increased exposure to violence is claimed to increase one's acceptance of violence, then decreased exposure to violence should also mean a decreased acceptance of violence. Mill believed that there should be a predictable pattern and relationship between a cause and its alleged effect.

Mill also claimed that discovering whether the "method of agreement" between the cases was the same could test the consistency between cause and effect. He thus claimed, "If two or more instances of the phenomenon under investigation have only one circumstance in common, the circumstances in which alone all the instances agree is the cause (or effect) of the given phenomenon."[2] Turning again to the argument about violence on television and in video games, and the effect on behavior, an arguer would seek to determine if the subjects in the argument were alike in their video habits and in their proclivity toward violence, but dissimilar in other respects such as social status, income, children living in single parent homes, neighborhoods, and/or lifestyle. This inquiry might lead one to conclude that exposure to violence on television and in video games was or was not a more important factor in shaping their attitudes and behaviors with regard to violence than these other factors studied.

Finally, according to Mill, considering whether the method of difference between the cases compared is consistent can test the consistency between cause and effect. "If, for example, the instance where the phenomenon under investigation occurs and that instance where it does not occur have every circumstance in common except one, that one occurring only in the former, then the circumstance in which alone the two cases differ is the effect, or the cause of the phenomenon."[3] Returning again to our test case, one might cite an example of two boys who both grow up in a violent inner-city neighborhood, in single-parent homes, and with a single parent who unfortunately is abusive and alcoholic. One child becomes a violent felon and is sent to prison. The other becomes an ordained minister and community leader. The argument about the relationship between video violence and real-life violence would be supported if the arguer could establish that the minister's parents had not owned a television set, and consequently he was seldom exposed to the video violence that was the other boy's constant companion. Incidentally, although such an example would be very convincing, locating evidence this specific in the real world to establish causality is rare indeed.

All three of Mill's canons—concomitant variation, method of agreement, and method of difference—are essentially subsumed under the first test of a causal correlation, the test of the consistency of the association between cause and effect.

A second test of a causal correlation argument asks: Is the alleged association a strong one? This is often an empirical test. There are, for example, many children who watch violence on television and in video games who do not become violent adults. What percentages of those who see violent programs do become violent? How much violence did these children see? Is there some point up to which watching violence may not be harmful, but beyond which it is? Is there a certain age at which violent television programs become either more or less dangerous? All of these questions seek to determine the degree to which the statistical association between watching violent television programs and committing violent acts can be predicted.

A third test of a causal correlation asks: Does the movement of cause to effect follow a regular and predictable time sequence? For example, if one argues that children who are exposed to higher levels of lead suffer learning disabilities as a result, one should be able to argue definitively about the length of time it takes for the exposure to cause the harmful effect. Does it take hours, weeks, days, or months for the symptoms to manifest themselves? Furthermore, how long do the symptoms persist? Does the damage that a child faces from lead poisoning correct itself over time? Or can one expect that a child once so injured will suffer throughout his or her life?

Research into the AIDS virus has demonstrated the importance of carefully considering time frame as a test of argument. Doctors now understand that AIDS is unlike most other diseases. First, it takes a long time for medical tests to confirm that the patient has been exposed (perhaps as long as six months) because doctors can determine that patients are HIV-positive only after they begin to develop antibodies to fight the infection. Second, even after these antibodies appear, most patients will continue to be healthy for many months or even many years before beginning to develop symptoms of the disease. Finally, even after patients develop AIDS symptoms it may be another extended period before their condition is identifiable as full-blown AIDS. In the early years of AIDS research, doctors interpreted this time lag as an indication that many, if not most, of the people who were HIV-positive would probably not come down with the disease. Doctors assumed that, because these patients had been infected but showed no symptoms, they would probably be able to fight the disease off on their own. Early estimates based on this reasoning predicted that only 10 percent of those infected with the virus would succumb to the disease. Then, as more and more patients became ill, doctors were forced to keep increasing their estimates—20 percent, then 30 percent, and so on. Ultimately, the doctors conducting AIDS research realized that virtually all patients who are HIV-positive would eventually come down with the disease unless they are given a rigorous program of state-of-the-art drugs to manage their viral loads and prevent the onset of full-blown AIDS. As a result, the notions about the lag time from exposure to the onset of the disease have been not only extended but also fundamentally reconsidered. Only with this new realization of the ways in which the disease progressed (the cause) was the real severity of the global AIDS epidemic understood (the effect).

The final question of causal correlation asks: Is the alleged association between cause and effect coherent? Essentially this asks the arguer to offer a persuasive explanation for the relationship between cause and effect. For example, several years ago in San Francisco an enraged city supervisor named Dan White murdered Mayor George Moscone and a fellow supervisor named Harvey Britt. The defense attorney claimed during the trial that White committed the murder because he was addicted to, and had been on a binge, eating junk food. This junk food, the attorney claimed, produced such a "sugar-high" that the murderer could not be held responsible for his actions. This so-called "Twinkie defense" won wide attention from the media but was criticized by nutritional experts as largely spurious. These experts argued that while there might be some association between physical behavior and diet, there is no coherent explanation to support an association between willingness to commit violent acts and one's diet.

It is surprisingly common for individuals to confuse the sequence of events with a belief in cause and effect. In the Middle Ages villagers whose crops withered in the field blamed the dead crops on the actions of individuals. The result was to ostracize those who were different, or sometimes to label them as witches and burn them at the stake. But such tendencies didn't die with the Enlightenment; even today we look to situate the cause for an effect. When students in Colorado were shot by disturbed classmates, some attributed causality for the murderous actions to music, others to video games, and still others to cliques at the school. We may never know what caused these abhorrent actions, but many are quick to try to find the reasons. Confusing "sequence of events" with "cause and effect" is called the *post hoc ergo propter hoc* fallacy. It literally means "after this, therefore, because of this." While sometimes we commit this fallacy purposefully, for example claiming that it rained because we forgot our umbrella, when we encounter arguments that attribute causality without adequate rationale, we should seek additional information, lest we be guilty of committing the *post hoc* fallacy.

Now that we have introduced the three primary forms in which inductive arguments might be developed, it is time to consider the different forms in which deductive arguments occur.

DEDUCTIVE ARGUMENTS

In deductive arguments one generalizes from theories or principles believed to be true to claims about individual cases. There are two types of deductive arguments.

Arguments from Sign

An *argument from sign* relies on the presence of certain attributes observable in a specific case to prove that it can be related to a generalization that is assumed to be true. When using this form of argument one identifies certain characteristics or signs and then seeks to account for them by tying them to a conclusion or claim. Consider the following examples:

- The lack of respect for other people's property—the graffiti and vandalism, as well as the increased incidents of violence—suggests that many American youths lack values.
- Bob is suffering from excessive fatigue, diarrhea, swollen lymph glands, and many mouth sores. He must have contracted AIDS.
- The students were hunched over their desks in apt concentration, and the quiet in the room was almost deafening. It was obvious that they were taking their required competency examinations very seriously.

There are three separate tests that can be used in the evaluation of a sign argument. First, are the cited signs always indicators of the general theory being cited? The symptoms cited in the example about AIDS, for example, might also be symptoms of many other medical conditions, none of them as alarming or as serious as AIDS. A doctor would not want to mention the possibility that the patient had contracted AIDS until these other possibilities had been eliminated. It would be cruel to cause a patient to worry unnecessarily.

Second, are there enough signs present to support the conclusion offered? The students who are hunched over their desks taking the examinations, for example, might simply be exhausted from a night of intense partying, and might not be concentrating on their tests after all. One might want to determine whether or not there are other signs that the students took the examinations seriously. For instance, did they study for them? And how well did they score?

Third, are contradictory signs present, and if so, have they been carefully considered? With regard to the argument about AIDS, for example, it might be that Bob is gaining weight despite all of his other symptoms. As it is highly unusual for an AIDS sufferer to gain weight, the arguer would need to account for the weight gain in order to support any conclusion ventured about the underlying cause for Bob's medical symptoms.

Those advocates who would have us move too quickly from a limited number of signs are guilty of the fallacy of *false reasoning by sign*. If we suspect that this might be the case, it would be to our benefit to examine the argument more closely.

Arguments from Causal Generalization

The second type of deductive argument is the *argument from causal generalization*. The causal generalization is the direct counterpart of the causal correlation that we have already discussed. While the causal correlation argues inductively from specific cases to seek to identify a connection between these cases, the causal generalization argues deductively from some general principles that are assumed to be true to judgments about specific cases under consideration. The following are examples of causal generalizations:

- It is well known that the AIDS virus is transmitted by the exchange of bodily fluids. This frequently occurs when drug addicts share hypodermic needles. Bob was an intravenous drug user, which probably accounts for his infection with AIDS.

- Steven is bound to abuse his children because he was himself abused as a child.

- It is unwise to raise interest rates. Every time interest rates have been substantially increased a recession has followed.

There are three tests of arguments from causal generalization. First, is the cause that is identified sufficient to produce the effect? The fact that Steven was abused as a child might influence his parenting style, for example, but there are many persons who were abused as children who are very good parents and who do not abuse their children. As a result, one can question whether his own abuse experience is sufficient to explain his behavior.

Second, might the cause result in other quite different effects? Perhaps Steven has such negative recollections of his own childhood experiences that he will be especially motivated to avoid them with his children. He might become a parent who is unusually sensitive and kind to his own children precisely because his parents were not sensitive and kind to him.

Third, might intervening factors preclude the expected relationship between cause and effect? In some cases an adjustment upwards of interest rates will stabilize and ultimately strengthen the economy. The increase in interest rates might slow demand, reduce inflation, respond to a tight labor market, and help to strengthen banks. All of these factors might serve to keep the nation out of a recession.

Fallaciously reasoning from a known generalization to a specific case is called the fallacy of *false reasoning by causal generalization*. Just as the other fallacies we introduced in this chapter, if you suspect that an advocate may be reasoning falsely in this manner, you should seek additional information before granting adherence to such a claim.

THE DEDUCTIVE SYLLOGISM

We can test all deductive arguments, whether they are arguments from signs or from causal generalizations, by phrasing them in syllogistic form and then examining their structural properties. A *syllogism* is a formal, logical type of reasoning. A syllogism consists of three statements. The **major premise** states a generalization: *All Men are mortal*. The **minor premise** relates a specific case or class to the generalization: *Socrates is a man*. And the **conclusion** is deduced from the two premises: *Socrates is mortal*.

The example about Socrates is what is known as a *categorical syllogism*—one that makes a statement about all cases within a given category. The major premise asserts a generalization that prescribes the category, the minor premise locates a specific case being argued within that category, and the conclusion is the deductive judgment that presents itself when these two premises are rationally or logically evaluated. The categorical syllogism is thus a very straightforward and simple deductive judgment. Another example of a categorical syllogism is:

Major Premise   All Christians believe in God.
Minor Premise   Fred is a Christian.
Conclusion   Fred believes in God.

Analyzing deductive arguments as syllogisms enables an arguer to assess their validity quickly. (A valid syllogism is one that meets the required characteristics of argumentative form). As we will discuss in detail later, logical validity is not the same as material truth. A syllogism that is not true may be valid, and an invalid syllogism may be materially true. Nonetheless, tests of logical validity are very useful to arguers and are easy to learn because they are often intuitive. These tests can be summarized as follows:

First, to be valid, a categorical syllogism must in its major premise so define the category in question that it can be determined for certain that the specific case cited in the minor premise will fall within it. In the most recent example, the category defined "All Christians" is so clear that once the minor premise labels Fred as a Christian we can immediately conclude that he believes in God. If, for example, the major premise had asserted only that *some* Christians believe in God, it would have been impossible for us, based on the information provided in the syllogism, to know whether or not Fred fell within that group.

Second, no term can be found in the conclusion that is not found in one of the premises. For example:

Major Premise   All tennis players are athletic.
Minor Premise   Jim is a tennis player.
Conclusion   Susan is athletic.

This syllogism cannot be presumed valid because the specific case Susan is not specified in either the major or the minor premise. We do not know from the information provided in this syllogism whether Susan is a tennis player or not. Thus, her specific case cannot be deduced from a generalization about tennis players.

Third, the major and the minor premises cannot both be negative statements. If both statements offer negative judgments it is impossible to derive a positive conclusion about a specific case based on the information provided in the syllogism. This is illustrated in the following example:

Major Premise   No Republicans favor tax increases.
Minor Premise   Senator Jones is no Republican.
Conclusion   (Who knows?)

Fourth, whenever the major or the minor premise is a negative statement the conclusion must also be a negative statement. For example:

Major Premise   No Democrats favor cuts in social programs.
Minor Premise   Senator Williams is a Democrat.
Conclusion   Senator Williams does not favor cuts in social programs.

You have no doubt discovered by now that most of these categorical syllogisms are fairly easy to evaluate. In order to further guide your assessments of the validity of a syllogism, however, you can construct what is known as a Venn diagram, named for its creator, the nineteenth-century mathematician John Venn. In a Venn diagram one takes the broadest category, which is established in the major premise, and draws it in a large circle. One then takes the more specific term of the major premise and draws it in a smaller circle. Finally, one takes the particular case to be categorized and draws it in the smallest circle. For example:

Major Premise   All Christians believe in God.
Minor Premise   Fred is a Christian.
Conclusion   Fred believes in God.

The Venn diagram would be constructed as follows:

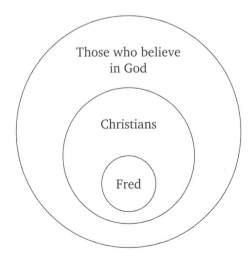

The Venn diagram reveals that this is a valid syllogism because the three circles are located within each other. We can thus visually determine that Fred, as a Christian, falls within the category of those who believe in God.

A Venn diagram can also reveal the invalidity of a syllogism:

Major Premise   No Republicans favor tax increases.
Minor Premise   Senator Jones is no Republican.
Conclusion   Who knows?

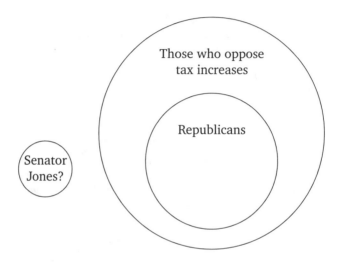

Because, in this case, we cannot place the term that we are seeking to define (Senator Jones) within the circles representing the two proposed defining characteristics, this Venn diagram reveals that the syllogism does not meet the requirements of formal validity.

The Conditional Syllogism

A conditional syllogism might best be described as an "if/then" syllogism. This type of syllogism asserts that if a particular thing occurs then some other particular thing will follow:

Major Premise   If students study they get better grades.
Minor Premise   The students will study.
Conclusion   The students will get better grades.

The antecedent, or "if" premise, sets up the reasoning process that makes the syllogism function. If the consequent, or minor premise, affirms the antecedent, the syllogism is presumed valid. However, if the consequent denies the antecedent, the syllogism cannot be presumed valid:

Major Premise   If students study they get better grades.
Minor Premise   The students will not study.
Conclusion   The students will get better grades.

This syllogism is not valid because the consequent does not meet the conditions specified in the antecedent.

The Disjunctive Syllogism

A disjunctive syllogism contains premises that are essentially "either/or" statements:

Major Premise   The University must either raise tuition or cut faculty and programs.

Minor Premise   The University is unwilling to make cuts.

Conclusion   Therefore tuition must be increased.

The disjunctive syllogism may be judged valid when the major premise includes all of the possible alternatives thereby allowing a conclusion to be drawn through the process of elimination. Frequently there are more alternatives than are provided for in the major premise. This flaw is less a failure of the syllogistic reasoning, however, than it is a test of the material truth or falsity of the syllogistic claim. This leads us to the next issue for discussion.

Structural Validity versus Material Truth

The evaluation of syllogistic form is useful as a demonstration of explicit logical deduction. By applying the tests of syllogistic reasoning, an arguer can readily determine whether or not a conclusion argued in a syllogism is valid. The same tests are not effective in determining the material truth underlying the argumentative claim, however, because material truths are assumed in the formation of premises. Consider the following example:

Major Premise   All cats have three legs.

Minor Premise   Felix is a cat.

Conclusion   Felix has three legs.

The syllogism is valid. It meets all of the tests of a categorical syllogism. Obviously, however, the syllogism is not materially true since we know that cats have four, not three, legs. The arguer who wishes to test a syllogism needs to remember that a syllogism's being valid does not make it true. The truth or falsity of a syllogism must also be evaluated by an examination of the material truth of the premises and the degree to which the claims offered in the premises are verifiable.

THE TOULMIN MODEL

Another approach to viewing arguments has been suggested by Stephen Toulmin, and has come to be known as the *Toulmin model*, or diagram, of argument.[4] (We have already discussed Toulmin's notion of argument fields in chapter 3). While few artifacts of argument exhibit all of the elements of the Toulmin model, and while abstracting an argument from its social context in order to diagram it risks distorting and oversimplifying it, the Toulmin model is a useful tool for understanding the components of argument, and it provides real insight into the reasoning process that arguers use. Once you understand the elements of an argument you can critically evaluate each one in turn. The six components are:

Claim: conclusion of the argument; that statement which the advocate wishes the audience to believe

Grounds: foundation or basis for the claim; the support

Warrant: reasoning that authorizes the inferential leap from the grounds to the claim

Backing: support for the warrant

Modality: degree of certainty with which the advocate makes the claim

Rebuttal: exceptions that might be offered to the claim

Before discussing each of these elements in greater detail we will examine an entire argument and diagram it.

Megan: The Dodgers will probably win the National League Pennant this year. (claim)

Sean: What are you basing this claim on? (request for grounds)

Megan: They have the best pitching. (grounds)

Sean: Maybe, but how does the fact that they have the best pitching lead you to believe that they will win the pennant? (request for the warrant)

Megan: The team with the best pitching usually wins. (warrant)

Sean: How can you make that claim? (request for backing of the warrant)

Megan: Well, that is what has happened the last few years. (backing)

Sean: How sure are you that they will win? Do you want to bet on it? (request for modality)

Megan: Well, I did say probably, so I don't want to bet too much. (modality)

Sean: Well, you seem pretty confident. Why don't you make a nice big wager?

Megan: There is always the possibility that the Dodgers will have a lot of injuries (rebuttal)

Following the Toulmin model, this argument would be diagrammed in this way:

Claims

The first component of an argument is the *claim*. The claim is the statement that the arguer seeks to convince the audience to accept. Claims may be made in past, present, or future tense. The following are examples of claims:

- It is time for you to start working on your term paper.

- The recession should be over by next spring.

- We should probably give more foreign aid to the people of Afghanistan.

Each of these claims is a declarative statement that expresses the advocate's belief. Claims are not always expressed in declarative statements, however.

"Won't deficit spending ultimately come back to haunt us?" is another way of asserting that it *will* come back to haunt us. There are several different types of claims that can be argued:

Claims of fact: potentially verifiable assertions as to the nature of things

- There are currently six million unemployed Americans.
- The number of high school dropouts is increasing.
- Millions of Americans have no health insurance.

Claims of value: indications of preference or judgment. Often values are predicated on facts, but they also contain value judgments.

- We should not tolerate a situation where so many are unemployed.
- The large number of dropouts demonstrates that our schools are failing.
- It is unacceptable that some persons are denied access to health care because they cannot afford it.

Claims of policy: assertions that something should be done. They are easily identified because they contain words like *should* or *ought*.

- We should create a jobs program to find people work.
- We should revise our school curriculums so that students will stay in school and get their diplomas.
- The federal government ought to create a program of national health insurance.

The first objective in analyzing a claim is to determine whether it is a claim of fact, value, or policy. Once you have identified the claim and categorized it you can determine whether you wish to challenge it.

Sometimes an advocate's claim is not readily apparent in his or her argument. This may occur simply because an argument is poorly developed and expressed. Often advocates themselves are not sure precisely what they are arguing. On other occasions advocates are reluctant to explicitly state their claims for strategic reasons. They may have a hidden agenda. In such situations you must infer from the information available to you what the advocate is claiming. This inference process is, of course, subject to great error, so the advocate who wishes to be clearly understood should explicitly state his or her claim.

Grounds

When asked, "What are you basing your claim on?" you are being asked for the *grounds*, or foundational assumptions, underlying your argument—the evidence you offer in support of your claim. The grounds may include examples or signs that you cite and then generalize from. Evidence should consist of such things as factual statements, statistical proof, the statement of accepted principles, and testimony.

Each type of evidence can be subjected to tests evaluating its quality. The grounds for arguments and the appropriate tests of evidence will be discussed in far greater detail in chapter 7.

Warrants and Backing

The next two elements of the Toulmin model are called the **warrant** and the **backing**. Just as a judge may issue a warrant authorizing the police to conduct a search of a suspect's dwelling, a warrant authorizes an advocate to make a claim based on the grounds provided. A warrant is the reasoning that permits an inferential leap; it works like a bridge connecting the grounds to the claim.

Backing refers to the support for the warrant. If a warrant has backing there is reason to believe that the warrant is legitimate. In essence, a warrant is a secondary claim. The backing for the warrant is thus the grounds for this secondary claim. There are several different types of warrants, which correspond to the different forms of reasoning we discussed in the beginning of this chapter. One can reason warrants from examples, analogies, signs, and causal correlations or generalizations. In addition, however, an arguer can use warrants that are drawn from authority (this claim is true because a significant, respected, and qualified source says it is true) or from principle (this argument is true because it depends upon a principle that virtually everyone would accept as true).

Earlier in this chapter we discussed the tests to which arguments from example, analogy, causality, and signs could be subjected. There are also tests to evaluate arguments from authority and principle. Arguments from authority depend on the quality of the authority cited, and arguments from principle depend on the principles being readily accepted and shared. These tests for arguments from authority and principle will be considered more fully in chapters 7 and 9.

Modality

The fifth element of the Toulmin model is called the **modality** and refers to the degree of certainty the advocate has that the claim is true. Words like *probably, possibly, might,* or *may* are illustrations of modal qualifiers. The absence of a modal qualifier in an argument makes a claim unequivocal—that is, certain.

Consider the following adverbs and adverbial phrases. Which of these communicate the greatest certainty? the least certainty?

very possibly	it would seem	presumably
apparently	certainly	quite likely

When attempting to discern the modality of an argument artifact you must be careful not to confuse those adverbs that modify other elements of the argument with those that modify the certainty of the claim. Modality refers only to those that modify the claim. For example, an advocate could argue "I definitely smell smoke, so it is likely that there is a fire." The modality of this argument is expressed by the word *likely*, and not *definitely*.

Modal qualifiers are a very important element of the argument model. Claims that are absolute, about which the arguer is certain, leave no room for doubt. The grounds must be equally certain. By diagramming an argument and identifying whether or not a modal qualifier is present, and what its relationship is to the grounds, you can begin to assess both the merits and the weaknesses of the argument.

Rebuttal

The final component of the Toulmin model is called the *rebuttal*. The rebuttal refers to exceptions, cases in which the claim would not be true. Understanding the nature of rebuttals, and being able to identify them, is important to the evaluation of arguments for two reasons. First, some advocates admit to rebuttals when presenting their arguments. For example, an advocate could argue that current deficit spending by the federal government has significantly drained capital resources (grounds), and that unless new sources of capital are discovered (rebuttal) continued deficit spending will bankrupt the economy (claim). In this case, the advocate has admitted that there could be an intervening factor that would deny the validity of the claim. If an advocate admits to a rebuttal, a critical audience can consider the possibility that this rebuttal will negate the claim. If the outcome suggested in the rebuttal actually appears probable, the arguer will not be likely to win adherence to his or her argumentative claim. It is noteworthy that this is precisely the argument that has taken place in the United States Congress; the Republicans have called for significant tax cuts even in the face of an ever-growing federal budget deficit because they believe that these cuts will stimulate the economy and ultimately lead to enhanced federal revenues.

Rebuttals are also important to opponents of an argument because they highlight a potential point for refutation. Since there may be an exception to almost any argument that makes the claim invalid, critical thinkers should draw upon their own knowledge and experience to identify and create rebuttals. Giving presence to the role of rebuttals in arguments thus facilitates such critical analysis.

SUMMARY

This chapter has considered arguments as complete logical claims and has focused on the ways that such claims can be constructed and analyzed. Two primary modes of argument, inductive and deductive claims were discussed. Inductive arguments can be developed from example, analogy, or causal correlation. Deductive arguments can be developed from signs or from causal generalization. Each type of argument can be tested, critically assessed, and responded to as is appropriate. We focused on the deductive syllogism as a formal test of argumentative reasoning. Principles for constructing and evaluating syllogisms were specified. Finally, the chapter discussed the utility of the Toulmin model as a means for arguers to both develop and analyze the component parts of argumentative claims.

Key Terms

deductive reasoning
   argument from sign
   argument from causal generalization
fallacy
false reasoning
   by analogy
   by causal generalization
   by hasty generalization
   by sign
inductive reasoning
   argument by example
   argument by analogy
   argument from causal correlation

syllogism
   major premise
   minor premise
   conclusion
Toulmin model
   claim
   grounds
   warrant
   backing
   modality
   rebuttal

Activities

1. Find an editorial or argument artifact in your local or student newspaper. Select a major argument advanced in the artifact. Identify what type of argument it is, and apply the appropriate tests of reasoning provided in this chapter.

2. Identify the type of argument used in the debate provided in appendix B of this text and apply the appropriate tests of reasoning provided in this text.

3. Locate a causal claim in an argumentative artifact, such as in the debate in appendix B. Utilize the tests of causal correlation or causal generalization to assess the validity of the claim.

4. Construct a categorical syllogism that is both structurally valid and sound.

5. Find a song and try to diagram it using the Toulmin model. What is the claim advanced by the songwriter? What grounds does the advocate provide as a basis for the claim? Is there a warrant provided? What type of reasoning does the warrant employ? If the warrant is not explicit can you provide it? Are any other elements of the Toulmin model included in the advocacy?

Recommended Readings

Arthos, John. "Where There Are No Rules or Systems to Guide Us: Argument from Example in a Hermeneutic Rhetoric." *Quarterly Journal of Speech* 89 (2003): 320–345.

Ikuenobe, Polycarp. "In Search of Criteria for 'Fallacies' and 'Begging the Question.'" *Argumentation* 16 (2002): 421–442.

Kay, Jack, Charles Dause, and George W. Ziegelmueller. *Argumentation: Inquiry and Advocacy.* 2nd ed. Englewood Cliffs, NJ: Prentice-Hall, 2000.

Klement, Kevin C. "When Is Genetic Reasoning Not Fallacious?" *Argumentation* 16 (2002): 383–401.

Lee, Ronald, and Karen King Lee. *Arguing Persuasively.* New York: Longman, 1989.

McGill, Ann L. "Counterfactual Reasoning in Causal Judgments: Implications for Marketing." *Psychology & Marketing* 17 (2000): 323–344.

Measell, James S. "Perelman on Analogy." *Journal of the American Forensic Association* 22 (1985): 65–71.

Reinard, John C. *Foundations of Argumentation and Critical Thinking: A Modern Approach.* Thousand Oaks, CA: Sage, 2004.

Rieke, Richard D., and Malcolm O. Sillars. *Argumentation and Critical Decision Making.* 5th ed. Boston: Addison-Wesley, 2000.

Rybacki, Karyn C., and Donald J. Rybacki. *Advocacy and Opposition.* 2nd ed. Englewood Cliffs, NJ: Prentice-Hall, 1991.

Secor, Marie. "Mill's Fallacies: Theory and Examples." *Argumentation* 12 (1998): 295–315.

Simosi, Maria. "Using Toulmin's Framework for the Analysis of Everyday Argumentation: Some Methodological Considerations." *Argumentation* 17 (2003): 185–203.

Toulmin, Stephen. "Strategies of Reasoning." *Communication Yearbook* 14 (1991): 445.

Toulmin, Stephen, Richard D. Rieke, and Allan Janik. *Introduction to Reasoning.* 2nd ed. Amsterdam: Pearson Education POD, 1997.

Warnick, Barbara, and Edward S. Inch. *Critical Thinking and Communication: The Use of Reason in Argument.* 2nd ed. New York: Macmillan, 1994.

Willard, Charles Arthur. "On the Utility of Descriptive Diagrams for the Analysis and Criticism of Arguments." *Communication Monographs* 43 (1976): 308–320.

Notes

[1] John Stuart Mill, *System of Logic* (London: Longmans, Green and Company, 1900), 255–266.

[2] Ibid., 255–266.

[3] Ibid., 255–266.

[4] This model of argument was originally discussed in the book, Stephen E. Toulmin, *The Uses of Argument* (Cambridge: Cambridge University Press, 1958). It was later modified, and it is the modified version of the model that is used here. See: Stephen E. Toulmin, Richard Rieke, and Allan Janik, *Introduction to Reasoning* (New York: Macmillan, 1978).

THE GROUNDS
FOR ARGUMENT

Humans across the globe have begun to ponder the consequences of their actions on the biosphere. One result of this environmental focus is an ongoing debate about global warming. One side paints a bleak picture. Humanity's heavy reliance on burning fossil fuels, they say, is releasing large amounts of carbon dioxide into the atmosphere. The result is the greenhouse effect: carbon dioxide traps the earth's heat, causing the planet to gradually become warmer. This, they contend, will melt the polar ice caps and lead to starvation, wars over resources, and significant economic dislocations. These advocates claim that we should take immediate steps to dramatically reduce the use of fossil fuels. The other side tells a different story. Current evidence, these individuals argue, does not support significant actions to discourage fossil fuel use. The data available to us now is insufficient to justify actions that could have significant economic dislocations.

A public controversy broke out in the early 2000s when the United States Environmental Protection Agency scientists issued a report about global warming that was critical of government actions taken to respond to the problem thus far. The scientists called for more draconian and costly policy solutions. The Bush administration objected to the language of the report and subjected it to a careful editing that softened both the language and the policy alternatives suggested. This resulted in a fierce battle about government attempting to censor scientists that spilled out onto the front pages of the nation's newspapers.[1] The public controversy starkly revealed the differences in the positions between those who view global warming as an imminent crisis and those who seem to believe that we can simply turn up the air conditioning.

The stasis of the dispute between these two views is in what should be done now. Each side might agree that global warming is undesirable and that if it were certain to happen, new policy initiatives would be necessary. However, they disagree about the nature of the evidence used as the foundation for their claims. This dispute illustrates how disagreement over the facts can be at the center of a long-standing and intense debate.

When an advocate is asked, "What are you basing this claim on?" the advocate is being asked for the grounds or evidence supporting the argument. Whether the argument is inductive or deductive, **_grounds_** serve as the evidence, support, or foundation for the claim. According to Aristotle, the basis for a claim may be one of two types depending on where it originates.[2] If the advocate is the creator of the support for the claim—if, for example, it depends on the reasoning, analysis, inspiration, or creativity of the advocate—it is considered an **_artistic proof_**. If, on the other hand, the starting point for the argument comes from someone else—for example, it is based on common knowledge, shared experience, or perhaps physical evidence—it may be considered **_inartistic proof_**. Both types of evidence may include premises, examples, statistics, and testimony.

In this chapter we focus on the support or grounds advocates use for their claims. We will identify the types of grounds used by advocates, present the tests many critical consumers of argument typically employ to assess the validity of grounds, and suggest ways advocates might choose supporting data that will increase the likelihood they will gain adherence to their claims.

PREMISES

All evidence acts as the premise or starting point of a claim. But as a premise, grounds function as an established point of agreement between advocates and their audiences. A **_premise_** therefore is a point accepted without the requirement of additional support.

The premises an advocate can use to support a claim are based on two types of knowledge: personal knowledge and cultural knowledge.[3] **_Personal knowledge_** is that which we know to be true because we have firsthand experience with it. Personal knowledge is an artistic proof.

We know that fire is hot, ice is cold, and rain is wet, and so on, because our senses provide us this information. We had to learn the labels, but the senses give us basic data that is easily recognizable because we have experienced these sensations before. Personal knowledge extends beyond such sensory data, however, and thus supplies premises. We know that snow may appear beautiful when it falls from the sky but also that it can be heavy to shovel off of our sidewalk and treacherous to drivers. We know when times are tough, because we may ourselves be unemployed, because we know others who are unemployed, or because we are given cause to worry that we, like the others around us, might soon become unemployed. We believe such things because we have experienced them and seen others who are close to us experience them. When an advocate uses a premise that taps into our personal knowledge we are likely to find fidelity in the argument, because the premise rings true with experiences that we know to be true.

There are other things we believe to be true that we have not experienced ourselves. We may hold these views because we are part of a culture. This **cultural knowledge** may consist of shared values or shared truths. It may be explicit—codified into rules, principles, or laws—or it may be tacitly derived from our behavior. It is contained in the stories we tell about ourselves, who we are, where we have been, and where we are going. Cultures are defined by the stories that are told about them, both by the people who live within them and by the outsiders who confront them. Cultures are thus created and maintained through communication.[4]

In our culture we teach a multitude of stories to our children: from the accounts of the Pilgrims crossing the stormy seas of the Atlantic on the crowded and tiny Mayflower to accounts of the suffering of the Continental Army soldiers under the command of General George Washington at Valley Forge; from accounts of President Abraham Lincoln speaking at Gettysburg to stories of Teddy Roosevelt and his troops charging up San Juan Hill, to accounts of President John F. Kennedy's speech in Berlin, to stories of the heroic firefighters climbing up the stairs of the doomed World Trade Center towers, attempting to rescue the people trapped inside. All of these stories reveal something about what culturally it means to us to be American. It is through the telling and retelling of these stories that we inculcate American values in our youth. And these values and "truths" about our public experiences may constitute the premises advocates use in their arguments. As an example, the heroism and the deaths of the New York City firefighters might be cited as an argument to pay public employees better salaries, as an argument about the contributions immigrants make in American culture (many of the firefighters were "ethnic" Americans), as an argument for better disaster planning, or even as an argument against the construction of new high-rise buildings.

Another way a culture reinforces its shared knowledge is through rituals. **Rituals** are behavior patterns so often repeated that the participants come to know them by heart and to expect them to be performed at precise times. From who sits where at a family meal, to the inauguration of a president, to the taking of an oath before providing testimony in a courtroom, many of our cultural practices are scripted by ritual.[5]

When you successfully complete your college degree you will be invited to participate in a commencement ritual. Participants will be suitably garbed in the vestments of the academic community. You will probably wear a black robe and a strange flat hat with a tassel hanging from it. Likewise the faculty members and senior academic administrators of the campus will wear their robes often accompanied by colorful hoods signifying the disciplines and universities where they earned their doctoral degrees. These robes may be traced back to the universities established in the middle ages. Indeed, in Germany when student protestors during the 1960s and 1970s expressed their rage against the conservatism and elitism of the university culture, they demanded many reforms. One of the first and most visible things that they sought to change was the wearing of academic robes by university faculty and students. The slogan: "The stink of a thousand years comes from beneath those robes," became a rallying cry for the student protestors, and today German graduates are among the few in the world who do not wear traditional academic garb on their graduation day. Of course, the very reason that the German student protestors opposed the gowns—that they signified this notion of cultural elitism—may be why so many Americans enjoy the day. The wearing of the graduation gown, the marching in the procession, the calling of each graduate's name, the receipt of the diploma, and the highly formulaic graduation speech are all ritualized activities that honor the achievements of the graduates and that welcome them into the ranks of the educated elite. It is through such rituals that universities, families, and cultures communicate their faith in the values of discipline, education, and intellectual development.

Symbols are yet another way a society teaches its values. Visit any state or national capital and you will undoubtedly see great monuments and halls devoted to governance. Must the chief executives of states reside in stately mansions such as the White House? Is it necessary to construct huge buildings with impressive rotundas, pillars, and lofty ceilings? No, of course these ornaments are not necessary. But these are the vestiges of monarchical tradition, and they are perpetuated to communicate the importance and the seriousness of the business conducted in these settings. Such buildings are also ways to honor the significance and the importance of the persons who work in these buildings. One of the enjoyable things to do on a visit to Washington, D.C., is to tour the neighborhoods where other nations maintain their embassies. Even small and poor nations typically make an effort to acquire impressive buildings to provide space for their ambassadors to work in and to represent the interests of their governments. The buildings, in some senses, come to serve as the image of the importance, substance, and solidity of the political system and the nationalistic cultures that they represent.

Shared premises enjoy *presumption* with audiences. That is, audiences tend to believe these premises until convinced otherwise. This is the concept of presumption. (The topic of presumption will be discussed in greater detail in chapter 10.) It is the idea that most people, most of the time, are comfortable with the way things are. We generally are apprehensive about the unknown. We stick to familiar beliefs, values, and policies until sufficient reasons are presented to convince us that they should be changed.

Advocates can successfully build arguments on shared premises by invoking them through their own arguments (artistic proofs) or by citing evidence that calls on shared premises (inartistic proofs). For example, most of us have little personal experience with governmental censorship. But just because we have not actually been arrested for something we have said or for a message that we posted to our Web site does not diminish the fervor with which we support freedom of speech. In this political culture, unlike in some other political cultures with histories of authoritarian leadership, we cherish the right to express our views freely. Consequently, an advocate who argues against attempts to censor the lyrics on recordings of popular music, or one who opposes attempts to restrict free speech on the Internet, can draw on this shared premise.

Where can an advocate look to discover shared premises? A good source might be the adages or proverbs that we all know. Here is a short list. Undoubtedly you can think of additional examples:

> Good triumphs over evil.
> Experience is the best teacher.
> Love conquers all.
> Hope for the best, but prepare for the worst.
> Good things come to those who wait.
> Haste makes waste.
> A penny saved is a penny earned.
> Good fences make good neighbors.

The slogans or manifestos that we profess faith in are another source of premises. Look, for example, to the articulation of our beliefs in the Declaration of Independence and in the Constitution. They express our collective political and cultural commitments to equality, liberty, and the freedoms of speech and religion; due process; the freedom to pursue happiness; property rights; and the rule of law. All of these beliefs provide an important source for the premises of arguments. Note, however, that often these freedoms are in conflict with each other. Thus, for example, freedom and equality may often be in conflict. Some advocates may place greater emphasis on the freedom to follow their own religious beliefs than on others' right to be treated equally. Thus, some may claim that since they believe homosexuality is a sin they should not have to rent their apartment to a gay couple. The gay citizens, on the other hand, may claim that they are entitled to the freedom to live in accordance with their own wishes, and should have equal access to housing without fear of discrimination. Thus, although audiences may generally grant adherence to shared premises, arguments predicated on accepted premises will not necessarily win automatic agreement. Critical consumers of arguments and advocates constructing discourse will have to evaluate the use of the premises in the support of individual claims. We identify three tests of the use of premises.

Testing Premises: Shared Premises

First, the premise employed by an advocate must be truly shared by the audience. While the definition of a premise presumes agreement, beliefs are not static. Some things that we believe now, we may have once rejected. People once scoffed at the ideas that the earth was round and that the earth revolved around the sun. But we do not have to go that far back into history to see examples of beliefs that have dramatically changed.

In the United States, at least from the time of the presidency of Franklin Delano Roosevelt until the 1980s, most people when asked would have indicated that they considered themselves to be "liberal." To be a liberal, in this era, meant to be modern, forward-thinking, in favor of progressive governmental programs to solve social problems, and tolerant. So many citizens had suffered during the Great Depression that a clear majority of Americans were supportive of "liberal" political positions. Beginning with the presidency of Ronald Reagan, however, this began to change. Reagan argued that government was more often the cause of and not the solution to public problems. Indeed, one of his most effective joke lines in his speeches was to declare: "Hi, I am from the government and I am here to help you." President Reagan was so wildly popular with the American voters that many people came to share his views. Today, it is clear that a majority of Americans would emphatically not consider themselves to be "liberal." One of the nastiest things that one candidate can say about another in a contemporary political campaign is that he or she is a "liberal." What changed over the years? Was it the notion about what the term "liberal" really meant? Was it the opinions people had about the effectiveness of specific policies? Was it changing convictions about the role of government in people's lives? Or changing views about the degree to which people should be responsible for their personal circumstances? Probably all of the above, to some extent have changed, and so advocates making use of shared premises need to be aware that agreement cannot merely be assumed.

Another difficulty with assuming that all audiences share the same premises arises from the increasing impact of different cultures. As a result of population migrations, the ease of communication, access to travel, and the impact of a global economy, we are experiencing changes that many experts have come to refer to as the "globalization" of our planet.[6] Due to globalization, we can no longer presume that the people whom we are trying to convince with our arguments will share the same cultural premises that we hold dear. These cultural premises themselves are now a source for disagreement and argument.[7] For example, some have argued that the American educational system now fails to teach the essential central values of Western culture. They argue that because our school children no longer read the same great classic books in their literature courses, or learn about the important Western philosophers and their theories, they will not be taught the principles that will enable us to sustain our political culture. Students today, they lament, are taught that all cultures are equally valuable, and as a result, they fear that our children will grow to become adults who do not share the same value system.[8]

Others have called for even greater inclusion of great books, philosophers, and the teaching of the values of non-Western cultures. They argue that American school children should be exposed to even more information about Eastern cultures or the cultures from the Southern hemisphere. Teaching from a multicultural perspective, they argue, validates the experiences of minority students and makes all citizens more sensitive to the differences between people.[9]

The continuing debate in higher education over the teaching of cultural perspectives reveals the difficulties in assuming that all audiences share the same premises. There may be differences between and within audiences because the persons composing them collectively or individually represent divergent cultures.

Testing Premises: Contradictory Premises

A second concern with the use of premises as grounds for a claim is that there are sometimes contradictions and conflicting claims under consideration. Bromides reflect American values; they also reveal the tension between competing wisdoms. Consider the belief that you should "Look before you leap," versus "He who hesitates is lost." Similarly, is it "Absence makes the heart grow fonder" or "Out of sight, out of mind"?

On a more serious level, Walter Fisher argues that one of the unifying elements in the American culture is what is known as the American dream.[10] Even though most citizens could tell you about the American dream and what it means to them, Fisher has persuasively argued that the American dream is actually derived from two frequently contradictory beliefs. The first is the belief in America as the land of opportunity. The opportunity to achieve unlimited material success is a fundamental cornerstone of capitalism. Hundreds of thousands of immigrants have come to the United States, often at the cost of great sacrifice and danger, to realize this aspect of the American dream. According to this dream, in America hard work will be rewarded, the children of blue-collar workers can gain university education and secure professional careers, and anyone can save their money and ultimately purchase their own home. This is the materialistic dimension of the American dream. The second dimension of the American dream is that the United States is the land of *equal* opportunity. Regardless of race, ethnic identity, religion, gender, age, or sexual preference, this aspect of the dream affords the promise of equal protection under law. This is the moralistic aspect of the American dream.

There are times when the materialistic and the moralistic components of the dream are in opposition. For example, some argue that affirmative action programs are moralistic attempts to redress inequities at the price of impinging on the materialistic endeavors of nonminorities. The steps taken to counter the history of racial discrimination and minorities' lack of access to adequate education means that nonminority students, who may by some measures be better qualified than minority students, may be denied spots in first-tier universities or professional schools. The 2003 U.S. Supreme Court case that reviewed the affirmative action remedies undertaken at the University of Michigan revealed the profound disagreement among the justices over the conflicting elements of the American dream. Ultimately, the Court held that affirmative action was permissible but also that hopefully such a remedy to past racial discrimination will be short-lived and no longer necessary in approximately 25 years.[11]

It often seems that the most hotly contested contemporary disputes have contradictory premises at their core. As an example, we can cite the controversy over the need to protect the citizens of the United States from the threats of terrorism versus the rights of our citizens to be free from unwarranted intrusions into their private lives. In the wake of the September 11 tragedy the government passed legislation known as the Patriot and the Homeland Security Acts. Both bills dramatically increased the power of government agencies to conduct surveillance on citizens via telephone taps, access to e-mail records, access to banking and financial transactions, and even access to confidential health information. Those who favored the legislation insisted that the government's obligation to protect "life, liberty, and the pursuit of happiness" meant a clear responsibility to protect our lives from those who would seek to kill us or otherwise damage our safety and security. Those who opposed these bills, however, argued that the real and potential losses of liberty and privacy from such bills would chill dissent, undermine our democracy, and provide the clearest evidence that the terrorists who were intent on attacking American capitalist democracy had in fact succeeded.[12] Clearly advocates who predicate their arguments on premises that are contradicted by other widely held beliefs risk the rejection of their arguments.

Testing Premises: Public vs. Private Beliefs

Finally, there are often discrepancies between our public and private beliefs. The values that a culture shares are not always exemplified in the actions of the individuals who comprise the culture. As a society, we abhor racism and bigotry. Yet, it would be naive to think that America has no racists or bigots. The progress of our contemporary society may have succeeded in partially purging public language and antisocial behavior, but many of the hostile attitudes toward people who are of another race persist. Social actors may have merely learned acceptable code words with which to express their prejudice. An audience that privately rejects a publicly shared belief is not likely to find appeals to such beliefs compelling. There are cases, by the way, where people find themselves in trouble, not necessarily for the beliefs that they hold, but for violating the social rules and disclosing those beliefs. It is, in such circumstances, often the disclosure that brings critical attention to a subject that others would prefer not be so illuminated.

For example, Senator Strom Thurmond led a long and remarkable career as a governor and then senator from South Carolina. A staunch segregationist, Thurmond left the Democratic Party to run for president in 1948 as a "Dixiecrat" on an anti–civil rights platform. Eventually, Senator Thurmond became a Republican and continued to serve the people of South Carolina until his retirement from the Senate in 2002 at the age of 100. On Senator Thurmond's retirement from the Senate, the Republican Senate Majority Leader, Trent Lott from Mississippi, was effusive in his praise, even going so far as to assert: "I want to say this about my state: When Strom Thurmond ran for president, we voted for him. We're proud of it. And if the rest of the country had followed our lead, we wouldn't have had all these problems over all these years, either."[13]

Although Senator Lott quickly apologized for his statement, and made clear that he was just trying to celebrate Senator Thurmond's long life and service to the nation, and not his segregationist platform, the apology was not sufficient to satisfy his critics who did not agree that the accomplishments in the area of civil rights should be referred to as the accumulated "problems over all these years." Senator Lott had himself long opposed virtually all civil rights legislation, but he had previously phrased his opposition in appropriate legalistic policy language.

In this public statement, however, he let his guard down and as a result revealed his own racist beliefs. After President Bush weighed in on the controversy, Senator Lott was forced to step down from the post of majority leader.

Advocates confronting uncertain situations must take pains to support the premises they employ and to use language that is consistent with those premises. Simply stating what one believes to be a widely shared premise may not be enough. Providing real support for a premise and then using that premise as the foundation for the next claim advanced is a preferred way to organize an argument.

EXAMPLES

Examples are specific instances or occurrences of a given phenomenon. They may be detailed or cursory. The advocate may provide an example from personal experience (artistic proof), or derive the example from another source (inartistic proof). In chapter 6 we identified the inductive process of using examples to reason to a generalization. In that chapter we discussed four tests for reasoning from examples.

1. Are there a sufficient number of examples offered to support the claim?

2. Are the examples that are selected typical of the category or class that the arguer is trying to generalize to?

3. Are negative examples sufficiently accounted for in the argument?

4. Are the examples that are cited relevant to the claim being advanced?

In addition to these tests, we would admonish advocates to provide whatever details are necessary to gain the audience's adherence. Listing several specific examples may enhance the validity of the claim for a given audience. On the other hand, detailed examples (also called *extended illustrations*) can give power to a claim by making it more memorable and by arousing the audience's emotions.

Consider the effect of briefly listing the names of five students who have died in alcohol-related automobile accidents. The use of these examples may provide sufficient basis for a claim that students should not drink and drive. But providing an extended illustration of how one student lost her life may have the same persuasive effect. In addition, hearing the details of the accident may enable the audience to visualize the events, and that may stir their empathy for the individual. Presenting additional information about the effect of her death on her parents, siblings, and friends may further humanize—and strengthen—the argument by getting people to recognize that the loss of their own life would have a devastating impact on those who care about them and who they themselves love.

Advocates can also seek to bolster the audience's faith in the examples by drawing them from sources the audience considers credible (inartistic proof). In this way they combine examples and testimony. Some advocates even attempt to emulate statistical methodologies and select examples randomly from the set of possible examples.

STATISTICS

Since the use of multiple examples may enhance the likelihood of their acceptance, and since time constraints may limit the number of specific cases that may be presented, advocates may choose to present statistics instead.

Statistics are numeric expressions of examples. There are two basis types of statistics: descriptive and inferential. ***Descriptive statistics*** are numeric representations that present the entire set of instances of a phenomenon. When advocates present, for example, the number of AIDS deaths worldwide since the epidemic was identified, they are attempting to describe the entire population of victims. Similarly, statistics about the total number of American soldiers killed in the Iraq War, the number of handgun accidents each year, the number of starvation victims in Somalia, or the number of motorcyclists who lose their life in traffic accidents, all attempt to describe all of the cases.

Inferential statistics are numeric representations that attempt to infer the properties of a population from inspection of a sample drawn from that population. The advocate who cites public opinion polls is providing inferential data—which does not literally present the views of the entire public, but rather a presumably representative sample or subset of the public is selected and described. Then the pollster infers that the views presented by people in the sample accurately represent the views of the entire public.

Testing Statistics: Methods of Gathering

Both kinds of statistics are useful as proof, and both have potential weaknesses. Whether advocates are presenting their own statistics or those from other sources, meeting certain tests enhances the likelihood that critical audiences will find the data convincing.

First, it may be important to know how the statistics were gathered. Understanding the methodology employed in counting the cases may reveal weaknesses in the evidence. One way statistics are often gathered relies on individuals reporting instances of the phenomenon. This method can lead to misleading statistics, due, for instance, to the problem of *underreporting* wherein disincentives for reporting instances of the phenomenon result in artificially low numbers of cases. For example, how much child abuse was there in the United States last year? Law enforcement and social service agencies compile the number of cases reported to them, but are all instances reported? Unfortunately, many abused children do not come forward, and most abusers, their spouses, and their relatives are reluctant to report the abuse. School teachers, school nurses, and pediatricians are required by law to report suspected cases of abuse, but are the official counts of abused children an accurate reflection of the actual number of cases of abuse? Obviously not, since underreporting is inevitable. Thus the true numbers of abused children is certainly far larger than the official statistics indicate.

There also may be incentives for *overreporting* cases of a phenomenon. During the Vietnam War, American soldiers were told to report the number of enemy soldiers that they killed in action. Critics argued that the military's desire to show that the United States was winning the war resulted in exaggerated body counts. Thus, when the statistical method is used to collect individuals' reports, the motive of those doing the reporting must be considered.

Inferential statistics rely on descriptions of a subset of the population and then the drawing of inferences that what is true of the sample is also true of the entire population. The method by which this subset is selected is consequently very important. The sample must be representative of its parent group, or else any general conclusions drawn will not be valid. Thus, most researchers use random samples. A *random sample* may be defined as a sample in which each element of the larger group has an equal and independent probability of being selected.

Let's assume we wanted to discover how the students at a particular university felt their student body president was doing in office. We could question all of the students on the campus (a descriptive statistic). This would clearly be the best method, because it would assure that the opinion of every student was considered. It would also, of course, be a very difficult method because it would involve a very large number of opinions. A more likely method then would be to randomly poll students in such a way as to assure that all students have an equal chance of being included in the study.

One way to assure that all students have an equal chance to be questioned is to use a technique called *simple random sampling*. Researchers using this method employ a random numbers table. This is a list of numbers randomly generated by a computer. For example, by assigning all of the students on campus a number, we could select a predetermined number of students to be surveyed as their numbers are chosen. If the number of students in our sample is sufficiently large we are relatively certain that we will have a sample that roughly mirrors the opinions of the student body.

A second way researchers generate random samples is by using an *interval sampling* system. With interval sampling we might construct our sample of students by including every twentieth student on the roster. As long as we randomly determine where to start choosing the students, each student would have an equal chance of participating.

Equality of participation, however, does not guarantee that we will have a representative distribution of graduate students, undergraduate students, part-time students, international students, males or females, and so forth. To make sure that such groups are included in numbers proportionate to their size, we could use a modification of the random and interval procedures called *stratified sampling*. Instead of sampling from the entire student population, in stratified sampling we would divide the population into groups that we might want in the sample. Once the population has been stratified, we could select students from each stratum using either the simple random number technique or the interval technique. The students are selected from the stratum in accordance with the size of each stratum as a percentage of the total population.

Professional pollsters and researchers employ sophisticated sampling techniques to assure the reliability of their results. When they report their findings they usually identify the *margin of error* as well. Gallup polls of voter preference during presidential campaigns, for example, will acknowledge that their statistics may be off by 2, 3, or 4 percent. This indeed is often a plus or minus percentage statistic. Thus, if a poll reports a margin of error of plus or minus 3 percent, a candidate that it shows having the support of 52 percent of the electorate may actually have the support of as few as 49 percent of the electorate to as many as 55 percent. Obviously that is a large gap in potential support. Polls that do not reveal their margin of error should be viewed with suspicion.

Respondents who change their minds or who do not vote further complicate presidential preference polls. The pollsters are thus often trying to determine new means to measure the intensity of support for a particular candidate. They also will generally ask respondents how likely they are to cast a ballot in the next election. Given that voter turnout in the United States is now embarrassingly poor compared to other democracies—sometimes as low as 10 to 12 percent of registered voters in local or primary elections, and as low as 45 percent of registered voters in presidential elections—the need to identify the likely voters is absolutely essential in predicting the outcome of an election.

Many periodicals and Web sites will survey and report the opinions of their readers. The use of these polls as evidence of what the population believes is profoundly unreliable, however, because the survey participants are self-selected. Only those who read the periodicals or go to the Web sites are asked to respond to the questions, and only those who are highly motivated to express their opinions are likely to exert the effort to respond. Thus, the conclusions drawn in such surveys are biased by the self-selection process and may bear little resemblance to the opinions of the overall population.

Similarly, phone-in polls have become increasingly popular on television and radio shows. Many television networks have nightly phone-in polls. In the past, some networks have asked viewers, for instance, to phone in with their opinions about who won the televised presidential debates. Yet only those with access to phones, who watched the show, and who bothered to take the time to call, are included in such polls. Special interest groups, such as political parties, activist groups, or lobbying groups (e.g., the National Rifle Association) have actively coordinated how their members will participate in such phone-in polls. Political campaigns have even been known to set up phone banks so that their supporters can make call, after call, after call. Naturally, excessive participation by any segment of the population distorts poll results.

The results of such phone-in polls are thus not scientific because they do not approximate the views of the overall population. Broadcasters often mention this, yet, surprisingly they continue to cite the results of these polls—sometimes treating the results as legitimate news stories. If the results are essentially meaningless we wonder why they bother. Perhaps either they can make money by charging for the calls or they believe that their audiences enjoy participating in such polls and therefore that conducting them builds viewer loyalty. It is unfortunate, however, that the effect of such polling is often only to mislead the public.

Testing Statistics: Defining Categories

In addition to potential problems that might arise with the ways in which the statistics are gathered, there is the second and equally significant issue of how research categories are defined. If the categories are not exact or precise, the counts of the numbers of cases falling within each category will be inexact.

When researchers assign particular occurrences to categories they often must make judgments about those occurrences. Sometimes the categories are forthright—"alive" or "dead" would be such categories. Yet there are often gray areas that make categorization difficult. For example, "employed" or "unemployed" appear to be fairly discrete categories requiring little interpretation by the researcher. Yet appearances can be misleading. If you are on a payroll and your salary is reported to the government, you are clearly someone who will be classified as employed. If you have been laid off and you are collecting unemployment, which requires that you be actively looking for a job, you will be classified as unemployed. If, however, your unemployment compensation has run out, or you have become discouraged and have quit looking for a job because you have been unable to find one, or you are not really actively looking for a job but would take one if you could find one that would accommodate your school schedule, or if you are a housewife, or a student, or someone who picks up "odd" jobs for a day or so at a time when they become available, you are not easily categorized as either "employed" or "unemployed." In such cases, even though you are not really employed, you are not unemployed either, because none of these situations matches how the government chooses to define "unemployed."

As another example, we all know that there are many instances of sexual harassment in the workplace. But how many cases are there? Since experts may disagree about what constitutes harassment, and since some people would see harassment in behaviors that others might see as only minor flirtations or boorish behavior, it is somewhat difficult to know how to proceed to count the numbers of cases. Some studies will as a result cite the number of grievances or complaints filed, but certainly this does not solve the problem either since we can imagine that many instances will go unreported and perhaps also because some cases may not be substantiated. So how many cases of sexual harassment in the workplace occur? The statistics and estimates, as might be expected, vary widely.

Testing Statistics: The Time Frame

The third test of statistics relates to *time frame*. The point at which one begins and ends a time period under statistical analysis can directly influence what the statistics will reveal. At the beginning of this chapter we discussed the issue of global warming. Some argue that the climate is warming, while others suggest that it may not be and we may only be witnessing temperature variations that are within the range of previous annual averages. There is some evidence to suggest, for example, that the Northern Hemisphere experienced cooling during the 1940s and the 1970s. Advocates who either began or ended their statistical analysis by drawing evidence focused on these two decades might succeed in convincing an uncritical audience that the earth's climate was actually cooling. But researchers, who look at longer periods of time, for example studying temperature averages over the last century, might find ample evidence to support theories of global warming.

In chapter 6 we also raised the time frame question with regard to the AIDS crisis. We noted that early in the crisis medical experts mistakenly believed that only some AIDS patients would develop full-blown AIDS. This occurred because it can take many years before the disease ultimately claims its victims. Then, after some of the new drug therapies to treat AIDS were introduced, there were others who claimed that AIDS could now be managed and need no longer be considered an always-fatal disease. Meanwhile, however, other experts cautioned that a much longer time frame of analysis would be required to study the long-term effects of these treatment regimens since it may be that some patients acquire new forms of infection that are drug-resistant or that after a time the drugs may simply not be tolerated by some patients.

Americans generally have faith in science and in scientific methods, although this faith may be waning. Consequently, American audiences often find statistical data very compelling. But Americans are also aware that statistics are susceptible to distortion—remember the old adage, "There are lies, damned lies, and statistics." Yet skilled advocates recognize that, although susceptible to distortion, statistics are compelling argumentative tools. They do not hesitate to use them or to provide as much detail as possible about the methods used to gather and categorize the data, as well as the time frame of the analysis.

TESTIMONY

A fourth type of grounds utilized by advocates is the provision of testimony. *Testimony* consists of observations and judgments by the advocate or sources cited by the advocate. Testimony may be descriptive or interpretive. *Descriptive testimony* refers to the observation of supposedly factual (verifiable) information. *Interpretive testimony* involves making judgments or drawing inferences from the facts in discussion. In each case a similar set of tests can be applied.

Before accepting an advocate's arguments, critical audiences evaluate the credibility of the advocate and that of the authorities that he or she cites. *Credibility* refers to the audience's assessment of the competence and trustworthiness of the source. It is important to emphasize that sources do not possess credibility, but rather, audiences attribute varying levels of credibility to them. Thus, a source may be quite credible to one audience, and wholly lacking in credibility to another. An arguer could attempt to support an argument, for example, by citing a statement by conservative radio personality Rush Limbaugh. This source may have credibility for conservative listeners, but even mentioning Limbaugh's name might be akin to waving a red cape in front of a bull for a liberal audience. Not only would the liberal be unlikely to find Mr. Limbaugh a credible source, the arguer's credibility might be diminished as well merely because of the decision to cite him as a source of evidence.

Testing Testimony: Competence

The first dimension of credibility is *competence*. Audiences assess whether or not the source is competent to make the proffered observation or interpretation by judging the source's capability and ability.

Capability refers to whether or not the source was able to make the observation. Have you ever heard someone claim to have seen something, when they could not have done so? Did you doubt the veracity of their claim? Then you have applied the test of capability. For example, in a courtroom a witness might testify that he heard someone make a verbal threat to a victim. If, however, it can be established that the witness was not even in the room at the time this is alleged to have occurred, then he could not be presumed capable of having heard such a threat. Or, if it is established that he was in the room, but it was a very noisy place and he was far away, his capability of hearing and properly accounting for what may have been said can certainly be called into question.

Source ability is a second measure of competence. Ability may be the result of education, training, or life experience. Most Americans believe, for example, that trained physicians have more ability to diagnose illness than do witch doctors. Why? Because anyone can claim to be a witch doctor, but physicians are required to complete years of specialized education and training. Does the fact that the physician finished a rigorous program of formal education guarantee that the physician will be correct and the witch doctor wrong? Not necessarily, but most American audiences will likely find testimony provided by a physician more credible than that provided by a witch doctor.

Of course, physicians may know less than witch doctors about the effectiveness of some herbal medicines found in nature. This illustrates the concept of field dependence in competence. Experts are only authoritative in their own fields. Several years ago Dr. Benjamin Shockley received widespread notoriety for his public statements theorizing that there were significant genetic differences between Africans and Caucasians. Dr. Shockley always referred to himself, and was introduced by others, as a Nobel Prize winning scientist. This was true. But, Shockley won the Nobel Prize for his work that contributed to the development of the transistor, not for his work in genetics. As a result, it is understandable that most who disagreed with his theories about genetics also challenged his expertise to advance such claims.

Celebrities testifying outside of their fields pose an interesting illustration of this issue of competence. If, for example, Tiger Woods is used in a testimonial advertisement to talk about the benefits of a particular brand of golf ball or golf clubs, we might afford him credibility. If, however, Tiger Woods is asked to give a testimonial advertisement for a particular brand of automobile, should he be accorded greater competence or credibility than any other figure? Interestingly, such questions may also loom large in contemporary political discussions. In California, for instance, the actor Arnold Schwarzenegger was elected governor. During the campaign reporters frequently pestered him with questions about his opinions on political issues and public policies. What qualifies "the Terminator" for such a role? Does he know any more about these topics than you do? Perhaps he does, but his success on the screen and at the box office does not necessarily translate into evidence of such competence.

Competence need not require extensive training. Life experiences can make people experts within a given field. If we wanted to know what it was like to be homeless in America, for instance, we might consult scholars who had written on the subject. But we might also find that the testimony of a homeless person on the subject would not only be more authoritative, it might also have greater impact and spark far more empathy and compassion in your audience.

Testing Testimony: Trustworthiness

Another dimension of credibility is *trustworthiness*, which is an audience's assessment of the integrity of the source. Source integrity concerns the source's motives. Is the source willing to report his or her observations and judgments fairly? Sometimes sources have something to gain from what they report. This potential may influence what they say, causing *source bias*.

When Congress holds hearings before enacting legislation they invite experts to present their views on the issue at hand. If the issue is, for example, auto safety, experts from the automobile manufacturing companies will likely be called to testify. Their statements, however, might reflect mostly their own corporate interests. Thus, Congress may also call for testimony from insurance companies, consumer groups, and independent scientific researchers. While their testimony might also reflect their own agendas, the net effect, we can all hope, is that our representatives hear a variety of conflicting views, which they can evaluate to make up their minds impartially.

Testimony of advocates or their sources that contains self-serving statements or bias is less reliable than testimony that seems not to be motivated by personal needs or bias. In fact, many audiences consider **reluctant testimony**, testimony given grudgingly because it does not serve the motives of the source, as the most reliable kind. Individuals who step forward and admit misdoings are generally considered more credible, for example, than those who admit culpability for something only after they have been confronted with incontrovertible evidence.

Evidence that demonstrates *internal consistency*, that is, it is free from self-contradiction, is usually considered better than testimony from a source who contradicts him- or herself. For example, the police often make use of this test to evaluate the integrity of a suspect. If a suspect changes her story when retelling it, the police will consider the inconsistency as evidence of duplicity. Parents have learned to apply the same tests. Consequently, if they think their children may be lying they may ask them to repeat their stories to see if retelling the stories some flaw or error will be uncovered.

The ability of advocates to provide several concurring sources is likely to encourage an audience toward a positive evaluation of the argument. This demonstration of **external consistency**—showing that the testimony is consistent with the testimony of others—strengthens the credibility of each cited source, since none of them are alone in their observations. Corroboration by other experts reduces the likelihood that the evidence is not trustworthy.

Verifiability is another component of trustworthiness. A source who cannot be verified, because he or she is neither available nor properly identified, is not likely to be given much credibility. For example, in the legal field hearsay evidence (testimony given by witnesses concerning what they heard others say) is with few exceptions considered inadmissible because, in part, the statements are not verifiable.

A final test of the trustworthiness of testimony is *recency*. Some advocates and audiences assume that the date of testimony is critical to its value. But the importance of recency depends on the nature of the testimony and the issue under consideration. Some evidence is outdated almost as soon as it is presented. For example, consider the win-loss record of your favorite major league baseball team. You need to know the team's record on the day you are using it as evidence or quoting it in some other way because it will likely change on the next day. Other testimony seems perpetually valuable—quotations from Aristotle generalizing about the principles of persuasion and argumentation, for example, are still very relevant today. The test of recency is most usefully applied when the advocate or the audience is asked to consider whether anything has happened between the date of the evidence and when it is used to support an argument that might make that testimony invalid. If nothing has changed in a significant way, then the observations offered in the testimony are sufficiently recent to be relevant to deciding the issue under consideration.

On some issues, of course, events change very quickly and thus recency is an especially important concern. Scientific, technical, medical, or economic issues for instance are very dynamic and thus an arguer has an especially important responsibility to present recent testimony. Issues involving moral, ethical, or philosophical testimony are probably less dependent on recency because these issues are less dynamic and less driven by events.

An interesting question about recency involves historical testimony. As we know, new histories are written every day. So which is more reliable, a history of the Civil War that was written by the soldiers, statesmen, or citizens who may actually have experienced the conflict, or a history of the Civil War written by contemporary academics plowing back through archives? Certainly an argument could be made for the value of both histories. The firsthand accounts would of course be informative and would create a real sense of the emotion and tenor of the times. On the other hand, would such writers be able to judge the events with detachment or might they instead present their own conduct in the most favorable light? Contemporary scholars are temporally removed from the events that occurred during the Civil War. Would they be likely to apply today's standards of behavior and morality to such events, perhaps doing a disservice to our genuine understanding of the times? Indeed, differences of opinion over the value of recency may themselves be the subject of very important arguments.

Of course, there are other issues that may affect the credibility of testimony. Research reveals that audiences are likely to view speakers whose arguments are well organized more favorably than those whose presentation seems scattered or disorganized. Thus, the clarity of a presentation, the structure of the text, and the degree to which an audience can reason along with the source will all influence the effectiveness of the message. Also, testimony that uses strong, dynamic, and active language communicates that the source is certain and has confidence in what is claimed. This also has influence on how testimony is perceived by audiences.

Testimony delivered by advocates who seem to demonstrate care and concern about their audiences and about their audience's well-being will also be accorded more trust. Remember our discussion of Brockriede's arguers-as-lovers metaphor in chapter 1. Advocates who seem to care about and to respect their audiences do not try to seduce or coerce them through arguments. Instead, such arguers have nothing to hide. They are explicit and clear, and they allow the best evidence to be revealed and evaluated. On the other hand, arguers who try to mislead, deceive, or play games with their audiences on one issue may find themselves embroiled in a credibility damaging controversy that spills out into other issues. As an illustration, President George W. Bush received withering criticism for a statement he made in his 2003 State of the Union Speech warning of Iraq's weapons of mass destruction. Bush's goal was to justify preemptive military action against Iraq. In the speech he argued that "the British have reported" that Iraq sought to buy weapons grade nuclear materials from another nation. He made this statement even though the evidence now suggests that the CIA had already told the administration that it had significant doubts about the reliability of this intelligence information, and indeed, our government had already communicated those doubts to the British government. A nasty finger-pointing exchange, seeking to determine who was responsible for the statement's use in the president's speech, resulted. A few columnists went so far as to argue that intentionally misleading the American public and taking them into a war on the basis of such deceptive arguments is an impeachable offense, far worse even than the crimes of Watergate that forced Richard Nixon to resign the presidency.[14]

Research has long supported the fact that audiences are more inclined to grant adherence to claims advanced by advocates who are perceived as likable and dynamic. If advocates seem personable and friendly, audiences may make allowances for them and grant them greater credibility than they might otherwise. Also, if audience members see an advocate as like them, as sharing in their interests and concerns, they will be more likely to accept the advocate's statements as credible.[15] Think about how you respond to your friends' statements or arguments as opposed to those of people you hardly know, or worse yet, dislike. We tend to find the claims of persons whom we like more compelling.

Finally, advocates who are excited about their claims and animated in their presentation send us cues that suggest they believe in their own arguments. These dimensions of a speaker's sincerity thus speak to his or her integrity. Of course, we are generally suspicious of those who attempt to conceal the weakness of their arguments by resorting to an artificially dynamic delivery, for example the overly polished smooth-talking salesperson, so even dynamism must be measured, lest it boomerang and become counterproductive.

Summary

In this chapter we have considered the grounds used by advocates when they make claims. We identified four specific types of grounds: premises, examples, statistics, and testimony. We pointed out that each type of evidence is subject to tests to determine the likelihood that critical audiences will accept or reject it. Critical decision makers will consider the grounds presented before they render a judgment on the advocacy of others. Advocates seeking to maximize the effectiveness of their arguments will consider what kinds of grounds are most likely to sway their audience.

Key Terms

artistic proof
competence
credibility
cultural knowledge
examples
external consistency
grounds
inartistic proof
internal consistency
interval sampling
margin of error
overreporting
personal knowledge
premise
presumption
random sample

recency
reluctant testimony
ritual
simple random sampling
statistics
  descriptive
  inferential
stratified sampling
symbols
testimony
  descriptive
  interpretive
time frame
trustworthiness
underreporting
verifiability

Activities

1. Examine an argumentative artifact. Once you have ascertained the claim, determine whether the grounds provided are artistic, inartistic, or both. Next, identify the kinds of grounds that are presented: premises, examples, statistics, or testimony. Then apply the appropriate tests to determine whether or not you find the grounds convincing.

2. Find a public opinion poll in a newspaper or magazine. Examine the polling sample, the questions asked, and the definitions of the statistical categories. Does the statistical evidence pass the appropriate tests?

3. Examine a speech by a public figure. Identify the types of data the speaker employed and apply the appropriate tests do determine whether or not you find the evidence compelling.

4. Look through a popular magazine and locate three advertisements. What kinds of grounds do the advertisers utilize? Apply the appropriate tests to determine whether or not you find the grounds compelling.

5. Select a public controversy of interest to you. Take a position on this controversy and then find grounds drawn from each of the four types to support your position.

Recommended Readings

Aristotle. *Rhetoric and Poetics of.* Translated by W. Rhys Roberts. New York: The Modern Library, 1954.

Best, Joel. *Damned Lies and Statistics: Untangling Numbers from the Media, Politicians, and Activists.* Berkeley: University of California Press, 2001.

Bettinghaus, Erwin P., and Michael J. Cody. *Persuasive Communication.* 5th ed. New York: Holt, Rinehart and Winston, 1994.

Burke, Kenneth. *Attitudes Toward History.* 2nd ed. Boston: Beacon, 1959.

Murray, David, Joel Schwartz, and S. Robert Lichter. *It Ain't Necessarily So: How Media Make and Unmake the Scientific Picture of Reality* Oxford: Rowan and Littlefield, 2001.

O'Keefe, Daniel J. *Persuasion: Theory and Research.* 2nd ed. Newbury Park, CA: Sage, 2002.

Pickering, Barbara. "Women's Voices as Evidence: Personal Testimony in Pro-Choice Films." *Argumentation and Advocacy* 40 (2003): 1–22.

Rumsey, Debra. *Statistics for Dummies.* New York: For Dummies Press, 2003.

Stauber, John, and Sheldon Rampton. *Trust Us We're Experts: How Industry Manipulates Science and Gambles with Your Future.* Los Angeles: J. P. Tarcher, 2002.

Notes

[1] For example, see Andrew C. Revkin and Katharine Q. Seelye, "Report by the E.P.A. Leaves Out Data in Climate Change," *New York Times*, June 19, 2003.

[2] *The Rhetoric of Aristotle*, trans. Lane Cooper. (Englewood Cliffs, NJ: Prentice-Hall, 1932), 8.

[3] For additional information on the subject of personal and cultural knowledge see: Michael Polanyi, *Personal Knowledge: Towards a Post-Critical Philosophy* (Chicago: University of Chicago Press, 1974); and Lloyd Bitzer, "Rhetoric and Public Knowledge," in *Rhetoric, Philosophy, and Literature*, ed. Don M. Burks, 67–93 (West Lafayette, IN: Purdue University Press, 1978).

[4] For an interesting discussion on this topic see, Clifford Geertz, *The Interpretation of Cultures* (New York: Basic Books, 1973).

[5] For interesting discussions of the importance of rituals see, Mircea Eliade, *Cosmos and History: The Myth of the Eternal Return* (New York: Bantam Books, 1972); and Joseph Campbell, *Myths We Live By* (New York: Bantam Books, 1972).

[6] For an excellent discussion of globalization see: David Held, Anthony McGrew, David Goldblatt, and Jonathan Perraton, *Global Transformations: Politics, Economics and Culture* (Palo Alto, CA: Stanford University Press, 1999).

[7] For an excellent discussion of cultural diversity see: DeWight R. Middleton, *The Challenge of Human Diversity*, 2nd ed. (Prospect Heights, IL: Waveland Press, 2003).

[8] For example see: Alan Bloom, *The Closing of the American Mind* (New York: Simon and Schuster, 1987); and E. D. Hirsh, *Cultural Literacy: What Every American Needs to Know* (Boston: Houghton Mifflin, 1987).

[9] See for example see: Robert G. Powell and Dana Caseau, *Diversity and Classroom Communication: Enhancing Instruction Practice* (Mahwah, NJ: Lawrence Earlbaum, 2004); and, N. Appleton, *Cultural Pluralism in Education: Theoretical Foundations* (New York: Longman, 1983).

[10] Walter R. Fisher, "Reaffirmation and Subversion of the American Dream," *Quarterly Journal of Speech 59* (April 1973): 160–167.

[11] Peter Schmidt, "Supreme Court Upholds Affirmative Action in College Admissions," *Chronicle of Higher Education*, June 23, 2003.

[12] For an excellent discussion of these conflicting positions see: Richard C. Leone and Greg Anrig, Jr., eds. *The War on Our Freedoms: Civil Liberties in an Age of Terrorism* (New York: Public Affairs, 2003).

[13] Trent Lott, *Daily Kos*, December 7, 2002. http://www.dailykos.com/archives/00651.html.

[14] For example see: Arianna Huffington, "If His Words Are His Bond We're in a Bind," *Los Angeles Times*, July 16, 2003.

[15] David K. Berlo, James B. Lemert, and Robert J. Mertz, "Dimensions for Evaluating the Acceptability of Message Sources," *Public Opinion Quarterly, 33* (1970): 56–76.

BUILDING ARGUMENTS

You are engaged in a conversation with a classmate who makes a claim that you intensely disagree with, perhaps for reasons that are not clear even to you. You know that you can express your own opinion, but you are not even sure why you hold that opinion. How can you possibly express it in such a way so as to convince a colleague whom you already know holds a different opinion? Such a situation, and of course, many other argumentative situations that you will often encounter, demands that you investigate the sources of your own beliefs so that you can create compelling and coherent arguments to convince others to share your views. This process demands research, so that you can identify appropriate grounds to establish your argumentative starting points, analysis, and of course, appropriate organization to tie the claims together into a coherent position.

In this chapter we will describe the research process, give some suggestions as to where to locate sources, and discuss how you can organize your research results to increase the likelihood that your arguments will gain the adherence of your audience.

DEFINING RESEARCH

As we have already explained, rational arguments contain three basic elements: the grounds used as the basis or premise to develop a claim; the reasoning that justifies the inferential leap from grounds to claim; and the claim itself, which is the conclusion drawn from the grounds and reasoning. Thus, grounds refer to the foundation or support for the claim the advocate wishes the audience to accept (see chapter 6). Like a house, an argument is only as solid as its foundation. Thus it is imperative that you provide grounds that will move your audience. But where do the data for these grounds come from?

The best answer is: from our life experiences. We argue based on what we know—what we have read, studied, and lived. That is why U.S. universities generally emphasize a liberal arts education—so that students can draw from a variety of perspectives. As an advocate you should always use what you know as the basis for your claims. Furthermore, you should take the preparation time in developing your arguments to expand your storehouse of information: read! Be an informed citizen and you will become both a better advocate and a better consumer of arguments.

Nevertheless, no matter how well read you are, or even how many interesting personal experiences you have had, there will come a time when your present personal knowledge is insufficient to convince your audience of the claim you want to advance. In many cases, you will also discover that your life experiences may even be contradicted by the life experiences of others. Then, to make a convincing claim, you will need to look elsewhere for support. Or, perhaps you have been asked to give a formal presentation of your views. If you wish to demonstrate the breadth of your knowledge, and you are committed to being an ethical communicator, you will need to supplement your knowledge with the facts and opinions drawn from other sources. Engaging in this process of inquiry to identify such material is what we consider to be argumentative *research*.

PLANNING THE RESEARCH PROCESS

Once you have decided to supplement your knowledge and explore the ideas of others, you will need to decide where to begin. The information available in good libraries can be overwhelming. This is not just a happy circumstance. It is the result of a conscious decision to create informed citizens and to give people the individual freedoms to read widely so that they might discover their own interests and notions about what is or is not true. Without ready access to the latest information we would be forced to make decisions in a vacuum, with a significant chance that we would err or be misled. Nevertheless, if millions of holdings in a library (or now on the Internet) are available to you, and potentially of use, you must have a *research plan* or strategy to determine what information you need and the best way to obtain it.

Our advice is to start with general sources and move on to more specific ones as your research progresses. By *general sources* we mean those that give a broad understanding of all aspects or sides in the issue or controversy under investigation. There are five benefits in starting with more general sources.

First, getting a broad overview of the topic will enable you to better understand the particular perspectives of the sources you choose to consult in greater detail and with closer attention later. Authors write because they believe they have something to contribute to an ongoing conversation. Sometimes it is very clear what has prompted them to write, and sometimes their agenda is not clear and must be inferred by the reader. For example, authors may respond directly to arguments that have already been advanced by others, or they may anticipate and preempt arguments that they believe others might raise. You can understand why both after-the-fact and preemptive information would be very valuable to your research. You can also see how easily you might miss this information if you do not understand the nature of the controversy. The result can be poor argumentation, or you may be compelled to return and reread material that you had already passed over. Neither outcome is efficient or desirable.

A second benefit of starting with more general sources is that doing so will enable you to generate a list of topic headings and synonyms. This can be invaluable because when you consult indexes you may need to look under several headings. A lack of familiarity with the overall picture can frustrate good-faith efforts to research a topic. We once assigned a group of students to research "ethos." They returned to class confused by the lack of material in the library on what they had been told was a major element in public speaking. As it turned out, the students had only looked under "ethos" in the indexes they consulted. A second visit to the library yielded better results because they tried looking for information about ethos under related topics such as "public speaking," "oratory," "source credibility," and "Aristotle."

The broad understanding of the controversy yielded by general sources offers a third benefit in that it enables the researcher to select those lines of inquiry that seem most promising. There may be many reasons, for example, to support handgun control in the United States. If you have less than ten minutes to convince an audience, however, it probably makes sense to limit the scope of your advocacy to a couple of positions. That means selecting the most compelling reason or reasons and building your case around them. Knowing your options early in the research process can save you a lot of time and can also make the time that you do invest in argument preparation much more productive.

A fourth benefit is the discovery of potential critical responses to your advocacy. In order to gain the adherence of a critical audience, you will need to know the likely objections to your arguments. Researching only one side of a controversy may not prepare you adequately. Whereas, understanding the arguments from both sides in a dispute enables you to anticipate possible refutations to your claims and thus prepare responses to those refutations.

The fifth and final benefit of focusing on general sources in your initial research efforts is that they tend to be easier to read and comprehend than more specific and technical writings. General sources tend to be written for lay audiences; terms used in their field are defined and explained. Authors of more specific or technical writings, on the other hand, usually presume that their audience already commands knowledge about the basics and is also familiar with the jargon of the field. They may also write using language, style, and references that impede your comprehension. For example, contrast reading a newsmagazine article on the technical challenges that doctors may face when separating conjoined twins versus reading an essay on the same topic in the *New England Journal of Medicine*. Ultimately, of course, you may need and want to know about the contents in the journal article, but we would urge you not to start with such essays. Start with sources that will provide you with a broad understanding of the controversy you are investigating and then move out to more specific information as you acquire greater knowledge, familiarity with the issues and vocabulary, and perspective on the topic.

SOURCES OF INFORMATION

Interviewing Experts

Having decided that you wish to start with broader sources of information, the next question is: Where should you go to find such information? A common first step in the research process, even a step recommended by some books on research, is to begin by interviewing experts on the subject matter. It is likely that faculty members on your campus are knowledgeable about the topic you want to investigate. They might make excellent subjects to interview. Representatives from public interest groups might also be good persons for you to talk to as you begin your research efforts. If your topic is about a controversy in society, there might be many groups of citizen activists who will have literature advocating one side of the controversy or the other. Although interviewing such persons might be valuable, it might not be the first thing you want to do. You need to be on guard so you are not easily misled by your interview subject, who may see you as a target for his or her advocacy. In short, you may not yet know enough about the topic at this point to critically evaluate the information that you are provided.

As with conducting research in books or the Internet, you should have a general knowledge of the topic or controversy before seeking more detailed information. If you ask your expert/subject to tell you everything he or she knows about your topic, the expert may not know where to begin. Instead, your subject expects you to give guidance by asking the right questions. If you do not have enough background information and understanding of the issues of controversy and the different opinions on the topic, it will be tough for you ask intelligent questions. As a result, you might end up wasting the expert's time. Even if the expert is generous with his or her time, the results may not be especially useful. Our advice therefore is that you should not conduct interviews until you have done preliminary reading on your topic and have acquired sufficient background information and knowledge to assure that your questions will be both probative and productive to your research effort.

In addition, statements made in personal interviews are frequently not accepted as valid by educated audiences. Since the advent of the printing press, Western culture has been dominated by the written word. For some reason, an idea that appears on the printed page makes it intrinsically superior to that delivered in oral speech.[1] Neil Postman has argued that in the academic world the published word is given greater credence than the spoken word. This emphasis, he argues, stems from the transitory nature of oral communication:

> What people say is assumed to be more casually uttered than what they write. The written word is assumed to have been reflected upon and revised

> by its author, reviewed by authorities and editors. It is easier to verify or refute, and it is invested with an impersonal and objective character . . . ; that is to say, the written word is, by its nature, addressed to the world, not an individual. The written word endures, the spoken word disappears; and that is why writing is closer to the truth than speaking.[2]

This emphasis on the written word perhaps accounts for why so many of us are not particularly good at monitoring what we say. When the spoken word constituted the preferred form of communication, we were probably better at communicating orally. Now that the emphasis has shifted to the written word, we are better writers but possibly less effective at communicating orally.

Just as we may suffer discomfort when we hear our recorded voice or see ourselves on videotape, it can be disquieting to see our spoken words written out in black and white. A frequent and understandable reaction to transcribed conversation is the desire to rephrase an utterance. In some cases we deny that such words could have come out of our mouths, or we insist that the words are misleading without the accompaniment of the other words that we used to surround them and to provide the context of our thoughts. This may account for the frequency of the claim that reporters have misquoted their subjects when conducting interviews.

A final reason why educated audiences may look dubiously on statements made in personal interviews may derive from their lack of verifiability. Published statements are potentially available to all and can be checked for accuracy and veracity. Personal interviews are not. Thus, we believe that you should save the interviews until you have specific questions to ask, and even then, you should focus on asking experts questions for which their sources of information are published and accessible to others.

General Sources

Having postponed interviews until later in the research plan, you will still need to find general sources that provide you with a broad view of your topic. Where should you turn in the library? We suggest that you allow the journalistic ethic to serve as your guide.

Reporters are generally taught to report both sides of a controversy. Presenting the competing views is considered balanced coverage. For our purposes, that means you should begin your research with sources that report the controversy, rather than those that advocate a single, particular viewpoint. Newsmagazines, such as *Time, Newsweek, U.S. News and World Report,* or the *Economist* tend to offer the perspectives drawn from advocates on both sides in their stories. Their stories also tend to be written in a style that is accessible to the lay reader. At this point in your research process you are trying to gain a breadth of information in a quick and efficient way, and newsmagazine stories tend to be short. The same generally is true for articles in newspapers. After consulting newsmagazines and newspapers, you may then wish to move on to articles that are a bit longer, are more likely to be analytical, and begin to stake out a position of advocacy, but that are still written for general audiences. Magazines such as the

Atlantic Monthly, Vanity Fair, the New Yorker, the New Republic, the Nation, the Weekly Standard, to name just a few, are often excellent sources for information on contemporary public controversies.

You can find articles in such news sources by consulting your library's various databases. LexisNexis and the Public Affairs Information Service (PAIS) are two popular databases for articles about current events. Many major newspapers are also indexed individually, so consider consulting indexes for the *New York Times, Los Angles Times, Chicago Tribune, Washington Post, Wall Street Journal, Christian Science Monitor*, or your local newspaper. When newspapers take positions on controversies, they do so in editorials. Editorials are indexed by each newspaper and will appear in the LexisNexis database, but a very interesting way to read and compare a variety of newspaper editorials organized by subject is in the publication *Editorials on File*.

Specialized Sources

Once you have read what some general sources have to say about your topic you will be ready to conduct a more focused search of *specialized sources*. These publications contain articles that are targeted to audiences who want in-depth information about a specific topic of field and who typically have background knowledge in the field. Having already covered a number of general sources, you should now be familiar with the issues in the controversy and know some of the key terms and jargon. There are four reasons why it will be beneficial for you to continue your research by consulting specialized sources.

First, articles written for the general public often report the conclusions of experts in the field, but they seldom explore a controversy in depth. While breadth means more individuals know a little about the topic, to discover where truth resides or to find material to gain the adherence of others, you need to read more deeply so that you can learn the rationale behind the conclusions drawn by the experts.

Second, as you gain more knowledge of your topic, you will discover the unstated assumptions of the experts. For example, we remember when it was widely reported that U.S. oil reserves would be exhausted in less than seventy-five years. This claim, of course, depends on many different assumptions, such as assumptions about consumption patterns, whether drilling will be allowed in areas that have been contested by environmentalists (e.g., off the Florida or California coasts, or in Alaska), the amount of oil we choose to purchase from foreign suppliers, the price of oil, and the technologies for extraction (that might make it physically and economically viable to remove oil that is harder to find and pull from the ground). We thus *may* deplete the U.S. oil reserves in seventy-five years, or even less if the S.U.V. craze continues, but such a claim obviously rests on many assumptions that you as a researcher should understand if you are to become an effective advocate.

Third, additional research uncovers specific information necessary to support the arguments you wish to convey. General sources may give you most of the information that you need to justify your position, but there may be gaps that need to be filled. For example, newsmagazines may provide basic informa-tion about the importance of childhood immunization programs, but they may not provide the details necessary for a compelling argument. Consulting jour-nals devoted to public health could yield statistics on the efficacy of immuniza-tions, examples of the consequences of failing to immunize children, or the procedures necessary to fully protect youngsters.

The most important benefit of consulting specialized sources of information is the opportunity to discover more about your topic than you think you need. Have you heard the saying "a little knowledge is a dangerous thing"? This adage refers to cases in which individuals assume that having some knowledge of a topic means they know the entire truth, when, in fact, they may only know a small part of it. Then, on that basis, they enter into a discussion and leap to an incorrect conclusion that has a negative effect on themselves or others. Achiev-ing a more thorough grasp of the subject by conducting more focused research should help you avoid sounding like you think you know it all when you don't.

Once you have decided to pursue the lines of research indicated by your general reading, you need to pinpoint what types of sources to consult and find them. We will present two types of specialized sources, but this is not to suggest that there are no others. However, these two types should get you well started on most topics.

Sources for Specific Disciplines

In any academic discipline, scholars are expected to contribute to the under-standing of the field by publishing the results of their research in professional journals. These articles are not written for the general public, but for readers familiar with the jargon of the field and with the important issues and contro-versies imbued in that field. Check the list below or consult your reference librarian for the index to the journals on the topics that interest you.

Selected Indexes to Scholarly Journals

ABC: Political Science Index	*Index Medicus*
Abstracts in Anthropology	*Index to Legal Periodicals*
Applied Science and Technology Index	*Philosopher's Index*
Education Index	*Social Science Citation Index*
Humanities Index	

Of course, there are also a wide variety of popular magazines that publish in-depth articles and editorials on subjects of concern. Although such essays may tend to be relatively one-sided, they can still be very helpful to your research efforts. For example, such magazines as *Science, National Geographic, Psychology Today,* and *Wired*, to name only a few, are not necessarily written in the same style and with the same degree of scholarly rigor as are most academic journals, but they nonetheless offer more detailed and thorough coverage of subjects within their sphere of influence than do other sources. Thus the more specialized popular magazines can prove to be very useful as research resources to support your arguments.

Many disciplines also have their own databases, but there are some that transcend particular fields. For example, we have found EBSCOhost and JSTOR to be very useful. Your topic area will naturally determine the database you will find most useful. When in doubt, do not hesitate to request assistance from a reference librarian.

Government Sources

Other, more specialized sources that can be immensely useful are government publications. The United States Congress holds hearings on almost every topic that is identified as a matter of national concern or where there will be a demand for legislative policy action. At these hearings experts from both sides of the controversy present sworn statements and answer questions from members of Congress. The experts usually testify as advocates in favor of, or in opposition to, proposed federal legislation. Consequently, the statements from these sources contain practically everything an advocate would need to construct convincing arguments. Similarly, congressional committees, independent agencies, cabinet departments, federal commissions, and a host of other agencies produce reports that are available via the Internet to the public.

To locate government publications you can consult *Firstgov.gov*. This Web site offers links to all three branches of the federal government, to some local and state government Web sites, and even to some Web sites of foreign nations. The *Library of Congress Internet Resource Page* contains similar links to government documents and Web sites.

Congress also prints a record of the debates that take place on the floor of the House and Senate. The *Congressional Record* is indexed to help you find useful information. Since senators and representatives can revise and extend their remarks, and even insert documents for the record, you can find a tremendous wealth of helpful research information in the *Congressional Record.*

Of course, some controversies that interest you may be more prominent in local discussions than in national discourse. Your state may publish information about their legislative or governmental proceedings. Consult your reference librarian for additional information about how best to locate such information for your state.

The Internet

The technological age is clearly upon us. As previously noted, much information from a wide variety of sources is now available on the Internet. The research process has been greatly simplified now as most of us can conduct our research from anywhere if we have a computer and a connection to the Worldwide Web.

One of the easiest ways to research a topic is to conduct an online search via the Internet. Indeed, many complain that the Internet makes researching too easy, and thus too many of us are satisfied with the results of hasty, superficial, and careless Web searches. The Google search engine is so popular that "to google" has become an accepted verb. Yahoo, Lycos, Ask Jeeves, and Netscape are also popular search engines that Web researchers may use to find sources of information on the Internet. Although Web searches are convenient and profoundly helpful, we identify four challenges to keep in mind.

First, not all Web sites have equal power, standing, respect, or editorial quality. Certainly many excellent sources of information can be found via the Web, but ascertaining the accuracy and reliability of information on the Web can be problematic. Major newspapers; broadcast news networks; magazines; academic journals; activist organizations; scientific, technical, and professional organizations; and individual experts maintain Web sites that are profoundly useful to researchers. You must remember, however, that it is easy to create a Web site and easy to post information on a Web site. A Web site that looks impressively official and reliable can be produced in someone's garage. As a result, if you do not know the reliability of the source you are consulting, you should be skeptical about the information you discover on the Web. Many Web sites exert very little editorial control over the information that is posted on the site. Weblogs (or Blogs), for example, have no restrictions on the content posted on them. The "blogger" can type anything from a passing thought to a well-crafted essay. Often the commentary resembles conversations more than carefully reflected upon essays. On the other hand, a Web site that quotes an authority is not automatic proof that the site is a valid source. We must always assess the credibility of a source when deciding whether or not to use the information provided by that source. Most of us put little faith in something reported in the tabloids that one finds at the checkout lanes in grocery stores, similar skepticism is in order when citing from previously unknown Web sites.

Second, we have already noted in this chapter that the printed word is generally considered more compelling because it goes through an editorial process and because it is potentially verifiable. Web sites may or may not use a similar editorial review process. It is common, for example, for academics to post lectures, working papers, and conference presentations on their Web sites. Certainly, such papers may prove very useful, and some of them will constitute outstanding work that represents the "state of the art" research on any given topic at that point in time. Yet, most of them will not have been through the kind of rigorous editorial review that is required of essays published in leading journals. As a result, errors in this work may go undetected, and the work will not have benefited from helpful editorial critiques by other experts in the field. In addition, Internet materials often lack permanence; what is accessible on the Web today may be gone tomorrow. That means revisiting or verifying information may be impossible.

Third, audiences may give less credibility to printed material accessed on the Web in contrast with material from traditional publications. For instance, declaring, "according to www.aboutviolence.com" is not as credible as saying "according to an editorial in the *New York Times*." If your audience does not perceive the source of the information that you present as credible, then you have gained little by drawing upon that source. If a Web site provides the name of a primary source of information, you would be better off looking up that source on the Web or in a library. Primary sources tend to be seen as more reliable than secondary sources—especially when you do not know the credibility of the secondary source.

The fourth concern to keep in mind about Internet searches is that the search engines typically reinforce "mainstream" thinking. The software team that designed and developed the search engine technology had to use some strategy to determine which 500 sites might appear when you punched in the words "handgun control"—or any other search terms that you used. Some search engines "order" the possible sites by identifying those sites that readers go to most frequently. Certainly this strategy favors mainstream sites over those that might stake out more controversial or potentially unpopular positions. Automatically marginalizing such alternative voices is antithetical to the goals for multivocality and diversity that are central to our text. Other search engines, however, use even more controversial and potentially counterproductive means to "order" the responses to search inquiries. They allow Web sites to pay a fee to get their Web addresses to come up first. The higher the fee they pay, the higher their place in the list. Now, there are even more troublesome technologies being used to manipulate your searches and to turn them into corporate profits. You can punch in, for example, the Web address for a travel site and the computer will automatically give you a "pop-up" window for a rival travel site that has paid them for providing this service.

Do these concerns mean that we do not think you should use the Web and the available Internet search engines? Of course not, but we do want you to avoid becoming overly reliant on them. Delving deeper into the extant literature through computer-assisted searches of books, journals, periodicals, and government sources will yield much better results, which in turn will enable you to construct compelling arguments for nearly any audience.

Computer Databases

Although we have cautioned you about relying too much on Web searches, we do believe that there are other computer databank searches that you will wish to use. Some of these services may not be available in all libraries (e.g., LexisNexis), and they may be expensive. Others, on the other hand, are free to any users. Indeed, many libraries have now moved to computerize their entire reference system. A computer search can often tell you about almost everything that has been published on your topic. Often now, sites such as HighWire and looksmart can also offer you free, online full-text articles, so you do not have to leave your computer terminal to read full journal articles.

Each library and each databank has its own procedures, so it is best to consult your reference librarian. However, most searches have some factors in common. First, they have databases. Some databases are limited to selected recent periodicals. Others are more extensive. Second, each online search system has to have a way to search the data. Usually this requires that the researcher provide key words to narrow the data fields just as is done for an ordinary Web search. The search engine then looks for articles that contain these times in the text of the articles in its database. The researcher is notified as to the number of articles that meet the search specifications.

If the number of articles located is too great to be managed, or the topics seem too broad, the researcher can modify the search terms to refocus the efforts of the search engine. Additional keywords can be added to the search, and searches can be limited by specifying the year or range of years to be searched. Each time the search is modified the number of matches is narrowed until only the articles of greatest interest are isolated.

Obviously, selecting the key terms is a critical component of this process. This again illustrates the importance of using general sources at the beginning of your research process to discover key terms. Using the right key terms for your computer search is a major time saver. As you become proficient at such searches, you will find these databases invaluable.

Books

In addition to periodicals, government documents, and computer based research access, most libraries have—not too surprisingly—books. The books that have been published on the controversy that you are researching may be very helpful to you. We have listed books last, however, because there are some real problems with focusing your research effort too much or too early in the process on books.

First, reading books can be very time-consuming. Although comprehensive research necessitates reading deeply and broadly on a subject, most of us lack the time to be as thorough as we should be. We thus need to obtain the greatest possible return for the time we invest. Because of their length and depth, books may not be as profitable as other sources of information. Second, a book will generally offer you the perspective of only one author. The same time invested in reading journal articles, for example, will likely offer a number of different perspectives and viewpoints.

Finally, it can take a long time for a manuscript to evolve into a published book. For some controversies, especially those focused on historical events, this is not a problem. However, in researching current events or some scientific or technical issues the recency of the information is critical to its value and accuracy. Regarding certain topics (e.g., where government policies may be changing, the nature of the problem is fluctuating, or technologies may be rapidly evolving), by the time a book reaches the public it may already be out of date. A book on the Internet may be out of date before it makes it to the shelves in the library because changes in online communication occur so quickly that no author or publisher can keep up with them.

So yes, you should read books in order to be fully informed on the topic that you are investigating, but do not turn to books too early in the research process and do not make them the only focus of your research.

HOW TO RECORD THE EVIDENCE

Having located an article, essay, or news story that interests you, it is time to record whatever information you will need to develop to support your arguments. In addition to recording the verbatim quotation (more about this later), you will need to record all of the information required by the citation system you will use.* If you are writing a scholarly essay or college paper you will need to know the requirements of the style manual so that you can record the required source information. It is very frustrating, and requires significant extra time, if you have to go back to the original source materials because you neglected to write down the complete information to fully cite your research according to the style manual you are using, so be sure to familiarize yourself with the requirements of that manual before you undertake your research. We recommend that you record the following five components:

1. **Author's name.** The first thing to record is the author's complete name. Some style manuals require that you provide only the author's last name and the initials of their first and middle names (e.g., APA); others require that you use the full name in your citation. If you do not know for sure which manual you will eventually use, it is always best to record the full name, that way you will have it if you need it.

   What do you do if there is no author identified? This frequently is the case with newspaper or magazine articles or with pamphlets. It means that the source—the newspaper, magazine, or the group that produced the pamphlet—should be considered the author. The same goes for articles written by staff writers. The words in such articles are, in a real sense, the words of the source.

2. **Author's qualifications.** None of the official style manuals that we have mentioned above require, or even permit, the inclusion of the author's qualifications in the reference section. These citation systems make no judgment about the quality or competence of the sources that an advocate chooses to cite. But audiences do evaluate, and are often heavily influenced by, the quality, training, reputation, and competence of the sources that an advocate uses. Advocates who cite sources that the audience views favorably (that is, sources that the audiences find to be especially credible), benefit from a "halo effect." If a source that the audience considers trustworthy and competent supports your argument, it makes your argument *and you* look better. Of course, the reverse is also true. Consequently, it is important that you record the author's qualifications. Doing so can then help you choose from among the different sources that you have identified to support your arguments, so that you cite those you believe will be most likely to strengthen the appeal of your claims in the eyes of your audience. If you are arguing about immunizations for children, for instance, a statement supporting your position from a medical doctor and epidemiologist from the Centers for Disease Control in

---

* MLA (Modern Language Association), APA (American Psychological Association), Turabian (developed by Kate Turabian), and Chicago Manual of Style (developed by researchers at the University of Chicago) are all organized style systems. Your instructor may assign one of these style systems for your particular assignment, or the choice of which style manual you follow may be left to you. All are available in the reference section of your library or in your college bookstore for you to consult. What is important, however, is that you faithfully and consistently follow whichever style manual you select.

Atlanta might have far greater credibility than a staff writer for the *Omaha World Herald*.

Occasionally, you will not know the qualifications of an author, and it is not provided in the material you are referencing. All you may know then is that he or she wrote an article or a book. Chances are good that you can find out more about the author by consulting sources such as *Who's Who*, and *Who's Who in America*. Both provide biographical information on many authors. There are other biographical indexes in many areas of specialization that a reference librarian can help you to locate. In addition, today you can often find very helpful information to assist you in learning more about a source by typing the source's name into a Web search engine. Many experts post biographical information, often including their academic or scholarly resumes on the Web.

Once you record the qualifications for the sources you intend to use, be sure to use them in the text of your advocacy. Your audiences may not know that your sources are experts unless you tell them. Therefore, it is to your advantage to include enough information about the author so that your audience learns about their many accomplishments, when you cite their words, ideas, or research.

3. **Source information.** Style manuals require that you provide enough information about the source so that members of your audience could locate the articles, essays, or books themselves. For a book, this usually necessitates the full title and the name and location of the publisher. For an article, you will need the title of the article, and the name and volume of the periodical. For a Web site, you will need the name of the site and the Web address (typically the address begins "http://www. . . ."").

   To be safe, you should consult the style manual you will be using to make sure you are aware of all the required information before you conduct your research. This is especially important if you are citing unusual sources such as pamphlets, sound recordings, translations, edited volumes, TV programs or videotapes, speeches, personal interviews, and so forth.

4. **Date.** In chapter 7, we discussed the test of evidence called *recency*. We argued that the date of the material is not as important as what has transpired since the material was written. Thus, some very recent data are already outdated, while other data will always be considered relevant. Nevertheless, it is of vital importance that you record the specific date that the material you cited was produced. Not only is this required by all of the style manuals, it is necessary if someone else is to locate the original source that you cited. Some style manuals, although not all, also specify that you must record the date you actually accessed any material that you found on the World Wide Web. This is because, as we have already mentioned, materials sometimes have a way of disappearing when the administrator of the host computer server elects to take down a Web site or to change the content. The date that you located the material on the Web, however, might help another researcher locate it in a Web database archive.

In many forms of communication it is also common to cite the date at the point you refer to such material, or in the text of your advocacy. Audiences may be greatly impressed if your evidence is very recent, and also if the date of the evidence is germane to the argument you are advancing.

5. **Page number.** If you intend to quote or paraphrase an author, style manuals require that you provide the specific page number where the passage appeared in the original source. In addition, the style manual may require that your list of references includes the beginning and ending page numbers for articles in journals or for chapters in edited books. Thus, it is very important that you develop the habit of conscientiously recording this information.

WHAT TO LOOK FOR WHEN RESEARCHING

You have, shall we say, been busily researching your topic and have located many great sources that will help you support the arguments you wish to develop. You have also carefully recorded the source information. Now you are reading the materials that you located in order to determine what to write down in your notes. How do you determine what information is going to prove relevant to your arguments? This is a difficult question. Experience will prove to be your best teacher, but we can offer some suggestions.

What Is Necessary to Gain Adherence

We have previously discussed the role of *stasis* and *stock issues* in argumentation (chapter 5). Think about the issues that must be addressed and where there will likely be disagreement with the claims that you wish to advance. To illustrate this, we will consider the deliberative arguments that develop in an instance of policy analysis.

Remember that the first stock issue in traditional policy analysis concerned the existence of a problem or the identification of an *ill*. Locating and demonstrating the existence of an ill—or refuting the existence of an ill that has been argued by your opponent—generates several questions:

- How many people are affected by the problem?
- How are they affected?
- To what extent are they affected?
- How are these effects manifested?
- What are the likely consequences of these effects?

Such questions get at the heart of the stock issue of ill. If you are trying to convince an audience that the status quo needs to be changed, you will want to show them the nature and extent of the problem. After all, there is no sense in changing the status quo if the problem is not a significant one. Evidence that directly answers such questions as those listed above should be recorded.

The second stock issue is *blame*. This issue concerns the cause of the problem and why our current policies may be inadequate. Some questions to consider here include:

- What is the main cause of the problem?
- Why are other potential causes unimportant?
- What is the status quo policy toward this problem?
- Why is this policy inadequate?
- Why have presumably "good" people tolerated the existence of this problem?
- Can the status quo policy be saved with minor changes?

The third stock issue is *cure*. This deals with whether or not the proposal would solve or ameliorate the problem. Questions like the following appear relevant:

- What specifically should the agent of change do?
- Who should initiate the change in order to secure the best results?
- What proof is there that a new policy would work better than the status quo?
- Has the proposed new policy been tried elsewhere? With what results?
- Would the new policy meet with likely resistance? How might such resistance be overcome?

Finally, consider the stock issue of *cost*. Remember, this issue asks the question, "Are there any disadvantages to the proposal that might outweigh the advantages?" Search for and record evidence that addresses questions such as the following:

- Will the proposed solution cause any new problems?
- Will the proposed solution exacerbate any existing problems?
- Will the proposed solution delay some other desired outcome?
- Is the proposal ethical?
- What is the likelihood that there will be some other unintended consequences?
- How much will the proposed solution cost and what sacrifices will be required to cover those costs?

Recalling the requirements of the various stock issues will help guide your research and help you to discover how to best support your arguments. Now you need to consider how to make your arguments as convincing and compelling as possible.

What Is Likely to Gain Adherence

In order to make your arguments as effective and as convincing as possible, you need to think about the audience that you will address and the argumentation field in which your arguments will be considered. Merely having the relevant facts may not be enough to assure that you have made a convincing case, since facts are subject to interpretation. You must not only secure the evidence necessary to gain adherence, you must also make sure it and the supporting materials persuade your audience to embrace your perspective or beliefs. From a narrative perspective, this means finding evidence that helps you to frame your story in such a way so the actors, the events, and the scene that you describe are vivid, compelling, and seem to match up with your audience's worldviews.

If, for example, your story depicts government public servants as loyal, competent, conscientious, and even heroic, you must find evidence that supports these characterizations. If, on the other hand, your story depicts government public servants as inattentive, uncaring, insensitive, incompetent, or even malicious, then evidence that supports these views is required. Similarly, the data you use as the foundation for you portrayal of the events and of the scene should reflect and support the narrative construction that you are creating. Quotations can be particularly effective, for the language of the authority may embody the label you wish to depict.

In addition, remember the importance of *examples* and *analogies*, which we have already discussed (see chapter 6). Not only do they serve as proof, they also make the argument more comprehensible to your audience. Consequently, it is useful to record examples and analogies you find compelling. You will probably convey them in your own words, so it won't be necessary to record them verbatim, but you will wish to acknowledge the source of this information. To do so will enhance your credibility and also protect you from the charge that you may have plagiarized the work of others.

When we discussed examples we noted that a single example might not be found typical of the set of other possible examples. Even a few examples might lead to a hasty generalization. *Statistics*, the numeric expression of examples, reduce the likelihood of such errors. So it is best to record statistics that show the extent of the point that you are trying to make. Nevertheless, statistics alone are rather cold and might not move an audience, therefore it is useful to combine them with examples. Examine your readings to see if there are statistics and examples that you can combine to make more compelling arguments. Then you can, not only illustrate your claims, but also clarify them. Keep in mind that with statistics it is often desirable to tell an audience how the statistics were gathered and by whom, so you should record this information as well.

Authoritative opinions can also be compelling. Examine what your experts have said. A concise quotation that directly supports a point that you are trying to make can be very effective, especially if the audience is likely to respect the source as an authority that is well qualified to make such a statement and free from potential conflict of interest. Thus, as a reminder, it is important to record the qualifications of your sources.

Be careful when recording quotations that you also include more information than just the author's conclusions. The reasoning that the author uses to develop his or her arguments is as important as the final conclusion that he or she reached. Audiences may find the reasoning compelling even in those cases where they might reject a one-sentence conclusion from the same author. After all, the reasoning reveals the author's analysis and argumentation. Merely quoting the author's concluding claims assumes that the audience will be convinced by the author's credibility alone. Perhaps they will, but a knowledgeable advocate would probably hedge that bet by including the author's reasons for advancing the claim.

Finally, when selecting data to record, be sure to consider the tests of data that we presented in chapter 7. Audiences, and opposing arguers, will be far more likely to listen respectfully and even to grant adherence to data that passes these rigorous tests.

In summary, we think the best advice is to think of the kind of claims that you will need to advance to make your arguments convincing. Then, go out and find the data that directly demonstrate that your claims are indeed well founded.

ORGANIZING YOUR ADVOCACY

Even the best arguments will fail if an audience cannot understand or make sense of them. That is why it is important that you construct your advocacy carefully. Part of this certainly entails making lucid and succinct claims. It also entails discovering relevant and convincing evidence. But even good arguments must be well organized if they are to move audiences.

Exactly how you choose to organize your arguments will depend on several factors: the occasion, the audience, your subject, and your own personal communication style. Each of these factors constrains advocates, and thus each will be discussed in turn.

The Occasion

Some occasions, circumstances, or situations lend themselves to structured arguments, others do not. Clearly, in the middle of an interpersonal discussion, it might be inappropriate to launch into an extended monologue advocating a specific point of view. Even in public speaking situations, which lend themselves to prepared addresses, there may be times when pointed advocacy is considered inappropriate. For example, we recently heard a commencement speaker who received distinctly mixed reviews because rather than focusing his remarks on the achievements of the graduating class or the ceremonial occasion, he devoted his time to arguing for a change in the way the city was administered. He might have been successful in making city governance a focus for his speech that day had he, for example, talked about the role that the graduates and those of their generation could play in making political reforms. However, he seemed to misunderstand his occasion, and as a result, he made arguments that failed to meet the demands of the situation or to respond to the expectations of his audience.

Two academic theorists have had much to say about the nature of rhetorical situations and the expectations of audiences. Lloyd Bitzer argued that a rhetorical situation not only invited utterance, it invited a particular kind of utterance, an utterance that genuinely met the audience's expectations and fit that situation.[3] A similar view was developed by Burke, who declared that appropriate rhetoric must meet the expectations of form. He then observed: "Form is the creation of an appetite in the mind of the auditor [audience], and the adequate satisfying of that appetite."[4]

The Audience

Audiences do not approach argumentative situations as blank slates. They bring with them to each new argumentative encounter a host of experiences, values, attitudes, and beliefs. Even those who are willing to suspend their judgment and give a full and impartial hearing to arguments do so from within the perspective of the value framework and the narrative experiences that have defined their lives. Advocates need to assess these perspectives in order to effectively organize their arguments.

The audience will also reveal something about the *field* of argumentation. We have already explained (see chapter 3) that the assumptions about the nature and tests of argument vary from field to field. The types of arguments expected or even demanded in one field may or may not be accepted in another. Thus, the advocate must take into consideration the field of argument embraced by the audience.

The Subject

We have identified three different types of propositions that arguers might be called upon to support: *fact, value,* and *policy.* Each type of claim will lend itself to different organizational patterns. Questions of fact generally are organized into main points, each of which constitutes the reasons why an advocate believes some statement of fact to be correct or not.

Value questions usually involve setting criteria for evaluation and arguments in support of or against the value judgment. For example, an advocate who claimed that Jack Nicholson was America's best male actor in 2004 would be required to offer two lines of argument: the first would involve establishing the criteria for selecting the best actor; and the second would demonstrate that Jack Nicholson met these criteria better than did other actors.

Finally, there are questions of policy. There are four ways policy advocates typically organize their advocacy. Each reflects a pattern of reasoning. The first method is called the **needs** (or stock issues) **case**. As you are aware, this entails organizing your arguments around the stock issues ill, blame, cure, and cost. This approach works most effectively when the advocate can clearly demonstrate that there is a significant and compelling problem, the advocate can identify who is responsible for the problem (where to place the blame), and an effective solution can be offered. An obese American population may be the problem. Changing Americans' dining habits may solve the problem. Altering how the purveyors of fast foods market their products may help change those dining habits and thus may be desirable.

A second organizational format, which stems from systems analysis, is called the **comparative advantage case**. In this approach, advocates present their policy proposal and then compare the status quo (what exists now) to what would exist after the introduction of alternative policy measures. The advocate's goal is to demonstrate whether or not the alternative policies would likely prove desirable. This organizational approach might be most effective when there are no significant and readily identifiable ills in the present system, but nonetheless, an advocate can convincingly argue that things would still be improved if the system were changed. An obese American population may be the problem. Changing Americans' dining habits may solve the problem. Educating persons to make better food choices might change their habits. Providing accurate and easy-to-use labels on the foods they purchase might help to educate people and influence their purchasing habits.

A third approach is a variant of the comparative advantage case called the *goals case*. With this approach, the advocate attempts to convince the audience that they share a commitment to a particular goal (helping people to lead long and healthy lives, for example). If the advocate can convince the audience that his or her proposal has a better change of achieving that goal than does the status quo alone, then the audience will be more likely to find the case compelling.

A fourth organizational pattern used by policy advocates is called the *criteria case*. When audiences agree that a problem exists (or when the advocate can convince them that a problem exists), but when they disagree as to what to do about the problem, the advocate may choose to present and defend specific criteria to guide them to the appropriate course of action. The criteria may be fairly self-evident: the new policy should be reasonably inexpensive, easily administered, and likely to be successful. Or, the criteria may be complex. For example, policies to change Americans' eating habits could focus on: educating consumers about viable choices, the costs of food, setting limits on portion sizes, the exposure to advertising, and food labeling.

Once an advocate establishes criteria, he or she then presents the policy that best meets the criteria. This organizational pattern entails three main points: a review of the existing problem, the presentation of criteria to judge the scope of the problem and potential solutions, and the application of the criteria to the specific policy (or policies) now proposed.

SUMMARY

In this chapter we have argued that research is an important component of the argumentation process and we have attempted to equip you with the basic skills of research to support sound claims. We began by defining the research process and urged you to construct a research plan. We then recommended that you begin with general sources and move on to more specialized materials. Next we considered what you should research and how to go about conducting research. We also identified the elements of full citations and advised you to consider, as you undertook your research, what you must prove in order to gain the adherence of your audience to your arguments. The final section of the chapter focused on how best to organize your claims.

Key Terms

comparative advantage case
criteria case
general sources
goals case

needs case
research
research plan
specialized sources

Activities

1. Select a controversy that you wish to research. Construct a research plan. Be sure to indicate what sources you will consult for each step of the plan, identifying your intentions to conduct both general and specific research.

2. Make a list of key terms and synonyms that you will use to conduct a survey of the controversy that you have selected.

3. Find an article, book, or essay relevant to your research using each of the following:

   a. The *Readers' Guide to Periodical Literature*

   b. The card catalog (it may be computerized)

   c. A newspaper index

   d. An index to scholarly journals

   e. A legal or government index

   f. The Internet

4. Record the full source citation and text of a quotation drawn from each of the sources that you found in question three.

5. Find a policy argument presented in an argument artifact and attempt to reorganize the advocacy using the four policy organizational formats provided in this chapter: needs case, comparative advantage case, goals case, and criteria case.

Recommended Readings

Chesebro, James W. "Beyond the Orthodox: The Criteria Case." *Journal of the American Forensic Association* 7 (1971): 208–215.

Chesebro, James W. "The Comparative Advantages Case." *Journal of the American Forensic Association* 5 (1968): 57–63.

Dresser, William R. "The Impact of Evidence on Decision Making." *Journal of the American Forensic Association* 3 (1966): 43–47.

Lewinski, John D., Bruce R. Metzler, and Peter L. Settle. "The Goal Case Affirmative: An Alternative Approach to Academic Debate." *Journal of the American Forensic Association* 9 (1973): 458–463.

Kruger, Arthur N. "The Comparative Advantage Case: A Disadvantage." *Journal of the American Forensic Association* 3 (1966): 104–111.

Mann, Thomas. *The Oxford Guide to Library Research.* London: Oxford University Press, 1998.

Newman, Robert P., and Dale R. Newman. *Evidence.* Boston: Houghton-Mifflin, 1969.

Smith, Craig R., and David M. Hunsaker. *The Bases of Argument: Ideas in Conflict.* Indianapolis: Bobbs-Merrill, 1972.

Zarefsky, David. "The Traditional Case—Comparative Advantage Case Dichotomy: Another Look." *Journal of the American Forensic Association* 6 (1969): 12–20.

Notes

[1] A number of scholars have commented on the influence of the printing press on the communication process. See, for example, Marshall McLuhan, *The Gutenberg Galaxy* (Toronto: University of Toronto Press, 1962).

[2] Neil Postman, *Amusing Ourselves to Death* (New York: Penguin, 1985), 21.

[3] Lloyd F. Bitzer, "The Rhetorical Situation," *Philosophy and Rhetoric* 1 (1968): 1–14.

[4] Kenneth Burke, *Counter-statement* (Berkeley: University of California Press, 1931, rpt. 1968), 31.

9

REFUTING ARGUMENTS

All of us, from time to time, find ourselves inclined to disagree with some statement that is uttered by another individual. We might be engaged in a discussion around a conference table or a kitchen table; we could be in the boardroom or a bedroom, a living room or a classroom. When such moments of disagreement occur, we must make a decision about whether or not we should voice our disagreement. Is the disagreement worth pursuing? Or, would we be better served to keep silent? If we conclude that it is worthwhile to express our disagreement, we then have to give consideration to how we might best formulate and present our arguments. Unfortunately, even the best arguments that we can muster to support our convictions might not be adequate to convince others to agree with our views. They may be persuaded, however, if in addition to presenting our own views we simultaneously point out the weaknesses in their claims. This process is called *refutation*.

Even when we are not actually engaged in direct conversations with other advocates we may automatically, and almost instinctively, be subjecting the advocacy offered by others to similar refutational processes. Why? Because it is natural for us to critically evaluate the claims that others offer for our consideration. Humans are not sheep that can be led wherever or whenever another person wishes to lead them. Humans are actors; we have choice over our actions; and, as actors, we naturally evaluate the claims advanced by others because we have learned that the uncritical acceptance of advocacy directed our way can lead to undesirable consequences. So we scrutinize the messages we receive. Some we accept, others we reject. Understanding the refutation process will enable you to more carefully evaluate the arguments that you personally

159

encounter, and it will give you the tools to identify why you reject a claim, should you agree to verbalize your objections.

In this chapter we will first, define the refutation process. Then we will systematically guide you through the steps necessary to critically evaluate an argument, formulate a response, and verbally present your refutation.

THE REFUTATION PROCESS DEFINED

To refute an argument is to deny its validity and refuse to agree with it. The *refutation process*, therefore, is a series of actions culminating in the denial of an argument advanced by another. It is not simply attacking another's argument, instead, it is figuring out an appropriate strategy to develop and organize a response to another's claim. Refutation may occur to written or to oral arguments. In this discussion, however, we will primarily focus on refutation aimed at oral arguments. We believe that the refutation of an oral argument involves four steps:

1. listening in a focused way
2. critically evaluating the arguments
3. formulating a response
4. presenting that response

FOCUSED LISTENING (STEP ONE)

Listening versus Hearing

Have you ever had a conversation where you remember hearing the other person speak but you cannot recall what was actually said? Of course you have. Odds are good that this has happened in a classroom. You were hearing a lecture, but not really tuned in to what was being said. This is a case where you were hearing but not listening. Hearing is passive. We have no control over it. Surely at some time or another you have been stuck in a car or a small room where someone has tuned the radio to a station that is playing annoying music. Try as you might, blocking out the noise is almost impossible. We cannot choose not to hear. But listening is active. It requires concentration or focus. This applies in reading too. If you ever find yourself rereading something because you do not remember what you just read, it could be because you lost your concentration. There are several reasons why people may be considered poor listeners.

Factors Affecting Listening

Selective Exposure

Psychologists tell us that we seek out discourse (in either written or oral forms) with which we agree and that we avoid discourse with which we do not agree. It is more cognitively comforting to be reinforced in our own opinions and thinking by the other messages that we confront. Consequently, we may not even expose ourselves to messages that we believe will be contrary to our beliefs. For example, liberals probably do not tune in to Rush Limbaugh.

Distortion

If we are exposed to messages that we disagree with, the experience can often be unsettling. Since we prefer not to be unsettled, our minds may help us by distorting the message into something that we find more palatable. We may also distort messages because we anticipate the rest of a message before actually hearing it in in its entirety. Did you notice that the word *in* was repeated in the prior sentence? Some readers will have skipped right over the repeated word because they anticipated the end of the sentence. We can distort advocates' arguments the same way—by thinking we know what they are going to say prior to their actually saying it.

Intrapersonal Argument

Another common human reaction when hearing something is to turn our attention away from the discourse to a discussion occurring within our own heads. When we argue with ourselves or focus on what we are going to say, instead of attending to the comments being offered by someone else, we are not doing a very good job of listening.

Externalities

Distractions can also prevent us from being good listeners. Noise draws our attention away from what is being said. Many different things can constitute such noise. For example, it could be a whirring fan in the background, or the sound of freeway noise, or perhaps the annoying couple behind you talking all through a film. But you can also think of "noise" in a different sense. Noise could also be the very attractive person who walks by and suddenly steals your attention, or even the smell of the potato chips that the person sitting next to you is eating in class. Any external factor that draws your attention may diminish your ability to be an effective listener.

Internalities

Just as external factors can interfere with your reception of messages, internal factors can distract you too. If you are not feeling well that day, perhaps you have a headache or an upset stomach, you will not be as good a listener. If you did not get a restful sleep, you will not be as effective a listener. If you are upset about something, it might distract you and cause you not to be a good listener. Sometimes the person who is arguing with you will, intentionally or unintentionally, manage to hit your "hot buttons." "Hot buttons" are those sensitive, psychological points that whenever they are mentioned they invariably upset you. It sometimes seems that relatives, and especially siblings, are adept at hitting those buttons, and they seem to know just what to say to get us riled up—a skill no doubt derived from years of practice! But when we react emotionally to these triggers, we lose our ability to listen effectively.

So the first step in effective listening is to attend to the discourse so that you can comprehend it and understand exactly what it is that the advocate is arguing. But active listening is only half of the task of being an effective listener. You also have to develop your critical ear. A critical ear is one that is intently listening in order to identify the potential flaws or weaknesses in the arguments advanced by other advocates.

CRITICALLY EVALUATING ARGUMENTS (STEP TWO)

In this text, we have been trying to teach you to be skeptical of the advocacy advanced by others. Many of the issues presented in this book come together in the refutation process. Listening actively is a good start, but it is only a start. The product of active listening is accurate reception of the other person's argumentation—correctly hearing what the other person has said. But you will still be faced with the need to evaluate the message that you received.

Determining What the Advocate Is Arguing

To evaluate another's arguments you should begin by trying to determine what it is that the other individual is actually arguing. Sometimes this is not as easy as it sounds.

Some advocates just do not argue well. As a result, they can be very difficult to follow. Others may deliberately try to conceal their objectives. The intentional attempt to disguise or conceal one's real argument may be considered *obfuscation*. There are at least two reasons why an advocate might resort to obfuscation: to be kind or to be tricky.

Advocates may deliberately use language that is not explicit because they wish to shield the listener from unnecessary pain or discomfort. One way this is accomplished is through the use of euphemisms. A *euphemism* is a mild or inoffensive term that can be used in place of language that might offend or suggest something unpleasant. A friend of ours described an interesting example. She taught her three-year-old son that when he went to dinner at someone else's house, if he did not care for the food that was served, he should tell the hostess that it was "interesting." All seemed to be going fine. The child was served a cooked vegetable and without prompting declared it to be "interesting." Then he brightly looked up and told the hostess: "When I say something is interesting, that means I don't like it!" The child had sort of mastered the art of using a euphemism. What he had not yet learned is that euphemisms generally work best if you leave it to the listener to decode their meaning.

There are many examples, such as the one above, where language is used euphemistically to achieve relatively benign purposes. Think of the language used to refer to someone who is dying: people pass away, they go to a better place, they leave this earth, they move on, or they go to sleep. Such terms are intended to soften the impact of declaring that someone is dead.

Cultures also have many names given for what individuals do in bathrooms. Some printable examples include: powdering one's nose, going to the john, freshening up, and answering the call of nature. Indeed, the entire process of using the proper language to excuse yourself from a group so that you can perform natural bodily functions that everyone else in the group also has to perform is part of a cultural ritual.

At other times language may be used perniciously to confuse or conceal. This type of language is called *doublespeak*. The use of doublespeak is especially common in times of war. Prisoners of war, for example, might be called "detainees" rather than prisoners. Innocent civilians who are killed might be referred to as "collateral damage." Indeed, the weapons of war themselves may be referred to as "patriot missiles," "smart bombs," "peacekeepers," or "Minutemen." Such names are important because they symbolically distance us from the acts of violence that may be conducted in our name when we go off to war.[1] Doublespeak is the strategic use of language to conceal meaning. "Taxes" become "revenue enhancements." Workers are not "laid off," they are "transitioned," or they accept "voluntary severance."

There are at least two specific ways in which language can conceal.

Ambiguity

When advocates deliberately employ language that is overly broad or unclear, they are utilizing *ambiguity*. Such a situation may result in our having only a vague understanding of what it is that they are actually advocating. Politicians who wish to avoid alienating voters often speak so vaguely that what they say is almost indecipherable. For example, support for "family values" is a popular political battle cry. But what does that expression really mean? Different political candidates have, of course, given the term different meanings. Does it mean opposition to abortion rights? Does it mean support for paid family leave to take care of sick relatives? Does it mean after-school programs for children? Does it mean welfare reforms that make it harder for unwed mothers to move out on their own and get their own apartments? Does it mean requiring the V-chip in television sets so that parents can prevent their children from seeing violence on television? Does it mean encouraging "stay at home" moms? Does it mean subsidized day-care centers? Does it mean taking a position either in favor of or in opposition to same-sex marriages? Obviously, the term "family values" can mean many different things to many different people, some of which seem to advance a liberal political agenda and others a conservative agenda.

Equivocation

Making the same stance take on two different meanings at different times is *equivocation*. For example, political candidates may equivocate so that different audiences assign different meanings to roughly the same words. In this fashion, they try to ensure that potential voters are not alienated from their candidacies by the strong stands they might take. As an illustration, former Governor Gray Davis of California frequently asserted how "tough" he was on crime and criminals. His "toughness" was illustrated during his 2002 reelection campaign when he declared his opposition to legislation that would permit illegal aliens in the state the right to get drivers licenses. Davis was not responsive at the time to arguments that said permitting the two million illegal immigrants the right to get drivers licenses would permit them to secure proper training, insurance, and the opportunity to safely move back and forth to work. He declared that it would be wrong to permit persons who were in the United States illegally to secure legal documents affirming their residency. The governor also warned that easier access to the licenses might make it easier for terrorists to move about in the state.

One year later, faced with the prospect of a recall election, Governor Davis announced his enthusiastic support for a bill that would permit undocumented aliens to get drivers licenses. Now he argued that if the Department of Motor Vehicles' files contained photographs, thumbprints, and addresses of illegal immigrants, it would be easier to find immigrants who may have committed crimes. Again this position can be offered as evidence that the governor was "tough" on crime. The governor's office also issued a statement declaring that the governor had not changed his mind in response to the upcoming recall election or because the bill was endorsed by organized labor (a constituency that was very important to his campaign).[2] While opponents of the bill complained that the governor's change of mind illustrated that he was "willing to sacrifice the very lives of law-abiding Americans and legal residents in exchange for [Latino] votes to stay in office," the sponsor of the bill argued that it showed that the governor recognized "that on national security and national traffic safety issues, this is good policy."[3]

Did the governor intentionally deceive the voters of California about his true position on this issue in 2002 when he was attempting to appeal to centrist and Republican voters? Did the Governor cynically change his position on the issue in 2003 when he felt the need to mobilize his political base within the Democratic Party to defeat the recall effort? Or did he actually change his mind and/or allow his position on this issue to evolve in response to new arguments presented in support of the bill? Advocates who equivocate may use language that purposely confuses or hides their real motivations. In such cases, it may be necessary to ask questions of the advocate and to read between the lines. You should also look for cues in the information that is available to you. Can you glean anything from your knowledge of the context for the argument? How about from your knowledge of the advocate? Do other messages that emerge at the same time shed light on what might motivate the advocate? Such analysis is an important way to critically evaluate arguments in order to better understand the advocate's intentions and goals.

Evaluating the Reasoning

We have previously discussed the reasoning process (chapter 6) and the data used to support claims (chapter 7). These are the starting points for the critical assessment of ideas that is central to the refutation process.

In chapter 6 we presented different forms of inductive and deductive reasoning. The first step in evaluating the reasoning employed by the advocate is to determine what kind of reasoning is being used and to apply the appropriate tests for that type of reasoning. Thus, examples, analogies, causal correlations, sign arguments, and causal generalizations all have appropriate tests to determine if the arguments are well reasoned and sound. If the reasoning appears to pass those tests, you should then consider the additional tests of arguments presented below. An argument that uses flawed reasoning may be considered *fallacious*, and the tests below are known as *fallacies of reasoning*.

Argument scholars have identified many examples of fallacies. While each audience, in each field, determines whether it will grant adherence to a story or not, it is useful to understand and to know how to recognize different types of fallacies. We present three categories of fallacies and offer several illustrations of each.

Fallacies of Irrelevant Reasoning

Some advocates base their claims on what most argument scholars consider irrelevant reasons. We identify seven.

1. **Ad populum.** If an advocate attempts to prove a claim is correct by arguing that most people agree with that claim, the advocate is committing the *ad populum* (appealing to the people) fallacy. For example, poll data may indicate that the majority of Americans believe that public schools fail to do a good job in educating students. Yet, for an advocate to offer this poll data as proof that public schools are failing may be fallacious. The majority could be wrong. It is much more important to know why people may believe that the schools are failing. What are their reasons? When these reasons for the public perceptions are presented, they can be examined like any other reasons. Simply because a majority believes something is true does not make it correct. Majorities once believed the world was flat, that slavery was morally acceptable, and that kings were divinely chosen. Now, these beliefs have not only been rejected, they would not even be given a moment's consideration by contemporary audiences.

2. **Ad hominem.** We recall hearing a friend providing dietary advice to a colleague. The colleague later rejected the advice. He justified dismissing the generally sound advice about avoiding certain kinds of fats because the friend who provided it to him was himself overweight. Does the friend's own weight problem invalidate his argument?

   If an advocate argues that an idea should be rejected and offers as justification, not something wrong with the idea, but something wrong with the person presenting the idea, he or she is engaging in **ad hominem** (attacking the person). Even the worst person—someone who lacks good judgment or good character—can have a good idea. You should seek to argue about the merits of the claim that is offered and not just the qualities of the source. We are not arguing that as an advocate you should ignore the credibility of a source or the integrity of an advocate. We do believe, however, that the validity of *ad hominem* arguments may vary from field to field, but that advocates should never presume that it is sufficient to refute an argument only by attacking its source.

3. **Appeal to pity.** On rare occasions the only basis for a claim will be a statement intended to provoke pity. When the claim calls for compassion, pity may be a relevant reason. For example, audiences might be justifiably moved to act on the basis of an argument that produces pity for children who could be denied life-saving medicines or surgery because their parents lack the means to pay for treatment. On the other hand, a student who attempts to petition a teacher for a higher grade on an examination on the basis of an appeal to pity is not making a very strong claim.

4. **Appeal to fear.** The threat "your money or your life" relies on fear to convince someone to agree to hand over his or her cash. Such appeals do not provide real choice, and thus they are not really reasons for agreement—even if they are sometimes successful in gaining compliance.

5. **Tu quoque.** Defending one's actions by pointing out that others acted in a similar fashion is not really an appropriate or sufficient defense (*tu quoque* means you're another). Thus if you are pulled over for speeding a judge will not likely be persuaded by a defense that says others were also speeding so it is unfair for you to have been the one detained. The fact that others were violating the speed limit too does not invalidate the charge against you.

6. **Appeal to tradition.** Because something has always been done a particular way may or may not be a good reason to continue to do it that way. Determining whether it is appropriate to do something in the way it has customarily been done requires an evaluation of the reasons. For example, a congressman argued that the United States should hold elections on Saturdays instead of Tuesdays in order to increase voter turnout. He reasoned that since more people were off work on Saturdays they would be more likely to cast their vote. Another congressman, who opposed increasing voter turnout (probably because his own candidacy and perhaps his party was advantaged by lower turnout), argued that the United States has always voted on Tuesdays and thus always should so do. Although there may be other good reasons not to change the day on which Americans cast their ballots, merely invoking tradition is probably an insufficient reason not to more fully consider alternatives.

7. **Slippery slope.** If you have ever started down an ice-covered hill, you have experienced how difficult it is to stop your momentum once it starts. As you gain momentum, you run the risk of not stopping and/or becoming injured. When an advocate objects to something not because it is itself undesirable but because it may eventually lead to something else that is undesirable, the advocate is recalling this experience. For example, some conservatives have opposed extending civil liberties to gays (including the recent court decisions striking down laws that uniquely prohibited sodomy between persons of the same sex) because they believed that any court actions acknowledging the rights of gays would inevitably lead to a legal protection for gay marriages. To return again to the case of the ice-covered hill, while it may be difficult to stop, it is almost always possi-

ble to stop. This illustrates that the slippery slope claim is a fallacy. One can almost always take an action that may be desirable without causing other undesirable outcomes to follow. Therefore, an arguably undesirable but not inevitable outcome (and we want to make clear that we do not believe gay marriage would be an undesirable outcome) does not constitute a compelling reason to reject an otherwise desirable idea.

Fallacies of Miscasting the Issue

Sometimes advocates commit errors in reasoning by casting the dispute in fallacious terms. We present three such fallacies.

1. **Fallacy of composition.** This fallacy is committed when an advocate argues that what is true of the parts is also true of the whole. For example, we recently heard someone argue that the faculties of the state university system were creative in dealing with problems and thus the budget cuts that were being proposed would not be devastating to students. The fact, that faculties had developed the capacity to make do with less, however commendable that may be, does not suggest that the entire university system would be creative or that individual students would not suffer from cuts that decreased the number of classes available to them, increased average class sizes, and shrunk budgets for library acquisitions and student aid.

2. **Fallacy of division.** This fallacy is the reverse of the fallacy of composition. The advocate who claims that what is true of the whole must be true of the individual parts is committing the fallacy of division. For example, a U.S. Army unit serving in Iraq was accused of having badly mistreated Iraqi civilians who had been arrested as suspected terrorists. The military commander responded to the complaint by asserting that the case must not be true because the U.S. military was committed to discipline and to treating prisoners in accordance with established laws of war. It may, of course, be true that institutionally the military is committed to discipline and to protecting the rights of detainees, but this does not mean that all individual soldiers are similarly committed. Thus such an assertion does not deny that this case of abuse may have occurred.

3. **Fallacy of false dichotomy.** Life is rarely all black or all white. There often are gray areas. An advocate who casts an argument in either/or terms may be falsely dichotomizing the issue. On September 20, 2001, President George W. Bush declared "war on terrorism" by asserting that nations could decide to be either "with us or with the terrorists."[4] Many Americans seemed to take the president at his word; when our long-time allies, the French, German, and Canadian governments, declined to support U.S. military intervention in Iraq there were loud public protests and opposition to their disloyalty. Indeed, American tourism to these nations steeply declined, and there were even attempts to boycott imports from these nations. Nonetheless, the argument that opposition to an American incursion into Iraq constituted support for terrorism was not very well reasoned or compelling, at least if viewed from a perspective less infused with patriotic emotion.

Fallacies of Misdirecting the Issue

The final category of fallacies concerns those occasions when advocates avoid proving their own claims by distracting the audience.

1. **Shifting the burden of proof.** Instead of proving their own claim, some advocates challenge audiences to disprove the claim. "There is no end to the universe, and I challenge you to prove that there is!" Perhaps the claim is true. But the advocate who advances the claim has the responsibility to prove it. There is no burden to rebut an unproven claim.

2. **Begging the question.** An advocate who essentially restates his or her claim and offers it as the only reason in support of the claim is guilty of begging the question. "I think I should have received an A on this paper," said a student. When asked why, the student said, "Because it is an A paper." The student's reason is the same as the claim. The argument has thus not been advanced or supported. Had the student given some data, or offered some arguments, such as: the paper was thorough, well researched, carefully organized, clear, coherent, and well written, then there would have been reasons offered in support of the claim.

3. **Straw man fallacy.** It is not difficult to knock over a man made of straw. Nor is it particularly difficult to refute an opponent's argument if you get to present your claim in an unfair fashion. Some advocates, for example, have attacked arguments for reforming the health-care delivery system in the United States by calling such proposals attempts to offer socialized medicine. Then they move to attack socialized medicine. Yet for the most part, these advocates fail to argue how the proposed policies equate with the notion of "socialized medicine"; they fail to delineate specific objections to the new proposal; and they therefore fail to refute the arguments for the new system on their merits. The result is often that they have attacked a straw man in order to divert attention from a substantive analysis of the actual proposal. This constitutes a form of fallacious reasoning.

In each of the foregoing fallacies the reasoning offered is flawed, and as a result, the argument is a ***non sequitur***, which means that the conclusion does not follow from the claim.

Once you have subjected the reasoning offered in support of a claim to critical scrutiny, it is time to turn your attention to the advocate's narrative and to the grounds or evidence offered.

Evaluating the Narrative and the Grounds

In chapter 4 we considered how advocates use language to construct their arguments. We specifically discussed the elements of a narrative: actors, scene, and events. With each, we discussed what constituted effective argument. As the audience of another's argument you should also carefully examine these depictions. Analyze how the advocate depicts these narrative elements. Are the characterizations fitting? Are they consistent? Are there alternative and more appropriate constructions? Similarly, if the advocate employs a metaphor, the critical consumer will want to evaluate whether this particular metaphor is appropriate. Are there weaknesses in the comparisons it makes?

In chapter 8 we presented four types of data that advocates use to support their arguments: premises, examples, statistics, and testimony. We also identified ways in which you can test the data to see whether audiences will consider it compelling. Now we will discuss strategies for refuting the data.

FORMULATING A RESPONSE (STEP THREE)

Once you have discovered what it is that an advocate has said, and evaluated the discourse to determine whether the argument is faulty or not, you must determine how you wish to respond. If the argument is not faulty, you may find that you actually agree with it. If, on the other hand, you find that you still disagree with an argument, you must decide on the most appropriate manner to express that disagreement.

Sometimes the best response to an argument is to offer no response at all. In some cases an opposing advocate's argument may be so weak that it falls on its face and does not even merit a response. On other occasions, the price that you might pay by engaging in an argument may be too great. Individuals who continually find fault with the advocacy advanced by others are considered argumentative. Most people prefer not to associate with argumentative people. Thus, we urge you to choose your arguments carefully. Once you do decide to refute an argument, you must develop a strategy that best expresses your opposition and that best exposes the weaknesses in the opposing arguments.

Strategy

Your first decision at this point is to determine which of your opponent's arguments you believe to be most vulnerable to refutation. It is likely that not all of your adversary's arguments are faulty, but even if they were, you might not wish to spend the time and energy required to attack them all. Your choice of which arguments you will oppose will vary from situation to situation, with the nature of the arguments advanced, and in response to your insights about the audience for your claims.

If you are engaging in interpersonal argument then you may have little time to present your views before you are interrupted. In such circumstances, you would probably be wise to decide what the most critical point is and start there. If you are engaging in an audience debate, you may have more time and you may be able to advance a number of objections. So, consider the situation you are in when choosing your strategy.

You should also consider the nature of the dispute. Is this a disagreement over a claim of fact, value, or policy? The stock issues for each kind of dispute are fairly well established (see chapter 5), and you may choose which of them you wish to dispute. Policy advocates, for example, must convince neutral audiences that there is a problem with the status quo, that the current policies cannot solve the problem, that the proposed policy will solve the problem, and that there are no significant disadvantages to the new proposal. If you are attempting to refute a policy argument using this approach you can choose which of these stock issues you will address. You need not refute them all. There is no reason to adopt a new policy if the existing problems that have been identified are really not all that significant (ill), if the new policy that has been advanced will not be likely to solve the ill(s) identified (cure), or if the current mechanisms already in place will ultimately be able to remedy the problem (blame). Selecting the point of stasis is an important component of strategic planning.

Finally, take into consideration the values and beliefs of the audience. The field of argument determines the standards for what constitutes good evidence. Arguments that might work in a legal context, accusations of hearsay evidence, for example, might be irrelevant in interpersonal argument situations. Further, the values of the audience will certainly influence the efficacy of your argumentation. You may believe that capital punishment is immoral, but knowing your audience does not share this belief should influence the way in which you choose to construct your arguments.

Tactics

Having decided what arguments you wish to refute, you must now go about the business of refutation. You still face some strategic choices that could influence the effectiveness of your arguments.

Refutation by Denial

Sometimes an advocate seems completely wrong. He or she makes a statement that you believe cannot be supported. As an illustration, we cite the claim that one of our students made: "There are absolutely no significant ideological differences between Democrats and Republicans." If you believe someone has made a statement that cannot be supported, you are justified in selecting a strategy of denial. This entails attempting to prove that the conclusion(s) offered by that advocate is erroneous. Such a strategy will, in all likelihood, necessitate that you have material that supports your opposite conclusion. But such supporting material alone may not be sufficient. Your opponent and your audience should not be left with contradictory arguments without also having a basis for determining which conclusion is the better one.

To be successful in refutation by denial you must be able to account for why the two conclusions conflict and why the conclusion that you prefer is indeed the more compelling one. Perhaps you can point out how the opposing advocate has made erroneous assumptions in constructing his or her argument. Or, perhaps the evidence that you present in support of your argument can be demonstrated to be superior. Or, there may be cases in which you discover that this argument advanced by the other advocate contradicts some other claim that the advocate previously offered. It certainly strengthens your argument if you can offer a convincing case for deciding why the view that you are espousing is superior. In the case of the example above, you might want to select two or three very concrete issues that illustrate the significant differences between the ideological commitments of the Democratic and Republican parties.

Refutation by Mitigation

The effect of refutation by mitigation is to minimize the impact of the advocacy you wish to undermine. Perhaps the other advocate has, in your mind, exaggerated the claims that he or she has made. Maybe the reasoning offered is dubious, the characterizations are spurious, or the evidence that has been provided is questionable. In any case, it is doubtful that these arguments alone will convince the advocate or an undecided audience that the advocate is completely wrong. At best such refutation will diminish the strength of the advocate's claims, but some probative argumentative force will probably remain. Thus, the strategy of mitigation must be used in conjunction with other arguments.

Refutation by Additional Consideration

The opposing advocate may also offer arguments that you find are both logically correct and convincing, in which case it may not be possible for you to either deny or mitigate the advocate's position. This does not leave you without recourse, however, for you might still be able to identify ways in which the advocate's reasoning may be incomplete. We will consider two possibilities.

Reducing the Argument to Absurdity. The Latin term for this is *reductio ad absurdum*. With this tact you attempt to take the opposing advocate's reasoning to its logical conclusion, which hopefully reveals how it is flawed.

Consider the arguments that may have been advanced for the legalization of cocaine. One reason that has been advanced by those who support this position is the claim that laws forbidding the use and sale of drugs are unenforceable. You might oppose this argument by noting that the assumption of this claim is that if a law cannot be enforced it should be abandoned. Indeed then, any law that seems to have been frequently violated is a law that might by this standard appears unenforceable. Should this reasoning then logically extend to laws against speeding, drunk driving, assault, or even murder? Examining the advocate's reasoning this closely may illustrate the faulty assumption of the argument—that the inability to adequately enforce a law means that the behavior that it prohibits should be legalized.

Turning the Tables. It is possible that the advocate is correct, as far as the reasoning goes, but the consequences he or she opposes are actually desirable. In academic debate this type of argument is called a *turnaround*. It simply means taking a negative position and turning it into a positive, or taking a positive position and demonstrating how it is really a negative one.

Suppose an advocate argues that some policy might have adverse consequences for the U.S. economy. For example, an advocate might claim that failure to resolve the conflict in the Middle East might lead to escalating and unstable oil prices that could damage the prospects for long-term economic growth. The opposing advocate, however, could argue that gasoline prices in the United States are actually too low—much lower, for example, than the prices paid by Europeans. These low prices, it could then be argued, have encouraged wasteful practices such as people driving to work alone, the purchase of gas guzzling sport utility vehicles, and the use of energy-inefficient appliances. Higher oil prices, on the other hand, might lead to conservation, might encourage the development of new and efficient mass transit systems, and might also improve the quality of our air and water. It could even be argued that higher oil prices might make it more possible for our economy to grow at a somewhat slower but more sustainable level that would improve economic conditions over the long term.

Preparation for Refutation

Deciding on the strategy and tactics that you wish to use will be much easier if you have had the opportunity to prepare for the refutation process. While preparation is unlikely in the case of interpersonal arguments, it is possible to be prepared in more formal situations, that is, in fields like debate, in the case of an academic or scientific dispute, or in a legal dispute. In such situations you should anticipate what your opponent might argue and prepare for different contingencies: consider the stock issues that need to be addressed. Gather your supporting materials ahead of time. These materials may be prepared in the form of briefs (sometimes called blocks of arguments) or organized on note cards.

Briefs are a series of arguments, claims, and the requisite supporting evidence and/or analysis organized to support a specific point of clash. A well-prepared advocate prepares for a variety of different contingencies and probably has many more briefed arguments than he or she would use in a particular dispute. For example, attorneys anticipate which witnesses the opposition might call and outline the questions that they intend to ask. They even anticipate the cross-examination of the other side and their questions to follow up that cross-examination. Debaters anticipate the arguments their opponents will raise, prepare responses, and in some cases anticipate what the opponents will say to those responses and prepare extension briefs to answer those points. (See the sample brief on p. 171.)

Presenting Your Response (Step Four)

Only when you have completed the first three steps are you really ready to present your arguments. We will now discuss two processes for refuting an advocate's arguments: declarative refutation and refutation by questioning.

Declarative Refutation

The first refutation process involves the systematic assertion of one's objections to an argument. In a well-organized, thorough, carefully reasoned manner, one "declares" a series of criticisms or beliefs that counter the opponent's arguments. There are four steps to presenting your declarative refutation arguments.

1. **Identify the point to be refuted.** You must tell the advocate and the audience what argument you wish to refute. Is it a specific point or sub-

point offered by the other advocate? Are you grouping a number of points together and responding to them collectively? Or, are you responding to the essence of their entire case?

2. **Label and signpost your refutation.** What is the essence of the point you want to make? Try to state your argument succinctly. For example, note the way the arguments are labeled in the sample brief provided below. This is the claim that you intend to offer in response to the advocate's argument, and this is what you will want the opposing advocate

---

Sample Brief

If you were to argue that "fish-farming" or what is sometimes known as aquaculture might solve the world's hunger, an opponent could argue that fish-farming is damaging to the environment and may lead to the production of fish that have high levels of toxicity. In anticipation of such an argument, you might develop a brief to refute these claims.

Responses to "fish-farming" damages the environment

1. All forms of agriculture potentially damage the environment.

   "A New Way to Feed the World," *The Economist,* August 9, 2003, 9.

   "If modern agriculture were invented today, it probably wouldn't be allowed. It pollutes the environment with pesticides, fertilisers [sic] and nutrients from feed and animal waste. Farming damages wild habitats and wildlife. And domesticated animals are stocked at high densities and pumped full of growth hormones and antibiotics, with the result that they are often unhealthily fatty compared with their wild relatives."

2. There are good and bad forms of fish-farming.

   "A New Way to Feed the World," *The Economist,* August 9, 2003, 9.

   "One of the world's most respected fisheries biologists, Daniel Pauly at the University of British Columbia, argues, naturally enough, that there are good and bad forms of aquaculture. The good forms include plant-eating fish such as tilapia—popular in America—and filter-feeding creatures such as scallops, mussels and oysters. Tilapia, he argues, could become the chicken of the sea and produce a net increase in the world's supply of fish."

3. International environmental regulation is necessary.

   "A New Way to Feed the World," *The Economist,* August 9, 2003, 9.

   "In the future, much aquaculture will occur on the high seas, beyond the boundaries of individual nation states. If fish farming starts to become a big business in international waters, it could become a big, hard to regulate and polluting industry: in other words a tragedy of the commons. Before that happens, and before large investments are made and governments feel obliged to start defending national interests, mariculture needs common international standards."

4. On balance aquaculture is desirable.

   "A New Way to Feed the World," *The Economist,* August 9, 2003, 9.

   "Aquaculture's promise is that, within the next three decades, it could produce most of the world's marine produce. At the same time it could help to alleviate poverty and food shortages in some of the world's poorest countries."

and your audience to remember, so clarity is of vital importance. If there are several points to your refutation you need to enumerate them to help your audience to identify them and keep them in mind.

3. **Support the refutation.** You have already labeled your argument, now you must fully develop it. What is your reasoning? What supporting evidence (premises, examples, statistics, or testimony) can you present to support your claim?

4. **Show the impact of the refutation(s).** What effect do your arguments have on the entire dispute? Did you win this particular argument? Did you at least mitigate or diminish the other advocate's claims? What must the advocate do in order to answer your refutation? If indeed you do believe that you have convinced your audience that you won this point, what effect does winning this particular argument exchange have on the other issues that are under dispute? Do not trust the advocate or your audience to resolve these questions on their own. They may see the outcome of the controversy differently than you do. You must provide direction for positively evaluating your arguments.

These four steps should be repeated for each point that you wish to refute. Your refutation is considered to be effective if you have convinced a neutral listener of the merits of your position.

Refutation by Questioning

Asking questions is an important part of almost all argumentative interactions. In academic debate and the law, the process by which one refutes another through the use of questioning is known as direct examination or cross-examination. Each of these fields has specialized guidelines for the process. We will present some general orientations that apply to all contexts in which arguers use questioning.

The chance to question an opponent can be very inviting. Some individuals get swept up in the process, however, and engage in tactics that undermine their credibility and likability. We encourage you to remember the golden rule and to treat the person you are questioning in the manner in which you would want to be treated yourself. Do not badger. Ask questions in a way that they can be answered and in a way that does not unfairly bias the answer (e.g., when did you stop beating your wife?). Finally, make sure that you allow the other advocate time to answer the question. Do not cut him or her off or interrupt.

Questioning can serve three important purposes. It permits you to clarify what an opponent has argued, to probe an argument so that you can expose potential weak points, and to highlight those weaknesses of which you might already be aware. This latter purpose can be very useful for setting up arguments that you will make later. It is unlikely that your opponents will concede their arguments during questioning, so concession is not a purpose that should motivate your strategy in choosing your questions or the style of your interaction.

Just as declarative refutation has several steps that you should systematically follow, so too does questioning.

1. **Identify the point about which you wish to question your opponent.** Don't merely ask questions out of the blue. Something that your opponent has said has prompted you to want an answer to your question. Tell your opponent and the audience what that point was.

2. **Ask your question succinctly.** Try to be brief. Questioning time is best not used to make lengthy speeches. The most effective questions are those that are both direct and specific. Avoid asking compound questions or questions that require elaborate preparation; they take too long to set up and may in fact cause you to be interrupted. You should also avoid asking *loaded questions*. Loaded questions direct your opponent as to how to respond, for example: "Do you support wasting millions of dollars on building a new generation of space shuttles?" No one would answer that question affirmatively. But if your opponent favors space research, he or she won't simply take such a question lying down. He or she will object to your phrasing and you will likely find that you have lost ground with your audience.

3. **Ask follow-up questions.** Only occasionally will one question accomplish all that you wish to achieve. Listen to the answer and probe it. Try to uncover its unspoken assumptions. Probe as well the characterizations and the reasoning that are implicit in the answer that you have been provided.

4. **Move on.** When you have accomplished what you wanted to accomplish you should not continue to ask questions. Just as moving on too quickly by not asking an appropriate follow-up question can prevent you from exposing the potential weaknesses in an argument, dwelling too long on a point with unnecessary and/or unproductive questions can undercut your effectiveness, distract your listeners, and waste time.

5. **Use the information you acquire.** The information you glean from questioning can help you to construct subsequent arguments. In some argumentative contexts, such as academic debate, cross-examination is only effective if the answers are used to develop arguments that are made in subsequent speeches.

Whether you present your refutation declaratively or through questioning, if you have chosen your strategy and tactics well and conveyed the refutation clearly, you will be in a position to reap the rewards of your thoroughness.

SUMMARY

In this chapter we have considered the process of refutation. We defined the refutation process as a series of actions culminating in the denial of the argument advanced by another. This process includes four specific steps: focused listening, the critical evaluation of argument, the formulation of a response, and lastly, the presentation of your points of refutation. It is our belief that those who wish to actively refute someone else's claims, and those who merely intend to become critical consumers of argument, benefit from carefully thinking about refutation from a strategic perspective.

Key Terms

ad populum	fallacy of false dichotomy
ad hominem	loaded question
ambiguity	non sequitur
appeal to fear	obfuscation
appeal to pity	reducing to absurdity
appeal to tradition	refutation by additional consideration
begging the question	refutation by denial
cross-examination	refutation by mitigation
direct examination	refutation process
doublespeak	shifting the burden of proof
equivocation	slippery slope
euphemism	straw man fallacy
fallacy of composition	tu quoque
fallacy of division	turning the tables

Activities

1. Observe two or more individuals engaged in an argument on a radio or television talk show. Try to find indications of flawed listening, and then identify which of the factors affecting listening provides the best explanation for the failure.

2. Assess your own listening behavior. Listen to an individual engaged in public advocacy on a talk show. As you listen, apply the five factors that affect listening to your own listening behavior.

3. Construct an example for each of the different types of fallacies of reasoning presented in the text.

4. Select a public controversy that interests you and take a position on one side of the controversy. Identify a claim made by the opposition. Now construct a brief refuting that opponent's claim.

5. Have a friend or a classmate help you practice your questioning techniques. First, reread the section of the text on questioning. Then have your colleague take a position on a public controversy and ask him or her questions. Be sure to follow the golden rule.

Recommended Readings

Babitsky, Steven, and James Mangraviti. *Cross-Examination: The Comprehensive Guide for Experts.* Falmouth, MA: Seak, 2003.

Bridges, Dick A., and John C. Reinard, Jr. "The Effects of Refutational Techniques on Attitude Change." *Journal of the American Forensic Association* 10 (1974): 203–212.

Chichi, Graciela Marta. "The Greek Roots of the Ad Hominem Argument." *Argumentation* 16 (2002): 333–349.

Cragan, John F., and Donald C. Shields. "The Comparative Advantage Negative." *Journal of the American Forensic Association* 7 (1970): 85–91.

Dudczak, Craig A. "Direct Refutation in Propositions of Policy: A Viable Alternative." *Journal of the American Forensic Association* 16 (1980): 232–235.

Hansen, Hans Vilhelm. "The Straw Thing of Fallacy Theory: The Standard Definition of 'Fallacy.'" *Argumentation* 16 (2002): 133–156.

Hollihan, Thomas A. "The 'Turnaround' as Argument Strategy: A Rationale for Use and Standards for Evaluation." *Speaker and Gavel* 22 (1985): 45–51.

Johnstone, Henry W. *Philosophy and Argument.* University Park: Pennsylvania State University Press, 1959.

Kahane, Howard, and Nancy Cavender. *Logic and Contemporary Rhetoric: The Use of Reason in Everyday Life.* Belmont, CA: Wadsworth, 2001.

Kimball, Robert H. "Moral and Logical Perspectives on Appealing to Pity." *Argumentation* 15 (2001): 331–349.

Wellman, Francis L. *The Art of Cross-Examination.* 4th ed. New York: Touchstone Books, 1997.

Notes

1 For an excellent analysis of the power of language and naming in war, see: Charles Kauffman, "Names and Weapons," *Communication Monographs* 56 (1989), 273–285.

2 Carl Ingram, "License Bill Draws Mixed Response," *Los Angeles Times,* 29 July 2003.

3 Ibid., B1.

4 George W. Bush, *Address to a joint session of Congress and the American people.* The White House (Producer). [Online] September 20, 2001, http://www.whitehouse.gov/news/releases/2001/09/20010920-8.html (retrieved 9/15/2004).

PART II

ARGUMENTATION IN SPECIALIZED FIELDS

The remaining chapters will focus on argumentation in selected specialized fields. As we have already discussed, the norms and practices that characterize argumentation differ according to context. You will likely not find yourself arguing the same way in an ordinary conversation between friends as you might in an academic debate, as a candidate engaged in a political campaign, in a court of law, or at work in a business setting. The requirements for establishing acceptable proof, the style of presentation, and the criteria for evaluating knowledge claims are substantially different in each case.

The fields selected for discussion in the following chapters are intended to reflect some of the differences found when one argues in alternative settings. Thus the selection is representative rather than exhaustive. We do not claim that these chapters will identify or represent all of the important differences found in argument fields, and in fact, we could have selected other fields for discussion. We chose these fields because they are substantially different from each other and because it is likely that you will come into contact with each of them at some point during your lives.

Chapters 10 and 11 consider the field of academic debate. Chapter 10 introduces the rudiments of debate as a field, and chapter 11 gives you a glimpse of some of the more complex theoretical issues that emerge in debate competitions. Many teachers of argumentation assign debates as class requirements because these contests provide an outstanding way to teach students the practical skills of argumentation. Academic debate was first developed as a kind of model of what reasoned argumentation should look like. It is a contest activity designed to teach the skills of research and oral argumentation. We encourage you to read these chapters and to try your hand at debating. It is both an enjoyable experience and an outstanding way to expand your mind.

Chapter 12 focuses on the arguments that surface in politics and political campaigns. These arguments fix our attention on the vital political issues of the day and involve all of us as citizens and hopefully as voters. Political arguments shape our public life and organize our collective energies. These arguments represent the very fabric of our system of pluralistic democracy. Warts and all, the political campaign practices of today represent the culmination of more than 200 years of experimentation in representative democracy and electoral politics. This chapter should interest all of you and should help you to fulfill your civic responsibilities.

Chapter 13 considers the argumentation that takes place in our courts. These arguments also involve all of us. Some of you may become litigants, others may experience careers as attorneys or judges, and many more of you will serve as jurors. All of us, however, will be affected by the argumentation that takes place in our courts because the courts reflect our social values, resolve our most significant public controversies, and create what passes for justice in our frenzied contemporary society.

Chapter 14 examines argumentation in business and organizations. This chapter is included because almost all of you will someday find yourselves working in an organization. Your effectiveness in achieving your career goals may be very much influenced by how well you can represent your ideas through both spoken and written arguments. Although we would caution all readers that organizations differ and that the specific requirements for arguing in any particular organization may be unique to that organization, we believe that there are general characteristics to arguments created in business and organizational settings. You can learn some of these characteristics and, once mastered, they will help you to become a much more effective member of that organization.

Finally, chapter 15 discusses arguing in interpersonal relationships. This chapter also affects all of us because were are all engaged in creating, managing, nurturing, and sometimes disengaging or terminating interpersonal relationships. The method for managing the disagreements or conflicts in these relationships is argumentation. Our goal is to make you a more effective, sensitive, and strategic arguer in these interactions—in short, to help you win friends and influence people!

ACADEMIC DEBATE
OVERVIEW

Academic debate is a special field of argumentation, distinguished by the problems it addresses and the methods used to evaluate disputes. Each year thousands of high school and college students participate in this activity. Some do so within classes, others represent their schools in competition against students from other institutions. There are several types of debate and each has its own rules and terminology, but they share some theoretical orientations. This chapter provides an overview to academic debate. In the next chapter we will examine the most popular types of debate in which college students engage.

THE DEBATE ORIENTATION

In this text we have approached argumentation as part of the natural process of life. It is one way we make sense of our world and negotiate our understandings with others. Our intent has not been to teach you how to win arguments; rather, we have given you the tools to reach your own decisions and to construct your own advocacy. We have also contended that through argument you can discover the best conception of probable truth.

Academic debate is a somewhat different proposition. It is a laboratory for practicing the skills of argumentation. Students are frequently assigned to debate both sides of a controversy, so clearly their arguments do not necessarily reflect their own opinions or their own best conception of truth. Rather, debaters offer the best arguments they can find for the position on a topic that they have been asked to defend. Although it is hopeful that competitors in debate will emerge from the activity with a more informed position on the issues that they debated, and thus perhaps with a better understanding of where the truth might lie on those issues, nonetheless, the focus of this activity is competitive and as a result, the more truthful arguments may sometimes not emerge as the most successful arguments. The intent of debate is to have fun, refine your argument skills in a structured environment, get some feedback and critiques from those who serve as your audience, and, if your skills are up to the challenge, to win.

Although there is widespread agreement within the argumentation community as to the value of academic debate, there are few explicit rules governing the activity of debating, and there are a number of different debate formats. Consequently, if you will be involved in academic debating, your instructor will likely give specific instructions regarding what you should expect and how you should prepare.

THE RESOLUTION

The focus of any debate is the proposition. The proposition is a statement that expresses the subject of the dispute. In academic debate the proposition is called the *resolution*. Because debate is a formal setting for argument, the resolution is explicitly worded prior to the debate. It may be a proposition of fact, value, or policy. Because it is less rewarding to debate on a proposition that can be easily falsified if someone produces definitive physical or empirical evidence, as can happen with a proposition of fact, most contest debates utilize either value or policy resolutions, and these will be the focus of this chapter and the next.

The purpose of the resolution is twofold. First, it announces to all participants the topic of the debate. This gives both teams an equal opportunity to prepare for the contest. Second, it divides the ground for the two teams and thus delineates their argumentative tasks and responsibilities.

Affirmative Burdens

Almost all debates divide the propositional ground into those who favor the resolution, the *affirmative* (in parliamentary debate this is called the government) and those who oppose the resolution, the *negative*.

In that the resolution typically proposes a change from currently held beliefs, values, or policies the affirmatives are also known as the advocates of change. The affirmative's burden is to convince the audience and/or the judge assigned to render a decision that the resolution is truthful, correct, or desirable. To do so, they must explain what they believe the resolution means and then present sound reasons in support of that resolution.

Negative Burdens

The resolution also conveys certain argumentative obligations to those who say "no" or who oppose the resolution. These individuals, known as the negative team (called the opposition in parliamentary debate), have the **burden of rejoinder**. This is the obligation to disagree with or refute the affirmative position. Implicit within this burden is the obligation to clash (discussed in detail in chapter 5) with the arguments presented by the affirmative. Clash refers to responding directly to the arguments the affirmative advanced. Often this is done point by point. Sometimes negatives group arguments and respond to them. Either way, effective advocacy demands that the negative develop a strategy to refute the affirmative's arguments. As representatives of current belief, negatives are not required to persuade the audience that the resolution is false. They are merely obliged to rebut the story advanced by the affirmative. Negative debaters may show that the affirmative's narrative lacks probability or fidelity. This may be best accomplished by presenting a competing narrative. If a competing story better accounts for the facts, then it will seem likely that the affirmative's narrative is not true.

Presumption and the Burden of Proof

Although all arguers have a burden to support their arguments, affirmative debaters have the **burden of proof**. They must prove the resolution true. This necessitates that they present and defend a **prima facie case**: a narrative that, on its first presentation, would meet the burdens necessary to persuade a reasonable audience that the resolution is true.

Affirmatives have the burden of proof because they must overcome **presumption**. In the field of law, this principle assumes that an individual is innocent until proven guilty. In academic debate, we presume that current beliefs are justified until there is good and sufficient reason for a change. In most debates, presumption resides with the negative and against the resolution.

Assume the resolution for an academic debate is: *Resolved: that the United States should significantly strengthen its trade restrictions on imports coming from Japan*. Both teams would know that the affirmative team would be calling for the imposition of stronger trade restrictions by the United States, and that the negative team would be obliged to rebut the imposition of such new trade restrictions. The burden of proof would be placed upon the affirmative, for the affirmative is advocating a change in policy. Presumption would be against such change. Both teams would also know that the debate would focus on U.S.-Japanese trade policies. This would enable them to investigate the relevant literature to discover and prepare for the issues likely to figure in this debate.

THREE TYPES OF ACADEMIC DEBATING

Fact Debates

Sometimes debates focus on questions of fact. Typically this involves giving some descriptive characteristic to a referent. Is today (referent) Tuesday (descriptive characteristic)? Did Iraq possess weapons of mass destruction immediately prior to the U.S. invasion of that nation in 2003? Does watching violence on television cause viewers to be more likely to commit acts of violence? To each of these questions, there is a yes or no answer. Either today is Tuesday or it some other day of the week. Either Iraq possessed such weapons, or it did not. Either watching TV violence causes more violence, or it does not. There is no judgment about whether either of these is good or bad (a value judgment), nor is there a recommended course of action (a policy judgment). The outcome of such debates would merely establish the facts that are in dispute.

Addressing such disputes results in an even greater focus on the terms within the resolution than do other types of resolutions that might be debated. This results from the importance of determining the criterial attributes of the important terms. In the resolution, *Resolved: That the war against Iraq was just,*[1] the debate would focus on the nature of a "just" war. What are the criterial attributes of this type of war? How does a "just" war differ from a war that is not just? The debate would also focus on whether or not the U.S. invasion of Iraq should be considered to have met the criteria for inclusion in the category of "just" wars. The opposition could challenge the criterial attributes of a just war and/or argue against inclusion of the war in Iraq in that category.

Value Debates

In *value debates* the affirmative asks the audience to agree to a judgment stated in the resolution. There are two components to this evaluation: a value object and a value judgment. For example, the topic may be: *Resolved: that the Pledge of Allegiance is inappropriate expression in public schools.*[2] In this case, the value object is the "Pledge of Allegiance" and the value judgment is that reciting the Pledge in public schools is "inappropriate." To support this resolution the affirmative would need to present a value criterion for determining how to judge what is "inappropriate" and by implication what is "appropriate." This would, of course, constitute a value judgment and whether or not the Pledge is deemed "inappropriate" would depend on the values supported in explication of the words "appropriate" and "inappropriate." For example, an affirmative might argue that expression in public schools that supports religion is "inappropriate." The underlying value would therefore be separation of Church and State, and the public school would be viewed as an extension of the state. The affirmative would need to be able to defend this criterion and then would need to contend that reciting the Pledge of Allegiance constitutes support for religion. This provides the negative with the opportunity to clash with the criteria presented by the affirmative as well as with the specific example as to whether or not the expression of the Pledge of Allegiance does actually support religion. Winning either argument would spell victory for the negative.

Policy Debates

In *policy debate* the affirmative team is generally asked to present a specific proposal or plan to implement the change called for in the resolution. Imagine the resolution is: *Resolved: That the United States Federal Government should sub-*

stantially increase federal control throughout Indian Country in one or more of the following areas: child welfare, criminal justice, employment, environmental protection, gaming, resource management, taxation.[3] The affirmative would present a plan that detailed how they think the United States ought to substantially increase federal control throughout Indian Country in one or more of the specific areas delineated. To justify such a change, the affirmative would need to prove that the current policies are not working well (by identifying an existing ill in the current system and by assigning blame or responsibility for the existence of that ill) and that increasing federal control would result in a superior policy (a proposed cure). Most affirmatives would compare the status quo (the current policies in this area) with the status quo as modified by the affirmative plan. They would argue that the status quo + plan are significantly better than the status quo alone. The negative would be called upon to refute this viewpoint. Since the current system enjoys presumption, negatives do not have to prove that the status quo is better than the status quo + plan. They merely have to argue that the proposed change would not be better. A "tie" goes to the negative because of the principle of presumption already discussed.

FORMAT

Most academic debate is conducted in a format in which two-person teams face each other, although other formats of debate also exist. For example, one-on-one debate, known as Lincoln-Douglas debate, is also common. The nature of speeches, the speaker order, and the time limits of each speech are referred to as the **debate format**. The specific formats used in each type of debate will be presented in the next chapter.

The Order of Speaking

While there is some variety in the specifics, all common debate formats share some traits. The most important shared trait is that the format is designed to provide balanced competition; neither side is given a unique advantage from the format. Another is that the proponent of change—the affirmative—both initiates and concludes the debate. This is the case because the affirmative generally has the burden of proof. In the first speech the affirmative defines the terms and establishes the grounds of the debate. If the affirmative did not speak first, there would be nothing for the negative to negate. The affirmative also gets to present the last speech in the debate. The rationale is that the affirmative must persuade the audience that the present policies or beliefs are problematic and this burden of proof is challenging. The advantage of speaking first and last is offset by the fact that the negative team always retains presumption.

Other speeches in the debate alternate between affirmative and negative speakers. The one exception is that in order to have the affirmative start and end the debate it is generally necessary to have two consecutive negative speeches at some point. This is called the *negative block* and is generally considered a significant advantage, because the negative gets to hold the attention of the adjudicator for a significant amount of time.

Constructive Speeches

Each participant in a four-person academic debate presents a *constructive speech*. In this speech you can present any argument you consider relevant. This is the opportunity to construct the positions you believe should be the focus of the debate. It is also the occasion for presenting your initial responses to the positions developed by the opposition.

Rebuttal Speeches

Each participant in a four-person academic debate also presents a *rebuttal*. In this speech you will rebuild your initial constructive positions and extend your attacks on the opposition. Because rebuttal speeches take place in the latter part of the debate, debaters are prohibited from initiating new arguments. You can extend your own arguments and refute the arguments developed by your opponents. You are permitted to provide further evidence and analysis to support the arguments that you initiated in your constructive speeches, but you cannot start a brand new argument.

For example, consider the trade topic illustration we used earlier. If the negative had not discussed in their constructive speeches the possibility that Japan would respond to new trade restrictions on Japanese goods bound for the United States by implementing their own restrictions on American goods coming into Japan, it would be too late to bring this up in rebuttals. If this is an important argument to the negative's case, it should be introduced in one of the negative's constructive speeches and not saved for the rebuttals when the affirmative might not have an opportunity to respond to it. The requirement that arguments be first introduced in the constructive speeches is a way of encouraging a more complete and careful examination and consideration of these positions. The prohibition against introducing new arguments in rebuttals also prevents the affirmative from coming up with new reasons to support their policy in their final rebuttal, when the negative would have no opportunity to respond.

Rebuttal speeches are shorter than constructive speeches. This means that speakers must adapt to the rebuttal situation. Sometimes this means offering a much briefer and thus less complete explanation of your arguments. Sometimes it means choosing which arguments you believe you need to discuss and dropping others. It is important to remember, however, that if you do not discuss an argument in your last rebuttal, it is likely that the audience or the judge will not consider this argument when deciding who won the debate.

Final rebuttals are also the last opportunity for you to convince the audience or the judge why you have won the debate. This means that you should explain why you believe you should be considered to have the superior arguments on certain issues, why those issues ought to be considered important to the outcome of the contest, and how the issues that you have won in the debate outweigh those issues that your opponents may be winning. Putting the arguments presented in the debate together into a coherent story that can be readily understood and evaluated by your hearers is at this point a very effective strategy.

Cross-Examination

Most debate formats incorporate question periods. In debate this is called *cross-examination* (once again parliamentary debate is different, and those differences will be discussed in chapter 11). Each debater asks questions of, and is questioned by, the opposition. The individual asking the questions is called the *questioner*. The debater who has just concluded a constructive speech and is now being questioned is called the *witness*.

You may decide to use this time to clarify what the opposition has argued. While this may be necessary because, after all, one cannot refute what one has not heard, it is not the most effective use of cross-examination time. Asking questions that probe an opponent's argument can be a more profitable use of this time. Arguments and evidence often are predicated on unproven assumptions. Discovering these assumptions may permit you to dispense with arguments in a very expeditious fashion. Also, if you know what the weaknesses of an opponent's arguments are, it can be useful to highlight these weaknesses during the questioning period and before you develop and present the arguments in your next speech. This strategy permits you to reference the admissions gleaned in your cross-examination.

We discussed the art of argumentative questioning in depth in chapter 9, but debate cross-examination is a little different. In most contexts argument is regulated by the norms of polite conversation. If you are abusive or uncooperative, people will probably stop interacting with you. Two rules govern the cross-examination required of debaters, and they are quite strict.

First, the cross-examination period is controlled by the questioner. If you are the questioner, you get to ask the questions, the witness does not. You can also politely interrupt the witness if you feel the need. This may happen because you think you have the answer you need, or because the witness is not answering the question you thought you had asked. But you may not badger the witness or demand yes-or-no answers. Some questions cannot be adequately answered with a "yes" or "no," so it is unfair to make such a request. You are not permitted to assert a new argument during cross-examination, even if you intended to give the witness a chance to respond. Arguments and evidence must be presented during a speech.

Second, witnesses must cooperate as fully as possible. This means that if you are the witness you should answer the questions as clearly and as succinctly as possible. You should not attempt to stall or obfuscate. Nor are you permitted to read new evidence. Of course, you are permitted to refer to the evidence you presented in your speech, and you may be asked by the questioner to reread evidence that you just presented in your speech.

Time Limits

Each team receives an equal amount of speaking and cross-examination time. This is another attempt to maintain the competitive balance of the activity. These time limits are strictly enforced, and when your speaking time has expired, you must end your speech.

Now that you have an idea of how a debate operates, we can discuss in greater detail the types of debate arguments typically advanced.

THE NATURE OF DEBATE ARGUMENTS

As one might expect, most of the arguments advanced in debate focus on the reasons why the audience should accept or reject the resolution. These are called *substantive arguments*. There are some arguments, however, that may precede the substantive ones.

Procedural Arguments

Procedural arguments are those that must be resolved prior to the consideration of substantive issues. These arguments are customarily initiated in the first two speeches (first affirmative constructive or first negative constructive). The most important procedural argument is topicality. We will also discuss criteria arguments that are used in value debating.

Topicality Arguments

We have already noted that the affirmative burden is to prove the resolution. The affirmative therefore has the *right to define* the key terms of the resolution. But the affirmative must do so in a nonabusive manner. If the arguments presented by the affirmative deal with something other than the resolution, the affirmative will not have proved the resolution true. A negative argument alleging that the affirmative has strayed from proving the resolution true is called a *topicality argument*.

Typically, the affirmative first defines the key terms of the resolution and then develops the arguments supporting the resolution. In policy debate the plan proposed by the affirmative, or the policy change under consideration, is the focus of the topicality question. If the plan were topical, that is, if the proposed plan does what the topic calls for, the advantages that flow from the plan would prove the resolution true. If the plan is not topical, the advantages would not be relevant, and they would not serve as reasons why the resolution ought to be implemented.

For example, if the affirmative defined trade restrictions as tariffs and quotas, the plan must specify how U.S. tariffs and quotas would be modified. The advantages of such a policy must then be shown to stem from these changes.

In value debate there is no plan. Thus, a different determinant of topicality is used. With value resolutions the issue of topicality focuses on the relationship between the definitions and the arguments advanced by the affirmative in support of the resolution. Let's take, for example, the resolution *Resolved: that the welfare system exacerbates the problems of the urban poor.* The affirmative might choose to define the key terms: *welfare system, exacerbates, problems,* and *the urban poor.* The affirmatives would then present reasons why they think the resolution is true. If they argued that public schools do not adequately prepare the urban poor for careers, and the negative team did not think schools should be rightfully considered as part of the welfare system, the latter could issue a topicality argument.

Although topicality is an affirmative burden, it is generally presumed that an affirmative will present a topical case. Thus, it is generally the first negative speaker who initiates a topicality argument if one is warranted.

Criteria Arguments

In fact and value debates there is a special kind of definition presented, an argument about the criteria to be applied in judging the resolution. With propositions of fact affirmatives must present **criteria** for the key terms. This means determining those defining attributes that separate one object from another, for example, a just war from an unjust war. Similarly, in value debates the affirmative must present a value that focuses the decision making. It is the affirmative's right and obligation to present reasonable criteria to help in rendering a judgment about what value to use in determining the truth of the proposition. You will recall that in the value proposition about the Pledge of Allegiance, we suggested that one criterion might be an argument about which team best meets the long accepted principle from the United States Constitution that there should be a separation of Church and State.

Negative speakers can respond to affirmative criteria arguments by accepting or rejecting them. If they accept the affirmative criteria then the audience will use them as a filter to evaluate the arguments presented in the debate. Therefore, in a value debate, if preservation of life is paramount, the audience will look first to determine whether the affirmative or the negative arguments best uphold this value. Arguments that address other values, such as the protection of human rights, would not flow through the criteria filter and should therefore not enter the debate. Since the affirmative can select their criteria, and since this selection often provides a strategic benefit, many negatives choose to clash with the criteria that have been proposed by the affirmative. To do so, the negative must give reasons why the affirmative criteria are not acceptable and then present **countercriteria** that are arguably better than those presented by the affirmative.

Whether the criteria used in evaluating the outcome of the debate are presented by the affirmative or the negative, they should be defined and the rationale behind their selection should be presented and defended. The team that does the better job of debating about criteria will convince the audience to use their criteria for evaluating the debate.

Substantive Arguments

While topicality and criteria arguments are both potentially decisive, most debates focus on the **substantive arguments** that remain. In a substantive debate on matters of value the vision may be only of the status quo. In a substantive debate on a question of policy the affirmative is called upon to envision and depict two worlds: the world of the status quo and that of the status quo plus the plan. We will consider each in turn.

Substantive Issues in Value Debates

Once the criteria analysis has been presented, affirmatives in a value debate must show that the status quo should be negatively evaluated. This is usually accomplished through the presentation of a story that demonstrates the validity of the value judgment. For example, in arguing that the welfare system exacerbates the problems of the urban poor, an affirmative could present independence as the value to look to when determining the truth of the resolution. Then in their arguments they would need to show that the welfare system frustrates the achievement of this value by the urban poor. This would probably entail the presentation of several ways in which the welfare system fosters dependence.

The relationship between the procedural and the substantive issues in a value debate should now be clear. The substantive elements of the case demonstrate the failings of the present system with regard to the value criteria presented earlier.

In responding to the substantive issues presented by the affirmative, the negative would challenge the story presented. The negative would look to the motives and behaviors attributed to the actors in the affirmative's story. Are those on welfare dependent? Do they seek independence but are frustrated in their attempts to get off the welfare rolls by some policies of the welfare system? Are there counter-causalities, such as discrimination, poor education, lack of jobs, inadequate access to child care, which are more likely causes or at least significant contributing factors to welfare dependence?

In addition, most negatives present arguments against the value criteria. An argument of this type is often called a **value objection**. This is an argument that says embracing the value favored by the affirmative would have adverse consequences. For example, some affirmative values focus on the rights of individuals. The negative could argue that basing decisions on individual rights is a bad idea because individual rights reinforce the notion that individuals are more important than the group. This, some authorities contend, has adverse consequences on society. They contend that our wasteful, throwaway, pollution-filled society is the result of elevating the individual above the group. Therefore, the negative could maintain that argumentative criteria that focus on individual rights should be rejected and shared or community rights and responsibilities should be viewed as more important. If the affirmative fails to win the argument about individual rights that they have established as criteria for the evaluation of the arguments in the debate, it is unlikely that they can win the arguments regarding the superiority of the value judgment presented in the topic. This would, in turn, permit the negative to argue that the affirmative failed to prove the resolution true; or, at the very least, this becomes another reason to support the superiority of the use of the negative's criteria instead of the criteria offered by the affirmative.

The substantive arguments—including the clash over whether or not the status quo achieves the value criteria and the debate over the merits (including the potential harms or risks of harms outlined in the value objections)—are then evaluated alongside any procedural arguments that have been introduced into the debate, and the judge formulates his or her decision as to whether the proposition has been affirmed or negated.

Substantive Issues in Policy Debates

In examining the status quo, the policy affirmative presents a story about the world as they see it. This entails describing the actors, the scene, and the events in narrative terms. In order to win, the affirmative must convince the audience that their proposed change would result in more advantages than would clinging to current policies existing in the status quo.

Needs Case.   Traditionally, affirmatives presented a world with problems that needed to be resolved. An affirmative story of this type is called a *needs case* (see chapter 8). These problems (the stock issue known as the ill) must be significant and inherent to the status quo (the stock issue known as blame). If the ills of the status quo are insignificant then there would be no sense in enacting a new policy. If the problems are not inherent to the present system, that is, if we do not know the cause of the problem and why current policies are inadequate, then a new policy might not solve the problem. Finally, we must have good reason to predict that the proposal will actually solve the identified problems (the stock issue known as the cure). If the plan accrues no advantage, then it should not be enacted.

The negative refutes a needs case by challenging the story told by the affirmative. They may do this by showing that there is not a significant problem with the status quo (thus that no significant ills exist), or that the present system is solving the problems that have been identified or could solve these problems with minor adjustments that are typically referred to as minor repairs (this is thus related to the stock issue known as "blame"). The negative will often also choose to argue that the proposal advanced by the affirmative will not solve the problems that have been identified and thus it should not be adopted (this is the issue of "cure"). Most negatives will choose to argue a mix of arguments that address the significance of the harms that have been identified, that propose minor repairs, and that also create doubts about the affirmative's ability to enact a cure. It is important to remember that to win the debate the negative does not have to win each and every one of the stock issues. The negative can conceivably win the debate by winning in a convincing way one of those stock issues or by otherwise demonstrating that the affirmative proposal will not yield significant advantages when compared to the status quo.

Comparative Advantage Case.   It is common for debaters to construct narratives that merge the three stock issues (ill, blame, and cure) and present a *comparative advantage case* (see chapter 8). In such an approach, the affirmative presents a plan and argues that the advantages of the plan compare favorably to the status quo. Thus, there does not have to be a significant problem (ill) with the present system, just a significant advantage (cure) that results from enacting the plan. The question of blame becomes part of the solvency issue. If the plan compares favorably to the status quo, then the inherency burden has been met—unless the negative can show that the same inadequacies that thwarted status quo efforts will also thwart the affirmative's proposal.

In order to refute a comparative advantage case the first substantive decision the negative must make is how to respond to the affirmative's depiction of the status quo (the issues of ill and blame). Suppose the affirmative is claiming that health-care assistance programs in Pakistan are failing and that, as a result, thousands will die. There are three potential responses to this claim. First, the negative can accept this depiction but clash with another aspect of the affirmative's case. This is risky because it grants the affirmative the point that the problem they address is significant. If their case shows even the potential to protect thousands of lives they will have gained an important advantage in the debate.

Second, the negative can attempt to deny the depiction of the current situation in Pakistan. Perhaps there is evidence that, contrary to the affirmative's claim, health assistance programs in Pakistan are working and the health of the population is improving. Usually when teams are contending polar opposite positions there is some explanation for the differing views offered in empirical evidence and in the testimony of experts. Sometimes these differences are the result of conflicting definitions of important key terms, sometimes there is difference in the time frame provided for the study data used in the evidence, sometimes the qualifications or interests of the experts' account for the divergence of opinion, and sometimes it is a matter of unstated assumptions behind the conclusions. There are certainly situations, for example, where experts are guided by their own ideological and political convictions, which are different from each other's, and these differences result in very different opinions about complex issues. The negative should try to figure out why their data or expert evidence differs from that offered by the affirmative, and they should also strive to explain why their evidence and thus their arguments are superior to what has been offered by the affirmative.

Third, the negative can attempt to minimize the significance of the affirmative's depiction of conditions in Pakistan. For example, it could be that the numbers presented by the affirmative represent a worst-case scenario, and therefore the loss of life will probably be significantly less than the affirmative has argued. Minimization of the significance of the affirmative case, however, is a strategy that must usually be accompanied by some other tactic. The negative is not likely to win by saying only that the problem in the status quo is not as significant as the affirmative depicts. An audience is likely to conclude that even if the negative wins their arguments there are still sufficient problems in the status quo to warrant the adoption of the affirmative plan.

Solvency Attacks.   The negative will often choose to refute the affirmative's depiction of the status quo while also attacking the affirmative's claim that their proposed plan would be superior to the status quo. First, the negative may try to deny that significant advantages will result from implementing the plan. Such arguments challenge the affirmative prediction that the proposed policy will solve the problems of the status quo; hence they are called **solvency** attacks.

There are several reasons why a plan may not accrue the advantages predicted by the affirmative. The negative must research the proposals to find out why they have not already been adopted. If the proposal really is likely to accrue significant benefits, a natural question to be considered is: why have we not already adopted it? There are often good reasons, and these reasons may provide the negative with strong arguments against the proposed plan.

- *Sometimes the proposed plan cannot be considered practical.* If one scholar or policy analyst has argued for a specific proposal it is possible, perhaps even likely, that another has critiqued that proposal. If the plan is modeled after a policy in a foreign country you should study the situation in that country and examine the policy to see how well it is actually performing.

- *Sometimes proposals are not adopted because special interests oppose them.* Debaters may be able to argue that the plan will not work because it is open to **circumvention**. In such a case you are arguing that people who have the will to thwart the new proposal will find a way to get around it. To construct a circumvention argument you need to show that there is both a motive and the means for someone to get around the proposal. For example, during Prohibition people had the motive—the appetite for alcoholic beverages and the profits to be made from smuggling—and the means—home-distilled beverages and illegal importations from Canada and Mexico under mob control—to circumvent the law. As a result, the policy was largely ineffective. If an affirmative suggests a similar prohibition, for instance a ban on cigarette smoking or an attempt to limit excessive political campaign contributions, the motive and means may exist for circumvention of these new policies as well.

A negative who fails to clash with an affirmative's solvency arguments ends up conceding to the affirmative their solvency claims. This greatly enhances the appeal of the affirmative's case and also raises the threshold level that must be overcome in the construction of the stock issue of "cost."

Disadvantage Arguments.   The stock issue of cost provides the negative with the opportunity to argue that even if the affirmative policy did produce some benefit or advantage over current policy it would end up resulting in some noteworthy drawbacks or costs that should be carefully considered and evaluated. Such a negative argument is called a **disadvantage**. A disadvantage is an argument, typically related in the form of a story, that says that there will be undesirable consequences should the affirmative's policy be adopted. Disadvantages usually assume affirmative solvency. But predicating a disadvantage on the conditional acceptance of solvency does not preclude the negative from also attacking the affirmative's solvency. Rather, our understanding of the negative contention is that even if the plan were solvent we would not want to do it because of its disadvantages.

There are several types of disadvantages. Each disadvantage is a story involving actors, events, and scenes. Debaters must be cognizant of how they depict the actors in their arguments. Inconsistency can destroy the validity of the story.

- *Sometimes proposed policy actions might create problems where none currently exist.* For example, you could argue that an affirmative case that prohibited the private ownership of handguns might leave the citizenry defenseless against home invasions by criminals or even against an invasion by a foreign power. Or, a negative could also argue that the second amendment to the U.S. Constitution is considered so fundamentally important to many of our citizens that any attempt to tamper with it would lead to the formation of reactionary militia movements opposed to our own government. This, one might argue, could also spawn the production of more characters such as Timothy McVeigh, the Oklahoma City bomber.

- *The newly proposed affirmative policy might exacerbate existing problems.* Pollution is already a serious concern. The negative could argue that the affirmative plan that promises to dramatically increase employment opportunities and to spur economic growth in the United States would also result in increased energy consumption, increased levels of pollution, speed the impact of global warming, and perhaps result in the melting of the polar ice cap. This in turn could produce a kind of economic disaster previously unknown to humankind.

- *New policies also may be a step in an undesirable direction.* For example, an affirmative might argue in favor of a policy change that creates a constitutional amendment to ban the possibility of same sex marriage. The negative could counter such a policy by arguing that the United States of America has been moving for many years toward the creation of a more egalitarian state. This is evidenced in the extension of voting rights and equality of opportunity for women, persons of different races and ethnic backgrounds, the elderly, and the disabled. An affirmative plan that specifically halts the progress toward full equality for gays and lesbians would thwart this progress toward greater equality and increase the likelihood that resistance to equal rights for all of these different classes of persons would again become common. Thus, a desirable movement toward equality for all citizens would be undermined and because of this, the affirmative plan should be rejected.

- *Plans can be attacked on moral or philosophical grounds.* This necessitates developing a value justification. If you are arguing against a policy that calls for the death penalty for drug pushers, you could oppose the plan on moral grounds. If so, you might argue that capital punishment is immoral, that civilized nations around the world have been abolishing state executions, and that the morality of a policy action is an important consideration that should not be ignored by decision makers.

Burdens.   Regardless of the type of disadvantage, the negative must meet several burdens. First, the negative must demonstrate a clear **link** to the affirmative policy. This means that the negative must show that there is a clear causal connection between the affirmative plan and the disadvantage.

Second, the disadvantage must be **unique.** To be unique, the affirmative plan must be the sole cause of the disadvantage. If many things can cause the disadvantage you would have to show the unique increment in the disadvantage that the affirmative plan causes. Third, the negative must show the affirmative plan is sufficient to cause the disadvantage. There are two ways this may be accomplished.

- *Some disadvantages presuppose that the present system is on the **brink**, or precipice, of a disadvantage.* With this kind of argument you need to contend that the affirmative action is enough to push us over the cliff. For example, perhaps the affirmative has proposed to build a high-speed rail system, such as those that exist in Japan or Western Europe, to address transportation problems and to reduce the consumption of fossil fuels.

  The negative could argue a disadvantage that claims many cities in the U.S. West (e.g., Phoenix, Las Vegas, and the Palm Springs area) already face a very serious water shortage. Then the negative could argue that access to high-speed rail transportation in the region would dramatically increase housing developments in the desert and spur further increases in population as people moved to these cities but used the new trains to commute to work in Southern California where land and housing prices were prohibitively expensive. Then the negative might argue that this rapid development would greatly aggravate the water shortage, perhaps destroy the underground aquifer, and lead to an ecological catastrophe.

  The affirmative can deny the validity of the brink if they can show that alternative sources for water exist (perhaps desalinization of ocean water), can defend other strategies for limiting development and growth, or can establish that credible programs of water conservation can be developed. They might also be able to diminish the credibility of the brink argument by claiming that threats of impending doom have been issued for years, but despite those threats and very rapid development in these regions, the catastrophe has never materialized.

- Other disadvantages are *linear*. This means that each increment is undesirable. We know additional pollution would be a bad thing, so if the affirmative policy causes additional pollution it would seem to be a bad idea. With such disadvantages you may be required to show how much more pollution the affirmative would cause and the impact of this additional increment of pollution.

Finally, *time frame* may be critical. If the affirmative plan could cause a significant disadvantage before it accrues its advantage that could be a reason to reject the proposal. If the achievable affirmative advantage has a shorter time frame than the eventual disadvantage, the audience may decide to accept the eventual risk of the disadvantage for the nearer term benefit of the affirmative proposal.

Affirmative Responses.   The negative must be wary when presenting disadvantages, for the affirmative has two options for response. One option is called a ***take out***. This is an argument that simply denies the chain of events in the story. Its name stems from the idea that if you take out one link in a chain, the chain falls apart. Similarly, if you break the sequence of events in the story the negative tells, you deny the validity of the story. If the negative story is that assisting

Pakistan may anger the leaders of India and lead to war, the affirmative could agree that India would be angered, but deny the next step in the story: that India would go to war.

The second kind of affirmative response to a disadvantage is particularly dangerous to the negative. Affirmatives may present arguments called **turnarounds**. A turnaround is an argument that takes a disadvantage and turns it into an advantage for the affirmative. There are two ways a disadvantage can be turned.

- *First, an affirmative may turn the link.* If a negative argues that implementing the U.N.'s declaration on human rights is undesirable because it reinforces the domination of male leadership in the world, an affirmative may respond by claiming that, rather than reinforcing the patriarchy, the U.N.'s declaration is a tool for enhancing the role of women in the world because it extends the protection of women to corners of the world where women are still viewed as male possessions. Thus, if patriarchy is a bad thing, it is more advantageous to implement the declaration than not to. In this line of argument the impact of the disadvantage is untouched and is claimed as an advantage by the affirmative.
- *The second kind of turn is an impact turn.* If the negative argues that changing health aid to Pakistan is disadvantageous because the new health aid will foster internecine conflict there, an affirmative could grant this scenario but claim that rather than a disadvantage, such civil unrest would be desirable because it could lead a more democratic form of government and perhaps also diminish the power of fundamentalist warlords. Thus the impact, internal strife, is turned from an undesirable outcome to a desirable one.

Policy debaters are not particularly interested in determining the likelihood that their proposals will actually be enacted. Rather, they prefer to concentrate on the merits of the proposed policies. The wording of policy debate resolutions does not say that the policy *will* be enacted. Instead such debate topics use words that indicate that a policy "should" or "ought" to be adopted. As a result, you should not spend your time trying to determine whether or not Congress or the executive branch of government would actually pass the proposed affirmative policy. You should, however, focus on whether or not the proposed policy should or should not be adopted based upon its desirability.

FLOW SHEETING AS SYSTEMATIC NOTE TAKING

When good students listen to lectures they take notes so that they may return to this information later and study for examinations. Debaters must also take notes, but their notes do not have to be as complete because they will be using their notes in a few minutes. The system of note taking in debate is referred to as *flowing*. It is a very important part of the debate process. In order for debaters to be sure that they have answered all of the arguments raised by their opponents, and to be sure that they have extended all of their own, they must write down what people have said. They also must record their notes in a fashion that makes them easy to read while they speak. In addition, they must write their notes quickly enough that they succeed in recording everything important that their opponent argues. This is not an easy task. But it should be clear that it is an essential task.

Here are some tips that may make the process a little easier.

1. Use at least two legal pads. Draw lines that divide the paper horizontally into eight equal sections. You now have room to record the arguments advanced in each of the eight speeches of the debate. Do not worry about flowing cross-examination, but be sure to listen to it. One pad will be the *case flow*. The other pad will be the *off-case flow*. On the case flow you will record the first affirmative and all of the arguments, negative and affirmative, which directly deal with the affirmative case. On the off-case flow you will record all of the procedural arguments and any disadvantages or value objections.

2. When you record a speaker's arguments, do not cross the lines you drew on the flow pads. To avoid crossing the lines you will need to write very small and you will need to abbreviate.

3. Record the enumeration employed by a speaker. If a speaker says this is the "first argument," write down: *#1*. If a speaker says "subpoint A" you should write that down too. We suggest you also circle the enumerated structure of the affirmative case as presented in the first affirmative constructive and all subsequent references to the affirmative case structure. That will make these numbers stand out. Then in later speeches when a debater says, "On their B subpoint I will have three responses," you can easily find the B subpoint on your flow.

4. Leave space between groups of arguments. Sometimes arguments expand as the debate develops and you may want more room to record them. Leaving space also helps you to find the group of arguments quickly.

5. Use arrows and lines to show which argument applies to which. If the first negative speaker has three arguments against the IB2 subpoint of the first case, it helps to draw a line to that subpoint.

6. Record the number and claim of the argument. As you get better you will be able to record the source citation and the essence of the evidence as well. If you miss something, ask your partner or ask about it during cross-examination.

7. Alternate the colors of the fine point pens you are using, one color for the affirmative arguments and another for the negative arguments. That way you can tell at a glance who said what.

8. Before it is your turn to speak, try to write down the arguments you intend to make. If you have your arguments on the flow pad, all you have to do is read your flow from left to right. You will have, right in front of you, what your opponent said and what you plan to say.

TRUNCATED SAMPLE FLOW*

Topic: Resolved that implementation of the United Nations' universal declaration of human rights is more important than preserving state sovereignty.

First Aff Const	First Neg Const	Second Aff Const
(1) Definitions	(1)	(1)
UN- intern'l org		
implmt- fulfill	OK	granted
UDHR- doc of HRts		
presrv- sustain		
st sov- legal concpt		
of governance		
(2) Crit- HRts	(2)	(2)
(A) HRts prereq 4	(A)	(A)
civilization	1. must arise w/in	implmnt=assist & ed
- humanity &	-only when fought 4	so = arise w/in
progress tied to	are rts valued	
recog of HRts		
(B) HRts O/w st sov	(B)	(B)
- states trample HRts	1. only sov guar	1. demo=guar too
& that's bad	safety	eg, USA
	-purpose of sov to	2. Rts more imprtnt
	presrve st & Rts of	fight to presrv Rts
	people	
(I) UDHR protects	(I)	(I.)
Democracy	(A)	(A)
(A) UDHR respcts		
other views	OK	granted
- when writ=respct		
4 divrgnce		
(B) UDHR plants	(B) & (C)	(B)
seeds of Demo	Demo Bad	1. nations do move
- adopted by all to	1. aid=dependency	away
accpt demo goals	- aid fosters reliance	-eg, Korea
	2. - ! repression	2. others ask for aid
	- aid—alignmnt of	-many nations reqst aid
(C) Demo=freedom	classes, presrvd	1. aid=rep
- demo protcts a	w/repression	past exmpls prove
variety of Rts		2. UDHR solves rep
		- purpose=protct Rts

* This truncated sample flow only shows parts of the first three speeches of the debate.

Explanation of Truncated Sample Flow

The First Affirmative Constructive

Observation ① Definitions

UN—United Nations

Implmt—implement

UDHR—Universal Declaration of Human Rights

presrv—preserve

st sove—state sovereignty

Observation ② Crit-Criteria; HRts-Human Rights

The affirmative is arguing that "more important" will be determined by examining which preserves human rights better, implementing the UDHR or state sovereignty

Subpoint Ⓐ HRts prereq 4 civilization—Human Rights are a prerequisite for civilization

evidence: humanity and the progress of humanity throughout history have been tied to a recognition of human rights

Subpoint Ⓑ HRts o/w st sov—Human Rights outweighs state sovereignty

evidence: nation states have trampled human rights and such abuse is not warranted

Contention ①. UDHR protects Democracy

Subpoint Ⓐ UDHR respects other views

evidence: when then UDHR was written it was written with a recognition of and respect for divergent viewpoints

Subpoint Ⓑ UDHR plants seeds for Democracy

evidence: the UDHR has been adopted by all of the members of the UN and that means they all accept the goals of a democracy

Subpoint Ⓒ Democracy preserves freedom

evidence: democracies are established to protect a variety of rights of their citizens

First Negative Constructive

Observation ① OK—we have no arguments with the definitions

Observation ②

Subpoint Ⓐ

claim: human rights must arise from within a nation

evidence: only when people have fought to obtain them are rights valued by the people

Subpoint Ⓑ

claim: only state sovereignty guarantees the safety of the people

evidence: the purpose of sovereignty is to preserve the state and the safety of the people and in doing so, it preserves the rights of the people

Contention ①

Subpoint Ⓐ OK—we have no arguments with this subpoint

continued

Explanation of Truncated Sample Flow (*continued*)

Subpoint (B) and (C) are grouped together
    claim #1: foreign aid promotes dependency in the recipient nation
    evidence: a nation which receives aid from other nations becomes dependent on that aid
    claim #2: dependency leads to increased repression
    evidence: aid leads to class differentiation, the haves and the have nots. Those who administer the aid attempt to perpetuate their status through repression

The Second Affirmative Speech
Observation (1) the negative granted our definitions
    explanation: the definitions cannot be challenged in subsequent speeches
Observation (2)
Subpoint (A)
    claim: by implementation we mean assistance and education
    explanation: our definition of implement was to fulfill the UDHR through assistance and education, so the rights will arise from within the nation
Subpoint (B)
    claim #1: democracy guarantees safety too
    explanation: the United States is a democracy and it guarantees the rights of its citizens
    claim #2: Rights are more important
    explanation: democratic nations have gone to war to fight to preserve the rights of the people. This shows that rights are more important than safety
Contention (I)
Subpoint (A) The subpoint was granted by the negative
Subpoints (B) and (C)
First Negative Argument #1
    claim #1: many nations do move away from aid
    evidence: at one time South Korea received significant American aid. It has now become self-sufficient
    claim #2: Other nations ask for aid
    evidence: requests for foreign aid from the U.S. are significant
    explanation: other nations wouldn't request aid if it were so bad
First Negative Argument #2
    claim #1: aid does not lead to repression
    explanation: many nations have received aid without it leading to repression
    claim #2: UDHR solves repression
    evidence: the purpose of the UDHR is to protect those rights of individual recognized by the UN

If you have been flowing correctly, you will be able to see how an argument unfolds during the course of a debate. You should be able to follow the argument across your paper, hence the term *flow paper*.

In most situations you will need to respond to each argument or group of arguments raised by your opponent, even if only to say, "We grant that point to the other team." You will also want to extend your own arguments, especially if your opponent had nothing to say about them. A good flow will enable you to do this.

SUMMARY

In this chapter we have examined the argument field of academic debate. We have presented the theory and practice of fact, value, and policy debate. The debate format was identified and both affirmative and negative burdens were generally considered. We discussed the different kinds of procedural and substantive issues that can be raised.

Key Terms

affirmative	negative
brink	off-case flow
burden of proof	policy debate
burden of rejoinder	presumption
case flow	prima facie case
circumvention	procedural arguments
comparative advantage case	rebuttal
constructive speech	resolution
countercriteria	solvency
criteria	substantive arguments
cross-examination	take out
debate format	time frame
disadvantage	topicality argument
flowing	turnaround
linear	unique
link	value debate
needs case	value objection

Activities

1. Select a value or policy proposition and construct an affirmative case for it. Be sure that your case addresses the issues required by the type of resolution you choose. For a guide to the specifics of an affirmative case, see also the debate in appendix B.

2. Select a point of stasis in the resolution you have chosen and construct a negative-brief that addresses this point. Be sure to include the enumer-

ated claims, the full source citations, and the text of the data you intend to present in your brief.

3. Construct a disadvantage to implementing the change advocated by the affirmative. This should include the structure and data, including the full source citation, which supports the subdevelopment of your argument. For samples of disadvantages, see the debate in appendix B.

4. Prepare an affirmative brief responding to one or both of the arguments you constructed in the two preceding exercises.

5. Practice taking a flow of a debate by having someone read you the transcript of the sample debate included in appendix B.

Recommended Readings

Freeley, Austin J., and David L. Steinberg. *Argumentation and Debate: Critical Thinking for Reasoned Decision Making*. 10th ed. Belmont, CA: Wadsworth, 1999.

Knapp, Trischa. *Elements of Parliamentary Debate: A Guide to Public Argument*. Boston: Pearson, Allyn and Bacon, 1998.

Meany, John, and Kate Shuster. *Art, Argument, and Advocacy: Mastering Parliamentary Debate*. Harrisburg: IDEA Books, 2002.

Patterson, J. W., and David Zarefsky. *Contemporary Debate*. Boston: Houghton Mifflin, 1983.

Pfau, Michael, David A. Thomas, and Walter Ulrich. *Debate and Argument*. Glenview, IL: Scott, Foresman, 1987.

Phillips, Leslie, William S. Hicks, Douglas Springer, and Maridell Fryer. *Basic Debate*. 4th ed. Lincolnwood, IL: National Textbook, 2001.

Thompson, Wayne N. *Modern Argumentation and Debate: Principles and Practices*. New York: Harper and Row, 1971.

Notes

[1] This topic was debated by the participants of the final round of the National Parliamentary Debate Association's National Championship Tournament in 2003.

[2] This topic was debated by participants at the Macalester National Parliamentary Debate Tournament in 2002.

[3] This topic was debated by participants of the National Debate Tournament during the 2001–2002 academic year.

ACADEMIC DEBATE
ADDITIONAL INSIGHTS

Academic debate is practiced in a variety of contexts: in-class debates, audience debates, and intercollegiate debates, among others. In chapter 10 we presented the general information needed to participate in any of these contexts. But to keep the ideas manageable, we also skipped some of the thornier aspects of debate theory, and we treated debate in general rather than looking at the different types of debate that one may wish to try.

This chapter will delve more deeply into specific areas of debate not fully covered in the preceding chapter. The issues we discuss should prove useful to anyone wishing to gain additional insight into academic debate. We will also present the formats and general nature of debate that occurs under the auspices of the National Debate Tournament Committee (often referred to as NDT style), the National Parliamentary Debate Association, the National Forensics Association (Lincoln-Douglas debate), and the Cross-Examination Debate Association.

THE RESOLUTION

In chapter 10 we identified the resolution as the focus of debate and indicated that the affirmative is obligated to present a topical case. We also suggested that affirmatives present definitions of the key terms of the resolution. We think this is a good idea for beginning debaters. In policy debate tournament competitions, however, it is more common for experienced debaters to define their terms operationally.

Operational Definitions

When an affirmative uses *operational definitions*, the audience and the negative are expected to ascertain what the affirmative thinks a term means by looking at their plan or their arguments. In short, the definitions are not explicit but rather are implicit. For instance, if you want to know how an affirmative defines a key phrase in the resolution such as "substantially change its development assistance policies" you look at what policies the affirmative plan would modify. Only if such operational definitions are challenged by the negative (typically in the form of topicality attacks, a type of procedural argument also discussed in chapter 10) will the affirmative present formal definitions.

Constructing Topicality Arguments

In chapter 10 we explained how a negative who believes the affirmative is not debating the resolution fairly can present a topicality argument. This is the argument that seeks to convince the audience that the affirmative interpretation of the topic is illegitimate. Fortunately, policy topics are worded today with language that is often very specific, and thus topicality is not an issue in most debates, but should it become an issue where you choose to clash with the affirmative case you will need to know how such an argument is constructed.

Usually a topicality argument has three components: standards, violation, and impact. The negative typically presents *standards* that they wish the audience to use when evaluating whether or not the affirmative is topical. Years ago in academic debate all an affirmative team needed to do was argue that their interpretation of the resolution was reasonable. But reasonableness is vague and often difficult to assess. What constitutes reasonability? How does one determine that an affirmative has crossed the line from reasonable to unreasonable? There is no way to predict what an audience will consider to be reasonable. Consequently, most scholars now agree that when there is a disagreement concerning what definition to use, the one offered by the affirmative or the one offered by the negative, the *better definition* should be used. But this is still somewhat vague. How does one determine which is the better definition? This is where the notion of applying argumentative standards comes into play.

Standards

There are a variety of means employed to determine the better definition. We will consider several common standards presented by negatives. These are also used by affirmatives as counter-standards.

Unique Meaning. This argument is premised on the assumption that each word has a **unique meaning**. This seems self-evident. Even Alice in Wonderland knew that we cannot make words mean whatever we want. Yet debaters sometimes interpret the resolution in such a way as to render some words meaningless. For example, if the resolution calls for a change in *development assistance policies,* and the affirmative's interpretation of the topic is that all assistance policies are in essence developmental, then the affirmative has rendered the term *development* meaningless. A better definition might be one that preserves the unique meaning of each word in the resolution.

Precision.   The **precision** standard argues that the more specific or concrete definitions are, the more clearly they mark the boundaries of what is topical and what is not topical. Arguing that *urban* refers to those who live in cities, rather than those who live near such communities, is more precise because it is easier to determine who lives in a city than it is who lives near a community. Therefore, the better definition is that which more precisely defines a resolutional term.

Limiting and Breadth.   The broader the resolution the more latitude affirmatives have in locating ground for constructing a topical case and hence the more likely it is that the negative will have to prepare to debate a very broad range and number of different cases. Such a situation greatly increases the burden on negative teams to find evidence and to prepare arguments against these different affirmative cases. Consequently, affirmatives gain a tactical advantage if they can broaden the range of topical cases. To offset this advantage, negatives sometimes argue that the **limiting definition** is a better one, which establishes manageable boundaries to the scope of the topic.

For example, if any public assistance program is considered to be a part of the welfare system, then the negative will have to be prepared for a wider range of cases than if the welfare system is defined more narrowly as only including income transfer policies. In the former case the negative might have to be prepared to refute cases focused on health care, housing, education, as well as other cases. If the narrower definition is used, the negative would only have to be prepared to oppose cases with a focus on cash assistance programs.

Thus, while negatives typically favor a limiting definition, affirmatives usually present the opposite view as their counter-standard; they generally argue for **breadth**. The view here is that broader topics are more challenging, less tedious, and require more research. Broader topics, say affirmatives, mean debaters learn more. The better definition, then, either limits or broadens the topic and individual judges might choose to apply one standard or the other depending upon their assessment of the arguments for that standard introduced by the debaters.

Field Definitions.   The **field definition** standard maintains that the better definition is one that would be commonly used by members of the field (or participants in the discipline) that is the focus of the resolution. The rationale behind this standard stems from the understanding that each field tends to bring its own meanings to the terms it employs. The term "campaign" has a different meaning in a military context for example, than it does during a political contest. Since jargon varies from field to field, it would be better to use definitions from the appropriate field.

Context.   I. A. Richards, among many others, has argued that a word gains its meaning from the **context** in which it is used.[1] Defining a word without considering the other words in the sentence will likely lead to error and will mislead your audience. Define *red* and *herring* separately, and you are not likely to come up with the same meaning as you would for *red herring*. As Richards writes, "a word or phrase when isolated momentarily from its controlling neigh-

bors is free to develop irrelevant sense which may beguile half the words to follow it."[2] Consequently, it makes sense to define words in the contexts of a set of
terms whenever it is possible.

These common definitional standards are used selectively by affirmatives
and negatives. Speakers choose a standard that supports the definition they
wish to use in a given debate. If the definition they wish to read does not meet a
particular standard, the standard is not presented. Of course, as reasonable as
each of these standards sounds, there are indictments of each, so debaters must
be prepared to defend them.

Furthermore, just as there is an incentive for the affirmative to define the
resolution broadly so that it makes it possible for them to create many different
types of cases, and also to make the case areas somewhat obscure and difficult
for the negative to attack, so too is there an incentive for the negative to define
the resolution narrowly so that there are very few possible affirmative cases. If
the negative definition is so narrow that the affirmative may not have a reasonable chance to win, the affirmative will argue that this is an unfair standard.

Regardless of the standard or counter-standard presented, debaters must
convince the audience that their standard is superior and should be used, or
they must use the standard that has been proposed by their opponents.

Violation

The second component of a topicality argument is the **violation**. Once the
negative has presented the standard they wish the audience to use, they must
present their definition, state why they think this is a better definition (because
it more closely adheres to the standards they have previously presented), and
explain why they believe the affirmative violates this specific definition.

If the affirmative believes they *do* meet the negative definition, they may
accept the negative standard and just respond to those negative arguments
alleging that the case violates the definition of the topic.

Impact

Finally, negatives must indicate, as with all of their arguments, what **impact**
their topicality argument has on the debate. In policy debate topicality is a voting issue. This means that if the negative convinces the audience that the affirmative case is not topical, the negative wins. All other arguments then become
irrelevant. Why? Because if the plan is not topical, no matter how advantageous
it is, the advantages do not prove the resolution true.

In value debate the impact of a topicality argument depends on what part
of the affirmative case is not topical. If, for example, an affirmative presents
three ways in which the welfare system worsens the plight of the urban poor,
and only one of these is not topical, many audiences will simply disregard the
nontopical part of the case. What remains may still be sufficient to carry the
debate for the affirmative.

Reverse Voting Issue

Some affirmatives argue that since the negatives can win the debate with a
topicality argument, negatives will argue topicality even against cases that most

debaters and audiences consider topical. To discourage frivolous topicality arguments some debaters will argue that topicality should be a *reverse voting issue*. This means that if the negative loses the topicality argument, the negative should lose the debate. Virtually no argumentation theorists support this position, however, because it simply does not make much sense.

Use the court system as an analogy to consider this type of argument. Imagine a situation where an attorney argues before a judge that the court does not have appropriate jurisdiction to adjudicate some dispute and thus the charge should be dismissed. If the judge rules against this claim and decides that the court has jurisdiction the case is allowed to proceed. The judge does not say, however, that because the case can go forward that the attorney who argued for the motion to dismiss and failed should be considered to have already lost his or her case.

In a sense topicality represents a similar jurisdictional argument. The negative is saying that the terms of the resolution do not give the judge the power to consider the affirmative case because it advances a rationale outside the jurisdiction of the topic. A finding for the affirmative on the issue of topicality is not akin to a finding on the merits of their entire argument; it simply should mean that the debate can also proceed. Also, implementing the "reverse voting issue standard" would make it too risky for negatives to argue topicality. This would give the affirmatives even greater latitude to run cases of questionable topicality. But negatives must be prepared for the possibility that affirmatives will argue this position and must have their responses ready.

HASTY GENERALIZATIONS

We have indicated that the affirmative burden is to prove the resolution true. But this claim glosses over a controversy in value debate. In policy debate it is commonly accepted that the resolution serves as a parameter for determining the range of cases that may be presented. As long as the case is topical, the case proves the resolution to be true. This approach has come to be known as *parametrics*. The resolution acts as a parameter, laying the boundaries for what is topical. All the affirmative must do is fall within the parameters to be topical and to prove the resolution true. There may be many cases that prove the resolution true, but the affirmative is required to present and defend only one such case. In value debate this is not necessarily true.

Value resolutions tend to be generalizations. For example, "Advertising degrades the quality of life" is an unqualified claim—a generalization. If the parametric approach to topicality is used with such a resolution, the affirmative need only select one example of the topic and then prove the truth of this one example.

Permitting affirmatives to argue only one example of the resolution results in at least two potentially significant advantages for them: first, they do not have to defend examples of the resolution that are untrue. For instance, if some advertising degrades and some does not, the affirmative could choose to present only an example of advertising that does degrade. Second, affirmatives can dismiss arguments that are not specific to the case they present. Just as a policy debater can dismiss a disadvantage that does not link to the mandates identified in the affirmative plan, a value debater can dismiss arguments that are not specific to the affirmative case.

We believe the net result of such a focus is to reward teams, either affirmative or negative, that have the resources to prepare to debate many conceivable examples of the resolution. This could potentially limit the ability of some students to compete effectively. We also believe the theoretical foundation for such an approach is flawed.

In policy debate the focus of the debate is the plan. The plan is the operational definition of the resolution. The resolution calls for a change from the present system, and the plan identifies that change. If the plan is proved to be advantageous, the resolution is proved to be true. Value debate, generally, has no plan. In addition, in argumentation one proves a generalization to be true either by arguing at the level of the generalization or by arguing inductively from examples to a generalization. An affirmative may therefore present examples of the resolution and argue that what is true of the examples is true of the generalization; or an affirmative may argue the **whole resolution**.

Affirmatives who argue by example cannot dismiss counterexamples, for as we mentioned in chapter 5, generalizations established by examples must account for counterexamples. An affirmative who reasons by example may be charged with committing a hasty generalization. Permitting affirmatives to reason by example gives the negative at least two potentially significant advantages.

First, negatives do not have to prepare for the affirmative examples; all they have to do is present the same counterexamples and the same hasty generalization argument in every debate. We do not believe this would promote much learning. Second, it is nearly impossible to find a generalization that divides ground fairly yet does not have some counterexamples. If a single counterexample invalidates an unqualified generalization, then affirmatives would be unable to win some resolutions.

If both the parametrics and the inductive approach are flawed, what is the affirmative to do? The answer seems to reside in resolutional **intrinsicness**. According to this view there are certain qualities that are inherent to the value object.[3] The affirmative should identify these and argue that the value judgment is causally related to these intrinsic attributes. For example, are there certain qualities that are present in all advertising? Does the degradation identified by the affirmative stem from one such inherent quality? All advertising sells. Is selling degrading? All advertising creates a need or desire on the part of the consumer. Does the creation of this appetite or desire necessarily degrade?

Some scholars contend that there is no suitable way to ascertain the intrinsic qualities of a value object. Consequently, they argue, intrinsicness is not an appropriate definitional standard.[4] There is no consensus at this point in value debate. As a result, many debates are still characterized by extensive numbers of arguments about debate theory and especially about the burdens of the affirmative.

PLANS AND COUNTERPLANS

In chapter 10 we indicated that the affirmative in policy debate is called upon to articulate the details of the proposal enacting the resolutional change. Here we examine the role of plans in detail, as well as the negative's option of presenting their own proposal or counterplans.

Value debate is arguably prepolicy, and the vast majority of debates remain at that level. Yet some say that it is possible to present quasi-policy proposals in a value debate. Consequently, many of the comments we will make about plans and counterplans are relevant to value debate as well as policy debate.

There are two reasons plans are receiving increasing use in value debate. First, they can give affirmatives tactical advantages (any advance in debate theory that gives one team or another tactical advantage will eventually be tried). Plans permit affirmatives to focus the debate on those aspects of the topic that they consider especially relevant. For instance, the topic calling for a comparison between implementing the U.N.'s universal declaration of human rights and preserving state sovereignty resulted in a fair number of affirmatives giving the details of the term *implementation* in something that strongly resembled and sometimes was actually called a plan. This permitted affirmatives to focus the debate on the process of implementation they selected and to dismiss methods of implementing the universal declaration of human rights that were less desirable.

Second, plans appear to be warranted by some topics. One way to reveal the inadequacies of the welfare system, for example, is to compare the current system with a modified system, presumably one modified by an affirmative plan.

As a result, the following comments about plans and counterplans may be as relevant to value debaters as they are to policy debaters.

Plans

In order to clarify the change being advocated, the affirmative sometimes specifies the elements of the plan of action they support. The specificity of the resolution directly influences the level of detail required of a plan. In general, plans typically have five components.

1. **The agent.** In this plank of the plan the affirmative identifies who will implement the plan. This may be the federal government or a specific agency of government, such as the Environmental Protection Agency, the Federal Communications Commission, or the Department of Energy, etc.

2. **The mandates.** These are the specific actions called for in the plan. For example, if the affirmative wishes to change development assistance policies by significantly increasing or decreasing agricultural assistance programs, the details of these actions are presented in the plan mandates.

3. **Funding.** If the proposal necessitates the expenditure of monies, some affirmatives specify where that funding will come from. Others rely on the normal funding processes, such as the general revenues of the federal government.

4. **Enforcement.** Policies requiring enforcement may have those provisions identified in this plank of the plan. Enforcement planks may specify the agent responsible for enforcement and the penalties for violating the mandates of the plan.

5. **Intent.** In order to clarify the purpose of the proposal, in case there is ambiguity in its wording, the affirmative may elect to present a summary statement of the plan. This plank derives from the judicial process of examining legislative history in order to clarify the intent of legislation.

Affirmatives occasionally incorporate other components in their plans, which preclude disadvantages and/or counterplans. These are called *plan spikes*. For example, the affirmative may seek to avoid giving the negative a link to a disadvantage about the negative consequences of increased government spending by arguing that their plan will also reduce governmental spending for something else such as agricultural subsidies for tobacco farmers. Such plan spikes are controversial in that many such planks that neutralize disadvantages (and occasionally even result in the affirmative claim that they are accruing additional advantage—e.g., a reduction in the amount of tobacco produced) do not constitute topical actions. Thus, the negative might choose to argue that a particular plan plank may yield a nontopical advantage.

Counterplans

Traditionally, presenting a *counterplan* was predicated on an explicit admission by the negative team that there was a problem in the status quo that could not be solved, but that the affirmative plan should be rejected because there was a different and superior way to solve the problem. In order for the counterplan to be a reason to reject the resolution, it must meet two standards: it must be nontopical and competitive. Usually the negative reads the counterplan (it is written just like a plan) and argues that it meets those standards. Most contemporary scholars believe that these requirements, like procedural arguments, must be presented in the first negative speech.

The negative can construct nontopical counterplans either by employing a nontopical agent of action or by advocating a nontopical action. Advocating a topical counterplan provides another rationale for accepting the truth of the resolution. Consequently, topical counterplans are not a reason to reject the resolution.

Competitiveness is a more difficult issue. To be competitive is to support rejecting the resolution. To support rejecting the resolution, counterplans must be mutually exclusive or net beneficial.[5]

For a plan and counterplan to have *mutual exclusivity* they must be unable to coexist.[6] Consider two mutually exclusive strategies that politicians have presented to balance the federal deficit. One group wants to cut personal income taxes to spur the economy thereby generating more jobs and more taxable income. Another group wants to raise personal income taxes to reduce the deficit. These two plans are competitive because they cannot coexist. No one can cut and raise the same taxes at the same time. On the other hand, we could simultaneously raise income taxes and cut capital gains taxes. Since these two actions "could" coexist, they would not be mutually exclusive.

Some negatives abuse this standard by artificially creating mutual exclusivity. For example, some negatives include a counterplan plank that prohibits adopting both the affirmative plan and the negative counterplan. Others steal the same funding planks. These are arbitrary and artificial because they do not pertain to the substantive mandate planks of the counterplan. Similarly, arguments that the two plans are redundant and/or philosophically incompatible are not tests of whether the plans could coexist. They are arguments that the plans should not coexist, which more correctly fall into the net benefits test.

The **net benefits standard** says that it is more advantageous to implement the counterplan than it is to implement either the affirmative plan or both the affirmative plan and the counterplan. A counterplan that is net beneficial when compared to the affirmative plan does not in and of itself warrant rejecting the resolution. Suppose, for example, the affirmative plan is to establish national health insurance, and the affirmative says that this will save thousands of lives a year. If the negative were to counterplan with a foreign aid plan that saves millions of lives a year, the counterplan would not be a reason to reject the resolution, for we could do both. In this example, the counterplan is not net beneficial when compared to the affirmative plan and the counterplan together. If, however, the negative can demonstrate that the federal government should not do both plans because doing both would destroy the economy, then the counterplan alone would be better than doing both.

If the counterplan cannot coexist or should not coexist, then the counterplan is a reason to reject the resolution and it is therefore competitive. If the counterplan is also not topical, the negative should win.

Permutations

In response to negative counterplans that artificially establish mutual exclusivity, affirmatives initiate something called a **permutation**. This is a tactic whereby the affirmative illustrates the artificiality of the mutual exclusivity by proposing to amend their plan by rewriting sections (e.g., the funding mechanisms) in order to reveal the artificial nature and the lack of clash in the counterplan's mandates.[7]

Fiat

In debate, **fiat** refers to the assumption that if the affirmative can demonstrate a proposal *should* be adopted, we can assume that sensible policy makers would adopt it through normal means. If the agent of action is the United States federal government, then "normal means" refers to the democratic processes typically followed when legislation is enacted. To dispute whether the plan *would* be enacted, rather than *should* the plan be enacted is called a **should/ would argument** and is generally dismissed.

The enactment of legislation is no guarantee, however, that the legislation will be solvent. If adverse attitudes preclude the status quo from accruing the advantages now, the enforcement of the new legislation may be thwarted by the same pernicious attitudes. Fiat is no magic wand. It does not automatically over-come attitudes. It only, theoretically, for the purpose of argument, implements the legislation.

An understanding of fiat is necessary to avoid or point out situations of fiat abuse. We have heard both plans and counterplans that abuse fiat. One plan called for the nations of the world to eliminate their militaries. The team then argued that the United Nations would then be the only entity with access to mil-itary force. Needless to say, the plan was advantageous when compared to the status quo where practically everyone has their own military and conflicts between nations are rife. Could this plan be implemented through normal means? What are the "normal means" by which the nations of the world abolish their militaries? We believe the plan was an abuse of fiat because it attempted to "set aside" and avoid debate over precisely those issues that an advocate would need to refute to evaluate the merits of the affirmative's case.

THINKING STRATEGICALLY

Since debate is an intellectual contest, it is important that you approach it that way. Some debaters have better tactical skills than others—perhaps they can speak more succinctly or more rapidly, or they have more or better evi-dence. They may simply have more experience than you. Some of these advan-tages can be minimized through strategic planning: anticipating how the debate may unfold and preparing accordingly.

Controlling the Ground

The affirmative has an advantage in that they get to start and end the debate. Starting the debate means selecting how they want to go about proving the truth of the resolution. This is their ground. Anyone familiar with sports will confirm that there is usually a home court advantage. The same is true of aca-demic debate. As much as possible, the affirmative will want the debate to unfold according to their terms. In policy debate, they will construct the plan and case so that the focus is on the issues that they think they are most likely to win. Similarly, in value debate experienced debaters are very adept at present-ing criteria that make it difficult for them to lose.

Some negatives are skilled at capturing the ground. If the negative presents several off-case arguments, the focus of the debate can shift from the affirmative case to the off-case. The off-case is the negative's turf. They get to select, from all of the possible off-case arguments, those they feel best able to win. Arguing one's own issues should be an advantage.

Planning for the End of the Debate

What do you think will be the telling issue or evidence at the end of the debate? If you think in terms of how the audience will eventually make sense of the round, it may help you decide how or when to present an argument.

When you first begin to debate it is difficult enough to come up with what you can say in your constructive speech, but as you gain experience, you will start to think in terms of what your opponent will say in response to your arguments, and then what you will say about your opponent's argument. Good chess players think several moves ahead. So do good debaters.

In fact, just as chess players lay traps for their opponents or divert their attention from their real objectives, so do debaters. Knowing what an opponent will say in response to your initial argument enables you to decide, in advance of the debate, what to say to defeat that response. If you cannot beat the response, perhaps you should not make the argument in the first place.

Winning in Rebuttals

Advanced debaters often attempt to narrow the debate to a limited number of issues in the final rebuttals. This means selecting those issues or arguments a team is most likely to win.

The negative often has several arguments that they could choose to extend in the final rebuttal: case arguments, procedural arguments, a counterplan, and/or several disadvantages. Because of time constraints, however, it may be difficult to cover all of them. As a result, many negatives grant answers that destroy the reasoning of a disadvantage or ignore an argument in their final rebuttal. This essentially removes these arguments from the final decision-making calculus. It also permits affirmatives to more fully explain and extend the remaining arguments.

The art of deciding what to go for in the last rebuttals is central to understanding what argumentation is all about and is also a place where your skills in reasoning, analysis, and refutation meet up with your ability to analyze and persuade your audience.

Maximizing Your Strengths

Some basketball teams walk the ball up the court. Others run it. Some football teams like to run the ball on every down, while others prefer to throw it. Why? Because teams know their strengths and try to take advantage of them. In determining their strategies teams will develop plays that permit them to capitalize on their resources. Think about your strengths in debate. Are you good at explaining arguments? Are you a quick talker? Do you have a lot of evidence or a little? You should always seek to discover your strengths and weaknesses and then construct your strategy accordingly.

We have known debaters who were prepared for almost any argument an opponent might raise. Such debaters maximized their strengths by constructing a broad affirmative case. But we have also coached teams whose strength was dealing with a limited number of arguments. Such debaters were better off with a case that invited fewer arguments but that permitted them to explain their positions more fully.

SPECIALIZED DEBATE FORMATS

Throughout this and the previous chapter we have focused on the most common formats for engaging in academic debate. Here we would like to introduce you to some of the specifics of the various types of debate.

National Debate Tournament and Cross-Examination Debate Association Debate

The oldest intercollegiate debate association is the *National Debate Tournament (NDT)*.* The first National Debate Tournament was held at the United States Military Academy at West Point in 1947. Every year since that first tournament, the best debate teams from across the nation have competed against each other, each seeking to qualify for a coveted spot in the annual National Debate Tournament. NDT teams debate policy topics at invitational tournaments that are hosted by different colleges and universities from September until April. Teams may qualify for the NDT either on the basis of their outstanding performance at these invitational tournaments (what is known as an "at-large" bid) or by winning one of the bids to NDT by doing well in their district qualifying tournaments.

In 1971, the *Cross-Examination Debate Association (CEDA)* was created as an alternative to NDT debate.† The original motivation for the creation of CEDA was to create a form of debate where students used a more persuasive and communicative delivery style, where they spoke more slowly and where debates could be more easily understood by untrained audiences. For many years CEDA operated as a completely separate entity. Frequently it utilized value resolutions and, in an effort to decrease the importance of evidence and increase the importance of communication, the CEDA debate resolution changed in mid-season so that debaters were challenged to undertake research on a second topic each season. Several years ago the two organizations enjoyed a rapprochement and now they share the same resolution throughout the year. As a result, even though the NDT and CEDA each hold their own national championship tournament, there now seems to be very little difference between the style and form of debate sponsored by each organization.

Format
The format for an NDT/CEDA debate is as follows:

9 minutes	First Affirmative constructive
3 minutes	negative speaker cross-examination of the First Affirmative speaker
9 minutes	First Negative constructive
3 minutes	affirmative speaker cross-examination of the First Negative speaker

---

* For more information about this form of debate contact the home page of the National Debate Tournament. It may be found at http://www.wfu.edu/organizations/NDT/.

† The home page for the Cross-Examination Debate Association is http://cedadebate.org/.

9 minutes	Second Affirmative constructive
3 minutes	cross-examination of the Second Affirmative speaker by the other negative speaker
9 minutes	Second Negative constructive
3 minutes	cross-examination of the Second Negative speaker by the other affirmative speaker
6 minutes	First Negative rebuttal
6 minutes	rebuttal by an affirmative speaker
6 minutes	Second Negative rebuttal
6 minutes	rebuttal by the other affirmative speaker

Each speaker thus gives a constructive speech and each speaker presents a rebuttal. Each debater is asked questions and also gets to ask questions during a cross-examination period. The affirmative both initiates and concludes the debate. As is the case in almost all debate formats, both sides get the same amount of time to speak.

Preparation Time

Each team also receives a total of ten minutes of **alternate use time**. This time is used by the debaters as preparation time. It is time that they can use to discuss strategy, find the evidence they wish to present, and prepare the notes that they will use when they speak. Judges or time-keepers typically are responsible for keeping track of this time.

The Resolution and Evidence

By vote of its membership, an NDT/CEDA resolution is chosen in late July and used throughout the year. This permits debaters a great deal of time to delve deeply into the extant literature on a resolution. In recent years the NDT/CEDA has moved to more specific wording of its resolutions. This decreases the breadth of cases for which students must prepare. Nevertheless, the NDT debate places a heavy emphasis on supporting one's claims with evidence drawn from credible, published sources; consequently, the research demands for NDT/CEDA debate are extensive. But the resulting depth of understanding of the arguments, pro and con, is also extensive. Research skills for experienced debaters are also highly refined. The 2003–2004 NDT/CEDA resolution was:

Resolved: that the United States Federal Government should enact one or more of the following:

- withdrawal of its World Trade Organization complaint against the European Union's restrictions on genetically modified foods;

- a substantial increase in its government-to-government economic and/or conflict prevention assistance to Turkey and/or Greece;

- full withdrawal from the North Atlantic Treaty Organization;

- removal of its barriers to and encouragement of substantial European Union and/or North Atlantic Treaty Organization participation in peace-keeping in Iraq and reconstruction in Iraq;

- removal of its tactical nuclear weapons from Europe;

- harmonization of its intellectual property law with the European Union in the area of human DNA sequences;
- rescission of all or nearly all agriculture subsidy increases in the 2002 Farm Bill.

The National Forensics Association's Lincoln-Douglas Debate

Most debating in post-secondary education is done by two-person teams. Nevertheless, there is increasing opportunity for one-on-one debate. This style of debate is known as *Lincoln-Douglas* or *L-D Debate*. It is named after the historic debates between Abraham Lincoln and Stephen Douglas. The sponsoring organization for most L-D Debate in the United States is the National Forensics Association (NFA).* The NFA was founded in 1971 to promote individual events (contests in such speaking events as oratory, extemporaneous speaking, oral interpretation of prose and poetry) and to crown national champions in these events. In 1990 the NFA expanded its competition to include L-D Debate.

Lincoln-Douglas debate is a variant of NDT/CEDA debate. It uses policy topics, and the stock issues of ill, blame, cure, and cost are the focus of the adjudication. But there are also substantive differences. In addition to being one-against-one debate, L-D is persuasion orientated. NDT and CEDA both permit, some would say encourage, speaking at very fast rates—rates that are much faster than one normally hears from a public speaker. Jargon and gamesmanship are also encouraged by the lack of rules and willingness to let debaters challenge norms during NDT and CEDA debate rounds. L-D Debate specifies in its rules that speaking too quickly is "antithetical to the purpose and intent of this event."[8] The NFA is not the only debate organization that emphasizes persuasive and reasoned communication rather than high speed-speaking either, another similar organization that sponsors its own debate tournaments is the American Debate Association.[†]

Format

In Lincoln-Douglas Debate, as with team debate, the affirmative speaks first and last, both speakers question and are questioned during cross-examination periods, and both sides have an equal amount of speaking time. Typical time limits for NFA-LD are:

6 minutes	First Affirmative constructive
3 minutes	cross-examination by negative
7 minutes	First Negative constructive
3 minutes	cross-examination by affirmative
6 minutes	Second Affirmative constructive
6 minutes	Second Negative constructive
3 minutes	affirmative rebuttal

---

* The home page for National Forensics Association's Lincoln-Douglas debate is http://www.bethel.edu/college/dept/comm./nfa/nfa-ld.html.

[†] Information about the American Debate Association can be found at http://www2.bc.edu/~katsulas/welcome.html.

You may have noted that there is only rebuttal. The negative speaker must use part of the Second Negative Constructive to summarize the arguments against the resolution. The Affirmative cannot bring up new argument in the rebuttal. This rule is true of all forms of academic debate.

The Resolution and Evidence

Members of the National Forensics Association select the topic to be used and it has always been a policy resolution. Claims need to be proven, but the reliance on evidence is balanced by the need to persuade the judge. The amount of evidence is about that which would be used in well-supported persuasive speech. The first time a source is cited the debater must provide a full-source citation. The resolution for the 2003–2004 season was:

> Resolved: that the United States Federal Government should substantially increase environmental regulations on industrial pollution.

Judges

Unlike NDT/CEDA tournaments, L-D Debate is held in conjunction with Individual Events (IE) tournaments. Frequently debaters are also participants in other such events. Judges for L-D also serve as judges for the IE competitions. That means that the judges frequently have limited experience in coaching and judging debate. This is also by design. The result is that debaters must talk to the judges as if they are reasonable people but lack expertise in debate. This also minimizes jargon and increases the emphasis on communicating effectively.

National Parliamentary Debate Association Debate

Most intercollegiate debate emphasizes argument to such an extent that public speaking skills are too frequently neglected. This is not the case in ***parliamentary debate***. Such debate rewards wit and rhetorical skill. It is loosely modeled after the kind of debating that occurs in the British House of Parliament. While there are several types of parliamentary debate (e.g., American Parliamentary Debate Association and World's Style), we will focus on that sponsored by the National Parliamentary Debate Association (NPDA).* NPDA began in 1993 and is now one of the largest debate associations in the nation. You will note many similarities between parliamentary debate and the other forms of debate previously examined, but you will also note significant differences.

The Resolution

In traditional intercollegiate team debate, a resolution is announced and the same resolution is used for a year, semester, or, at minimum, a tournament. In parliamentary debate the resolution changes each round. Fifteen minutes (plus walking time) before a debate is scheduled to begin, the topic is announced. This results in debates that call upon the general knowledge of the participants, rather than on precompetition research. In fact, inartistic proofs cannot be intro-

* The home page for the National Parliamentary Debate Association is http://www.bethel.edu/college/dept/comm./npda/. Information about the American Parliamentary Debate Association can be obtained at http://www.apdaweb.org/. Information about the World's Style of debate can be obtained at http://www.debating.net/Flynn/.

duced into the debate. Debaters can consult any written materials they brought to the tournament, but they cannot cite these sources during the debate. This results in a truly extemporaneous quality to the debate. Robert Trapp, one of the founders of NPDA, considers its extemporaneous nature to be one of the primary differences between parliamentary debate and NDT/CEDA.*

Parliamentary debate resolutions may be fact, value, or policy propositions. They may also be metaphorical. Metaphorical resolutions require interpretation or translation by the debaters. At a recent tournament students debated the resolution, "This House would rather be in than out." While some debaters undoubtedly took the topic literally and argued the pros and cons of trying to fit in, others discussed very complex and significant policy issues, such as whether or not the United States should seek membership with the other signers of the Comprehensive Test Ban Treaty, the Land Mine Treaty, and the World Court of Justice.

The Audience

The principle distinction, and the reason that speaking skill is rewarded, stems from the audience perspective. Parliamentary debate either utilizes or envisions lay judges instead of judges skilled in the rules and jargon of academic debate. Even coaches who judge parliamentary debate typically approach judging as nonexperts. The debaters, understanding this, avoid jargon and talk to the judges as if a larger audience were present.

Format

Another difference is that debaters are not referred to as affirmatives and negatives; rather they are known generally as the proponents and opponents of the resolution. Each debater is given a role in the format used at most tournaments:

7 minutes	Prime Minister
8 minutes	Leader of the Opposition
8 minutes	Member of the Government
8 minutes	Member of the Opposition
4 minutes	Leader of the Opposition
5 minutes	Prime Minister

Parliamentary debate does not permit preparation or alternate use time. Debaters must go to the podium and begin their speech as quickly as possible after the previous debater has concluded speaking.

Points of Information, Privilege, and Order

While other debate formats set aside time for asking and answering questions, in parliamentary debate there is no predetermined time for cross-examination. Instead, debaters can stand up and seek the floor during any constructive speech—except during the first and last minute of the speech, which is protected time. The debater currently speaking can yield for a **Point of Information (POI)** or indicate that he/she is not willing to yield at this time. If the speaker yields, the questioner can ask a question or make a short statement. The clock does not stop during the POI.

---

* Robert Trapp. Parliamentary Debate. Available on-line at http://www.bethel.edu/college/dept/ comm./npda/parliamentary.html.

In addition, debaters can rise for a *Point of Personal Privilege (PPP)* and a *Point of Order (POO)*. A Point of Personal Privilege is raised if the debater believes that his or her words have been grievously misconstrued or if the debater has been personally insulted by the opponent. A Point of Order is raised if a debater thinks that another debater or the judge has violated the rules of parliamentary debate. This could occur if there is a breach of ethics. It is a serious charge and must not be raised unless there is a serious matter. The clock is stopped for both PPPs and POOs and the judge rules immediately.

Even when not seeking the floor, the other debaters need not sit quietly. That is because heckling in parliamentary debate is perfectly acceptable. Usually such commentary is limited to a "well said" encouragement to a teammate, or a "shame, shame" to the opposition if the speaker mischaracterizes an argument. But heckling can go further. According to Theodore Scheckels and Annette Warfield, "A heckle is a brief, witty, and somewhat substantive remark hurled at the speaker so that everyone can hear it."[9] The purpose of such heckling is often refutation; it helps to call attention to what one side may see as a weak or preposterous argument offered by their opponents. A good parliamentary speaker masters the art of responding to the heckling with a witty retort and then proceeding on without sign of having been ruffled. Keeping a firm check on one's temper when faced with heckling is often an important test of one's ability to engage in this form of debating.

Summary

We have examined more fully the focus on the resolution, discussing such aspects as topicality, hasty generalizations, and parametrics. We have also considered the nature and functions of plans and counterplans. We have moved beyond specific tactics employed in debates to offer advice as to how debaters can think strategically. Finally, we have considered three increasingly popular forms of intercollegiate debate: NDT/CEDA, NPDA, and L-D Debate. Some of the issues we have addressed are controversial. Needless to say, we have presented our views of these issues. Readers are encouraged to pursue those issues that interest them by reading the articles noted in this chapter or by consulting the recommended readings.

Key Terms

alternate use time
better definition
breadth
competitiveness
context
counterplan
Cross-Examination
  Debate Association (CEDA)

fiat
field definition
impact
intrinsicness
limiting definition
Lincoln-Douglas (L-D) debate
mutual exclusivity
National Debate Tournament (NDT)

net benefits standard

operational definitions

parametrics

parliamentary debate

permutation

plan spikes

Point of Information (POI)

Point of Order (POO)

Point of Personal Privilege (PPP)

precision

reverse voting issue

should/would argument

standards

unique meaning

violation

whole resolution

Activities

1. Examine the sample debate presented in appendix B. Then construct a negative topicality argument against the affirmative case presented. Be sure to include the three elements of a topicality argument: standards, violation, and impact. If you think the affirmative case is topical, attempt to create a similar, but nontopical case on the same topic.

2. Now approach the question of topicality from the affirmative perspective. Construct an affirmative topicality brief answering the topicality argument constructed in activity # 1. You may clash on one or more of the three elements of the negative topicality position.

3. Examine the sample value debate in appendix B. Construct a negative countercriteria argument. This should be supported with data and should include a criticism of the affirmative criteria as well as a countercriterion for the debate.

4. Construct an affirmative brief supporting the original criteria presented in the sample value debate. This brief should respond to the arguments constructed in activity # 3.

Recommended Readings

Branham, Robert James. *Debate and Critical Analysis: The Harmony of Conflict*. Hillsdale, NJ: Lawrence Earlbaum, 1991.

Herbeck, Dale, and John P. Katsulas. "The Affirmative Topicality Burden: Any Reasonable Example of the Resolution." *Journal of the American Forensic Association* 21 (1985): 133–145.

Herbeck, Dale, John P. Katsulas, and Karla K. Leeper. "The Locus of Debate Controversy Reexamined: Implications for Counterplan Theory." *Argumentation and Advocacy* 25 (1989): 150–164.

Knapp, Trischa. *Elements of Parliamentary Debate: A Guide to Public Argument*. Boston: Pearson, Allyn and Bacon, 1998.

Madsen, Arnie. "General Systems Theory and Counterplan Competition." *Argumentation and Advocacy* 26 (1989): 71–82.

Madsen, Arnie, and Allan D. Louden. "The Jurisdiction/Topicality Analogy." *Argumentation and Advocacy* 26 (1990): 151–154.

Meany, John, and Kate Shuster. *Art, Argument, and Advocacy: Mastering Parliamentary Debate*. Harrisburg: IDEA Books, 2002.

Murphy, Thomas L. "Assessing the Jurisdictional Model of Topicality." *Argumentation and Advocacy* 26 (1990): 145–150.

Perkins, Dallas. "Counterplans and Paradigms." *Argumentation and Advocacy* 25 (1989): 140–149.

"Special Forum: Debate Paradigms." *Journal of the American Forensic Association* 18 (1982): 133–160.

Thomas, David A., and John P. Hart, eds. *Advanced Debate—Readings in Theory, Practice and Teaching*. Skokie, IL: National Textbook, 1992.

Notes

[1] I. A. Richards, *The Philosophy of Rhetoric* (London: Oxford University Press, 1936).

[2] Ibid., 55.

[3] Kenneth Bahm, "Intrinsic Justification: Meaning and Method," *CEDA Yearbook* 9 (1988): 23–29; and David M. Berube, "Hasty Generalization Revisited, Part One: On Being Representative Examples," *CEDA Yearbook* 10 (1989): 43–53.

[4] Bill Hill and Richard W. Leeman, "On Not Using Intrinsic Justification in Debate," *Argumentation and Advocacy* 26 (Spring 1990): 133–44.

[5] These are the classic determinants of the counterplan presented by Allan J. Lichtman and Daniel M. Rhorer, "A General Theory of the Counterplan," *Journal of the American Forensic Association* 12 (Fall 1975): 70–79.

[6] Kevin Baaske, "The Counterplan: A Reevaluation of the Competitiveness Standard," Western Speech Communication Association, 1985.

[7] For a thorough discussion of the issue of permutations, see Dale A. Herbeck, "A Permutation Standard of Competitiveness," *Journal of the American Forensic Association* 22 (1985): 12–19.

[8] See the NFA L-D Web site at http://www.bethel.edu/college/dept/comm./nfa/nfa-ld.html.

[9] Theodore F. Scheckels and Annette C. Warfield, "Parliamentary Debate: A Description and Justification," *Argumentation and Advocacy* 27 (Fall 1990): 88.

ARGUMENTATION IN POLITICS
CAMPAIGNS AND DEBATES

Although it is unlikely that American electoral politics were ever as clean, straightforward, or focused on substantive issues as many critics of present electoral practices would have us believe—there is much nostalgia for a golden age in American politics that never was—there is no doubt that the political landscape in America has changed over the years. One dramatic and noteworthy change is that paid political consultants have replaced the political parties as the controlling force in American politics. In the past, the political party bosses and a small group of party activists handpicked the candidates who ran for public office, either behind closed doors or in party conventions. The candidates were often selected because they had toiled in the party vineyards by working on past campaigns or because they possessed important connections that would help them gain election. Candidates were expected to follow the party platforms on issues, and voters were more likely to vote straight party tickets. The power of the political parties diminished for many reasons, including: the demise of urban political machines, the move to primary elections for the selection of party candidates, class mobility and population migrations that unhooked voters from the party membership that had been defined by their occupations and places of residence, and the fact that increasing numbers of voters began to declare themselves as independents rather than as Democrats or Republicans.

Today, those who participate in the electoral process are less likely to vote for the candidates of only one political party, or they often choose from a number of nominees within their own party through primary elections. Thus, voters must actively seek information about political candidates in order to make informed choices. Unfortunately, however, research suggests that fewer American citizens are interested in following politics or actively seek out political information. It now appears that fewer people attend political rallies or listen to candidates give live speeches today than two decades ago; fewer people watch political debates or pay attention to major party conventions; and more Americans are reporting that they rely on television for their political news rather than consulting the more complete information available from newspapers or newsmagazines.[1]

In this chapter we explore, from a narrative perspective, the elements on which candidates' focus to gain the attention, adherence, and support of voters. Because so many voters get their information about candidates from television, candidates work on projecting the proper image and displaying character traits that exhibit and command respect. We will examine how candidates use meaningful achievements and events from the past and the present in their stories to convince voters that their views, values, and dreams provide a solid and accurate foundation for their perspectives. We also look at the form and structure of political arguments and debates. We believe that American political campaigns and debates, and indeed the communication that shapes the pragmatic politics of legislation and governance in the United States, are fundamentally rational and argumentative in character. In fact, they are carefully orchestrated argumentative exercises aimed at engaging the electorate and convincing voters that their interests are being served and protected.

ISSUES AND VOTERS

People in general, and especially people as voters, are attuned to issues that directly affect their own lives and situations. Thus, farmers are predictably drawn to candidates who support policies that are helpful to agricultural producers, union members seek candidates who are willing to support the rights and power of unions, small business owners back candidates whose positions on issues will likely enhance the profitability of their businesses, and the parents of young children favor candidates who focus on issues such as improving education or expanded access to day care. In addition to courting constituencies such as these, however, political candidates also seek to appeal to voters who hold strong positions on other key political issues; some voters, for example, are so focused on the issue of abortion that they decide to vote either for or against a particular candidate on the basis of that candidate's position on this single issue. For other voters gun control, environmental regulations, or gay rights may be the issue that decides their votes. Candidates must seek to develop positions on these important single issues that will win them more votes than they will likely lose. Obviously a strongly pro-life voter is unlikely to vote for a strongly pro-choice candidate.

Although candidates attempt to appeal to particular interests held by voters, they must also try to avoid appearing so beholden to special interest or single-issue voters that they ignore the broader interests of other constituencies. In addition, candidates must attempt to create images, public personas, and stories that are consistent. A candidate who emphasizes certain issues to build support with a particular constituency also attempts to appeal to other voters with similar interests. Candidates develop ideological constituencies in order to preserve a sense of harmony and predictability in the stories that they tell.

As an example, we will return briefly to Walter Fisher's explanation of the power of the "American Dream" metaphor, which we discussed in chapter 7. Fisher argued that two political *myths* or stories have long dominated American electoral politics.[2] The first he calls the *materialistic myth*. This myth emphasizes economic issues, material well-being, and the drive to succeed and improve one's own life and the lives of our families in a material sense. We are all concerned about the state of the economy, our job security, the promise of the future, and our ability to support our families and ourselves, today and in our retirement years. The materialistic myth drives such shared cultural values as our beliefs in the work ethic, self-reliance, individual initiative, and ingenuity.

The second myth Fisher calls the *moralistic myth*. This myth celebrates the principles of equality, justice, unity, collective responsibility, and concern for our fellow citizens. While the materialistic myth stresses that government should stay out of our way so that we can take care of ourselves and "do our own thing," the moralistic myth says that government has a responsibility to protect the weak and less fortunate and to elevate the spirit of humankind.

Fisher argues that virtually all Americans have at least some allegiance to both of these myths, and that both of them shape our values, our political identities, the American political culture, and the argumentative appeals that candidates make to voters.[3] While Fisher cited the 1972 McGovern campaign as an illustration of the conflict between these two competing myths, this conflict can be found more recently when candidate George W. Bush argued that he was a "compassionate conservative." By using these words he was clearly attempting to appeal to both the materialistic and the moral myths. As a "conservative," he expressed his conviction in self-reliance and individual effort and ingenuity, with minimal governmental intrusion. As a person who is "compassionate," however, he claimed that he also sought to look out for those who are less fortunate and who need governmental assistance. Although many liberal critics complained that this rhetoric was short on specifics, it obviously won support from a substantial number—although not a majority—of American voters in the 2000 presidential election. Furthermore, Bush used the same words to describe himself in his 2004 presidential nomination acceptance speech (see appendix A).

VOTER ATTITUDES

People complain about politics and politicians for being inconsistent as well as for other reasons. Some voters are unhappy because they believe politicians do not really listen to them or represent their interests. Young voters, for instance, complain that politicians do not focus on the issues that are important to young people but instead spend most of their time talking about social security or the need to fix Medicare. It is not surprising that politicians do not spend much time talking about the issues that are important to young people, however, when it is older Americans who constitute the most likely and the most reliable voters in any election. Why should politicians spend their energy talking about issues that are important to young people who will not turn out to vote anyway? Others lament the fact that regardless of whom they vote for, their problems never seem to end and things never seem to change. Still others protest that the candidates seem so dependent on special interest groups and large campaign contributors that they ignore the needs of their constituents.

A study by the Shorenstein Center of Harvard University reported that approximately 17 percent of adult Americans are politically apathetic, meaning that they "have no sense of civic duty," "aren't interested in politics," and "have no commitment in keeping up with public affairs." Another study reported that roughly a quarter of all adult Americans were classified as either "alienated" ("the angry men and women of U.S. politics who were so disgusted with politicians and the political process that they've opted out") or "disenchanted" ("nonvoters who aren't so much repelled by politics as they are by the way politics are practiced"). In short, these voters are not at all apathetic to contemporary politics, instead they are so unhappy with politics that they have actively decided not to participate.[4]

In terms of voter participation, the United States ranks about thirty-sixth among the world's fifty most-industrialized nations.[5] In the 1996 presidential race less than half of those eligible to vote bothered to do so, resulting in the lowest voter turnout since 1924. In the midterm elections held in 1998 the turnout averaged from 36 to 38 percent of eligible voters.[6] Although turnout slightly improved in the 2000 presidential race, it was poor again in the 2002 midterm elections. Different theories to explain the low voter turnout have been offered, ranging from political apathy to the claim that voters are largely satisfied with the way things are and hence see no need to vote, but most analysts attribute the low levels of participation to citizens' disgust with the conduct of campaigns and cynicism about politics.[7]

In what may represent an even more ominous sign for the future, young people seem to be especially disconnected from political discussions and from voting. Young voters, 18 to 24 years of age, are the least likely of all eligible voters to cast their ballots. One study reported that only 27 percent of younger people reported that keeping up with politics was important to them.[8] Halstead argued that these younger nonvoters are "less politically or civically engaged, exhibit less social trust or confidence in government, have a weaker allegiance to their country or to either political party, and are more materialistic than their predecessors."[9]

Despite the cause or causes for the declining rates of political participation and the dissatisfaction with the political process, however, all of us have an interest in addressing the problem of low voter turnout. The stability of our nation and the vitality of our political system depend on a high level of political participation and involvement by our citizens. When people do not vote because they do not believe that their vote makes a difference, a pervasive feeling that the system does not work develops. If people do not participate in the political process, and in fact feel alienated from that process, then they are less likely to be committed to its preservation. As W. Lance Bennett argued: "Restoring public interest in government, trust in leadership, and commitment to a livable society . . . are essential steps toward real solutions for problems like crime, homelessness, drug abuse, education, economic revitalization, and other obstacles to the 'good life.'"[10]

CAMPAIGNS AS STORIES

That so many Americans are no longer following politics or even bothering to vote has, of course, increased the political power and the impact of those voters who do go to the polls. It has also created a political caste system in the United States. Those voters who are most politically engaged and involved—the active electorate, composed of persons who follow the issues, are informed about competing candidates, and often have strong opinions—have a wealth of political information available to them via newspapers, magazines, all-news cable television channels, talk radio, and the Internet. These voters often tend to decide who they will vote for early in a campaign, and they actively seek political information that will confirm their already strongly held opinions.

There are often not enough such voters to decide closely contested elections, however, so candidates often spend their energy and their resources during political campaigns trying to reach potential voters who are less interested in politics, who do not have strong partisan commitments, and who are not actively seeking political news or information. These citizens may not vote in many elections, but if they do decide to go to the polls, they may decide whom they will vote for much later in the course of a campaign. These voters admit that they get most of their political information from broadcast news or even from paid political advertisements; indeed, many of these citizens report that they get much of their political information from late-night entertainment programs like the Jay Leno or David Letterman shows.[11]

Because these voters are so volatile, because they often cannot be motivated to vote, or because they may swing their support from one party to the other, from one election to the next, they often find themselves as the primary targets for many political campaign messages.[12] How exactly do political candidates successfully target citizens who are not especially curious or motivated to seek information about political issues or candidates? This is indeed the challenge. The answer, in recent campaigns, has been through paid political advertisements, and the accepted political wisdom has become that such ads must be so numerous that they are ubiquitous and thus cannot be avoided.

Because political advertising, whether in the form of direct mailings, newspaper ads, billboards, or radio or television spot ads, is expensive, most candidates must seek to simplify their messages and present them in the briefest possible form. Because undecided voters are not well informed about politics, they can best be reached and persuaded by the simple messages. Political advertising also is constrained by voters' preexisting beliefs about a candidate's attributes and about the existing political situation. Thus, Kathleen Hall Jamieson argued that "advertising, whether brilliant or banal, is powerless to dislodge deeply held convictions anchored in an ample amount of credible information."[13] The result is a system in which candidates are increasingly packaged into attractive media personalities and then sold to the voters in much the same way the products are sold to consumers.[14]

In our earlier discussions of the storytelling perspective of argumentation, we emphasized that the world is made up of competing stories, each vying for public acceptance. Electoral campaigns provide excellent settings for watching these competing stories develop and emerge. As with any story, campaigns have main characters (the candidates) with whom the audience identifies in some way. Two attributes that play an important role in "identity" are image and character. Larry K. Smith, a former manager of a presidential and several senatorial campaigns, has observed that: "A campaign is a morality play . . . a contest over values and norms, not issues. . . . Every campaign is a story about the candidate and the nation."[15]

Image

We have entered an era of *image* politics where candidates are evaluated on the basis of their public personalities. This era emphasizes such attributes as physical appearance, a winning smile, the ability to project warmth and empathy, the ability to give an effective speech, and indeed the appealing portrait or the perfect spouse and children more than it does political experience or even perhaps a coherent political ideology. It seems understandable, given this era, that celebrities are often suggested as ideal political candidates, despite the fact that one might naturally question what being an actor (e.g., Arnold Schwarzenegger or Warren Beatty), professional athlete (e.g., Bill Bradley or Jack Kemp), or a professional wrestler—someone who seems to work at the intersection of athletics and acting (e.g., Jesse Ventura) has to offer as a potential political leader.

Politics, as a morality play, consists of candidate images that are created rather than merely discovered. The candidates themselves in speeches and public statements create their images. These images are further refined and publicly shared by campaign consultants and made the focus of advertising campaigns. Images acquire further power in the statements offered by the candidates' supporters and opponents. Images are circulated, refuted, or recast by the press accounts of the campaign. Finally, images also come alive in the conversations that voters have with their friends and family members.

There may, of course, be many different dimensions of political image that candidates might wish to communicate to potential voters. Physical attractiveness, vigor, strength, integrity, sincerity, intelligence, independence, wisdom, and a sense of humor, among other attributes, have been demonstrated to increase public support for particular candidates.[16] Given this public penchant for selecting candidates on the basis of their image rather than their expressed positions on the issues one might question what role argumentation really plays in American political campaigns. The answer, as you can expect given the bias of this book, is a very important one.

Character

An important element in the consideration of a candidate's image is the notion of **character**. Voters naturally seek candidates whom they believe are honest, trustworthy, and competent. We seek elected officials who will keep their promises and be true to their word. Perhaps even more important, however, is that we seek candidates who see the world as we do—who share our stories and who have the same values that we have. As an example we will cite a political advertisement that California gubernatorial candidate Cruz Bustamante ran in his campaign against Arnold Schwarzenegger. The ad shows Bustamante speaking before a large audience composed of racially diverse Californians. Bustamante declares: "Schwarzenegger does not share our values. He is not like us. He is from *Planet Hollywood!*"* The ad is thus a blatant attempt to convince largely blue-collar and middle-class Democratic voters in California that a wealthy Hollywood actor would not be sympathetic to their interests and their worldviews.

Voters seek candidates who share their values, beliefs, and worldview.[17] They want candidates who are like them, but not *just* like them. In short, voters seek candidates who can understand their needs, but who are just a little bit better than they are themselves—a bit more intelligent, a bit more experienced, a bit more courageous, and perhaps even a bit more morally perfect.

One of the most common techniques that political candidates use to attempt to identify with potential voters is to emphasize their own humble origins. For example, President George W. Bush, during the 2000 presidential campaign emphasized his childhood in Midland, Texas, far more than he did his attendance at an elite East Coast boarding school as a high school student or his college years at Yale University. Likewise, in that same campaign, Vice President Al Gore emphasized his summers spent working on the farm in Carthage, Tennessee, and not his childhood living in the prestigious Mayflower Hotel in Washington, D.C. Candidates eager to emphasize the importance of their own identity have now been known to write their autobiographies (e.g., the very popular life story written by Arizona Senator John McCain that recounts his own heroic experiences as a prisoner of war in Vietnam, and the life stories of his father and grandfather, both of whom served as admirals in the U.S. Navy).

Another strategy that has proven popular is the creation of the biographical video. The best example that we have seen is the 1992 video that Bill Clinton used to introduce himself during the Democratic Convention. The video described how Clinton grew up poor in the village of Hope, Arkansas. Clinton lived in a lower-middle-class home with an outhouse in the backyard. He was forced to endure his stepfather's excessive drinking, violent mood swings, and physical and emotional abuse. Despite these hardships, however, Clinton's life was defined by his own efforts to succeed. Through his own hard work and the

* The reference to *Planet Hollywood* refers not just to Schwarzenegger's celebrity status as an actor but also to his investment in the financially unsuccessful restaurant chain by the same name.

unyielding support of his loving mother he graduated from a first-rate university, became a Rhodes Scholar at Oxford University, and was admitted to Yale Law School. Then, when he could have accepted a highly paid job in the East, he gave up this opportunity to return to his home state and build a career of public service. This was a compelling narrative that conveys to the public that Bill Clinton is a simple person much like them, but also intelligent, gifted, and ambitious enough to lead them.*

The issue of a candidate's character takes on strong moral dimensions. Earlier in the 1992 campaign Governor Clinton had been charged with having an extramarital affair. While affairs are certainly common in contemporary America, and no doubt many of the voters had also been unfaithful at some point in their lives, there is a desire to hold our political candidates up to moral standards that we may be unable to meet ourselves. So who was Bill Clinton? Was he the unfaithful husband, selfishly pursuing his own gratification outside of the bonds of marriage, a slick politician who would do or say anything to get elected? Or was he the humble, honest, devoted man of the people suggested by the biographical film shown at the convention? Much later, of course, during his second term, it became well known that his sexual appetite caused him all kinds of grief and even led to consideration of his impeachment. This outcome, however, did not fully reveal whether or not a majority of the public believed that an extramarital affair should disqualify someone from public office. Some voters certainly wanted Clinton removed from office because they believed him morally unsuited to govern. Others, however, believed that his marital infidelity should be considered a private issue and that there is an important difference between morality in one's personal life and morality in one's public life.

While many critics lament the emphasis on a candidate's character, we see this as an inevitable dimension of the storytelling that occurs in contemporary political campaigns. An important measure of a story's narrative probability is its **characterological coherence**.[18] In testing a political narrative, voters seek to answer three questions related to the candidate's character: Is this candidate the person that he or she claims to be? Does this candidate's character suit the demands of the political office that he or she seeks? And, can I trust that my interests and the public interests that I hold as most important will be served by this candidate's election to office? These seem to us to be very relevant and important questions for voters to consider before casting their votes.

Stories of History, the Present, and the Future

All political campaigns provide **historical narratives** that seek to explain our past and also how it is that we have happened to find ourselves in the cir-

---

* The very moving 12-minute-long Clinton video, featuring footage found in the John F. Kennedy Presidential Library archives, emphasizes Clinton's small-town roots. It shows Clinton as a 17-year-old high school boy shaking hands with President Kennedy during a visit to the White House in 1963. Clinton also talked about the father he never knew (he died before his birth) and his feelings for his wife and daughter. The video was produced by Harry Thomason and Linda Bloodworth Thomason. See David Lauter, "Clinton: Nominee Tries to Show Bush as Failed Leader," *Los Angeles Times*, July 17, 1992.

cumstances we are in now. Thus, virtually any candidate's political rhetoric will emphasize those aspects of history that enrich and provide foundational support for the story that he or she wants potential voters to accept. Both Republican and Democratic candidates draw freely on the Founders of the American Republic for their inspirational messages about our political system. In addition, Republicans celebrate the achievements of the great Republican leaders from the past and the Democrats celebrate the legacy of their great leaders. In fact, after an ex-president has been dead for many years it even becomes possible for him to be claimed by politicians from the other party. Thus, both Republicans and Democrats may invoke the name of Abraham Lincoln, Theodore Roosevelt, Harry Truman, John F. Kennedy, or Ronald Reagan.

These nostalgic recollections for the great political leaders of the past are more than idle memorializing. These leaders have come to represent the ideological history of the different political narratives that live on in American politics. To invoke the name of Franklin Roosevelt is thus to invoke the New Deal dream of proactive governmental involvement designed to enrich the condition of the masses. To invoke the name of John F. Kennedy is to remember the optimism, vitality and youthfulness of his administration and of the "New Frontier" thinking that initiated the space race. To invoke the name of Ronald Reagan is to express nostalgia for the time of relative prosperity and pride that marked his administration. Certainly all of these presidents faced stiff opposition during their administrations. Nonetheless, we often find ourselves actively engaged in the creation of public memories that encourage us to forget the disagreements and disappointments as we actively search for the achievements and moral lessons of an era bygone and as we set our political compass to guide our present actions.

When we argue about the events of the Watergate scandal, the Vietnam War, or the Clinton impeachment drama, we are seeking to use these historical events to shape our understanding of the world that we live in today. We are creating historical accounts to serve contemporary needs and interests. Did we fail in Vietnam because it was an immoral war that we never should have fought in the first place? Or did we fail because we lacked the will to see the fight through to the finish? The answer to this question can help to determine what course of action we should follow in other conflicts, such as the conflict in Iraq that occurred over thirty years after the Vietnam War. If the lesson of Vietnam is that we should avoid involving ourselves in civil wars supporting puppet dictators, we would presumably conduct our foreign policy very differently than if we tell a historical story that celebrates the moral justice of our involvement and only condemns the fact that we lacked the will to fight to win.

The Vietnam War continued to rage as a political issue; during the 2004 presidential campaign, candidates Bush and Kerry tussled over the nature of their military service in the Vietnam era and over Senator Kerry's vocal opposition to the war once he left military service. It is in some respects curious that even as the war in Iraq was heating up and the U.S. death count went over 1,000 soldiers killed, it was the morality of the Vietnam conflict and the issue of what constituted an appropriate patriotic response during and following that war that dominated campaign conversations.

Historical stories thus provide material that is drawn upon in interpreting present problems and choices and also in articulating *future narratives*. All political candidates seek to emphasize that if they are elected, and their proposed policies are enacted into law, the world will be a better place and the quality of all our lives will be improved. On important public issues the competing candidates will construct very different but competing depictions of history, accounts of the present, and views of the future. The historical stories must, of course, account for the facts of history and thus cannot merely be fabricated to achieve a specific candidate's purposes.

Likewise, stories of the present must account for life as we know it. For example, President George W. Bush argued throughout most of the summer and fall of 2003 that the U.S. economy was pulling out of the recession, that his tax cuts were stimulating new investments, and that Americans would soon be reaping the benefits of economic expansion. Despite the president's best efforts to act as a cheerleader for the administration's policies, however, the news media, during this same period, seemed to tell a different and much grimmer story. Instead of focusing on the expansion of the economy many press accounts told continuing stories about job losses. For example, during the last week of September 2003 press accounts emphasized that the United States had actually lost jobs during the Bush administration, that the job losses had been most acute in the manufacturing sector where the wages were higher than in the service sector of the economy (which had reported some growth in the number of jobs), and that fewer people had access to health insurance than when this administration took office.

Perhaps even more damaging to the credibility of the president's optimistic stories about the growth in the economy were articles and commentaries that focused on individual families, companies, and communities. For example, again during the last week in September 2003, the media reported that the Levi Strauss Company, a firm with a more than one hundred years of history, and indeed an iconographic symbol of American manufacturing and even of American culture, had now decided to close its last manufacturing plant in the United States so that it could ship all of its production capabilities offshore. These mediated accounts of continuing economic problems in the United States are made even more compelling to people who begin to hear stories of friends, neighbors, and family members who lose their jobs due to economic cutbacks. Anxiety is of course common during any economic recession, and as most economists are well aware, anxiety prevents the kinds of spending and investment that can help shorten a downturn in the business cycle. As is well known, "if your neighbor loses his job we are in a recession. When you lose your job, it becomes a depression."

Stories about the future are far more flexible than stories about either the past or the present. Political candidates always seek to persuade voters that the world will be a much more prosperous, harmonious, and pleasant place if they are elected to office. Often arguments of this type are so overly optimistic, they describe a world so perfect that it is unlikely it will ever exist. For example, we routinely hear presidential candidates claim that if they are elected we will find an America where every child has access to an excellent education, all families have health insurance, our streets are safe and free from the scourge of illegal drugs, everyone has access to a well-paying job, and our environment is protected. Yet, year after year, these problems seem to persist.

THE STRUCTURE AND FORM OF CAMPAIGN ARGUMENTS

Because political campaigns are essentially narrative in form, the arguments offered to the voters seldom resemble the more formal arguments that might be used in an academic debate, in a courtroom, or even in a business meeting. Consequently, political campaign arguments may have very loose rules of evidence, lax standards for evaluation, and sometimes seem to intentionally obfuscate rather than clarify issues. There is a tendency in much political arguing, for example, to tell only partial truths, or at the very least to embellish and exaggerate the facts in support of one's position. Vice President Al Gore made himself the subject of ridicule during the 2000 presidential campaign when he claimed to have been responsible for the creation of the Internet. Although the vice president had indeed been a big supporter of developments in new communication technologies during his service in the U.S. Senate, this claim seemed so exaggerated that it lacked credibility and may actually have undermined the vice president's campaign.*

While some level of exaggeration might be expected in politics, there can be a profound credibility gap if it begins to appear that political candidates or elected officials are willing to outright lie or deceive the public. For example, both President George W. Bush and British Prime Minister Tony Blair were subjected to withering criticisms for having exaggerated the threats posed by Iraq's strongman ruler Saddam Hussein in order to justify a preemptive strike against Iraq. Both leaders argued for the war in rhetoric that linked Hussein's regime to the international battle against terrorism and by claiming that Iraq was developing weapons of mass destruction. Yet, when no such weapons were discovered, many began to complain that the case for war was trumped up (or in the British vernacular "sexed up") and that these were instead "weapons of mass deception." Although President Bush seems to be weathering the political storm at this point in time, Prime Minister Blair's poll numbers have plummeted, and some pundits have gone so far as to argue that this incident could ultimately cost him his office.[19] Perhaps an even more significant potential consequence of exaggeration and deception in a political leader is that citizens will begin to distrust virtually everything the elected official tells them and thus will be discouraged from following politics, voting in elections, or participating in civic life.

Obviously the media have a responsibility to listen carefully to, record, research, and evaluate the arguments advanced by political candidates and elected officials in order to help the public judge the quality and veracity of their

---

* The vice president got himself into even deeper trouble when he also claimed that he and his wife Tipper may have been the real-life couple that inspired the creation of the characters in the book and film *Love Story*.

rhetorical claims. When covering political campaigns, the media must do more than treat them as they would a horse race: they must focus on the issues and arguments advanced by the candidates. The voters, in turn, must act upon the information provided to them. Americans have to be encouraged to read newspaper accounts, listen to news broadcasts, and expend the energy to evaluate the arguments offered by political candidates and elected officials.

If voters become more attentive to the quality of arguments advanced by the candidates there is some hope that candidates will become less inclined to deliver simplistic, sophomoric arguments. As Roderick Hart declared, candidates need to focus less on how "audience predispositions can be exploited" and more on "how citizens' needs can be met."[20] Our political leaders speak for us and they speak for America. They should be creating arguments that challenge us, stimulate us, educate us, and motivate us to learn more about political issues, to take positions, and of course, to vote. What elected officials and political candidates should not be permitted to do is to massage our egos and make vague promises to fulfill our self-interests by making only the arguments that their polling tells us we want to hear.

POLITICAL DEBATES

The one format for political argumentation celebrated for its promotion of rational and deliberative discussions of issues is the political debate. Political debates are praised because they provide an opportunity to observe the candidates in face-to-face interactions about the issues. Certainly these contests have value, but it may be misleading to refer to them as debates. They certainly are not the same as the formal academic debates that we discussed in the previous chapters. They are also not the same as the type of debating that is routinely conducted in a legislative chamber or parliament. Instead, what passes for a political debate in a U.S. election campaign is more like a joint press conference where more than one candidate is questioned before the same audience.

In most U.S. political debates the candidates respond to questions from a single reporter or from a panel of reporters. In some contests the candidates have responded to questions directly from audience members in what has become known as a "Town Hall" format. In all such contests the quality of the debates are in large part determined by the resourcefulness and creativity of the questioners. If the candidates are asked tough and penetrating questions that expose their positions on issues and the potential gaps in their understanding and/or experience, then these contests can have terrific probative value for the electorate. If, on the other hand, the candidates are lobbed easily fielded softballs that permit them to mouth only platitudes—or to simply make use of their slogans and buzzwords from their campaign speeches and paid advertisements—then the debates are of far less value.

Indeed, political candidates and those who help them prepare for these debates have learned both from their personal experiences and from research studies that audiences seem not to listen to political debates very closely. This permits candidates to avoid answering the question they are asked, to reinterpret the question to one that may lend itself to a more helpful answer, to skirt the issues, or to deflect attention from their failure to answer the question with a criticism of their opponent. Sometimes these "slips" and "dodges" are detected by vigilant reporters who point out that a question was not answered, but sometimes they are not. Potential voters who are watching and listening to these debates should seek to focus both on what is being said and on what is not being said so that they can learn as much as possible from these exchanges. The application of critical listening techniques will help make these debates much more useful to audiences seeking to make their own evaluations of the candidates.

Research in political campaign debates has confirmed that substantial argumentative clash occurs in these debates and that candidates do make use of more analysis and evidence in debate speeches than in other forms of campaign discourse. Research has also suggested, however, that many who view debates are not able to identify whether or not a candidate has offered either evidence or analysis to support his or her arguments in a debate. Viewers are able to determine which candidate was more aggressive in the debate and which candidate was more defensive, and as you might expect, candidates were helped in the evaluation of their performance by being perceived as aggressive; they were harmed if they appeared overly defensive.[21] Most candidates seem to have gotten this message. They often aggressively pursue their opponents in the debate, but they seem to be somewhat more averse to responding to the attacks made on them, perhaps because they lack the skills to do so or perhaps because they do not wish to appear defensive. The result is that many political debates contain a lot of histrionic mudslinging but little in the way of probing, constructive argumentation.

Another problem with contemporary political debates is that they have become mediated campaign events where the press and the voters seem to focus less on the substance of the discussion than they do on the candidates' momentum in the campaign. The media and the public expend so much energy trying to determine who *won* the debate, and which candidate's campaign was most helped by his or her performance in the debate, that there is far less meaningful emphasis on the actual issues discussed or on the differences in the candidates. The emphasis on winning has led to some interesting consequences. For example, research suggests that voters questioned immediately after hearing the media's analysis of the outcome of a debate may have different impressions of the contest than they would if they were questioned a few days later, after they had time to reflect on what the candidates said, and after they have been exposed to press discussions of the debate.

That voters' opinions are heavily influenced by press reports of the outcome of the debate[22] has also resulted in the post-debate phenomena known as the "spin." Each campaign sprinkles spokespersons throughout the hall to be available for press interviews following the debate. Not surprisingly, the task of each spokesperson is to help shape how the just completed debate is reported, seen, and understood by anyone who will listen. The campaign spinsters would never admit that their own candidate was anything short of brilliant and insightful or that the opposing candidate managed to accomplish anything in the debate. The process might be truly humorous if it did not go so far toward trivializing politics in the United States.

Yet another hallmark of contemporary political debate practice is the search for the most significant slip, error, gaffe, or misstatement in the debate. The press and the public alike have become used to the notion that if one or the other candidate makes such a key mistake, then this is what should determine the outcome of the contest. For example, in perhaps the most significant gaffe to date, in 1976 President Gerald R. Ford declared that Poland could not be considered to be under the domination of the Soviet Union. The remark seemed so clearly to be a misstatement that the moderator gave the president an opportunity to clarify what he meant. Instead of admitting his error President Ford reaffirmed his conviction that Polish citizens would not consider themselves to be under Soviet domination. The post-debate press commentary focused almost exclusively on this one remark, all but ignoring the rest of the debate.[23] This focus on identifying, preventing, and punishing gaffes often seems to distract public attention from the more substantive issues in the debate.

There have also been many controversies regarding the debate formats that are used and their consequences. Even the determination about which candidates should be invited to participate in the debates has sparked controversy. There is a clear audience benefit, for example, to a debate format that pits the two leading candidates against each other with only a minimum of intervention from other speakers, including reporters. Candidates who are given an opportunity to make statements, address questions to each other, and respond to arguments offered by each other have a better likelihood of making known their positions on the issues, revealing their differences from their opponents', and highlighting the choices for voters. Such debates are often criticized because they exclude third-party or minor candidates, however. Still, when the minor candidates are accommodated in the debates as occurs in primaries, for example when the nine or ten candidates who may be competing for the nomination all share a stage, other problems emerge. First, it is very difficult for candidates to get enough time to speak or to distinguish themselves from their peers. Second, there is a tendency for those trailing in the polls to gang up on the front runner. Finally, because many candidates lack significant debating experience, they may need the assistance of a moderator to ask them questions and to control the flow of the conversation.

In recent presidential elections several different formats have been used. The decision about which format will be selected for a given debate is usually negotiated by the candidates and their handlers in consultation with the sponsoring agent for the debates. Regardless of what format is selected, or how well the individual arguers may perform in the contest, research suggests that audiences do find debates to be informative,[24] even though most studies also suggest that viewers' own partisan belief structures tend to influence their perceptions of the candidates' performance. In short, Republicans tend to think that the Republican candidate usually did the best job in the debates, and Democrats usually think that the Democratic candidate did the best job in the debates.[25]

Summary

The quality of the issues and arguments advanced by political candidates to gain the support of voters has a profound effect on the vitality of the American electoral process. Some studies suggest Americans are increasingly disinterested in learning about politics, following campaigns, or even voting.[26] Well over half of the adult population in the United States asserts that they have little interest in politics and agree with the proposition that "government is too difficult to understand."[27] Furthermore, many people feel that they can have little trust in their elected officials or control over them. A 2000 study found that 75 percent of respondents agreed with the statement "political candidates are more concerned with fighting each other than with solving the nation's problems."[28]

In order to restore public confidence and trust in our political leaders we should strive to improve the substance and the quality of political argumentation. Candidates need to demonstrate greater respect for the intellect and wisdom of the voters, and they need to be honest and forthcoming about their positions on the issues. Voters need to invest more energy in learning about the issues and the candidates' stands on them. Only an involved and informed electorate can expect to have influence over its elected officials. Voters will not respect elected officials until they demonstrate their respect for the voters.

Key Terms

character
characterological coherence
future narratives

historical narratives
image
myths

Activities

1. Consider why almost half of the potential voters do not participate in general elections. Write a short essay presenting the reasons for this lack of participation and suggest changes that might encourage greater participation by the electorate.

2. Read the text of the presidential nomination acceptance speeches in appendix A. Identify whom each candidate presents in the speech as the heroes, villains, and victims. Describe also how the speech depicts the scene and the events that account for the conditions in the world.

3. Examine the nomination speeches in appendix A. Identify the historical figures and events that are cited in those speeches. How are these historical elements used as arguments in these texts?

4. Summarize and critique the political advertising strategies used by the candidates in the 2004 political campaigns. How did these candidates make use of alternative argument strategies to influence audiences?

5. Presidential debates are often criticized for being too superficial. What changes in debate formats or practices might improve these contests?

Recommended Readings

Joan Didion. *Political Fictions*. New York: Vintage, 2001.

Nina Eliasoph. *Avoiding Politics: How Americans Produce Apathy in Everyday Life*. Cambridge: Cambridge University Press, 1998.

Stanley B. Greenberg. *The Two Americas: Our Current Political Deadlock and How to Break It*. New York: St. Martin's, 2004.

Thomas A. Hollihan. *Uncivil Wars: Political Campaigns in a Media Age*. New York: Bedford/St. Martin's, 2001.

Kathleen Hall Jamieson. *Everything You Think You Know About Politics and Why You're Wrong*. New York: New Republic Books, 2000.

Chris Matthews. *Hardball*. New York: Touchstone, 1988.

Thomas E. Patterson. *The Vanishing Voter: Public Involvement in an Age of Uncertainty*. New York: Alfred A. Knopf, 2002.

Whaley, Bryan B., and Rachel Holloway. "Rebuttal Analogy in Political Communication: Argument and Attack in Sound Bite." *Political Communication* 14 (1997): 293–306.

Notes

[1] Hollihan, *Uncivil Wars: Political Campaigns in a Media Age* (New York: Bedford/St. Martin's Press, 2001), especially chapter 10.

[2] Walter R. Fisher, "Reaffirmation and Subversion of the American Dream," *Quarterly Journal of Speech* 59 (1973): 161–163.

[3] Ibid.

[4] Cited by Joan Didion, *Political Fictions* (New York: Vintage Books, 2001), 10–11.

[5] D. Finnigan, "Mock the Vote," *Los Angeles Reader,* January 26, 1997, 7.

[6] Hollihan, 177.

[7] See for example: Jeff Greenfield, *The Real Campaign* (New York: Summit Books, 1982), 30. Also: E. J. Dionne, *Why Americans Hate Politics* (New York: Touchstone Books, 1991).

[8] M. P. Wattenberg, "Should Election Day be a Holiday?" *Atlantic Monthly*, October, 1998, 42–46.

[9] T. Halstead, "A Politics for Generation X," *Atlantic Monthly*, August, 1999, 33–42.

[10] W. Lance Bennett, *The Governing Crisis: Media, Money and Marketing in American Elections* (New York: St. Martin's Press, 1992), 2.

[11] For an interesting discussion of the impact the late night comedians had on the 2000 presidential campaign see B. Weinraub, "Elections Barometer: Barbs of Late-Night TV," *New York Times,* January 19, 2000.

[12] For an excellent study of contemporary politics see: Thomas E. Patterson, *The Vanishing Voter: Public Involvement in an Age of Uncertainty* (New York: Alfred A. Knopf, 2002).

[13] Kathleen Hall Jamieson, *Packaging the Presidency: A History and Criticism of Presidential Campaign Advertising* (New York: Oxford University Press, 1984), 412.

[14] See, C. Atkin and G. Heald, "Effects of Political Advertising, *Public Opinion Quarterly* 40 (1976): 216–228.

[15] Cited by Wendy Kaminer, "Crashing the Locker Room," *The Atlantic Monthly*, July 1992, 63.

[16] For a discussion of the impact of political image see Hollihan, 55–72.

[17] Bruce E. Gronbeck, "The Presidential Campaign Dramas of 1984," *Presidential Studies Quarterly* 15 (1985): 386–393.

[18] Walter R. Fisher, *Human Communication as Narration: Toward a Philosophy of Reason, Value, and Action* (Columbia: University of South Carolina Press, 1987), 47.

[19] For example, see "Blair's Court," *The Economist,* August 30, 2003, 39–40.

[20] Roderick P. Hart, *The Sound of Leadership: Presidential Communication in the Modern Age* (Chicago: University of Chicago Press, 1987), 200.

[21] For a discussion of this research see: Hollihan, 164–176. For a more general discussion of presidential debates and research findings see, Diana Carlin and M. McKinney, eds., *The 1992 Presidential Debates in Focus* (Westport, CT: Praeger, 1994).

[22] G. Lang and K. Lang, "The Formation of Public Opinion: Direct and Mediated Effects of the First Debate," in *The Presidential Debates*, ed. G. Bishop, R. Meadow, and M. Jackson-Beeck (New York: Praeger, 1978).

[23] "The Blooper Heard Around the World," *Time*, October 18, 1976, 16.

[24] A. H. Miller and M. MacKuen, "Informing the Electorate: A National Study," in *The Great Debates: Carter vs. Ford, 1976*, ed. Sydney Kraus, 269–297 (Bloomington: Indiana University Press, 1978).

[25] S. A. Shields and K. A. MacDowell, "Appropriate Emotions in Politics: Judgment of a Televised Debate," *Journal of Communication* 37: 78–89.

[26] See Hollihan, 177–194.

[27] W. R. Neuman, M. R. Just, and Ann Crigler, *Common Knowledge: News and the Construction of Political Meaning* (Chicago: University of Chicago Press, 1992), xv.

[28] Thomas E. Patterson, *The Vanishing Voter* (New York: Knopf, 2002), 51.

ARGUMENTATION
AND THE LAW

The most formalized and ritualized setting for the creation and evaluation of arguments is the courtroom. It is in the resolution of legal disputes that our expectations for arguers are most carefully delineated. To be successful, disputants must carefully research both the facts in their cases and the relevant statutes and laws; they must present their arguments in accordance with carefully constructed rules; the evidence they introduce should be probative without being unduly prejudicial; the arguments are to be weighed by independent jurors who typify the values of the community; and the entire process is controlled by a trained and impartial judge. The U.S. legal system also allows for appeals. A litigant who loses a case may appeal the decision to a higher court if he or she can establish that there was an error in the first trial.

The United States is a very litigious society. Ronald J. Matlon observed that "in 1950, there were approximately 220,000 lawyers in America. That number grew to over 300,000 by the mid-1960s, and stood at nearly 650,000 in 1985."[1] Since 1985, the number of attorneys has continued to grow. By 2003 there were more than a million lawyers in the United States and there was no indication that the growth rate in the profession would slow in the future, as the number of students sitting for the Law School Admissions Test (or LSAT) continued to grow each year.[2]

The increasing complexity of modern society, the tremendous number of new regulations created since the 1960s, the fact that the courts now recognize that defendants in criminal trials have a right to legal counsel, and the fact that there are simply more lawyers today trying to make a living have led to far more demand for attorneys and to increasingly crowded courtrooms. The court docket is so crowded in some U.S. cities that it takes more than five years for a case to make it to trial.

There are essentially two types of cases that come before the courts: *civil* cases and *criminal* cases. In civil cases litigants typically sue someone for financial damages that they believe they have sustained as a result of the other party's actions or negligence. You might sue for civil damages if you paid to have a house built and the contractor did not complete all of the work, if a surgeon made a mistake and amputated your right leg when it was your left that had been injured, or if someone ran a red light and hit your car when you were legally driving through an intersection. Criminal cases are, of course, those wherein a defendant is charged with violating the established laws of the community. In these cases litigants are charged by the district attorney on behalf of all of the citizens of the jurisdiction whose laws were violated. Thus the charge of lewd behavior involving a minor against Michael Jackson was listed on the court docket as: *The People of the State of California v. Michael Joe Jackson*.

Before discussing the importance of argumentation theory and argumentation principles in legal settings, we will briefly consider the organizational characteristics of the U.S. judicial system.

THE U.S. JUDICIAL SYSTEM

In the United States we have courts that are operated by local jurisdictions, such as cities, counties, and states, and courts that are operated by the federal government. Each state has primary responsibility for its own courts, and the decisions in one state court do not impact court decisions in another state. The structure of court systems varies somewhat from state to state, but typically states will have municipal (sometimes called circuit) courts, district courts, and/ or superior courts. The municipal or circuit courts are generally reserved for minor criminal cases or civil cases in which the amount of damages sought is fairly small. These courts may be subdivided further into traffic courts (where traffic offenses are adjudicated), probate courts (where challenges to wills are considered), domestic courts (where marital and custody matters are handled), small-claims courts (which rule on small civil suits not requiring attorneys), and petty crimes courts. More substantial and important cases are decided in district or superior courts. The latter typically cover greater territory and jurisdiction and are noteworthy because the judges are appointed or elected and may have more stature in the community and in the legal profession. Each state also has state appeals courts and a state supreme court to rule on the cases that have been decided by these lower courts. There are more than 3,500 courts of general jurisdiction in the United States.[3]

The federal courts resolve violations of federal laws and especially focus on interstate crimes. These include: violations of laws on federal lands or in national parks, as well as such offenses as environmental pollution that crosses state boundaries, immigration violations, income tax evasion, trafficking in drugs, treason, kidnapping that crosses state boundaries, and unlawful flight from one state to another to avoid capture. The federal court system is composed of 94 district courts and eleven federal appellate courts. Decisions from any of these federal courts, or even decisions from any of the state courts, could ultimately be appealed all the way to the United States Supreme Court.

The crush of activity in both the state and federal court systems has given attorneys, judges, and litigants increased incentive to divert cases from the docket and free the courts' time for hearing other cases. Thus only a small percentage of the cases that are initially filed, either civil or criminal, actually end up going to trial. Civil cases can be extremely expensive and the fees paid to lawyers can be more than the awards paid to the defendants. Consequently, litigants are encouraged to reach a settlement before the trial begins. Similarly, only one in ten criminal prosecutions actually is settled by a trial. In the other cases, prosecutors and defense attorneys agree to a plea bargain (in which a defendant agrees to plead guilty to a lesser offense than the one originally charged) in order to save the time and cost of a full trial. Simply because a case never goes to trial does not mean that argumentation plays an unimportant role. These bargaining and negotiation sessions, in which settlements are agreed on, are dependent on the argumentative skills of the participants. Building and presenting as strong a case as possible in these sessions increases the likelihood that the other side will agree to settle the case.

THE ASSUMPTIONS OF THE SYSTEM

The U.S. judicial system, which was modeled after the British system, is *adversarial* in nature. This model assumes that the best way to determine truth is to have litigants, each taking incompatible positions, present the best arguments in support of their cases and let an impartial third party evaluate the truthfulness of their arguments. Furthermore, this system assumes that even highly complex and technical legal questions at the trial level can be best resolved by untrained citizen jurors. Different states have created different standards for when litigants are entitled to a trial by jury, but typically, all civil cases beyond a certain level of damages (which varies from state to state), all felony criminal trials, and many misdemeanor trials can be decided by a citizen jury if the litigant demands it. Alternatively, a defendant can waive the right to a jury trial and have the case decided by a judge; such trials are known as "bench" trials.

Citizen Jurors

One might ask why our society has placed such faith in untrained citizen jurors. Certainly the jury system is costly and troublesome. Citizens do not eagerly come forth and volunteer their time for jury duty. In many jurisdictions it is a constant challenge to the courts to find suitable jurors to fill all of the jury panels needed. Many citizens actively seek to avoid jury service. Persons who must provide care for children or the elderly and those who can prove that their work is essential to the community and that they could not easily be replaced, such as teachers, doctors, police officers, or firefighters, often win excuses from jury service. In addition, those who are self-employed and who might face financial hardship are frequently excused from jury service. Those who have employers who will pay for a short term of jury service but not for the time required to hear longer, more complicated, and arguably more important cases will also frequently be excluded from such cases. As a result, juries in the United States are increasingly composed of elderly and often retired persons, of public employees, and of blue-collar rather than professional persons.

Thus, even though in many ways the law has become more and more complex, our jurors may be less well-educated and less prepared. In some areas of the law, for example, in such technically sophisticated areas as medical malpractice, antitrust prosecutions, complex tort actions, and even many criminal prosecutions that rely on scientific evidence, jurors may not be able to fully understand the evidence. In such cases it might be desirable to have these decisions rendered by experts and not by citizen jurors. Instead of turning to experts, however, our system emphasizes the ability of ordinary citizens to make these complicated decisions. The reasons for this commitment to citizen jurors are numerous and varied.

First, there is a general belief that citizen jurors are capable of making good decisions. They are careful and conscientious in the verdicts that they render, and they take their responsibility seriously. Research has suggested that judges agree with the verdicts rendered by juries most of the time.[4]

Second, even though the entire court system is organized and structured to assure litigants impartial and fair verdicts that will resolve complex questions of fact, one benefit of the jury system is that jurors are by their very nature not dispassionate arbiters of fact. Jurors are an important part of our legal system precisely because they temper their judgments with emotion and with pathos. The jurors bring with them into the courtroom the emotions and values of their community. Their judgments are shaped by their sympathy and or anger both for the victims or plaintiffs and for the defendants. In this sense the jurors reflect the public will. The presence of citizen jurors in the process protects the litigants from the potential capriciousness of the state, and ensures that the courts are not merely the instruments of existing state power and control, but reflect the wisdom and the will of the people themselves.

Indeed, one of the most significant issues to have emerged in recent years has involved the question of "juror nullification," or the power and the willingness of jurors to disregard their instructions and to refuse to find defendants guilty on some charges, even in the face of compelling, or in some instances even overwhelming, evidence of guilt. One example of this has been attempts in California to prosecute those who grow marijuana for or even distribute marijuana to cancer sufferers who use it to reduce the disabling side effects of chemotherapy. The voters in California passed a ballot initiative legalizing medical marijuana. The federal courts declared the law unconstitutional and both local and federal courts went about the routine business of trying to enforce prohibitions against the cultivation, distribution, or use of marijuana. Jurors, however, by refusing to find for the prosecution in many of these cases, have made the enforcement of these prohibitions very spotty and uneven.

Third, the opportunity to serve on a jury provides a kind of civic involvement that is unrivalled by any other experience in our society. Jurors learn about the legal system, feel themselves much more a part of their government, and are likely to be more committed to the protection and preservation of our important civic institutions. This civic participation is thus a central public ritual that helps sustain the health and vitality of the U.S. democracy.

Dispute Resolution

Because the U.S. legal system involves untrained jurors in the decision-making process at the most critical junctures of cases, the courtroom becomes an interesting field for argumentative study and inquiry. As we have already discussed, different fields develop specific standards for argument evaluation based on the need to resolve unique problems and to make effective decisions within the objectives of that field. In the law, for example, the key challenge is to decide how to categorize events. This categorization is sought through several kinds of questions. Some of these questions are factual: Did the alleged assault occur? Did the defendant commit the assault? Other questions may focus on the character of the act. Even if it can be clearly established that an assault occurred, and that the defendant committed the assault, one could still question the nature of the assault: Was this action taken in self-defense? What was the character of the situation, and did this situation have implications for the defendant's actions? Did the defendant simply lose control and strike out without thinking? Or was the act planned in advance and coldly calculated?

There are also questions of **precedent** (relevant decisions in previous court cases). In classifying and categorizing events legal arguers attempt to assure that like actions will be dealt with in like fashion by the courts. If all people are truly viewed as equal under law, an assault by a white defendant on an African American victim should be dealt with in the same way as an assault by an African American assailant on a white victim. The courts consider legal precedent as well as statutory guidelines to assure that the law protects the interests of its different constituencies equally well and is applied to events in a predictable and patterned way.

The work of the courts is primarily designed to resolve factual disputes and to classify and categorize actions and behaviors; therefore the propositions being disputed are propositions of fact. The specific wordings of the propositions in dispute will be very carefully framed to reflect the demands for legalistic precision. In criminal indictments the proposition considered will be a formal complaint, a charge in which the district attorney alleges that the named defendant broke a specific statute, on a specific date. Because we presume people to be innocent until proven guilty, the **burden of proof** in such a complaint clearly rests with the prosecution, and the prosecutor's arguments must be sufficient to overcome a *reasonable doubt*. What constitutes reasonable doubt is of course a matter of argument. Most judges will advise jurors that it does not mean the resolution of all doubts, but that a reasonable person would be inclined to find the evidence and the arguments presented by the prosecution sufficient proof that the complaint is true.

The complaints filed in civil cases are somewhat less precise than in criminal cases but still demand that the specific allegation be explicitly understood and spelled out. If, for example, the plaintiff is claiming that the defendant caused her injury when he struck her with his car, the plaintiff's attorney will have to prove that the accident was the defendant's fault and that the resulting injury was sufficiently severe that the plaintiff should be compensated for actual losses and perhaps also for pain and suffering. While the standard for determining culpability in a criminal case is beyond a reasonable doubt, in a civil case the standard for ascertaining responsibility is the *preponderance of evidence*. To meet this standard the plaintiff must persuade the adjudicator that the facts in support of the suit are more probable, that is, better than fifty-fifty. A very slim margin in favor of one side or the other can determine the outcome.

One important difference between a criminal case and a civil case, however, is that in a criminal case the verdict is typically guilty or not guilty, with little opportunity to create a middle ground (although in some jurisdictions, and with some kinds of crimes, a defendant could be convicted but for a lesser offense). In a civil case, on the other hand, verdicts quite often involve compromises in which, for example, the defendant is able to reduce the amount of damages claimed by arguing that while he should shoulder some responsibility for the accident, there was also negligence by one or more other parties in the case. In civil cases a verdict in favor of the plaintiff still leaves the question of the amount of damages to be awarded up to further deliberation. In determining the amount of the financial award, the jurors are asked to temper their findings with feeling for both the plaintiff and the defendant in the case.

THE ATTORNEY-CLIENT RELATIONSHIP

The role of an attorney is, by its very definition, argumentative. Your attorney is your advocate in any legal case; in criminal cases the prosecutor is the "people's advocate," who reflects the community's will in having its laws enforced. From the time an attorney is first introduced to a client, she or he is gaining information, undertaking a critical analysis of that information, and beginning to construct a theory of the case.

During this first meeting the litigant and the attorney discuss the possibility of a case. In a civil case the client seeks out an attorney either in hopes of filing a cause of action against another person or because someone has filed a complaint against him or her. In a criminal case the prosecuting attorney likely begins by interviewing the police officers who investigated the criminal complaint and identified a probable suspect. Likewise, in a criminal case the defendant is often interviewed by counsel only after a criminal complaint has been lodged.

During the interview the attorney seeks information that will facilitate an assessment as to whether this is a winnable, or deserving, case. Attorneys rarely want to spend their own time or the court's time on a case that they probably cannot win. This is why a defense attorney will urge a settlement or a plea bargain if the facts seem to suggest that it is unlikely that an outright acquittal can be achieved for their client.

The initial attorney-client interview also provides the attorney and client an opportunity to begin to get to know each other. Trust is an important dimension of the attorney-client relationship. Because most citizens lack understanding of the law, and because we typically call upon attorneys only when we really need their expertise, trust is highly important. It also works both ways. Just as it is important that clients trust their attorneys, attorneys must trust their clients. It is helpful to attorneys if clients are honest and forthright with them, for there is nothing worse than clients who lie to their attorneys, and then get caught in those lies when their cases go to trial.

THE ROLE OF ATTORNEYS IN PRETRIAL PHASES

Much of the work of an attorney is accomplished long before a case ever comes to trial. This stage is called the pretrial phase. It includes all of the activities of investigators and attorneys prior to the opening gavel. Many cases are won or lost in the pretrial phase.

The Discovery Phase

Once an attorney decides to represent a client, she or he begins the process of researching the facts of the case to locate and link the material evidence to the client's claims. This is called *discovery*. Discovery typically includes additional interviews with witnesses or interested parties, an examination of important documents that might prove or deny the case, and the consultation of law books to both illustrate the specific statutes in dispute and to examine relevant case precedents.

The evidence that the attorneys assemble may take many forms: letters, contracts, legal documents, financial records, photographs, statements or affidavits from witnesses, and so on. Sometimes witnesses will be identified so that they can be subpoenaed to testify in court at a later date, and at other times their statements are introduced in the form of sworn depositions, given under oath and in the presence of a trained legal stenographer.

From this vast amount of information, the attorney begins to organize the facts into a case that supports the client's position. The case is organized so that the key issues on which the case might turn are highlighted and accessible for discussion and scrutiny. Naturally attorneys seek to construct their case so that those facts that are helpful to their client are given greater attention and prominence in the presentation, while those that may be seen as harmful to their client are obscured and perhaps even obfuscated.

The attorney should always interview her or his own witnesses before either a deposition is taken or the trial begins so that the attorney knows what answers will be given. Witnesses should also be prepared for testifying in court. Since jurors evaluate not only what a witness says but also the credibility of the witness, making recommendations about the manner in which the witness presents his or her testimony is common. Exactly how far an ethical attorney can go in coaching, or what is known as "wood shedding," is open to interpretation. It would be unethical and unlawful for an attorney to tell a witness to say something that is not true or even permit a witness to say something he or she knows to be untrue. That is called suborning perjury and it is illegal.

Developing the Theory of the Case

What an attorney must be thinking about when interviewing a client is a *theory of the case*. Attorneys use their knowledge of the law in an attempt to adapt general legal principles, statutes, and precedents to fit the specific situation of the client's case. The theory of the case is the underlying idea that unites the legal principles to the factual background and ties the evidence into a coherent story that puts the client's position in the best possible light. The fact that human decision makers rely on stories in the creation and evaluation of arguments has already been established. Consequently, it should come as no surprise that courtroom arguments also emerge in the form of stories.

The stories that the attorneys tell, like all other stories that listeners evaluate, will be judged on the basis of their narrative probability and fidelity. With regard to narrative probability, or whether or not the story is coherent, attorneys must consider questions such as: Is the structure of the story satisfying and complete? Does it account for the chronology of events? Does it account for the material evidence that has been revealed? Do the actors in these stories perform their roles and fulfill the expectations of their characters in a reasonable and convincing manner?

The defendant's attorney seeks to convince the jurors to sympathize with his or her client. The plaintiff's counsel or the prosecuting attorney wants the jurors to empathize and feel pity for the victim and seeks to portray the defendant in the worst possible way. The defense attorney, of course, seeks to portray the defendant as sympathetically as possible and even seeks to demonstrate ways in which the victim does not really suit that role very well.

In the Michael Jackson case briefly mentioned above, for example, the prosecution wants to convince jurors that the singer is a predator who actively seeks out children to fulfill his sexual desires, even plying them with alcohol to numb their inhibitions. The victim will be cast as a vulnerable and young cancer sufferer from a broken home, certainly unable to protect himself from being used by an older man. The defense, on the other hand, will characterize the singer as a caring, empathetic, and "childlike" waif himself, and as someone who deeply loves children, who is very generous toward them, and who would never do anything to cause harm or injury to a child. Indeed, the charges will themselves be characterized as the result of sick and twisted minds that cannot come to understand let alone appreciate the purity and goodness of Michael Jackson's character. Meanwhile, the defense will claim that the real villains in the case are the parents and their greedy lawyers who are willing to make such spurious charges in the pursuit of financial gain.

The second test of stories is that of narrative fidelity. Does the story seem likely to be true: Does it coincide with the stories that jurors have known or experienced in their own lives or in the lives of friends or family members, with stories they have read about in the press, and even with the fictional accounts of characters that they have come to accept as reasonable and lifelike? Returning to the Michael Jackson example, is it credible that an adult male would invite children to share his bedroom and perhaps his bed and not have sexual gratification in mind? Does such a story seem believable given other stories that we have heard throughout our lives and have thus come to believe as probably true?

Two researchers, W. Lance Bennett and Martha S. Feldman, observed criminal trials in the Superior Courts in King County (Seattle), Washington, for a year. During their studies, they noted that:

> In order to understand, take part in, and communicate about criminal trials, people transform the evidence introduced in trials into stories about the alleged criminal activities. The structural features of stories make it possible to perform various tests and comparisons that correspond to the official legal criteria for evaluating evidence (objectivity, reasonable doubt, and so on). The resulting interpretation of the action in a story can be judged according to the law that applies to the case.[5]

Bennett and Feldman discovered that attorneys presented their legal arguments in the form of stories and that stories provided the means by which jurors organized information, recollected that information, and systematically tested and evaluated information.[6]

As we have argued in earlier chapters, it is understandable that listeners make use of their capacity for telling and evaluating stories in their role as jurors, for storytelling comes naturally to us. The greatest benefit to the use of stories as a means of legal reasoning is that:

> Stories have implicit structures that enable people to make systematic comparisons between stories. Moreover, the structural form of a completely specified story alerts interpreters to descriptive information in a story that might be missing, and which, if filled in, could alter the significance of the action. The inadequate development of setting, character, means, or motive can, as any literature student knows, render a story's action ambiguous. In a novel or film, such ambiguity may be an aesthetic flaw. In a trial, it is grounds for reasonable doubt.[7]

The best stories are those that not only account for all of the evidence presented in the case but are also simple, relatively straightforward, and easy for jurors to follow. The more complex a story is, the greater the likelihood that the opposing counsel can find ways to poke holes in it and reveal its flaws. It is also helpful if attorneys create stories that they themselves find believable. Attorneys should try not to argue a case that they themselves do not find plausible, for in doing so they might reveal their lack of faith in the case to the jurors, and as a result, poorly represent the interests of their client.

Because the burden of proof is always placed on the plaintiff (or the prosecutor in a criminal case), it is especially important that the plaintiff presents a unified, compelling, and forthright story. Complexities, plot twists, and inconsistencies of almost any kind prove especially troublesome to the construction of a compelling case by the prosecutor or plaintiff, because they enhance the likelihood that a defense attorney can introduce an element of doubt in the jurors' minds.

It is best if the defense counsel can also present a unified defense story that clearly contrasts and is incompatible with the opponent's story but that also accounts for all of the material evidence that is present. Unfortunately, it is often difficult for the defense to construct such a unified story. In these cases, the defense counsel might choose to present multiple stories all of which compete with and therefore cast doubt on the prosecutor's or plaintiff's story. In some cases, the defense attorney might even decline to present any story at all, and instead choose to present only a refutational case. Such a strategy tries to capitalize on the fact that the prosecutor or plaintiff has the burden of proof and seeks to demonstrate reasonable doubt only by probing the potential weaknesses in the opponent's case. Because the jurors have such a strong preference for narrative reasoning, however, this is a dangerous strategy for the defense to use. The jurors will likely be seeking to construct rival stories to challenge the prosecutor's or plaintiff's story on their own. If they are unable to identify such a story, and if the defense counsel has also failed to present such a story, a verdict against the defendant is likely.

The preparation of the case and the pretrial work that goes into the development of the case is every bit as important, if not more so, than the trial presentations. Given that very few cases even get to trial, it is clear that most cases are won or lost during the pretrial investigations and the construction of the case arguments. The decision as to whether or not to take a case to trial is often the most important one an attorney will make, and it can be made only after a careful consideration of the evidence, the appropriate legal statutes, and the theory of the case that is to be advanced.

Pretrial Motions

Not all of the evidence acquired before a trial can be used in court. Sometimes, for example, there are questions about whether the evidence was gathered and maintained properly. In such situations, attorneys representing the two sides of the dispute engage in pretrial motions. Evidence obtained by the police without a warrant or probable cause may be suppressed (excluded) by a judge. This is called the exclusionary rule and it is designed to deter the state from violating an individual's right to privacy. If illegally obtained evidence leads to additional evidence, that too is excluded as "fruit of the poisonous tree." Once seized, the state must maintain a "chain of custody" for any physical evidence. This means the state must be able to demonstrate that the evidence, as it moved from hand to hand, was always under someone's protection or locked up so that there is no possibility that the evidence was tampered with or degraded.

There are many additional types of pretrial motions, from a change of venue motion, to requests for separate trials for codefendants, to motions that argue that evidence is too inflammatory to be presented to a juror. Whole courses at law school are devoted to these matters. Regardless of their nature, pretrial motions must be argued effectively before a judge. The matter may be decided strictly on the basis of legal arguments or litigants may call witnesses to corroborate or support an argument. In both situations, finding and citing relevant prior court cases, or precedents, that support one's advocacy is an important component of this process.

Jury Selection

The selection of the jurors also occurs before the trial begins. The attorneys seek jurors whom they believe will be most sympathetic to their case. The assumption of the jury system is that jurors are selected so that they represent a cross-section of the community and will thus make up, for any defendant, a jury of one's peers. Consequently, jury panels should include persons with racial, ethnic, religious, economic, and gender attributes that are proportionate to those that are found in the general population. Jury pools are drawn from voting registration lists, driver's license lists, tax rolls, and other public records in order to represent all segments of the community. Jury service is a legal responsibility; once called, jurors must serve unless officially excused. We have already discussed the issue of exclusion, but as a reminder, jurors may be excused because of a physical limitation (poor health, disabilities of hearing or sight, and the like), because they have to care for others (children or elderly relatives, for instance), or in some instances because of their professional responsibilities.

The lists of jurors are then gathered together into pools in such a way as to reflect the desire to achieve balance. These pools are then slated for specific cases. Trial judges actually seat the jurors on cases following a process known as *voir dire*. During the *voir dire* process the attorneys (or, in some jurisdictions, the judge) direct questions to the jurors in order to probe for and reveal any potential bias. The questions can probe many dimensions of the potential juror's life including: occupation, political beliefs, religious beliefs, personal opinions, hobbies, relatives, reading habits, and so on. During *voir dire* the attorney seeks to determine if the potential juror is likely to be sympathetic to the client and capable of rendering a verdict in the case. Attorneys also use the *voir dire* in order to attempt to establish a relationship with the potential jurors, to make a good impression on the jury, and to begin to win their favor.

There are three types of challenges that can be made to prevent someone from being seated on a jury. First, there is a *challenge to the array*. This is a claim that the entire jury panel was selected in an inappropriate way. Such challenges are very infrequent in contemporary society, because most court jurisdictions are very careful in the selection of jury panels. Years ago, however, jury panels were sometimes selected by means that did not assure that the balance of the community was represented. Minorities were often excluded from jury service, and in some instances people could even volunteer to serve on a particular jury. In both cases the fairness of the jury might be undermined, either because the resultant jury might not be appropriately sympathetic to the litigant's case or because the jury might then include a juror who already had strong opinions about the case. Challenges to the array are unlimited. An attorney may make as many as he or she wishes, but they are rarely sustained by the judge because the procedure for selecting jury panels is, by now, so routine.

A second type of challenge is known as a *for cause challenge*. In this kind of challenge an attorney can argue to the judge that a particular juror should be excused because he or she might be unable to be impartial. Someone who has been raped might, for example, be excused from jury service in a rape trial. Someone who had a son or daughter murdered might be excused from a jury in a murder trial. Close relatives of police officers might be excused from cases in which there are charges of police misconduct. Any juror who already has an opinion on the outcome of the case or who has learned a great deal about the case through pretrial publicity might also be excused for cause. Finally, any juror who admits to racial or ethnic prejudice might be dismissed from a jury for cause. The attorneys in a case have an unlimited number of challenges for cause, but each challenge must be ruled on by the judge.

The final type of challenge that can be raised is what is known as a *peremptory challenge*. These challenges can be raised by either attorney for any reason, and the reason does not have to be stated. Attorneys may decide to eliminate potential jurors because they did not like their political bias, were concerned about their religious beliefs and how these might influence the jurors' judgment, because they wanted a better or less well educated juror, and so forth. The number of peremptory challenges available to each attorney is strictly limited (although it varies by jurisdiction) so they must be exercised very carefully.

The selection of the jury requires thoughtful analysis on the part of the attorney. Attorneys evaluate potential jurors by considering their appearance, expressions, and answers to direct questions. But they also call upon certain stereotypical assumptions they are likely to have about jurors. Thus, for instance, defense attorneys often seek to find jurors who are like their client in the case, while prosecutors or plaintiffs seek to find jurors who are like the victim. Conventional wisdom also suggests that political liberals tend to favor the defense, while conservatives favor the prosecution. Minorities are more likely to favor the defense, while Caucasians might be more inclined to be sensitive to the prosecution. While there are most certainly exceptions to these stereotypical assumptions, they nonetheless guide the attorneys as they make their selections.[8]

Many large law firms now employ consultants who specialize in providing litigants with jury selection advice, although providing this advice is very costly, so it is the well-heeled litigant who is typically in the position where he or she can profit from the work of a trial consultant. Trial consultants may also test the story (or potential stories) to be presented in court before "mock" juries—juries that resemble the jury pool. By presenting their cases before mock juries, attorneys may be able to discover which arguments work best, which type of juror is most likely to find in their favor, and even how best to present and organize the arguments in their case.

The pretrial process, while time consuming and expensive, can easily influence the quality and nature of the evidence and arguments made in the courtroom. It can therefore be the difference between winning and losing the entire case.

THE ROLE OF ATTORNEYS IN THE TRIAL

Opening Statement

Once the jury panel is seated, the trial can begin. The prosecutor or the plaintiff begins the trial by presenting an opening statement. The opening statement provides the attorneys an opportunity to briefly introduce their stories of the case and to offer an explanation as to how the evidence will be drawn together to support the case. The opening statement is probably the most important moment in the case, especially for the prosecution or the plaintiff (for the purpose of clarity, future references will be to the prosecutor or the prosecution, and we will assume a criminal rather than civil action is being described). If the case does not seem clear and comprehensible to jurors on first hearing, before the defense has had its chance to speak, it is unlikely that the case can be won. Most of the trial evidence will be presented through the testimony of different witnesses and may come out in a somewhat disorganized and chaotic manner. The opening statement provides a framework for jurors to use in pulling this evidence together. An effective opening statement should stay in their minds throughout the case and should go with them into the jury room. In short, this statement provides the defense attorney and the prosecutor the opportunity to create the context for the presentation of all of the ensuing evidence in the trial.

The defense counsel may waive the right to make an opening statement, preferring to present the opening argument after the prosecution has presented its case. Generally, however, the defense will seek to make some sort of an opening statement, even if it is just to alert the jury to the fact that the other side has the burden to prove its case. However, the defense attorneys will choose not to make an opening statement if, for instance, they do not yet have a clear story of their own case, they plan a purely refutational case strategy, or they wish to wait to hear their opponent's case before they commit themselves to a particular argumentative strategy.

Direct Examination and Cross-Examination

Following the opening statements, the prosecution presents its case. The legal case is presented through the introduction of the testimony of relevant witnesses and the introduction of the physical evidence. The evidence becomes the substance of the legal case and can consist of physical evidence (such as contracts, the murder weapon, blood evidence, or the drugs seized) as well as testimony. The evidence is introduced to the court through the question and answer process. The prosecutor introduces the witnesses and builds a case through what is known as *direct examination*. Then, after the prosecutor's questions elicit the relevant evidence for the court, the defense attorney will ask questions of the witness. This is known as *cross-examination*. The direct examination and cross-examination portions of the trial are especially important to the trial's outcome, for they are the means by which jurors hear the assembled evidence and also hear the challenges to that evidence.

Unlike on television, however, witnesses rarely melt under the withering questions of the attorneys, and there are usually no profound surprises produced during these examinations. If the attorneys have done their pretrial homework, they have a very good idea as to what the witnesses will say in response to their questions. Neither counsel wishes to risk asking a witness a question that they do not already know the likely answer to, for doing so could jeopardize their case.

In the questioning process, attorneys seek to develop questions that put their cases in the best possible light and that minimize the credibility of the opponent's stories. Questions are best asked in a simple and straightforward manner and in such a way as to prevent the witnesses from providing lengthy elaborations that might only confuse the jurors or that might spark questions that would not otherwise occur in the jurors' minds. The attorneys also try not to antagonize witnesses, even the opponent's witnesses, because it may enhance the witnesses' appeal for the jurors while undermining the attorney's appeal, likability, and trustworthiness.

Some people, of course, are better witnesses than others. Ideally a witness should be a person of integrity and good moral character who will be believed and viewed sympathetically by the jury. In addition, a good witness is one who demonstrates a good memory, seems thoughtful and conscientious, is able to provide clear and focused answers, and does not seem to be attempting to qualify every answer given. Some witnesses pose very special problems to attorneys, including problems of character (the convicted felon, the philandering husband, the youth who demonstrates a willingness to fib), poor communication habits, (long-windedness, an antagonistic style, an unpleasant personality), or certain limitations (for instance, age or infirmities). An attorney who calls such a witness takes a calculated risk as to how the witness will hold up under cross-examination and how he or she will be perceived by the jury.

There are many other issues that attorneys must consider in presenting the witnesses in support of their case. Who should be called? In what order should they be called? If more than one witness can corroborate the testimony then how many witnesses should be called? If there are weaknesses in the testimony of the witness, should they be introduced by the side who called the witness rather than left to be possibly discovered by the opposing counsel? The wise attorney is careful and conscientious in the construction of the case and weighs the different strategic elements of the case in deciding these issues.

The cross-examination of the witnesses is also a great challenge for the attorneys. When examining witnesses whom one has called to testify, one has a good idea as to what the witnesses will say, having already interviewed them.

When examining witnesses who have been called by the other side, however, the situation is far more difficult. The attorney may have learned through pre-trial disclosure what the witness is to testify about, but the courtroom sometimes provides the first opportunity to speak directly to this witness. It is dangerous to risk asking questions that may actually strengthen the opponent's case by helping the witness to enhance her or his credibility with the jury. In conducting cross-examinations, the counsel must carefully study the depositions that were introduced and the material evidence that the witness may be presenting. In addition, the counsel should carefully structure and phrase all questions. This is no time for a hunting expedition. A good attorney also knows when to stop questioning a witness, so as not to undercut the progress already made with a line of questioning. Matlon provides the following example of a defense lawyer cross-examining an eyewitness:

Q: Where were the defendant and the victim when the fight broke out?

A: In the middle of the field.

Q: Where were you?

A: On the edge of the field.

Q: What were you doing?

A: Bird-watching.

Q: Where were the birds?

A: In the trees.

Q: Where were the trees?

A: On the edge of the field.

Q: Were you looking at the birds?

A: Yes.

Q: So your back was to the people fighting?

A: Yes.

Q: Well, if your back was to them, how can you say that the defendant bit off the victim's nose?

A: Well, I saw him spit it out.[9]

Attorneys should ask clear and direct questions; they should vary their inflection and pacing so that the examinations do not become monotonous for jurors; and they should always remember that they are working to win jurors over to their side of the case. Consequently, they should not appear to badger or treat the witness rudely, even if the witness is an undesirable character, for they do not wish the jury to begin to sympathize with the witness rather than with them. The most important thing that attorneys must remember in cross-examination, however, is that they must have a strategy in mind. They must know what they hope to accomplish; they must prepare their questions in advance;

and they must be able to use the questioning process to tell their story of the evidence and events.

There are some limits as to the types of testimony that may be elicited. Hearsay evidence, for example is rarely permitted. You might think that this rule exists because confidence in the testimony would be diminished if it has passed through more than one person. Think of the telephone game where a statement is passed from person to person. By the time it completes its trip around the room it frequently bares little relationship to the original statement. But probably juries could be trusted to weigh this evidence in light of its secondhand nature. We trust that jurors will ignore testimony that a judge tells them to ignore and we also trust juries to evaluate the credibility of witnesses. The main reason that hearsay evidence is excluded goes back to the philosophy of our system of justice. A key element of that system is the right to confront one's accusers. If someone has evidence to give against a defendant, that person must come forward. The defendant has the right to hear what the person has to say, and the defendant has the right to subject that testimony to the rigors of cross-examination.

Another limitation on testimony is the prohibition against asking witnesses to offer expert opinions unless the witness is introduced and accepted as an expert. Witnesses are generally asked only to testify to that which they saw, not speculate as to why someone did something. A psychologist or psychiatrist may be able to explain the motivation behind an act, but most of us are ill prepared to render such judgments. The use of experts in courts is another practice that is burgeoning.

Summary Judgment

Once the prosecution has completed its case it is time for the defense to present its case. Often the defense attorneys will approach the judge at this point with a motion to dismiss the complaint on the grounds that the prosecution's case is insufficient to overcome a reasonable doubt, in other words, that the prosecution has failed to present a *prima facie* case. Such motions, called summary judgments, are usually dismissed out of hand by the judge, because as we have already mentioned, the court dockets are so crowded that very few frivolous cases actually make their way to trial in the first place. In rare circumstances the defense counsel's cross-examination of the prosecution's witnesses has been so effective that the judge may in fact grant this motion. If it is granted, the trial is ended and the complaint against the defendant is dismissed. More likely, however, the judge will rule that the prosecution has met the burden of overcoming reasonable doubt, and the defense will be instructed to present its case. The defense now has the opportunity to present its witnesses under direct examination, and the prosecutor has the opportunity to cross-examine those witnesses.

Although the prosecution must show a crime was committed and that the defendant had the motive, opportunity, and means to commit the crime, the defense can win if it raises substantial doubt about just one of these issues. For example, the defense may be able to provide an alibi for the time during which the crime was committed. Or the defense may raise substantial doubt about the defendant's ability to commit the crime as it was described by the prosecution.

Or the defense may raise the possibility that there are others who have a better motive, opportunity, or means to commit the crime.

Closing Arguments

Following the presentation of the defense case the trial proceeds to the next phase, the presentation of the closing arguments. The prosecution presents its closing argument first, then the defense, and then the prosecution can present a rebuttal closing argument if it deems it warranted. These statements allow the attorneys to pull all of the evidence and testimony together and to tell their stories. Attorneys cannot use these speeches to present evidence. The time for introducing evidence is now past. Rather, the attorneys now have to bring all of the evidence presented, both pro and con, into a coherent narrative for the jury.

The prosecution obviously tries to tell as coherent and complete a story of the events as possible. Loose ends prove especially dangerous to the prosecutor's case, so there is an attempt to demonstrate that the narrative has probability and that it rings true with the way we know people act. The defense clearly wants to discredit this story, to find flaws in it that will convince the jury the defendant should not be found guilty.

Attorneys must be careful in closing arguments to faithfully recount the facts that were presented in the case. If the evidence is inaccurately described at this point, the opposing counsel will almost certainly object. The attorneys also have to decide what the key facts in their case are and emphasize those facts, rather than merely recount the entire case. Finally, it is important that the attorneys attempt to predict the flaws in their own case and seek to preempt arguments that either the opposing counsel or the jurors themselves might advance as they consider the evidence. The attorney who can predict the key turning points in the consideration of the case, and resolve jurors' uncertainties regarding those turning points, will have a much better chance of securing a favorable verdict.

Closing arguments also offer attorneys a final opportunity to win over the jurors with their communication skills. Attorneys seek to communicate directly with the jurors and to impress them with their competence, fairness, and thoroughness in presenting their cases. Often they will resort to emotional appeals in their closing arguments in order to win sympathy and/or empathy for their clients or for the victims they represent. If the attorneys made the right choices in jury selection, they should have created a panel that will be open to these arguments. They will now seek to take full advantage of these sympathies and to win the jurors over. It is especially important that the closing argument be simple, straightforward, and easy to follow. Often the attorneys will resort to such well tested argumentation strategies as the use of analogies and metaphors because, as we have already discussed, these argument techniques are proven to be effective storytelling modes of reasoning.

Decision Making

Once the attorneys have presented their closing arguments, the judge will instruct the jurors as to their responsibilities. This portion of the trial is extremely important to the outcome, for the judge essentially creates the context in which all of the other information in the trial is to be considered. Judges direct the jurors about the law, about the admissibility of certain evidence, about their obligations in reviewing the relevant evidence, and about their burdens in delivering a fair and impartial verdict. Jurors are also reminded of the standard, beyond a reasonable doubt or the preponderance of evidence, which they should apply in rendering a verdict.

Judicial instructions to jurors are frequently cited as places in which the trial judge errs, and since these errors may provide the grounds for an appeal, some jurisdictions provide the judge with what are called *pattern instructions*. These instructions are standardized to fit the nature of the charge and to reflect the statutory rules of the particular jurisdiction. Standardized instructions, however, frequently do not address the needs of the specific case under review, so judges often have to add other guiding statements to these standardized instructions.

Once the judge has charged them, the jurors are sent to their chambers to deliberate and to reach a verdict. In the jury room the competing stories told by the opposing counsels are subjected to close scrutiny. The jurors may ask to reread portions of trial testimony, examine the physical evidence again, and ask questions of the judge, which are relayed through the court's bailiff. They should not have discussed with each other or anyone else their opinions of the case or the evidence prior to being sequestered in the jury room. Once the case is in their hands, the attorneys can have no further effect on the trial outcome and they can only wait along with the victims and the defendants for the verdict to be reached.

When the jurors have reached their verdict, the principal participants in the case are reassembled in the courtroom and the verdict is handed over to the bailiff and announced. The attorneys will often seek to interview the jurors in order to discover why they ruled as they did and to try to learn more about why their case strategy either succeeded or failed to persuade the jurors.

SUMMARY

The law is an especially important focus for argumentation. Attorneys use their argumentation skills in virtually every dimension of their professional lives, from their initial conversations with their clients, to the negotiations and settlement conferences they conduct, to the depositions and fact-finding phase, and finally in the courtroom itself. Many of the principles of effective argumentation discussed in this text are especially important in the courtroom. The advocates rely on a storytelling argumentative approach, and the jurors make their decisions based upon their judgments of who told the superior story. In this argument field, as in many others, the emphasis should be placed on careful research and preparation, for a well researched and reasoned case theory is likely to win over the jury.

Key Terms

adversarial   discovery
burden of proof   precedent
civil   preponderance of evidence
criminal   reasonable doubt
cross-examination   theory of the case
direct examination

Activities

1. Diagram the court system in your locale, from municipal to state supreme court.

2. Attend a criminal trial and observe the presentation of the opening arguments. Try to ascertain the theory of the case held by each side. Evaluate these opening presentations in terms of narrative probability and fidelity.

3. Attend a civil court proceeding and compare what transpires with what took place in the criminal court. What differences can you identify? What are the similarities?

4. We have elsewhere described the importance of symbols and rituals. Observe a court proceeding and identify the symbols and rituals of the judicial system. What role do these symbols and rituals play in the U.S. justice system?

5. Visit a small-claims court and compare what transpires there with what went on in the civil courtroom you visited. How does the participation of citizen advocates change the nature of the proceedings? What similarities are there?

Recommended Readings

Beach, Wayne A. "Temporal Density in Courtroom Interaction: Constraints on the Recovery of Past Events in Legal Discourse." *Communication Monographs* 52 (1985): 1–18.

Benoit, William L. "Attorney Argumentation and Supreme Court Opinions." *Argumentation and Advocacy* 26 (1989): 22–38.

Bycel, Ben, H. Mitchell Caldwell, and Michael S. Lief. *Ladies and Gentlemen of the Jury: Greatest Closing Arguments in Modern Law.* New York: Scribner, 2000.

Hasian, Marouf Jr. "In Search of 'Ivan the Terrible': John Demjanjuk and the Judicial Use of Ironic Argument." *Argumentation and Advocacy* 39 (2003): 231–253.

Hollihan, Thomas A., Patricia Riley, and Keith Freadhoff. "Arguing for Justice: An Analysis of Arguing in Small Claims Court." *Journal of the American Forensic Association* 22 (1986): 187–195.

Huhn, Wilson R. *Five Types of Legal Arguments.* Durham, NC: Carolina Academic Press, 2002.

Makau, Josina. "The Supreme Court and Reasonableness." *Quarterly Journal of Speech* 70 (1984): 379–396.

Nobles, Scott. "Communication in the Education of Legal Advocates." *Journal of the American Forensic Association* 22 (1985): 20–25.

Saks, Michael J., and Reid Hastie. *Social Psychology in Court.* New York: Van Nostrand Reinhold, 1978.

Shipman, Marlin. "Ethical Guidelines for Televising or Photographing Executions." *Journal of Mass Media Ethics* 10 (1995): 95–109.

Taylor, K. Phillip, Raymond W. Buchanan, and David U. Strawn. *Communication Strategies for Trial Attorneys.* Glenview, IL: Scott, Foresman, 1984.

Worthington, Debra L., and David G. Levasseur. "Charity and the American Jury: Exploring the Relationship between Plaintiff's Need-Based Arguments and Mock Juror Verdicts in Medical Malpractice Suits." *Argumentation and Advocacy* 39 (2002): 23–39.

Notes

[1] Ronald J. Matlon, *Communication in the Legal Process* (New York: Holt, Rinehart and Winston, 1988), 2.

[2] Del Jones, "Lawyers, Wannabes on the Rise," *USA Today* On-Line. Posted 12–25–03. http://www.usatoday.com/money/industries/2003-12-26-lawyers_x.htm.

[3] Matlon, 4.

[4] Matlon, 101.

[5] W. Lance Bennett and Martha S. Feldman, *Reconstructing Reality in the Courtroom: Justice and Judgment in American Culture* (New Brunswick, NJ: Rutgers University Press, 1981), 4.

[6] Ibid., 4–7.

[7] Ibid., 10.

[8] For a discussion of the jury selection process see Michael Fried, Kalman J. Kaplan, and Katherine W. Klein, "Juror Selection: An Analysis of *Voir Dire*," in *The Jury System in America: A Critical Overview,* ed. Rita James Simon, 47–66 (Beverly Hills: Sage, 1975).

[9] Matlon, 236.

ARGUMENTATION IN BUSINESS AND ORGANIZATIONS

The principles of argumentation that we have discussed in this text are not merely theoretical abstractions that you can commit to memory, regurgitate on a final examination, and then forget. Instead, these are concepts that you will use—whether you are conscious of them or not—throughout your life. Although most of you will not participate in formal academic debates once you have finished this class, and some of you may never be asked to create or evaluate arguments in a courtroom, all of you will find yourself creating arguments in your workplace. As members of business, governmental, academic, or professional organizations you will often be called upon to develop arguments in support of your positions. As a result, we have designed this chapter to serve as a useful and pragmatic guide to help you prepare for your professional careers. We want to help you develop the skills necessary to achieve effective advocacy in the workplace.

This chapter will help you learn to argue so that you can analyze the kinds of issues that are significant in business and organizational settings and so that you can advocate your positions in a forceful and convincing manner. We will suggest how you should prepare your arguments, assess your audience, create and present your messages, defend your ideas, and follow up on your presentations. The goal is to help you learn how to promote your ideas—and yourself—in an organization.

COMPETING INTERESTS IN ORGANIZATIONS

As is the case in other argumentative contexts, organizational arguers typically make use of narratives and evaluate arguments on the basis of their appeal as stories. In fact, many organizations have developed "company stories" that are often embedded within and integral to the formation of the ***organizational culture*** that defines the organization and distinguishes it vis-à-vis its competitors.[1]

To say that there is a shared company story, however, is not to say that there are never disagreements within organizations. Organizations are composed of people with different levels and types of education and expertise, and thus of people who have different worldviews and goals. Nevertheless, these people are bound together to perform certain tasks and to produce products or services.[2] They transform inputs into finished products or outputs. Communication among organization members is necessary to accomplish tasks. Because these individuals will often have different opinions, experiences, jobs, interests, and objectives they will at times find themselves in conflict. People differ about how to do their jobs and in their notions about steps to be taken to help their organizations to prosper. Making sound arguments can resolve these conflicts and help people to make good decisions.

In a large and complex business organization, for example, you may find a finance division, a research and development division, a manufacturing division, and a marketing and sales division. Even though the executives from these different divisions all work for the same company and should be pursuing enterprise objectives that will benefit that company, their different tasks, personalities, backgrounds, and specializations often lead them to very different views of how their company should be run and what decisions are in the company's best interests.

- *Finance Division.* Executives from the finance division are especially concerned with the company's bottom line, with the return of value to shareholders, and with the performance of the company in the stock market. These executives are sometimes referred to disparagingly as the "bean counters." They focus on improving income and reducing expenses. They tend to be protective of the company's assets and may be reluctant to commit funds for such purposes as developing new products, purchasing new plants or equipment, hiring new employees, or increasing employee compensation packages.

- *Research and Development Division.* Executives from the research and development division are especially interested in developing new products and in improving current products. They are the company dreamers and are always speculating about how things could be improved. In an effective organization the research and development executives are highly creative. They seek funding for the technology, facilities, newly trained expert employees, and innovative materials and practices, which they feel they need in order to either improve the products the company currently manufactures or develop new products. They may also have little regard for what their "needs" will cost, how hard the new products might be to manufacture, or even if there is a market for these products.

- *Manufacturing Division.* For their part, these executives are keenly aware of how difficult it is to actually produce the new products. They are often reluctant to take on new product lines and eager to continue operating as they always have in order to get the current products out on schedule, keep a ready flow of spare parts available, and maintain a stable workforce. New products require development money and new training programs, and they lead to quality-control problems. Manufacturing division executives often think that new products mean having the money to hire new employees, to secure more floor space, and to purchase new equipment—money that they feel the "bean counters" won't give them.

- *Marketing Division.* The executives from the marketing and sales division are concerned with selling the product. Consequently, they want innovative and new products to show to their customers, but not if the innovations threaten to undermine the secure markets and market share that they currently have with existing products. They also want reliable products that will sell at a competitive price, meet customers' needs, and be delivered on time. Such needs put pressure on all of the other divisions.

A well-managed company needs strong, effective, rational, and articulate executives in each of these divisions. The leaders of each division must represent the particular interests and concerns of their division and of the employees within their division in discussions with senior managers, especially with regard to business strategies and resource allocation. If any division is poorly led or does not make its interests known, the entire company might suffer as a result. Company chief executive officers (CEOs) are hired, and are often paid very generous salaries, because they have the know-how to make the tough decisions and to guide companies in deliberative management processes. Certainly some CEOs make better decisions than others, but any CEO is likely to be more effective and to make far better decisions in an organization that has created a healthy deliberative climate for the creation and evaluation of competing arguments that reflect the interests of the different parts of the organization.

Organizational conflicts are often productive and necessary.[3] Arguers in organizational settings should not assume that their colleagues already know the facts and understand their thinking. Instead they should view their argumentation as an opportunity to enlighten and inform their colleagues. In addition, it is important that organizational arguers not see conflicts as zero-sum games with winners and losers. They should address conflicts using arguments to initiate an investigative process that enables the decision makers to choose the best courses of action. This means that advocates should avoid personality attacks or personalizing the arguments directed against them. Arguments should be seen as a natural and important part of an organization's daily activity.

PREPARING ARGUMENTS TO MEET OBJECTIVES

The first consideration in developing arguments in an organizational setting, as in any other setting, is to clarify your objectives. What do you hope to accomplish? People may argue for many reasons: to advance an issue they believe is especially important, to effect change in the way the organization conducts its business or operates, to secure resources for a new project or procedure, to promote themselves or their work unit, or to defend themselves or their unit from attack or criticism. It is important for you to have a clear idea of precisely what your purpose is before you develop your arguments. If your ideas are unclear and your objectives are not well defined and carefully considered, you risk undercutting your purpose. For instance, say that you want to argue for a new innovation that reduces the layers of bureaucracy in order to streamline your company and help it to operate more efficiently and thus more profitably. This argument could, of course, backfire if the executives who have to approve your proposal believe that their jobs reside in the layer of bureaucracy that you believe is burdensome and should be eliminated! Carefully consider what you hope to accomplish and how you intend to go about accomplishing it before going public with your arguments.

Carefully assess the accepted communication or argumentation style in your organization. Different organizations reflect very different communication cultures. Some are very friendly, very supportive, and informal. In such organizations the chain of command is more loosely followed and the executives are open to interactions from below. The style of interaction in such organizations tends to be relaxed. Other organizations are very formal and require communication to flow along specific paths that conform to the organization's hierarchy. In such an organization interactions might be more tense, people may be somewhat more closed toward each other, and there may be greater emphasis on the important of preserving an explicit chain of command. Such an organization represses conflict and discourages open disagreements. Information in such organizations tends to flow downward much more easily than upward. Still other organizations are highly contentious, and conflict might not only be very common, it might be accepted as the norm. People feel free to openly disagree with each other and perhaps even to show signs of bad temper. You need to determine the nature of the organization that you have joined and attempt to respond accordingly. This is not to say that you should adopt the negative elements of the communication style of your organization. It is to say, however, that you should take care not to violate important communication standards of that organization because doing so might diminish your effectiveness as an advocate and might create discomfort and problems for you and your coworkers.

It is important to assess the audience for your arguments. Consider who ultimately makes the decisions about the issues that you intend to address. Once you have a clear idea of this you can attempt to determine what this person might be looking for and/or considering when he or she ponders the alternatives presented. What issues is this person interested in? Is this person likely to have a particular perspective based on his or her job requirements, or on time and experience with the company, or on experience gained from working at another company or organization? Has the person been shaped by the unique character of his or her academic training and by the disciplinary characteristics of that field? What values or goals seem to influence this individual and your organization and how might these goals or values shape your arguments?

Often the audience for your arguments in an organizational setting is your immediate boss. Consequently, you should always consider how to make arguments that your boss will find persuasive. Keep in mind, one way for you to prosper in an organization is to make your boss look good, which can have positive consequences for you.[4] Remember, in presenting arguments to your boss, your boss is an ordinary person with biases, fears, preoccupations, goals, strengths, weaknesses, and so forth. Too often bosses make poor decisions because they have been poorly trained or ill prepared for their jobs or because they fail to get good information from their superiors, their subordinates, or both. Subordinates may distort the information to protect their own interests or because of fear in relaying bad news.* Superiors may keep subordinates in the dark because of lack of trust or respect for the subordinate.[5] Your role as an arguer is to identify your boss's interests and objectives, come to know his or her idiosyncrasies, and seek to adapt your argumentative claims and strategies in accordance with them.[6] Then you should make every attempt to supply your boss with the information and the analysis necessary to make the best possible decisions.

SHAPING THE MESSAGE: DEVISING STRATEGIES

Once you have decided what your objectives are and have considered the audience to whom your arguments will be addressed, it is appropriate for you to consider from what vantage point you are arguing. What is your position in the company? How much authority, credibility, and *power* do you really have? If you have just been hired as a clerk in the mailroom, you may find that your ideas about how the company ought to be restructured will not receive much consideration. If, on the other hand, you have come to the company in a position of authority, the company's leadership may be expecting great things from you and might be eager to listen to your ideas. Careful consideration of your resources will help prevent you from overplaying your hand and getting yourself in trouble. It will also help you to understand that if you are in an uphill fight against someone who holds a lot more power and influence than you do you will have to adjust your argument strategies accordingly.

In addition to assessing your power in the organization you should begin to form *coalitions* for support.[7] Before brashly going to your boss you should cultivate support for the positions you want to advocate from peers and with other

---

* Sometimes the distortion and denial of access to information can have dramatic and even tragic consequences. One study has suggested, for example, that the great famine that killed millions of Chinese peasants during the period that was known as "the Great Leap Forward" during the 1950s was permitted to occur because Chinese Communist functionaries and bureaucrats refused to tell Party Chairman Mao Zedong that his efforts to increase steel production were producing disastrous results because farmers were being taken off the land and encouraged to produce steel in small backyard furnaces. Apparently the attempt to deceive Mao was so organized that when he traveled away from the capital to the provinces, the local party leaders would pile great stacks of grain along the railroad tracks to create an appearance of bountiful harvests even as the famine took a stronger grip on the public. For a fascinating discussion see: Li Zhi-Sui, *The Private Life of Chairman Mao* (New York: Random House, 1994).

important people in your organization who can help you and enhance your position. If these persons are supportive of your position, they can lend credibility to it. They provide what are known as "prestige referrals" for you, which are, in a sense, somewhat like endorsements in a political campaign. If these other persons turn out not to be supportive of your ideas, their feedback will enable you to reshape or bolster your arguments and to better anticipate the response that you may get from others in the organization.

There are some strategies that you can consider using if you find yourself at odds with a more powerful organizational advocate. You can seek out a mentor who might sponsor your position and also help protect you from the flak that your ideas might create in the organization. Ideally your mentor is someone at least as powerful as your principal adversary or is someone who has the credibility and the organizational stature to be respected in the organization. Second, when you present your suggestions to your boss, you can encourage your boss to take "ownership" and become an advocate for your ideas. One important way to do this is to convince your boss that your ideas were his or hers all along.

You should always think very carefully about who is likely to resist your arguments. Whose ox will be gored by your proposal? Whose interests will be undercut? How might these potential adversaries either be persuaded to come over to your side or, failing that, neutralized? How much power in the organization do your adversaries have and how entrenched are their views? Who will likely choose to ally themselves with your adversaries in the event of a confrontation? What compromises or accommodations might you offer that will win over those individuals? It is certainly preferable not to face determined and powerful adversaries, so how can you avoid such situations?

You should also seek strategies for presenting your arguments in a manner that discourages opposition without undercutting your objectives. For example, perhaps you wish to propose a solution to a problem that you have identified in your organization, but there will be active resistance to your ideas. You might consider presenting two alternative scenarios as potential solutions to the problem. The first scenario might be a conservative, inexpensive, and perhaps easily enacted approach to the problem but also one that may be demonstrably inadequate to fully solve it. The second scenario, in contrast, might be complex and expensive, replete with "bells and whistles." Although this scenario would solve the problem, its cost and complexity might make it a less than acceptable solution. Then, after your superior has shot down these two scenarios you can introduce a third—the one you actually favored all along—as a compromise to the first two. Scenario three, which might not have received careful consideration if proposed individually or initially, might now seem like a very reasonable approach compared to the first two scenarios.

In creating your arguments do not forget the importance of careful preparation. To succeed as an organizational advocate you must do your homework. You should begin by reviewing previous arguments that have been made in your organization regarding the issue that you are addressing. When the issue has come up for discussion before how did the advocates phrase their claims? What were the outcomes of those prior discussions? What happened as a result of the decisions reached before? Were those results positive or negative? What historical lessons should you and your supervisors learn from those prior discussions and the decisions that followed them?

You must also be careful to tailor your arguments to the primary decision maker(s) whom you are addressing. Be mindful or our earlier discussion of field theory. People in different fields often evaluate arguments differently. If you are talking to engineers you need to adapt your argument to that field. If you were talking to psychologists you would want to adapt your arguments to the forms of reasoning common in that field. You should also take care to assess the extent to which the audience that you are addressing has prior knowledge, expertise, or understanding of the issues that you are raising. Often you will have far greater expertise on the issue being discussed than will the person to whom you are appealing. Do not presume that the person fully knows what you know and adapt your arguments and your examples to his or her areas of expertise and experience. This situation is especially common in today's complex organizations where work is performed by narrowly trained specialists who understand a lot about very technical subjects but who are managed by senior executives who lack such specialized knowledge. Perhaps these executives came from another branch or division of the company, or perhaps the technological advances in the industry have occurred at a very rapid rate and have left them unprepared for the kinds of problems now being faced. Regardless of the reason, managers often report that they do not have as much knowledge and expertise as do the people whom they are charged with supervising. Making such complex technical organizations function effectively takes concerted effort by superiors and subordinates alike to make themselves understood.

You should pay special attention to the use of technical language or insider *jargon* in the arguments you present. If your listeners do not share your technical vocabulary, they are not likely to follow your arguments. Often people are very reluctant to ask for explanations or definitions because they feel that doing so reveals how little they understand and that they will be seen as ignorant or uninformed.[8] Be careful, on the other hand, not to demean the intelligence, background, or experience of your audience. Nothing puts people off more quickly than believing that someone has talked down to them. Assess the background of your audience before you begin your presentation, adapt your language to that background, define any terms that may be unknown to your audience, and carefully assess the feedback that you receive.[9]

You should also carefully consider the alternative formats available to you for sharing your arguments. Sometimes it is preferable to write an e-mail message or a memorandum advocating your position. Sometimes a phone call is better. At other times you may need to request a one-to-one meeting or perhaps a formal briefing. You can decide which form of communication is appropriate based on several factors, including:

1. How many people will have to be involved to implement your ideas? The more people who need to be involved the more interaction is probably needed to plan and discuss the proposal. If face-to-face meetings take place during the planning of the innovations, it may be easier to convince

people to accept the innovations and the people may be less likely to criticize them later.[10]

2. How complex are the issues that you are trying to communicate? The more complex an idea is the more people will feel a need to discuss it in order to gain confidence that they fully understand it.

3. How many feathers will be ruffled by your arguments? (This is a political consideration.) How much resistance can be expected? If you do anticipate encountering resistance to your ideas, it is probably best to present them in a briefing meeting. A memorandum can be too conveniently ignored, an e-mail is too easily forwarded to others for comment, perhaps in the process widening and deepening potential opposition to your ideas. A phone call can be too easily distorted or misrepresented when discussed with others. A briefing, on the other hand, permits you to explain your position in your own words so that all parties can hear for themselves what you are advocating.

If you decide to make a formal oral presentation you should systematically prepare for it. Conduct your research, outline your objectives, and prepare your appropriate *visual aids*. Today most business presentations include PowerPoint slides that can contain graphs, charts, tables, key points arranged as "bullets," and even photographs, film clips, and sound effects. Do not become too enamored with the technologies and the artful visual presentations. Remember that the essence of your arguments has to be revealed in the language that you select. Too many slides, too many special effects, and too much movement across the screen—bullet points magically appearing one after another on a slide—can distract from the essence of your argument. The rule of thumb should be to keep your slides simple and do not overload them with so much written content that your audience cannot keep up with your oral speech or finds themselves reading the slides rather than listening to you speak. Also, do not read what is on your slides to your audience word-for-word. This becomes very boring. The slides should contain brief key word prompts to help catch and focus your audience's attention. The slides should not contain the entirety of your message.

Most people are not very good at taking notes. If you wish your audience to remember key facts or arguments from your talk, you should be prepared to provide them with written copies of it. Some speakers actually give their PowerPoint slides as notes for people to take away with them. Be careful not to provide so much extensive reading material that your audience reads it while you are speaking and stops paying attention to you. Most people will flip through the material and read ahead of you, or they will occupy themselves by flipping through the pages, and once they have finished perusing the document they may begin to doodle in the margins. None of these activities help them to pay attention to your arguments. If you want to be assured that your audience pays attention to what you are saying, you should keep your handouts brief and pass them out section by section so that you have some control over when the audience begins to peruse them. You can invite your audience to write comments in the margins if they wish.

Too many organizational advocates are sloppy and careless in the preparation of their reports. Take care to organize your materials so that your arguments are clearly expressed and easy to follow. Make certain that you use font sizes and colors that stand out and are easy to follow. A slide with yellow coloring on a brown background can be very difficult to read. Be sure that you catch spelling errors and obvious mistakes that distract from the content of your messages. If your listeners become preoccupied counting all of the misspelled words in your handouts or on your slides, they are not likely to hear what you have said.

Remember how important appearances are to public presentations: you should make every effort to be well dressed, polished, prepared, and professional in you demeanor. This will communicate your competence and seriousness of purpose and will help enhance the appeal of your messages.

THE ORAL PRESENTATION

Most oral presentations succeed or fail on the basis of the quality of their advance preparation. The more time and attention you devote to analyzing the issues, developing your arguments, assembling your evidence, structuring and writing your remarks, and practicing your delivery, the better your talk will be. There are, however, some helpful tips that you should keep in mind.

1. Familiarize yourself with the setting for the talk. If it is a conference room or auditorium you should visit it and make sure that you can arrange where you will stand and where your visual aids will be projected and your computer placed to that you can access the key board and make reference to the slides to establish your points. Make certain that the room contains all of the equipment that you will need, such as an overhead projector and a screen. Locate the outlets, and make certain that you have the appropriate adaptors to connect your computer to the power source. If you are not bringing a laptop, make sure that the computer you will use will be able to read your disc. Nothing can be more unnerving than to devote hours to the preparation of a PowerPoint presentation that you cannot access or show for some reason or another.

2. Construct your talk so that you tell your audience a story that has a beginning, a middle, and an end. This allows you to create a new scenario to explain how things will be different if your proposed ideas are accepted, to paint a future that contrasts with the status quo, and to compare your story with the rival stories that might be circulating. Also, preface your story with an overview that lays out your objectives so that your audience can see where you are going. An axiom of these kinds of presentations is: tell them what you are going to say; say it; and then tell them what you said.

3. Consider preparing both long and short versions of your talk. Often presentations are scheduled in meetings at which several other persons are

speaking. If their talks run long you might find that you have only five minutes in which to make your fifteen-minute presentation. Do not try to present the same talk in five minutes that you would have attempted in fifteen; you will leave your audiences feeling rushed and confused. Instead, offer them a brief thumbnail sketch of the talk that you had hoped to give and leave them wanting more. Then attempt to reschedule your talk for a later day when you will have the time to make your more complete presentation.

4. Try to keep your presentation as brief as possible. The most frequently heard criticism in business presentations might be that they run on too long. Seek to determine how much background information your audience needs and give them just that much. Confine your comments to those that are germane to your topic. Never talk for twenty-five minutes when a ten-minute talk will do the job. Remember, people in the workplace almost always feel busy and rushed. The time spent in meetings hearing presentations is time away from their desks and their other responsibilities. Try to be respectful of other people's very busy schedules.

5. Use humor. Do not try to be Jay Leno—no one expects you to keep them in stitches. But people do enjoy a bit of humor and do want to relax and have a good time. If you do decide to tell a joke, however, make sure that it is clean and does not offend anyone. Never tell an off-color joke or one that ridicules anyone's gender, ethnicity, religion, or other social identity; such jokes only embarrass their tellers. Also, jokes work best when they are topically connected to the content of your speech. If you are not a good joke teller and cannot think of an appropriate joke that fits your topic, then do not attempt to tell a joke.

6. Make sure that you encourage questions and always try to leave time for questions. Answering questions gives you an opportunity to clarify your arguments, to respond to potential misunderstandings, and to get feedback on how your audience sees your arguments. Often arguers communicate verbally that they are willing to answer questions while simultaneously sending nonverbal cues that suggest that questions are not really welcomed or encouraged. Be careful not to do this. Also, be careful not to communicate an impression that you believe a question from someone in the audience is stupid or ill informed, for nothing can discourage questions more effectively than a hostile reception. Avoid becoming defensive when asked a question that seems hostile to your position. Answer questions carefully and honestly. If you do not know the answer to a question that you are asked, admit your ignorance. It is far better to admit that you do not know the answer than to make something up that may be wrong and that might discredit your entire presentation. The best response may be: "I do not know the answer to that question right now, but allow me to do some research into it and report back to you." Having made such a commitment, however, do be sure that you do in fact get back to the questioner with an answer.

ENCOUNTERING RESISTANCE

Organizational advocates often face *resistance* to their arguments. As we have already observed, organizations are composed of people with different opinions, interests, and objectives. There will probably be opposition to at least some of your arguments. However, if you have carefully researched and prepared your presentation, you may have anticipated this resistance and are prepared to respond to it. Here are some tips for dealing with resistance:

1. Stay calm. Opposition to your arguments is not the same as opposition to you as a person. It does not necessarily mean that the person who opposes you dislikes you, is out to get you, or wishes you to look bad. The more calm and cordial you are the more likely it is that the disagreement can remain at a professional and respectful level. If you become antagonistic and personalize the opposition, you can expect that your counterpart will respond in kind. If you remain calm, friendly, and professional, your adversary probably will too. It is generally best if it is your adversary who loses his or her temper and not you.

2. Clarify your position. Sometimes people oppose arguments because of what they think they are hearing rather than what was in fact said. As a result, you may find that a mere clarification of your arguments mitigates the opposition. If, however, the opposition is genuine, it still serves your interests and the interests of the adversary to fully understand that nature of the disagreement and what prompted it.

   Be especially wary of cases in which your adversary gives a false reason for his or her opposition to your argument in a public setting. Often people are reluctant to state the true reasons for their objections to arguments (you may have heard this phenomenon referred to as someone having a *hidden agenda*) because they fear that they will appear selfish, resistant to new ideas, or inflexible. In such situations you need to decide how direct you wish to be in your response. Do you confront someone with your belief that the person may be holding something back in the explanation of why he or she opposes your arguments? Or do you play along and just respond to the adversary's stated public objections and simply hope for the best? There is no single right answer to such a problem; it depends on the situation and the persons involved.

3. Be prepared to add new evidence or new analysis to support your arguments. Just as in an academic debate, in business or organizational arguments you should anticipate the refutation that your arguments might face and prepare answers to your opponent's arguments and extensions to your own positions. Do not retreat to your initial position and simply repeat your arguments when you are faced with opposition. Instead, add to your arguments to strengthen them and actively look for opportunities to identify weaknesses and mistaken assumptions or missing proof in the arguments offered by your adversary. Remember that the key is in refuting the arguments offered by your opponent.

Think also about the power of storytelling as a means of communication. Be prepared to expand your storyline to include new characters or actions. Think about the power of a shared story. We have been in meetings in which we were surrounded by statistical data that clearly suggested what the appropriate course of action should be, only to have someone in the meeting say: "Let me tell you about the last time we attempted to do something similar. . . ." Suddenly this narrative account of shared historical experience became a far more compelling reason to support an alternative course of action than was the previously offered statistical data.

4. When faced with what appears to be severe or intractable opposition, seek to minimize the differences between your positions and rival positions. Avoid dichotomies and either-or language. Look for ways to make accommodations and to adapt to other views. If a **compromise** is possible and will not undercut your argument, you should offer to compromise. Most decision makers are uncomfortable with conflict and resist making decisions that force them to support one strong-willed advocate while thwarting the will of another. Instead they prefer compromise and consensus. Remember also, if you can find a way to compromise, your adversary just might come around to agree with the newly modified position. The more "buy in" you get for a decision the more likely people are to stand behind it and not turn on you when something goes wrong.

5. Challenge your opponent to prepare and defend alternative positions. It is much easier to oppose and speak out against change than it is to develop and advocate alternatives. Try to force your opponent to present alternatives and then be prepared to refute those alternatives if you are so inclined. Focus the discussion on the comparisons between the alternative positions so that the decision maker can carefully weigh the benefits and disadvantages of the competing alternatives in making a decision.

6. Be a graceful winner or loser. Organizations typically reward people who can get along with their peers and not cause problems. Do not flaunt your successes over those whom you may have vanquished and do not stew over your losses. Instead, learn how to take both your successes and your failures in stride. Assume that during the course of your career you will have both wins and losses along the way.

FOLLOW-UP ACTIVITIES

One of the most common problems in organizations is that people do not carefully follow through after a decision has been reached. If you win support for your arguments or concessions to your positions, you should document what was decided and the commitments involved. Send a memorandum or an e-mail to the decision maker summarizing what you understood to be the results of the meeting, asking for a response to any portions of the communication that may not be accurate. Then keep a copy of that memorandum and any responses in your files. It is amazing how often commitments are "forgotten"; however, they are much more difficult to forget if there is a written record.

Schedule any required follow-up meetings as quickly as possible to demonstrate your commitment to this new project or proposal and to keep it fresh in people's minds. Do not let it fall between the cracks, or people will likely remember that they agreed to do something but that it must not have been successful—not that it failed due to a lack of effort on their part.

Take whatever actions are required of you personally and carefully document all of your activities. Ideally you should write progress reports to your supervisors keeping them posted on your activities and demonstrating that you are making progress toward achieving whatever goals you may have set or had set for you.

SUMMARY

Arguing in an organization is in many respects similar to arguing in any other context. Arguments are effective when presented in narrative form; arguments still need to be supported by evidence and analysis; careful preparation pays dividends; and arguments must take into account decision makers' self-interests. The key difference in the organizational context is that the person whom you are trying to convince may also be the person who signs your paychecks. Consequently, in this context more than in almost any other, it is important that you not allow personal antagonisms to develop. A clear track record of thoughtful, highly polished, and professional argumentative presentations will be most helpful in convincing your superiors that you are indispensable to the organizations and deserving of promotions.

Key Terms

coalitions   power
compromise   resistance
jargon   visual aids
organizational culture

Activities

1. Interview someone who holds a position in the profession you hope to enter when you have completed your education. How does he or she assess the organizational culture of his or her workplace? What is the assessment based on? How does the organizational culture affect his or her daily life? Be sure to keep your answers confidential.

2. Ask your instructors to reveal how they were taught the culture of their academic institution. Are there stories that were told to each new faculty member to introduce him or her to the culture? Are there rituals that identify the institution's values?

3. Construct a hypothetical memorandum in which you present arguments to your boss for more resources. Be sure to consider the advice we presented in this chapter.

4. Have a friend or classmate engage in a role-playing exercise with you. Assume the roles of a subordinate and of a supervisor. Have the subordinate orally present arguments for obtaining resources or a raise and have the supervisor provide resistance to these arguments. Then reverse the roles.

Recommended Readings

Andrews, Patricia Hayes, and John E. Baird, Jr. *Communication for Business and the Professions*, 7th ed. Long Grove, IL: Waveland Press, 2004.

Bennis, Warren. *On Becoming a Leader.* Boston: Perseus Press, 2003.

Fisher, Roger, William Ury, and Bruce Patton. *Getting to Yes*, 2nd ed. New York: Penguin Press, 1992.

Frost, Peter. "Power, Politics, and Influence." In *Handbook of Organizational Communication*, ed. Fred Jablin, Linda Putnam, Karleen Roberts, and Lyman Porter. Newbury Park, CA: Sage, 1987.

Hamilton, Cheryl, and Cordell Parker. *Communicating for Results,* 6th ed. Belmont, CA: Wadsworth, 2000.

Neher, William W., and David H. Waite. *The Business and Professional Communicator.* Boston: Allyn and Bacon, 1993.

O'Hair, Dan, Gustav W. Friedrich, and Lynda Shaver. *Strategic Communication in Business and the Professions.* New York: Houghton-Mifflin, 1994.

Pfeffer, Jeffrey. *Managing with Power: Politics and Influence in Organizations.* Boston: Harvard Business School Press, 1994.

Notes

[1] Terrence Deal and Anthony Kennedy, *Corporate Cultures* (Reading, MA: Addison-Wesley, 1982), 1–19.

[2] Charles Perrow, *Complex Organizations: A Critical Essay,* 3d ed. (New York: Random House, 1986).

[3] Gerald Goldhaber, *Organizational Communication*, 6th Ed. (Dubuque, IA: W. C. Brown, 1993). See also: George Cheney, Lars Thøger Christensen, Theodore E. Zorn, Jr., and Shiv Ganesh, *Organizational Communication in an Age of Globalization: Issues, Reflections, Practices* (Prospect Heights, IL: Waveland Press, 2004), esp. chapter 10.

[4] James Thompson, *Organizations in Action* (New York: Transaction Publications, 2003).

[5] Paul Krivonos, "Distortion of Subordinate to Superior Communication in Organizational Settings," *Central States Speech Journal* 33 (1982): 345–352.

[6] John Gabarro and John Kotter, "Managing Your Boss, *Harvard Business Review* 58 (1980): 92–100.

[7] Samuel B. Bacharach and Edward J. Lawler, *Power and Politics in Organizations* (San Francisco: Jossey-Bass, 1980), esp. chapter 4.

[8] Gary L. Kreps, *Organizational Communication: Theory and Practice.* (Boston: Pearson Education, 1990).

[9] Patricia Andrews and John Baird, Jr. *Communication for Business and the Professions,* 7th ed. (Long Grove, IL: Waveland Press, 2004).

[10] Increased participation in organizational decision making also results in increased employee satisfaction and decreased levels of job stress. See Eric M. Eisenberg and H. L. Goodall, Jr., *Organizational Communication: Balancing Creativity and Constraint,* 3rd ed. (New York: Bedford-St. Martin's Press, 2001).

ARGUMENTATION IN INTERPERSONAL RELATIONSHIPS

Disagreements are common in human interactions. The better we get to know someone the easier it is for us to express our disagreements with them. Upon just meeting someone most of us are too polite to engage in open disagreement. As we get to know people better, however, we become more comfortable in interacting with them. As our comfort level increases we become less self-aware about how we may be perceived and we allow more of our "real" self to appear, often making it easier for people to express their disagreements. A popular joke tells of a young boy who comes home from elementary school one day and enthusiastically reports to his parents: "Mom and Dad, did you know that in some cultures a man and a woman don't even know each other before they get married?" The boy's mom (or dad) responds by declaring: "Son, that's true in all cultures!"

In the formative stages of relationships people work especially hard to get along with others. As we become more comfortable in relationships we become more willing to openly disagree. This may be due to the fact that most humans are explicitly taught when they are young to make attempts to get along and to be agreeable. Part of the socialization experience of children emphasizes respect for the worth of others, the need to share, the importance of being polite, and the obligation to permit others to get their way. It is in this sense that children are actively taught not to disagree.[1] They are especially taught not to disagree with those who have more power or influence than they do personally. Thus children are told not to "sass back" to parents, caregivers, teachers, or others with power and control over them. Many theorists have commented that young girls are especially encouraged to be deferential to authority; as a result, as adults, women are less aggressive in their communication styles and less comfortable in situations characterized by disagreement.[2]

Although we would argue that most humans are socialized to try to avoid arguments, there are nonetheless critics who complain that Western society in general (and U.S. society especially) is far too focused on argumentation. The popular author Deborah Tannen described this tendency as "the argument culture," and lamented that: "In the argument culture, criticism, attack, or opposition are the predominant if not the only ways of responding to people or ideas."[3] Tannen's critique goes on to protest the fact that people in the West have a tendency to approach almost any issue, problem, or public person in an adversarial way.[4] She is particularly disturbed by the ways in which metaphors of war and symbolic slaying of one's adversaries make their way into public discourse. In essence, Tannen offers a very compelling argument for dialogue instead of rhetorical argument. This of course is not new, advocates for dialogue have since Plato been making the case against arguments by making arguments. What Tannen seems most concerned about is not arguments per se, but a "toxic culture" that is characterized by media and political practices that emphasize intense public squabbles at the expense of deliberative discussions and dispassionate reasoning and analysis.[5] The entire focus of this book has been on creating arguments that do not deteriorate into squabbles and on elevating the quality of argument in a wide range of contexts from public and mass mediated interactions to those that are interpersonal.

Our view is that it is sometimes necessary and even desirable for people to find ways to express their differences of opinion through arguments. The goal of this chapter is to help you find a way to express disagreements without appearing disagreeable. We believe that disagreements should not always be viewed negatively and that often the expression of disagreement is essential to effective analysis of problems and even to the development of healthy interpersonal relationships. All relationships will at some time or other experience conflict. Learning some techniques for **conflict resolution** can actually lead to improved interpersonal relationships.

This chapter will focus on how arguments develop and shape interpersonal communication interactions. Our focus is primarily on the process of arguing and how this process can be conducted in such a way as to enhance and enrich our relationships with others. The chapter will discuss the impact of arguing and conflict mediation strategies on relationships, a conversational theory of argument, the relationship of argument to self-esteem, and the importance of empathic listening.

ARGUING AND CONFLICT MEDIATION STRATEGIES

In interpersonal relationships, as in other argumentation contexts, people engage in storytelling. They test the quality of the claims that they hear by evaluating them as stories. One dimension of becoming an effective arguer in interpersonal conversation is learning to carefully construct and to convincingly present the stories that you believe to be true. Another dimension, however, is the ability to listen carefully and appreciatively to the stories that are told by others. Those with whom you find yourself disagreeing are probably just as convinced that their stories are correct as you are that yours are correct. The world is filled with opposing stories and with people who adhere to these differing stories. Awareness of the theory of storytelling should help you to better understand how it is that people come to adhere to rival stories and why many of the people with whom you will interact during the course of your life will not agree with you.

Disagreements are typically expressed through arguments, and people argue to achieve at least three objectives in interpersonal interactions. First, people argue to make decisions. When people have different opinions about what actions they should take, what values are most important, or even about factual statements they usually attempt to resolve these differences through the use of arguments.

Second, arguments provide a means to manage interpersonal conflict and to preserve the possibility of successful and rewarding future social interactions. The alternative to resolving conflict through arguments might be the use of coercion or force. Certainly having too many arguments can damage interpersonal relationships, but so too can fistfights! Also, some people actively avoid conflicts to such an extent that they fail to express themselves through arguments. This also can undermine interpersonal relationships. One of the authors of this book remembers a conversation that he had several years ago with two very close friends, a married couple. The couple explained with great pride that they never argued and had an almost perfect relationship. Certainly, you can guess what is to follow in this story. A few months after this conversation the same couple reported that they had decided to divorce. The divorce settlement, and the negotiation of a child custody and support agreement, was characterized by a long, nasty, and drawn out courtroom battle that cost both of them tens of thousands of dollars. One might naturally speculate that this couple would have been much better off had they learned how to argue in a productive and useful fashion earlier in their relationship.

Third, arguments are often about power in human relationships. Kenneth Burke wrote that people are "goaded by the spirit of hierarchy."[6] By this Burke meant that there is a certain hierarchical imperative that guides human symbolic action. All of us seek, in some way or another, to advance our place or standing in the hierarchy. All of us seek to be affirmed. We naturally want to be perceived as knowledgeable, competent, intelligent, valuable, and experienced. We want to be seen as necessary and even as irreplaceable. We communicate these needs both implicitly and explicitly in the positions (arguments and claims) that we develop and defend. Although this hierarchical urge is certainly stronger in some persons than in others, and thus it influences individual communicative choices differently, it is always a factor in human interactions.

Our goal should be to argue well not just in the strategic sense that we are making strong, convincing, and persuasive arguments, but also so that we are conducting our arguments in a socially productive and useful manner. Truly successful arguers have learned how to manage their disagreements so that they do not destroy their friendships, prevent them from working with their colleagues, or result in marital separation and/or divorce. This chapter is intended to help you to understand the role that your **argument style** plays in shaping effective social interactions. We hope that by making you more aware of the ways in which arguments function in interpersonal interactions you will become more sensitive and self-monitoring in your own argumentation as well as more tolerant of the argument styles and strategies that are employed by others. In short, we wish to help you create and preserve positive social relationships.

In chapter 1 we discussed Wayne Brockriede's theory of arguers as lovers and the importance of avoiding coercive and/or exploitative argument styles. It is appropriate to begin this chapter by reemphasizing Brockriede's belief in the importance of creating positive and mutually reinforcing argument techniques:

> One does not pursue the art of being human by coercing others through superior power or by manipulating them by charm or deceit to gain adherence to propositions from powerless or naive individuals. Instead, one seeks a dialogic acceptance of others as persons and develops a bilateral relationship by equalizing opportunities to express attitudes and intentions by enhancing everyone's capacity for arguing.[7]

Just as some people may be more skilled than others in the strategic dimensions of arguing, likewise some people are also more skilled than others in the interpersonal and social dimensions of argumentation. Some individuals are so shy and reticent about expressing their opinions and so eager to avoid conflict that they are unable or unwilling to assert themselves or to stand up for their beliefs. These individuals may become like sheep, meekly going wherever they are led, simply because they lack the ability to argue for their positions. Often such people have good ideas but their reluctance to speak up and argue for them undermines their effectiveness and prevents them from having the influence that they should have in a group's decision making.

Other people are very forceful and dynamic, perhaps even overbearing, in stating their opinions and achieving their desired outcomes, but they leave many bruised egos, damaged self-concepts, and embittered enemies in their wake because they do not use positive argumentative techniques. Sometimes these arguers fail to influence the outcomes of decisions or to convince others to adhere to their beliefs precisely because they do not use better argumentation strategies, and as a result their arguments never get a fair hearing. Certainly some people argue badly; they engage in name-calling, coercion, misrepresentation, and deliberate distortions. Some arguers fail to listen, refuse to acknowledge the worth of alternative points of view, and refuse to acknowledge, or perhaps even recognize, when their own arguments have been bested by others. We continue to believe, however, that arguers are capable of learning techniques that will enable them to make well-reasoned and civil arguments and to resolve conflicts and reach sound decisions.[8]

Effective interpersonal arguers also come to recognize that some arguments are not worth waging either because they are not winnable or because any win would incur too high a cost. People should learn how to differ with others without destroying their friendships or work relationships. It is entirely possible to disagree in a socially acceptable fashion. It means focusing on issues and not the other person. It also means learning how to avoid using emotionally charged language and terms that may be interpreted as demeaning or designed to provoke others to anger. It requires learning how to listen carefully and creatively so that points of agreement as well as disagreement are heard. That way, in the response, those sources of agreement can be emphasized while the extent of the disagreement is minimized. Finally, it requires that arguers learn how to remain calm and open to alternative ideas and ways of thinking. Of course, achieving these argumentative skills is not easy, and maintaining such a calm and dialogic argumentative style in the heat of an actual disagreement is also very difficult, but so too is the mastery of many other important social attributes that make us better and highly respected individuals.

A CONVERSATIONAL THEORY OF ARGUMENT

Despite the fact that disagreements are inevitable in human social interactions, researchers who have studied everyday human conversations have generally found that most people seek to avoid disagreements. In fact, Sally Jackson and Scott Jacobs argued that the very nature of our language system discourages disagreements. Their research demonstrated that arguments in everyday social conversations occur when one conversant or another violates an unstated but generally understood rule or convention in language. Specifically, Jackson and Jacobs introduced the notion of *adjacency pairs* to argumentation theory. These are linkages between types of statements that define their relationship to each other.[9] An adjacency pair might be said to exist when a first statement specifies or calls for a particular type of response. For example:

First paired-part	Second paired-part
request	grant/refusal
question	answer/refusal to answer
boast	appreciation/derision

In such adjacency pairs the first paired-part (or statement) establishes a "next turn" position in the conversation because it solicits or expects a particular second paired-part response. Conversational disagreement or arguments occur when a first statement is comprehensible but a *preferred* second paired-part (or response) is withheld.[10]

If, for example, a man asks the woman seated next to him for a date, he prefers to have his request met with an acceptance. If, on the other hand, the woman responds that she has other plans, and therefore signals her refusal with a *dispreferred* (undesired) response, then he can choose to ask for another evening or mumble his regrets and slink away with as much of his pride intact as possible. On some occasions, hopefully rare, the woman may respond with an even more overtly dispreferred response. For example, she might say: "How can you even think to ask me out when you know that I have been seeing your best friend?" This response is not merely a refusal to the request, it is also an attack on the man's character, his loyalty, and his commitment to his friend. Her conversation turn has thus been directly confrontational and it almost necessitates that he respond with a defense of some sort.

To further illustrate this process of conversational turn taking consider the following example of two baseball fans having an argument:

Bob: The National League has always been tougher than the American League.

Alexandra: No way. The American League has better hitting; look at how much higher the batting averages are.

Bob: Their hitting is better because they feast on all that American League pitching. Look at how many home runs they give up in the American League.

Alexandra: Well those home runs are because American League pitchers have to face designated hitters who can hit the long ball rather than other pitchers who can't even make contact with it.

Bob: Still, the National League has historically done better in the All-Star Game.

Alexandra: You're nuts! They got blown out this year, and they lost last year too.

Bob: Oh, yeah. I guess lately the American League is getting more respectable.

Alexandra: Wow, I can't believe you admitted even that much.

The above argument is typical of the kind of bantering that friends might engage in. Most conversations like this one are good-natured and even enjoyable to the participants. The participants in the conversation are expressing their disagreement as evidenced by the fact that they responded at several turns with dispreferred responses rather than with preferred responses. In the end, however, Bob acknowledges the superiority of Alexandra's arguments and Alexandra acknowledges a sense of satisfaction with her win and also with her continued good relationship with Bob. The conversation could, of course, have proceeded differently:

Alexandra: You're nuts! They got blown out this year, and they lost last year too.

Bob: Well that doesn't change my mind. I still think the National League is better.

Alexandra: Well, you are entitled to your opinion. No one expects a San Francisco Giants' fan to be rational.

Bob: Well, Giants' fans are every bit as rational as New York Yankees' fans.

In this example Bob refuses to acknowledge that Alexandra's arguments are powerful and declares that despite the facts and the quality of the opposing arguments he will not change his mind. This could, of course, lead to an even more negative interaction. Instead, however, Alexandra decides that she is too fond of Bob to permit this refusal to stand in the way of their friendship. Rather than escalating the disagreement she avoids continued conflict, makes an attempt at a joke, and defuses the situation. The conversation might, of course, have taken still a different turn:

Bob: Well that doesn't change my mind. I still think the National League is better.

Alexandra: Well, surprise, surprise, you're too bullheaded to listen to reason.

Bob: Oh sure, and you are always the reasonable one aren't you? You think you know everything.

Alexandra: Well at least I read the paper every now and then, and as a result I know who wins and loses All-Star Games.

Bob: Well I am glad that you at least read the sports pages. I am sure the news features and editorial pages are too difficult for you to comprehend.

Alexandra: You can really be a jerk.

Bob: And you are an idiot.

This last conversation is, as you can see, far less pleasant than the other two that preceded it. Neither speaker is willing to acknowledge the worth of the other's arguments. Furthermore, neither speaker views maintaining the friendship as important enough, in the heat of the disagreement, to be willing to modify his or her argument strategy. Consequently, a friendly and pleasant social interaction is permitted to become a hostile and most unpleasant interaction. In this case, the interaction degenerates into very juvenile personal attacks and name-calling, indeed the kind of conversation turn taking that children are actively taught to avoid by parents and teachers. Such interactions, even among adults, are of course, far too common, and may especially occur when the conversational partners are tired, insecure, harboring much anger or resentment toward others, depressed, or have consumed enough alcohol to diminish their reasonableness and judgment.

Jacobs and Jackson see conversational argument theory as a method for organizing our conversational activity and managing our social interactions.[11] William Benoit and Pamela Benoit, in their research on conversational arguments, suggest that arguments will be enacted when people realize that two conversation pairs are in opposition to each other and when they see the potential argument as worth the investment of time, energy, and risk. They also say arguments are terminated when someone capitulates, when consensus or compromise is reached, or when escapes are enacted (someone departs, someone chooses to remain silent, or someone shifts the topic).[12]

Arguments occur or do not occur because individual advocates decide whether or not to pursue their differences. Some people are very reluctant to engage in arguments. Even when they sense that they disagree with someone they may decide that an argument is not worth the investment or the risk. This may be because they dislike conflict; because they lack confidence in their own position, knowledge, or argumentative skills; or perhaps because they do not wish to jeopardize their relationship with the other person. For example, it may be very wise to choose not to argue with a person who holds power over you (for example with your boss or your teacher). It may also be that people decide that pursuing an argument will be like tilting at windmills, because it is unlikely that the other party in the disagreement will be open to changing his or her mind, even in the face of compelling reasons to reconsider his or her position.

Other people are, of course, very argumentative and are often not just willing but actually eager to engage in arguments and to pursue them with great intensity, even if doing so may prove futile, counterproductive, and perhaps politically unwise. Such people may lack the effective social judgment that is part of the self-monitoring process necessary for the maintenance of positive and rewarding social interactions.

Robert Trapp, in his discussion of arguments in interpersonal relationships observed:

> Argument episodes begin when one or both participants perceive some kind of incompatibility. Sources of incompatibility range from attitudes to values, to behaviors. . . . Once arguers perceive an incompatibility of significant magnitude, they must decide whether or not to confront their partners. As long as the cost of confrontation appears to outweigh the costs of continued incompatibility, arguing is avoided. . . . Once arguers decide to confront each other, they need to develop the content of the arguments they will make and the strategies they will use. They must invent and edit the arguments and strategies they think will be most effective and appropriate in the situation. Since people can develop their arguments and strategies without conscious reflection, this process is frequently conscious or mindless.[13]

Effective social arguers learn that the argumentative requirements and norms differ from situation to situation. One might employ very different argumentative strategies in an argument with one's lover than with a coworker or with one's boss. Regardless of the context for the argument, however, arguers need to avoid expressing hostility and/or demeaning others in their interactions. Again, we would remind you, that when author Deborah Tannen, whose work we discussed earlier, focused her attention on the "argument culture" she was emphasizing examples of such negative and hostile interpersonal interactions and taking them as somehow typical for almost all argumentative exchanges.[14]

Dominic Infante has introduced the notion of *verbal aggression* to describe people who rely on character attacks, competence attacks, personal appearance attacks, insults, brutal teasing, ridicule, profanity, and threats in their argumentative interactions.[15] Infante believes that people rely on such aggressive and counterproductive argument techniques because of their psychopathology, their disdain for other people who hold different opinions, their social learning—the argument style practiced in their families when they were growing up—and because they lack the skills for effective argumentation.[16]

While awareness of argumentation techniques and strategies will not change people's personalities, cause them to be more understanding and loving, or make up for communication style characteristics shaped by their family upbringing, we can hope to achieve some improvement in interpersonal argumentation by teaching people better argumentation strategies and techniques. That is the goal of this text.

STRATEGIC DIMENSIONS OF CONVERSATIONAL ARGUMENT

One of the primary ways an arguer can avoid having disagreements disintegrate into episodes of verbal aggression is to focus on the issues and not the personalities or other attributes of their opponents. Arguers should approach an argument in a conversation strategically, just as they should an argument conducted in a more formal or structured setting.

First, arguers should consider the likelihood that an argumentative resolution can be achieved. Is this an argument that you can win? Does a victory require that you change the other person's mind? What might be the repercussions if the conversation disintegrates into an exchange of arguments? How might having an argumentative disagreement affect your relationship with this person? Is this issue sufficiently important that it is worth arguing over? Based on your past experiences, how do you expect this person to respond to an expression of disagreement? Arguers should consider the fact that unlike in formal debate situations or in a courtroom setting, where winning means everything, in interpersonal arguments one can "win" and still lose. What good is securing a victory in an argument if the person you have argued with sees you as a bully, threat, or enemy? If someone begins to distrust you or dislike you as a result of an argument, the outcome of the interaction might not be worth the cost.

Effective interpersonal arguers should find ways to reach compromise and accommodation with their opponents and not merely seek to crush them with a total victory. Are there ways in which the rival stories that are competing with each other for acceptance can be made compatible, or at least is there room for the stories to coexist with each other? Trying to adopt a win-win philosophy rather than an "I win and you lose" philosophy may help arguers to improve the quality of the decisions they reach. A decision reached through consensus is far more likely to be embraced, accepted, enacted, and even defended from attack by others than is one that people feel has been forced upon them. Obviously it is not always possible to find agreement, to reach compromise, or to reach consensus. Some disputes (such as a dispute between an abortion rights advocate and a pro-life advocate) are so intractable that people are not willing to surrender any ground and there is almost no space in which rival stories are permitted to coexist. Nonetheless, in many circumstances the pursuit of inclusive stories and compromises preserves positive social relationships and fosters a respect for the worth of alternative perspectives.

Second, once an arguer declares an argument to be worth waging she or he should consider the source of the disagreement that has led to the conflict. Is the disagreement one that centers on differences in your and your adversary's fundamental values? If so, this may limit the chances of your reaching a resolution. It will also influence your strategies in shaping your claim and in responding to the claims advanced by the other person. Is the difference one of experience? If so, how can you help others to understand your experiences and how they influenced your opinions, especially if their experiences have been different? Likewise, how can you become sensitive to others' experiences? Is there appropriate evidence that you can muster to support your arguments? What evidence might be seen as credible and compelling? What stories do you share and how can these shared stories be used as a resource? If you can figure out the essential causes for the differences being expressed, you might be in a better position to find a way to accommodate your story so that it is no longer incompatible with your opponent's story.

Third, successful arguers must learn how to control their tempers. When we are angry, or when we have decided that we do not especially care for someone, it is difficult for us to separate these feelings from our consideration of the issues in dispute. This is not to say that being angry is not sometimes an understandable, legitimate, or even a strategically useful device; it can be. But anger should be controlled and managed. If you are angry all the time, you will get little if any strategic benefit from that anger for it no longer serves to punctuate extremely important situations where anger is a warranted response. On the other hand, if you rarely exhibit anger, getting angry will have a dramatic impact on a conversation through a carefully controlled and highly unusual display of temper. Such a display of anger becomes noteworthy precisely because it is likely understood as being out of character.

ARGUMENTATION AND SELF-ESTEEM

How people conduct themselves in interpersonal arguments says a great deal about how they conceive of themselves and of others. As we have already mentioned, our argument style may have been shaped by our formative interactions with our parents. For example, a child who grows up in a family in which conflict is expressed through very hostile and aggressive interactions, such as name-calling and demeaning personal attacks, might be more likely to continue behaving in this way as an adult. Lacking role models to demonstrate more positive argumentative behaviors, he or she mirrors the negative models that were provided at home.

People who have been demeaned or devalued by others' negative and verbally aggressive argument techniques may already suffer from diminished *self-esteem*. They may have been bruised and battered for so long that they have come to believe all of the disparaging things that have been said about them, and they may thus lack confidence in their own self-worth. It is in such repetitive interactions—abuse decreases self-esteem—that problems like the battered spouse syndrome can develop.[17]

As Trapp has observed: "The way people argue carries important messages about their self-concepts, how they see each other, and how they see their relationship. Every argument episode is about some content, but in its shadow is a larger relational issue."[18] Some of these relational issues are revealed in how the argument patterns of our loving relationships may change over time. All of us probably know couples, and some of you might have been in a relationship yourself, where there was a careful monitoring of communication behavior during the early formative stages of the relationship. Both people eagerly sought to please each other. They carefully monitored what they said and they attempted not to anger, provoke, or hurt the feelings of their partner. Yet as the relationship progressed and matured, perhaps not until after they were engaged or even married, their interest or willingness to closely monitor and limit their communications diminished. Now they are far more willing to say what they really think, even at the risk of hurting their partner's feelings. To an extent this new honesty might be a desirable characteristic. They feel more comfortable with the relationship and as a result are more willing to be themselves. Yet it may also, if taken to an extreme, signal a serious deterioration of the loving relationship. People find that they monitor their comments less and say what they really feel at the moment because they are becoming disinterested in the preservation of the relationship and thus much less committed to making it work or even last.

In relationships such as the one which we have just described we might see a very rapid deterioration. Every negative argumentative interaction may signal a willingness to get even more nasty and aggressive in the next interaction. If relationships continue to progress in this fashion people will eventually discover that they have fallen out of love and no longer have the will or the energy to try to patch things up.

Arguers need to learn to express their feelings in such a way as to achieve their objectives in an argument. Do they want to change someone's opinion or behavior? Do they want to punish someone and hurt their feelings? Do they want to sabotage or help terminate a relationship? Often arguers will maintain that they only wish to change someone's opinion when in a subconscious way they may in fact be seeking to undermine their relationship with someone. Arguers also need to consider how their relationship partners are hearing and reacting to their arguments. We know that communication is a process and that even though we may intend to say one thing our listeners may understand us to be saying something else. Many dysfunctional relationships develop because people become careless in framing their arguments and as a result they are misunderstood.

THE IMPORTANCE OF EMPATHIC LISTENING

Effective interpersonal arguers also need to develop their listening skills and especially their capacity for *empathic listening*. It is often difficult in an argumentative situation—when our aggressive instincts are at work, when our energy level is high, and when our creative strategic senses are agitated—for us to listen at all, let alone to engage in empathic listening. Yet the most effective interpersonal arguers are those who have precisely this capability. Instead of listening to others with a focus on refuting their ideas, empathic listeners seek to genuinely understand where their fellow arguers are coming from—what they are telling in their stories and in the arguments that they are presenting. Empathic listeners are tolerant and patient; they allow others to develop their positions; and they give these positions careful consideration before forming their response to them.

Empathic listeners are more likely to find ways to compromise because they are less likely to speak without thinking and thus to say things that they later come to regret. Empathic listeners allow themselves more time to carefully and strategically weigh their responses to arguments because they carefully consider the arguments made by others in the context of their search for a larger and more complete and compelling narrative. Nevertheless, this type of listening can be hard work, especially when we are distracted. There are also listening barriers such as laziness, closed-mindedness, insincerity, and boredom.[19] Listeners should expend the energy to be attentive and to overcome their distractions and also learn how to control their own emotions.

SUMMARY

There are no secrets to becoming an effective interpersonal arguer. The most important principles have to do with understanding the larger narratives that characterize an individual's sense of self, key values, and his or her style of argumentation. Also important are the interpersonal skills of being polite, respectful of others, and tolerant of alternative perspectives and worldviews. For most of us this means working on developing good communication habits in all of our interactions. Some conversations will certainly go better than others, but by working to improve our interpersonal skills we can hopefully resolve our own argumentative deficiencies.

Our ability to argue effectively in interpersonal interactions is a measure of our ability to analyze the circumstances, avoid destructive interactions, and determine what techniques will lead to productive exchanges with others. The husband who learns how to communicate love and respect for his wife while also expressing his disagreements with her will make a better marriage partner. The boss who knows how to argue with a subordinate while demonstrating respect for his or her opinions will make for a better employer. The son who learns how to argue with his parents without communicating disrespect for them will thus continue to nurture an important caring relationship. Our ability to reason—to use symbols to create and to evaluate the choices that are available to us—is our most important human capacity. It is a capacity that we should always be trying to develop and enhance as we try to create the good, harmonious, satisfying, and rewarding lives that we all seek.

Key Terms

adjacency pairs   empathic listening
argument style   self-esteem
conflict resolution   verbal aggression

Activities

1. An old but still effective means for improving your listening skills in interpersonal argument situations is to practice in the following manner: Have a friend or a classmate enter a conversation with you on a subject where there is disagreement. After your friend speaks, you are not permitted to respond with your own ideas until after you have paraphrased what your friend said. This paraphrase must be acceptable to your friend. Only then may you proceed with your comment. Similarly, before your friend may respond he or she must paraphrase what you have said to your satisfaction. While this process is arduous and cumbersome it is effective at forcing us to listen empathically to each other.

2. A similar exercise calls on communicators to label utterances and identify the preferred response before they are permitted to continue the conversation. Thus, if one person asks a question, the respondent would first identify the utterance as a question and then indicate the preferred paired-part that is an answer. The respondent could then answer as he or she wished. There is no requirement that the respondent provide the preferred paired-part because the purpose of the exercise is merely to reinforce the informal preferences that govern interpersonal argumentation and not to actually control the conversation.

3. Form three student interpersonal argumentation triads. Two students participate in an interpersonal argument of their choice. The third student acts as an evaluator of the argumentative process. If the third student observes argument behaviors that violate the norms of effective interpersonal argumentation—for example, if an individual exhibits verbal aggressiveness—the student evaluator should interrupt the conversation and identify the norm that has been violated. The two student discussants cannot challenge the student evaluator, but must repair the conversation and proceed. After a predetermined amount of time, the role of the student evaluator should be rotated. The process should continue until all three students have had the chance to participate as an evaluator. The concluding segment of the exercise should involve all three students in a discussion of the norms that were violated. How did this affect the conduct of the argument and the relationships among the participants?

4. Have a classmate or a friend engage in an argumentative interaction with you. Select a topic on which the two of you disagree. After about five minutes of argumentation switch sides. In other words, if you were pro, you must now be con. Try your best to present as reasonable a set of arguments for each side as possible. After another five minutes you should conclude your discussion by trying to reach a mutually agreed upon resolution to the controversy. Does one side possess probable truth? Or does the other? Or is truth found somewhere in between the opposing positions? Hopefully this exercise will help you to become less dogmatic in your views.

Recommended Readings

Benoit, Pamela J. "Orientation to Face in Everyday Argument." In *Argumentation: Perspectives and Approaches*, ed. Frans H. van Eemeren, Rob Grootendorst, J. Anthony Blair, and Charles Arthur Willard, 144–152. Dordrecht, Holland: Foris, 1987.

Benoit, Pamela J., and William L. Benoit. "To Argue or Not to Argue." In *Perspectives on Argumentation: Essays in Honor of Wayne Brockriede*, ed. Robert Trapp and Janice Schuetz, 55–72. Prospect Heights, IL: Waveland Press, 1990.

Canary, Daniel J. "Marital Arguments." In *Perspectives on Argumentation: Essays in Honor of Wayne Brockriede,* ed. Robert Trapp and Janice Schuetz, 73–85. Prospect Heights, IL: Waveland Press, 1990.

Dallinger, Judith, and Mark Callister. "Taking Conflict Personally, Solidarity and Relational Satisfaction: Interrelationships within Arguments." In *Argument in a Time of Change: Definitions, Frameworks, and Critiques*, ed. James F. Klumpp, 90–96. Annandale, VA: National Communication Association, 1998.

Hample, Dale, Pamela J. Benoit, Josh Houston, Gloria Purify, Vanessa Van Hyfte, and Cy Wardwell. "Naive Theories of Argument: Avoiding Interpersonal Arguments or Cutting them Short." *Argumentation and Advocacy* 35 (1999): 130–140.

Jacobs, Scott, and Sally Jackson. "Conversational Argument: A Discourse Analytic Approach." In *Advances in Argumentation Theory and Research*, ed. J. Robert Cox and Charles Arthur Willard, 205–237. Carbondale: Southern Illinois University Press, 1982.

Nussbaum, E. Michael, and Lisa D. Bendixen. "Approaching and Avoiding Arguments: The Role of Epistemological Beliefs, Need for Cognition, and Extraverted Personality Traits." *Contemporary Educational Psychology* 28 (2003): 573–596.

van Eemeren, F. H., Rob Grootendorst, Sally Jackson, and Scott Jacobs. *Reconstructing Argumentative Discourse*. Tuscaloosa: University of Alabama Press, 1993.

van Eemeren, Frans H., and Peter Houtlosser. "The Development of the Pragma-Dialectical Approach to Argumentation." *Argumentation* 17 (2003): 387–407.

Weger, Harry Jr. "Violating Pragma-Dialectical Rules in Arguments between Intimates." In *Advances in Pragma-Dialects*, ed. Frans H von Eemeren. Amsterdam: SICSAT, 2002.

Weger, Harry Jr., and Mark Aakhus. "Arguing in Internet Chat Rooms: Argumentative Adaptations to Chat Room Design and Some Consequences for Public Deliberation at a Distance." *Argumentation and Advocacy* 40 (2003): 23–38.

Notes

1. Barbara J. O'Keefe and Pamela J. Benoit, "Children's Arguments," in *Advances in Argumentation Theory and Research,* ed. J. Robert Cox and Charles Arthur Willard, 154–183 (Carbondale: Southern Illinois University Press, 1982).

2. Deborah Tannen, *You Just Don't Understand: Women and Men in Conversation* (New York: HarperCollins, 1990).

3. Deborah Tannen, *The Argument Culture: Stopping America's War of Words* (New York: Ballantine Books, 1999), 7.

4. Ibid., 8.

5. For a more complete critical response to Tannen's book see: James F. Klumpp, Patricia Riley, and Thomas A. Hollihan, "Beyond Dialogue: Linking the Public and Political Spheres," in *Argument at Century's End: Reflecting on the Past and Envisioning the Future*, ed. Thomas A. Hollihan, 361–368 (Annandale, VA: National Communication Association, 2000).

6. Kenneth Burke, *Language as Symbolic Action* (Berkeley: University of California Press, 1966), 15.

[7] Wayne Brockriede, cited in *Perspectives on Argumentation: Essays in Honor of Wayne Brockriede*, ed. Robert Trapp and Janice Schuetz, 41 (Prospect Heights, IL: Waveland Press, 1990).

[8] This view of argumentation is more fully developed in Klumpp, Riley, and Hollihan.

[9] Sally Jackson and Scott Jacobs, "Structure of Conversational Argument: Pragmatic Bases for the Enthymeme," *Quarterly Journal of Speech* 66 (1980): 251–265.

[10] Ibid., 253.

[11] Ibid., 255.

[12] William L. Benoit and Pamela J. Benoit, "Everyday Argument Practices of Naïve Social Actors," in *Argument and Critical Practices*, ed. Joseph W. Wenzel, 465–474 (Annandale, VA: Speech Communication Association, 1987).

[13] Robert Trapp, "Arguments in Interpersonal Relations," in *Perspectives on Argumentation: Essays in Honor of Wayne Brockriede*, ed. Robert Trapp and Janice Schuetz, 46–47 (Prospect Heights, IL: Waveland Press, 1990).

[14] Tannen, *The Argument Culture*, especially 8–9.

[15] Dominic Infante, *Arguing Constructively* (Prospect Heights, IL: Waveland Press, 1988), 24–27.

[16] Ibid., 21.

[17] For an excellent discussion of the development of self-concept see Dan O'Hair, Gustav W. Friedrich, John M. Weimann, and Mary O. Weimann, *Competent Communication* (New York: St. Martin's Press, 1995), 96–139. Also: Ronald B. Levy, "Relationships within the Self," in *Communication Concepts and Processes*, ed. Joseph DeVito, 227–237 (Englewood Cliffs, NJ: Prentice-Hall, 1976).

[18] Trapp, 54.

[19] For an excellent discussion on listening see: O'Hair et al., 228–274.

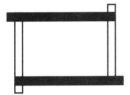

EPILOGUE

As you have no doubt already recognized, this book about argumentation is itself an argument for a particular view of the argumentation process. Through reading this book you have learned something about us—the authors, our biases, our ideology, and our values, as well as about the subject matter that we have discussed.

First, you have discovered that unlike many people, we are not averse to arguing. In fact, we are a couple of old debaters who enjoy the stimulation and challenge, indeed the sport, of a good argument. We believe that people can disagree yet nonetheless continue to like and respect each other and also to enjoy each other's company. Consequently, we do not believe that arguers should approach their interactions with a take-no-prisoners and win-at-all-costs attitude. Such an attitude will undermine the quality of the argumentative outcomes and needlessly destroy your relationships with others. Instead of trying to vanquish opponents you should try to achieve shared understanding.

Second, we are convinced that people are capable of making and evaluating well-reasoned arguments. We are committed to the narrative or storytelling view of argumentation, and we believe that people have the ability to judge the quality of stories. We have confidence in the intellectual abilities and the goodwill of our fellow human decision makers. We see the creation and evaluation of arguments as an essential dimension of human social activity. People argue to reach decisions, to resolve problems, to influence others, and to improve the quality of their lives. These are worthwhile goals and they often cannot be achieved except through the use of arguments.

Third, we believe that argumentation training can improve the quality of the public dialogue. While all of us are capable of evaluating narrative arguments and participating in important conversations about complex public issues, many of us lack the confidence in our argumentative abilities and in our own opinions. We hope that exposure to the principles discussed in this book will enhance your confidence, empower you, and help you to find your voice so that you can more fully participate in public life. We want you to speak out about those issues that most concern you, for this is the best means to assure that we have a government that is genuinely responsive to the needs and the interests of its citizenry.

Fourth, although it is rewarding to succeed when we argue—all of us are gratified by victory—it is important that we define our successes with a long-term view. A short-term view focuses our attention on our immediate interests and gratifications. A long-term view reveals that it is sometimes not in our interest to pursue an argument; the personal and interpersonal costs may be too high. A long-term view helps us to understand that we are sometimes better off to lose an argument rather than to win one, and that we are often judged more by the way in which we conduct ourselves in an argument than by our effectiveness in pleading our case.

In closing, we would remind you of Aristotle's declaration in Book I of the *Rhetoric:* "It is not true, as some writers assume in their treatises on rhetoric, that the personal goodness revealed by the speaker contributes nothing to the power of his [sic] persuasion; on the contrary, his character may almost be called the most effective means of persuasion he possesses."[1] As an advocate, your most precious asset is your reputation and your good name. Consequently, there can be no greater imperative for you to consider in forming your arguments than their ethical character.

Best wishes for your future arguments!

Note

[1] *Rhetoric and Poetics of, Aristotle,* trans. W. Rhys Roberts, (New York: The Modern Library, 1954), 25.

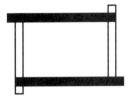

APPENDIX A
TWO POLITICAL SPEECHES

John Kerry
**Acceptance Speech for the Democratic Presidential Nomination,
Boston, July 29, 2004**

We are proud of what America is and what it can become.

My fellow Americans: we are here tonight united in one simple purpose: to make America stronger at home and respected in the world.

A great American novelist wrote that you can't go home again. He could not have imagined this evening. Tonight, I am home. Home where my public life began and those who made it possible live. Home where our nation's history was written in blood, idealism, and hope. Home where my parents showed me the values of family, faith, and country.

Thank you, all of you, for a welcome home I will never forget.

I wish my parents could share this moment. They went to their rest in the last few years, but their example, their inspiration, their gift of open eyes, open mind, and endless world are bigger and more lasting than any words.

I was born in Colorado, in Fitzsimmons Army Hospital, when my dad was a pilot in World War II. Now, I'm not one to read into things, but guess which wing of the hospital the maternity ward was in? I'm not making this up. I was born in the West Wing!

My mother was the rock of our family as so many mothers are. She stayed up late to help me do my homework. She sat by my bed when I was sick, and she answered the questions of a child who, like all children, found the world full of wonders and mysteries.

She was my den mother when I was a Cub Scout and she was so proud of her fifty year pin as a Girl Scout leader. She gave me her passion for the environment. She taught me to see trees as the cathedrals of nature. And by the power of her example, she showed me that we can and must finish the march toward full equality for all women in our country.

My dad did the things that a boy remembers. He gave me my first model airplane, my first baseball mitt, and my first bicycle. He also taught me that we are here for something bigger than ourselves; he lived out the responsibilities and sacrifices of the greatest generation to whom we owe so much.

When I was a young man, he was in the State Department, stationed in Berlin when it and the world were divided between democracy and communism. I have unforgettable memories of being a kid mesmerized by the British, French, and American troops, each of them guarding their own part of the city, and Russians standing guard on the stark line separating East from West. On one occasion, I rode my bike into Soviet East Berlin. And when I proudly told my dad, he promptly grounded me.

But what I learned has stayed with me for a lifetime. I saw how different life was on different sides of the same city. I saw the fear in the eyes of people who were not free. I saw the gratitude of people toward the United States for all that we had done. I felt goose bumps as I got off a military train and heard the Army band strike up "Stars and Stripes Forever." I learned what it meant to be America at our best. I learned the pride of our freedom. And I am determined now to restore that pride to all who look to America.

Mine were greatest generation parents. And as I thank them, we all join together to thank that whole generation for making America strong, for winning World War II, winning the Cold War, and for the great gift of service which brought America fifty years of peace and prosperity.

My parents inspired me to serve, and when I was a junior in high school, John Kennedy called my generation to service. It was the beginning of a great journey—a time to march for civil rights, for voting rights, for the environment, for women, and for peace. We believed we could change the world. And you know what? We did.

But we're not finished. The journey isn't complete. The march isn't over. The promise isn't perfected. Tonight, we're setting out again. And together, we're going to write the next great chapter of America's story.

We have it in our power to change the world again. But only if we're true to our ideals—and that starts by telling the truth to the American people. That is my first pledge to you tonight. As President, I will restore trust and credibility to the White House.

I ask you to judge me by my record: As a young prosecutor, I fought for victim's rights and made prosecuting violence against women a priority. When I came to the Senate, I broke with many in my own party to vote for a balanced budget, because I thought it was the right thing to do. I fought to put a 100,000 cops on the street.

And then I reached across the aisle to work with John McCain, to find the truth about our POW's and missing in action, and to finally make peace with Vietnam.

I will be a commander in chief who will never mislead us into war. I will have a Vice President who will not conduct secret meetings with polluters to rewrite our environmental laws. I will have a Secretary of Defense who will listen to the best advice of our military leaders. And I will appoint an Attorney General who actually upholds the Constitution of the United States.

My fellow Americans, this is the most important election of our lifetime. The stakes are high. We are a nation at war—a global war on terror against an enemy unlike any we have ever known before. And here at home, wages are falling, health care costs are rising, and our great middle class is shrinking. People are working weekends; they're working two jobs, three jobs, and they're still not getting ahead.

We're told that outsourcing jobs is good for America. We're told that new jobs that pay $9,000 less than the jobs that have been lost is the best we can do. They say this is the best economy we've ever had. And they say that anyone who thinks otherwise is a pessimist. Well, here is our answer: There is nothing more pessimistic than saying America can't do better.

We can do better and we will. We're the optimists. For us, this is a country of the future. We're the can do people. And let's not forget what we did in the 1990s. We balanced the budget. We paid down the debt. We created 23 million new jobs. We lifted millions out of poverty and we lifted the standard of living for the middle class. We just need to believe in ourselves—and we can do it again.

So tonight, in the city where America's freedom began, only a few blocks from where the sons and daughters of liberty gave birth to our nation—here tonight, on behalf of a new birth of freedom—on behalf of the middle class who deserve a champion, and those struggling to join it who deserve a fair shot—for the brave men and women in uniform who risk their lives every day and the families who pray for their return—for all those who believe our best days are ahead of us—for all of you—with great faith in the American people, I accept your nomination for President of the United States.

I am proud that at my side will be a running mate whose life is the story of the American dream and who's worked every day to make that dream real for all Americans—Senator John Edwards of North Carolina. And his wonderful wife Elizabeth and their family. This son of a mill worker is ready to lead—and next January, Americans will be proud to have a fighter for the middle class to succeed Dick Cheney as Vice President of the United States.

And what can I say about Teresa? She has the strongest moral compass of anyone I know. She's down to earth, nurturing, courageous, wise and smart. She speaks her mind and she speaks the truth, and I love her for that, too. And that's why America will embrace her as the next First Lady of the United States.

For Teresa and me, no matter what the future holds or the past has given us, nothing will ever mean as much as our children. We love them not just for who they are and what they've become, but for being themselves, making us laugh, holding our feet to the fire, and never letting me get away with anything. Thank you, Andre, Alex, Chris, Vanessa, and John.

And in this journey, I am accompanied by an extraordinary band of brothers led by that American hero, a patriot named Max Cleland. Our band of brothers doesn't march together because of who we are as veterans, but because of what we learned as soldiers. We fought for this nation because we loved it and we came back with the deep belief that every day is extra. We may be a little older now, we may be a little grayer, but we still know how to fight for our country.

And standing with us in that fight are those who shared with me the long season of the primary campaign: Carol Moseley Braun, General Wesley Clark, Howard Dean, Dick Gephardt, Bob Graham, Dennis Kucinich, Joe Lieberman and Al Sharpton.

To all of you, I say thank you for teaching me and testing me—but mostly, we say thank you for standing up for our country and giving us the unity to move America forward.

My fellow Americans, the world tonight is very different from the world of four years ago. But I believe the American people are more than equal to the challenge.

Remember the hours after September 11th, when we came together as one to answer the attack against our homeland. We drew strength when our firefighters ran up the stairs and risked their lives, so that others might live. When rescuers rushed into smoke and fire at the Pentagon. When the men and women of Flight 93 sacrificed themselves to save our nation's Capitol. When flags were hanging from front porches all across America, and strangers became friends. It was the worst day we have ever seen, but it brought out the best in all of us.

I am proud that after September 11th all our people rallied to President Bush's call for unity to meet the danger. There were no Democrats. There were no Republicans. There were only Americans. How we wish it had stayed that way.

Now I know there are those who criticize me for seeing complexities—and I do—because some issues just aren't all that simple. Saying there are weapons of mass destruction in Iraq doesn't make it so. Saying we can fight a war on the cheap doesn't make it so. And proclaiming mission accomplished certainly doesn't make it so.

As President, I will ask hard questions and demand hard evidence. I will immediately reform the intelligence system—so policy is guided by facts, and facts are never distorted by politics. And as President, I will bring back this nation's time-honored tradition: the United States of America never goes to war because we want to, we only go to war because we have to.

I know what kids go through when they are carrying an M-16 in a dangerous place and they can't tell friend from foe. I know what they go through when they're out on patrol at night and they don't know what's coming around the next bend. I know what it's like to write letters home telling your family that everything's all right when you're not sure that's true.

As President, I will wage this war with the lessons I learned in war. Before you go to battle, you have to be able to look a parent in the eye and truthfully say: "I tried everything possible to avoid sending your son or daughter into harm's way. But we had no choice. We had to protect the American people, fundamental American values from a threat that was real and imminent." So lesson one, this is the only justification for going to war.

And on my first day in office, I will send a message to every man and woman in our armed forces: You will never be asked to fight a war without a plan to win the peace.

I know what we have to do in Iraq. We need a President who has the credibility to bring our allies to our side and share the burden, reduce the cost to American taxpayers, and reduce the risk to American soldiers. That's the right way to get the job done and bring our troops home.

Here is the reality: that won't happen until we have a president who restores America's respect and leadership—so we don't have to go it alone in the world.

And we need to rebuild our alliances, so we can get the terrorists before they get us.

I defended this country as a young man and I will defend it as President. Let there be no mistake: I will never hesitate to use force when it is required. Any attack will be met with a swift and certain response. I will never give any nation or international institution a veto over our national security. And I will build a stronger American military.

We will add 40,000 active duty troops—not in Iraq, but to strengthen American forces that are now overstretched, overextended, and under pressure. We will double our special forces to conduct anti-terrorist operations. We will provide our troops with the newest weapons and technology to save their lives—and win the battle. And we will end the backdoor draft of National Guard and reservists.

To all who serve in our armed forces today, I say, help is on the way.

As President, I will fight a smarter, more effective war on terror. We will deploy every tool in our arsenal: our economic as well as our military might; our principles as well as our firepower.

In these dangerous days there is a right way and a wrong way to be strong. Strength is more than tough words. After decades of experience in national security, I know the reach of our power and I know the power of our ideals.

We need to make America once again a beacon in the world. We need to be looked up to and not just feared.

We need to lead a global effort against nuclear proliferation—to keep the most dangerous weapons in the world out of the most dangerous hands in the world.

We need a strong military and we need to lead strong alliances. And then, with confidence and determination, we will be able to tell the terrorists: You will lose and we will win. The future doesn't belong to fear; it belongs to freedom.

And the front lines of this battle are not just far away—they're right here on our shores, at our airports, and potentially in any town or city. Today, our national security begins with homeland security. The 9-11 Commission has given us a path to follow, endorsed by Democrats, Republicans, and the 9-11 families. As President, I will not evade or equivocate; I will immediately implement the recommendations of that commission. We shouldn't be letting ninety-five percent of container ships come into our ports without ever being physically inspected. We shouldn't be leaving our nuclear and chemical plants without enough protection. And we shouldn't be opening firehouses in Baghdad and closing them down in the United States of America.

And tonight, we have an important message for those who question the patriotism of Americans who offer a better direction for our country. Before wrapping themselves in the flag and shutting their eyes and ears to the truth, they should remember what America is really all about. They should remember the great idea of freedom for which so many have given their lives. Our purpose now is to reclaim democracy itself. We are here to affirm that when Americans stand up and speak their minds and say America can do better, that is not a challenge to patriotism; it is the heart and soul of patriotism.

You see that flag up there. We call her Old Glory. The stars and stripes forever. I fought under that flag, as did so many of you here and all across our country. That flag flew from the gun turret right behind my head. It was shot through and through and tattered, but it never ceased to wave in the wind. It draped the caskets of men I served with and friends I grew up with. For us, that flag is the most powerful symbol of who we are and what we believe in. Our strength. Our diversity. Our love of country. All that makes America both great and good.

That flag doesn't belong to any president. It doesn't belong to any ideology and it doesn't belong to any political party. It belongs to all the American people.

My fellow citizens, elections are about choices. And choices are about values. In the end, it's not just policies and programs that matter; the president who sits at that desk must be guided by principle.

For four years, we've heard a lot of talk about values. But values spoken without actions taken are just slogans. Values are not just words. They're what we live by. They're about the causes we champion and the people we fight for. And it is time for those who talk about family values to start valuing families.

You don't value families by kicking kids out of after school programs and taking cops off our streets, so that Enron can get another tax break.

We believe in the family value of caring for our children and protecting the neighborhoods where they walk and play.

And that is the choice in this election.

You don't value families by denying real prescription drug coverage to seniors, so big drug companies can get another windfall.

We believe in the family value expressed in one of the oldest Commandments: "Honor thy father and thy mother." As President, I will not privatize Social Security. I will not cut benefits. And together, we will make sure that senior citizens never have to cut their pills in half because they can't afford life-saving medicine.

And that is the choice in this election.

You don't value families if you force them to take up a collection to buy body armor for a son or daughter in the service, if you deny veterans health care, or if you tell middle class families to wait for a tax cut, so that the wealthiest among us can get even more.

We believe in the value of doing what's right for everyone in the American family.

And that is the choice in this election.

We believe that what matters most is not narrow appeals masquerading as values, but the shared values that show the true face of America. Not narrow appeals that divide us, but shared values that unite us. Family and faith. Hard work and responsibility. Opportunity for all—so that every child, every parent, every worker has an equal shot at living up to their God-given potential.

What does it mean in America today when Dave McCune, a steel worker I met in Canton, Ohio, saw his job sent overseas and the equipment in his factory literally unbolted, crated up, and shipped thousands of miles away along with that job? What does it mean when workers I've met had to train their foreign replacements?

America can do better. So tonight we say: help is on the way.

What does it mean when Mary Ann Knowles, a woman with breast cancer I met in New Hampshire, had to keep working day after day right through her chemotherapy, no matter how sick she felt, because she was terrified of losing her family's health insurance?

America can do better. And help is on the way.

What does it mean when Deborah Kromins from Philadelphia, Pennsylvania, works and saves all her life only to find out that her pension has disappeared into thin air—and the executive who looted it has bailed out on a golden parachute?

America can do better. And help is on the way.

What does it mean when twenty-five percent of the children in Harlem have asthma because of air pollution?

America can do better. And help is on the way.

What does it mean when people are huddled in blankets in the cold, sleeping in Lafayette Park on the doorstep of the White House itself—and the number of families living in poverty has risen by three million in the last four years?

America can do better. And help is on the way.

And so we come here tonight to ask: Where is the conscience of our country?

I'll tell you where it is: it's in rural and small town America; it's in urban neighborhoods and suburban main streets; it's alive in the people I've met in every part of this land. It's bursting in the hearts of Americans who are determined to give our country back its values and its truth.

We value jobs that pay you more, not less, than you earned before. We value jobs where, when you put in a week's work, you can actually pay your bills, provide for your children, and lift up the quality of your life. We value an America where the middle class is not being squeezed, but doing better.

So here is our economic plan to build a stronger America:

First, new incentives to revitalize manufacturing.

Second, investment in technology and innovation that will create the good-paying jobs of the future.

Third, close the tax loopholes that reward companies for shipping our jobs overseas. Instead, we will reward companies that create and keep good paying jobs where they belong—in the good old U.S.A.

We value an America that exports products, not jobs—and we believe American workers should never have to subsidize the loss of their own job.

Next, we will trade and compete in the world. But our plan calls for a fair playing field—because if you give the American worker a fair playing field, there's nobody in the world the American worker can't compete against.

And we're going to return to fiscal responsibility because it is the foundation of our economic strength. Our plan will cut the deficit in half in four years by ending tax give-aways that are nothing more than corporate welfare—and will make government live by the rule that every family has to follow: pay as you go.

And let me tell you what we won't do: we won't raise taxes on the middle class. You've heard a lot of false charges about this in recent months. So let me say straight out what I will do as President: I will cut middle class taxes. I will reduce the tax burden on small business. And I will roll back the tax cuts for the wealthiest individuals who make over $200,000 a year, so we can invest in job creation, health care, and education.

Our education plan for a stronger America sets high standards and demands accountability from parents, teachers, and schools. It provides for smaller class sizes and treats teachers like the professionals they are. And it gives a tax credit to families for each and every year of college.

When I was a prosecutor, I met young kids who were in trouble, abandoned by adults. And as President, I am determined that we stop being a nation content to spend $50,000 a year to keep a young person in prison for the rest of their life—when we could invest $10,000 to give them Head Start, Early Start, Smart Start, the best possible start in life.

And we value health care that's affordable and accessible for all Americans.

Since 2000, four million people have lost their health insurance. Millions more are struggling to afford it.

You know what's happening. Your premiums, your co-payments, your deductibles have all gone through the roof.

Our health care plan for a stronger America cracks down on the waste, greed, and abuse in our health care system and will save families up to $1,000 a year on their premi-ums. You'll get to pick your own doctor—and patients and doctors, not insurance com-pany bureaucrats, will make medical decisions. Under our plan, Medicare will negotiate lower drug prices for seniors. And all Americans will be able to buy less expensive pre-scription drugs from countries like Canada.

The story of people struggling for health care is the story of so many Americans. But you know what, it's not the story of senators and members of Congress. Because we give ourselves great health care and you get the bill. Well, I'm here to say, your family's health care is just as important as any politician's in Washington, D.C.

And when I'm President, America will stop being the only advanced nation in the world which fails to understand that health care is not a privilege for the wealthy, the connected, and the elected—it is a right for all Americans.

We value an America that controls its own destiny because it's finally and forever independent of Mideast oil. What does it mean for our economy and our national secu-rity when we only have three percent of the world's oil reserves, yet we rely on foreign countries for fifty-three percent of what we consume?

I want an America that relies on its own ingenuity and innovation—not the Saudi royal family.

And our energy plan for a stronger America will invest in new technologies and alternative fuels and the cars of the future—so that no young American in uniform will ever be held hostage to our dependence on oil from the Middle East.

I've told you about our plans for the economy, for education, for health care, for energy independence. I want you to know more about them. So now I'm going to say something that Franklin Roosevelt could never have said in his acceptance speech: go to johnkerry.com.

I want to address these next words directly to President George W. Bush: In the weeks ahead, let's be optimists, not just opponents. Let's build unity in the American family, not angry division. Let's honor this nation's diversity; let's respect one another; and let's never misuse for political purposes the most precious document in American history, the Constitution of the United States.

My friends, the high road may be harder, but it leads to a better place. And that's why Republicans and Democrats must make this election a contest of big ideas, not small-minded attacks. This is our time to reject the kind of politics calculated to divide race from race, group from group, region from region. Maybe some just see us divided into red states and blue states, but I see us as one America—red, white, and blue. And when I am President, the government I lead will enlist people of talent, Republicans as well as Democrats, to find the common ground—so that no one who has something to contribute will be left on the sidelines.

And let me say it plainly: in that cause, and in this campaign, we welcome people of faith. America is not us and them. I think of what Ron Reagan said of his father a few weeks ago, and I want to say this to you tonight: I don't wear my own faith on my sleeve. But faith has given me values and hope to live by, from Vietnam to this day, from Sunday to Sunday. I don't want to claim that God is on our side. As Abraham Lincoln told us, I want to pray humbly that we are on God's side. And whatever our faith, one belief should bind us all: The measure of our character is our willingness to give of ourselves for others and for our country.

These aren't Democratic values. These aren't Republican values. They're American values. We believe in them. They're who we are. And if we honor them, if we believe in ourselves, we can build an America that's stronger at home and respected in the world.

So much promise stretches before us. Americans have always reached for the impossible, looked to the next horizon, and asked: What if?

Two young bicycle mechanics from Dayton asked what if this airplane could take off at Kitty Hawk? It did that and changed the world forever. A young president asked what if we could go to the moon in ten years? And now we're exploring the solar system and the stars themselves. A young generation of entrepreneurs asked, what if we could take all the information in a library and put it on a little chip the size of a fingernail? We did and that too changed the world forever.

And now it's our time to ask: What if?

What if we find a breakthrough to cure Parkinson's, diabetes, Alzheimer's and AIDS? What if we have a president who believes in science, so we can unleash the wonders of discovery like stem cell research to treat illness and save millions of lives?

What if we do what adults should do—and make sure all our children are safe in the afternoons after school? And what if we have a leadership that's as good as the American dream—so that bigotry and hatred never again steal the hope and future of any American?

I learned a lot about these values on that gunboat patrolling the Mekong Delta with young Americans who came from places as different as Iowa and Oregon, Arkansas, Florida, and California. No one cared where we went to school. No one cared about our race or our backgrounds. We were literally all in the same boat. We looked out, one for the other—and we still do.

That is the kind of America I will lead as President—an America where we are all in the same boat.

Never has there been a more urgent moment for Americans to step up and define ourselves. I will work my heart out. But, my fellow citizens, the outcome is in your hands more than mine.

It is time to reach for the next dream. It is time to look to the next horizon. For America, the hope is there. The sun is rising. Our best days are still to come.

Good night, God bless you, and God bless America.

George W. Bush
Acceptance Speech for the Republican Presidential Nomination, New York City, September 2, 2004

Mr. Chairman, delegates, fellow citizens: I am honored by your support, and I accept your nomination for President of the United States.

When I said those words four years ago, none of us could have envisioned what these years would bring. In the heart of this great city, we saw tragedy arrive on a quiet morning. We saw the bravery of rescuers grow with danger. We learned of passengers on a doomed plane who died with a courage that frightened their killers. We have seen a shaken economy rise to its feet. And we have seen Americans in uniform storming mountain strongholds, and charging through sandstorms, and liberating millions, with acts of valor that would make the men of Normandy proud.

Since 2001, Americans have been given hills to climb, and found the strength to climb them. Now, because we have made the hard journey, we can see the valley below. Now, because we have faced challenges with resolve, we have historic goals within our reach, and greatness in our future. We will build a safer world and a more hopeful America—and nothing will hold us back.

In the work we have done, and the work we will do, I am fortunate to have a superb Vice President. I have counted on Dick Cheney's calm and steady judgment in difficult days, and I am honored to have him at my side.

I am grateful to share my walk in life with Laura Bush. Americans have come to see the goodness and kindness and strength I first saw 26 years ago, and we love our First Lady.

I am a fortunate father of two spirited, intelligent, and lovely young women. I am blessed with a sister and brothers who are also my closest friends. And I will always be the proud and grateful son of George and Barbara Bush.

My father served eight years at the side of another great American—Ronald Reagan. His spirit of optimism and goodwill and decency are in this hall, and in our hearts, and will always define our party.

Two months from today, voters will make a choice based on the records we have built, the convictions we hold, and the vision that guides us forward. A presidential election is a contest for the future. Tonight I will tell you where I stand, what I believe, and where I will lead this country in the next four years.

I believe every child can learn, and every school must teach—so we passed the most important federal education reform in history. Because we acted, children are making sustained progress in reading and math, America's schools are getting better, and nothing will hold us back.

I believe we have a moral responsibility to honor America's seniors—so I brought Republicans and Democrats together to strengthen Medicare. Now seniors are getting immediate help buying medicine. Soon every senior will be able to get prescription drug coverage, and nothing will hold us back.

I believe in the energy and innovative spirit of America's workers, entrepreneurs, farmers, and ranchers—so we unleashed that energy with the largest tax relief in a generation. Because we acted, our economy is growing again, and creating jobs, and nothing will hold us back.

I believe the most solemn duty of the American president is to protect the American people. If America shows uncertainty and weakness in this decade, the world will drift toward tragedy. This will not happen on my watch.

I am running for President with a clear and positive plan to build a safer world, and a more hopeful America. I am running with a compassionate conservative philosophy:

that government should help people improve their lives, not try to run their lives. I believe this Nation wants steady, consistent, principled leadership—and that is why, with your help, we will win this election.

The story of America is the story of expanding liberty: an ever-widening circle, constantly growing to reach further and include more. Our Nation's founding commitment is still our deepest commitment: In our world, and here at home, we will extend the frontiers of freedom.

The times in which we live and work are changing dramatically. The workers of our parents' generation typically had one job, one skill, one career, often with one company that provided health care and a pension. And most of those workers were men. Today, workers change jobs, even careers, many times during their lives, and in one of the most dramatic shifts our society has seen, two-thirds of all Moms also work outside the home.

This changed world can be a time of great opportunity for all Americans to earn a better living, support your family, and have a rewarding career. And government must take your side. Many of our most fundamental systems—the tax code, health coverage, pension plans, worker training—were created for the world of yesterday, not tomorrow. We will transform these systems so that all citizens are equipped, prepared—and thus truly free—to make your own choices and pursue your own dreams.

My plan begins with providing the security and opportunity of a growing economy. We now compete in a global market that provides new buyers for our goods, but new competition for our workers. To create more jobs in America, America must be the best place in the world to do business. To create jobs, my plan will encourage investment and expansion by restraining federal spending, reducing regulation, and making tax relief permanent. To create jobs, we will make our country less dependent on foreign sources of energy. To create jobs, we will expand trade and level the playing field to sell American goods and services across the globe. And we must protect small business owners and workers from the explosion of frivolous lawsuits that threaten jobs across America.

Another drag on our economy is the current tax code, which is a complicated mess—filled with special interest loopholes, saddling our people with more than six billion hours of paperwork and headache every year. The American people deserve—and our economic future demands—a simpler, fairer, pro-growth system. In a new term, I will lead a bipartisan effort to reform and simplify the federal tax code.

Another priority in a new term will be to help workers take advantage of the expanding economy to find better, higher-paying jobs. In this time of change, many workers want to go back to school to learn different or higher-level skills. So we will double the number of people served by our principal job training program and increase funding for community colleges. I know that with the right skills, American workers can compete with anyone, anywhere in the world.

In this time of change, opportunity in some communities is more distant than in others. To stand with workers in poor communities—and those that have lost manufacturing, textile, and other jobs—we will create American opportunity zones. In these areas, we'll provide tax relief and other incentives to attract new business, and improve housing and job training to bring hope and work throughout all of America.

As I've traveled the country, I've met many workers and small business owners who have told me they are worried they cannot afford health care. More than half of the uninsured are small business employees and their families. In a new term, we must allow small firms to join together to purchase insurance at the discounts available to big companies. We will offer a tax credit to encourage small businesses and their employees to set up health savings accounts, and provide direct help for low-income Americans to purchase them. These accounts give workers the security of insurance against major illness, the opportunity to save tax-free for routine health expenses, and the freedom of knowing you can take your account with you whenever you change jobs. And we will provide low-income Americans with better access to health care: In a new term, I will ensure every poor county in America has a community or rural health center.

As I have traveled our country, I have met too many good doctors, especially OB-GYNS, who are being forced out of practice because of the high cost of lawsuits. To make health care more affordable and accessible, we must pass medical liability reform now. And in all we do to improve health care in America, we will make sure that health decisions are made by doctors and patients, not by bureaucrats in Washington, DC.

In this time of change, government must take the side of working families. In a new term, we will change outdated labor laws to offer comp-time and flex-time. Our laws should never stand in the way of a more family-friendly workplace.

Another priority for a new term is to build an ownership society, because ownership brings security, and dignity, and independence.

Thanks to our policies, homeownership in America is at an all-time high. Tonight we set a new goal: seven million more affordable homes in the next 10 years so more American families will be able to open the door and say welcome to my home.

In an ownership society, more people will own their health plans, and have the confidence of owning a piece of their retirement. We will always keep the promise of Social Security for our older workers. With the huge Baby Boom generation approaching retirement, many of our children and grandchildren understandably worry whether Social Security will be there when they need it. We must strengthen Social Security by allowing younger workers to save some of their taxes in a personal account—a nest egg you can call your own, and government can never take away.

In all these proposals, we seek to provide not just a government program, but a path—a path to greater opportunity, more freedom, and more control over your own life.

This path begins with our youngest Americans. To build a more hopeful America, we must help our children reach as far as their vision and character can take them. Tonight, I remind every parent and every teacher, I say to every child: No matter what your circumstance, no matter where you live—your school will be the path to the promise of America.

We are transforming our schools by raising standards and focusing on results. We are insisting on accountability, empowering parents and teachers, and making sure that local people are in charge of their schools. By testing every child, we are identifying those who need help and we're providing a record level of funding to get them that help. In northeast Georgia, Gainesville Elementary School is mostly Hispanic and 90 percent poor and this year 90 percent of its students passed state tests in reading and math. The principal expresses the philosophy of his school this way: "We don't focus on what we can't do at this school; we focus on what we can do—we do whatever it takes to get kids across the finish line." This principal is challenging the soft bigotry of low expectations, and that is the spirit of our education reform, and the commitment of our country: No dejaremos a ningún niño atrás. We will leave no child behind.

We are making progress—and there is more to do. In this time of change, most new jobs are filled by people with at least two years of college, yet only about one in four students gets there. In our high schools, we will fund early intervention programs to help students at risk. We will place a new focus on math and science. As we make progress, we will require a rigorous exam before graduation. By raising performance in our high schools, and expanding Pell grants for low and middle income families, we will help more Americans start their career with a college diploma.

America's children must also have a healthy start in life. In a new term, we will lead an aggressive effort to enroll millions of poor children who are eligible but not signed up for the government's health insurance programs. We will not allow a lack of attention, or information, to stand between these children and the health care they need.

Anyone who wants more details on my agenda can find them online. The web address is not very imaginative, but it's easy to remember: GeorgeWBush.com.

These changing times can be exciting times of expanded opportunity. And here, you face a choice. My opponent's policies are dramatically different from ours. Senator Kerry opposed Medicare reform and health savings accounts. After supporting my education reforms, he now wants to dilute them. He opposes legal and medical liability reform. He opposed reducing the marriage penalty, opposed doubling the child credit, and opposed lowering income taxes for all who pay them. To be fair, there are some things my opponent is for—he's proposed more than two trillion dollars in new federal spending so far, and that's a lot, even for a senator from Massachusetts. To pay for that spending, he is running on a platform of increasing taxes—and that's the kind of promise a politician usually keeps.

His policies of tax and spend—of expanding government rather than expanding opportunity—are the policies of the past. We are on the path to the future—and we are not turning back.

In this world of change, some things do not change: the values we try to live by, the institutions that give our lives meaning and purpose. Our society rests on a foundation of responsibility and character and family commitment.

Because family and work are sources of stability and dignity, I support welfare reform that strengthens family and requires work. Because a caring society will value its weakest members, we must make a place for the unborn child. Because religious charities provide a safety net of mercy and compassion, our government must never discriminate against them. Because the union of a man and woman deserves an honored place in our society, I support the protection of marriage against activist judges. And I will continue to appoint federal judges who know the difference between personal opinion and the strict interpretation of the law.

My opponent recently announced that he is the candidate of "conservative values," which must have come as a surprise to a lot of his supporters. Now, there are some problems with this claim. If you say the heart and soul of America is found in Hollywood, I'm afraid you are not the candidate of conservative values. If you voted against the bipartisan Defense of Marriage Act, which President Clinton signed, you are not the candidate of conservative values. If you gave a speech, as my opponent did, calling the Reagan presidency eight years of "moral darkness," then you may be a lot of things, but the candidate of conservative values is not one of them.

This election will also determine how America responds to the continuing danger of terrorism—and you know where I stand. Three days after September 11th, I stood where Americans died, in the ruins of the Twin Towers. Workers in hard hats were shouting to me, "Whatever it takes." A fellow grabbed me by the arm and he said, "Do not let me down." Since that day, I wake up every morning thinking about how to better protect our country. I will never relent in defending America—whatever it takes.

So we have fought the terrorists across the earth—not for pride, not for power, but because the lives of our citizens are at stake. Our strategy is clear. We have tripled funding for homeland security and trained half a million first responders, because we are determined to protect our homeland. We are transforming our military and reforming and strengthening our intelligence services. We are staying on the offensive—striking terrorists abroad—so we do not have to face them here at home. And we are working to advance liberty in the broader Middle East, because freedom will bring a future of hope, and the peace we all want. And we will prevail.

Our strategy is succeeding. Four years ago, Afghanistan was the home base of al-Qaida, Pakistan was a transit point for terrorist groups, Saudi Arabia was fertile ground for terrorist fund-raising, Libya was secretly pursuing nuclear weapons, Iraq was a gathering threat, and al-Qaida was largely unchallenged as it planned attacks. Today, the government of a free Afghanistan is fighting terror, Pakistan is capturing terrorist leaders, Saudi Arabia is making raids and arrests, Libya is dismantling its weapons programs, the army of a free Iraq is fighting for freedom, and more than three-quarters of al-Qaida's key members and associates have been detained or killed. We have led, many have joined, and America and the world are safer.

This progress involved careful diplomacy, clear moral purpose, and some tough decisions. And the toughest came on Iraq. We knew Saddam Hussein's record of aggression and support for terror. We knew his long history of pursuing, even using, weapons of mass destruction. And we know that September 11th requires our country to think differently: We must, and we will, confront threats to America before it is too late.

In Saddam Hussein, we saw a threat. Members of both political parties, including my opponent and his running mate, saw the threat, and voted to authorize the use of force. We went to the United Nations Security Council, which passed a unanimous resolution demanding the dictator disarm, or face serious consequences. Leaders in the Middle East urged him to comply. After more than a decade of diplomacy, we gave Saddam Hussein another chance, a final chance, to meet his responsibilities to the civilized world. He again refused, and I faced the kind of decision that comes only to the Oval Office—a decision no president would ask for, but must be prepared to make. Do I forget the lessons of September 11th and take the word of a madman, or do I take action to defend our country? Faced with that choice, I will defend America every time.

Because we acted to defend our country, the murderous regimes of Saddam Hussein and the Taliban are history, more than 50 million people have been liberated, and democracy is coming to the broader Middle East. In Afghanistan, terrorists have done everything they can to intimidate people—yet more than 10 million citizens have registered to vote in the October presidential election, a resounding endorsement of democracy. Despite ongoing acts of violence, Iraq now has a strong Prime Minister, a national council, and national elections are scheduled for January. Our Nation is standing with the people of Afghanistan and Iraq, because when America gives its word, America must keep its word. As importantly, we are serving a vital and historic cause that will make our country safer. Free societies in the Middle East will be hopeful societies, which no longer feed resentments and breed violence for export. Free governments in the Middle East will fight terrorists instead of harboring them, and that helps us keep the peace. So our mission in Afghanistan and Iraq is clear: We will help new leaders to train their armies, and move toward elections, and get on the path of stability and democracy as quickly as possible. And then our troops will return home with the honor they have earned.

Our troops know the historic importance of our work. One Army Specialist wrote home: "We are transforming a once sick society into a hopeful place. . . . The various terrorist enemies we are facing in Iraq," he continued, "are really aiming at you back in the United States. This is a test of will for our country. We soldiers of yours are doing great and scoring victories in confronting the evil terrorists."

That young man is right—our men and women in uniform are doing a superb job for America. Tonight I want to speak to all of them—and to their families: You are involved in a struggle of historic proportion. Because of your service and sacrifice, we are defeating the terrorists where they live and plan, and making America safer. Because of you, women in Afghanistan are no longer shot in a sports stadium. Because of you, the people of Iraq no longer fear being executed and left in mass graves. Because of you, the world is more just and will be more peaceful. We owe you our thanks, and we owe you something more. We will give you all the resources, all the tools, and all the support you need for victory.

Again, my opponent and I have different approaches. I proposed, and the Congress overwhelmingly passed, 87 billion dollars in funding needed by our troops doing battle in Afghanistan and Iraq. My opponent and his running mate voted against this money for bullets, and fuel, and vehicles, and body armor. When asked to explain his vote, the Senator said, "I actually did vote for the 87 billion dollars before I voted against it." Then he said he was "proud" of that vote. Then, when pressed, he said it was a "complicated" matter. There is nothing complicated about supporting our troops in combat.

Our allies also know the historic importance of our work. About 40 nations stand beside us in Afghanistan, and some 30 in Iraq. And I deeply appreciate the courage and wise counsel of leaders like Prime Minister Howard, and President Kwasniewski, and Prime Minister Berlusconi—and, of course, Prime Minister Tony Blair.

Again, my opponent takes a different approach. In the midst of war, he has called America's allies, quote, a "coalition of the coerced and the bribed." That would be nations like Great Britain, Poland, Italy, Japan, the Netherlands, Denmark, El Salvador, Australia, and others—allies that deserve the respect of all Americans, not the scorn of a politician. I respect every soldier, from every country, who serves beside us in the hard work of history. America is grateful, and America will not forget.

The people we have freed won't forget either. Not long ago, seven Iraqi men came to see me in the Oval Office. They had "X"s branded into their foreheads, and their right hands had been cut off, by Saddam Hussein's secret police, the sadistic punishment for imaginary crimes. During our emotional visit one of the Iraqi men used his new prosthetic hand to slowly write out, in Arabic, a prayer for God to bless America. I am proud that our country remains the hope of the oppressed, and the greatest force for good on this earth.

Others understand the historic importance of our work. The terrorists know. They know that a vibrant, successful democracy at the heart of the Middle East will discredit their radical ideology of hate. They know that men and women with hope, and purpose, and dignity do not strap bombs on their bodies and kill the innocent. The terrorists are fighting freedom with all their cunning and cruelty because freedom is their greatest fear—and they should be afraid, because freedom is on the march.

I believe in the transformational power of liberty: The wisest use of American strength is to advance freedom. As the citizens of Afghanistan and Iraq seize the moment, their example will send a message of hope throughout a vital region. Palestinians will hear the message that democracy and reform are within their reach, and so is peace with our good friend Israel. Young women across the Middle East will hear the message that their day of equality and justice is coming. Young men will hear the message that national progress and dignity are found in liberty, not tyranny and terror. Reformers, and political prisoners, and exiles will hear the message that their dream of freedom cannot be denied forever. And as freedom advances—heart by heart, and nation by nation—America will be more secure and the world more peaceful.

America has done this kind of work before—and there have always been doubters. In 1946, 18 months after the fall of Berlin to allied forces, a journalist wrote in the New York Times, "Germany is . . . a land in an acute stage of economic, political and moral crisis. [European] capitals are frightened. In every [military] headquarters, one meets alarmed officials doing their utmost to deal with the consequences of the occupation policy that they admit has failed." End quote. Maybe that same person's still around, writing editorials. Fortunately, we had a resolute president named Truman, who with the American people persevered, knowing that a new democracy at the center of Europe would lead to stability and peace. And because that generation of Americans held firm in the cause of liberty, we live in a better and safer world today.

The progress we and our friends and allies seek in the broader Middle East will not come easily, or all at once. Yet Americans, of all people, should never be surprised by the power of liberty to transform lives and nations. That power brought settlers on perilous journeys, inspired colonies to rebellion, ended the sin of slavery, and set our Nation against the tyrannies of the 20th century. We were honored to aid the rise of democracy in Germany and Japan and Nicaragua and Central Europe and the Baltics—and that noble story goes on. I believe that America is called to lead the cause of freedom in a new century. I believe that millions in the Middle East plead in silence for their liberty. I believe that given the chance, they will embrace the most honorable form of government ever devised by man. I believe all these things because freedom is not America's gift to the world, it is the Almighty God's gift to every man and woman in this world.

This moment in the life of our country will be remembered. Generations will know if we kept our faith and kept our word. Generations will know if we seized this moment, and used it to build a future of safety and peace. The freedom of many, and the future security of our Nation, now depend on us. And tonight, my fellow Americans, I ask you to stand with me.

In the last four years, you and I have come to know each other. Even when we don't agree, at least you know what I believe and where I stand. You may have noticed I have a few flaws, too. People sometimes have to correct my English—I knew I had a problem when Arnold Schwarzenegger started doing it. Some folks look at me and see a certain swagger, which in Texas is called "walking." Now and then I come across as a little too blunt—and for that we can all thank the white-haired lady sitting right up there.

One thing I have learned about the presidency is that whatever shortcomings you have, people are going to notice them—and whatever strengths you have, you're going to need them. These four years have brought moments I could not foresee and will not forget. I have tried to comfort Americans who lost the most on September 11th—people who showed me a picture or told me a story, so I would know how much was taken from them. I have learned first-hand that ordering Americans into battle is the hardest decision, even when it is right. I have returned the salute of wounded soldiers, some with a very tough road ahead, who say they were just doing their job. I've held the children of the fallen, who are told their dad or mom is a hero, but would rather just have their dad or mom.

And I have met with parents and wives and husbands who have received a folded flag, and said a final goodbye to a soldier they loved. I am awed that so many have used those meetings to say that I am in their prayers to offer encouragement to me. Where does strength like that come from? How can people so burdened with sorrow also feel such pride? It is because they know their loved one was last seen doing good. Because they know that liberty was precious to the one they lost. And in those military families, I have seen the character of a great nation: decent, and idealistic, and strong.

The world saw that spirit three miles from here, when the people of this city faced peril together, and lifted a flag over the ruins, and defied the enemy with their courage. My fellow Americans, for as long as our country stands, people will look to the resurrection of New York City and they will say: Here buildings fell, and here a nation rose.

We see America's character in our military, which finds a way or makes one. We see it in our veterans, who are supporting military families in their days of worry. We see it in our young people, who have found heroes once again. We see that character in workers and entrepreneurs, who are renewing our economy with their effort and optimism. And all of this has confirmed one belief beyond doubt: Having come this far, our tested and confident Nation can achieve anything.

To everything we know there is a season—a time for sadness, a time for struggle, a time for rebuilding. And now we have reached a time for hope. This young century will be liberty's century. By promoting liberty abroad, we will build a safer world. By encouraging liberty at home, we will build a more hopeful America. Like generations before us, we have a calling from beyond the stars to stand for freedom. This is the everlasting dream of America—and tonight, in this place, that dream is renewed. Now we go forward—grateful for our freedom, faithful to our cause, and confident in the future of the greatest nation on earth.

God bless you, and may God continue to bless America.

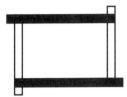

APPENDIX B
THE FINAL ROUND TRANSCRIPT*

National Parliamentary Debate Association Championship Tournament,
held at Portland State University, Portland, Oregon,
March 30, 2003

THE TEAMS

Government: University of Wyoming (Mike Owens and Josh Wilkerson)
Opposition: Pacific Lutheran University (Kyle Mach and Leah Sprain)

THE RESOLUTION

Resolved: The War in Iraq is Just

FIRST GOVERNMENT CONSTRUCTIVE SPEECH (7 MINUTES)

They told me my thank yous won't be timed, so they'll be very extensive. I would like to thank the coaching at the university of Wyoming, Matt Stannard, Jon Voight, (. . .),

* This is a transcript made from a sound recording. Oral speech often contains imperfections and nonfluencies as well as grammar errors that are more easily detected and avoided in written speech. We have made only insignificant edits to this transcript to promote clarity. For the most part, however, this debate reflects the speeches as uttered by the debaters.

Tara Stone, Julia Bohr, Luke Strikker, these are some of the people who have made us the debaters we are today. I of course want to thank my high school coach (. . .) who is one of the most important influences of my life. I also want to thank my partner Josh. He has really done a lot for me this year, as you can tell, so I'd like to thank him for that.

I'd like to thank the University of Wyoming squad and of course the University of Wyoming administration. I hear a lot of people in the debate community complain about their administrations not being supportive, that is certainly not the case at the University of Wyoming, our department is fully behind us, and always supportive, that's why I'd like to thank them. And finally I want to thank all of you for being here, judges, timers, people. This, I hope will be an interesting debate. We're glad that you turned out for it, and of course, we'll hope that regardless of your personal views in this round, that you will give all sides in this debate a chance to speak

And fourth, finally, thank you to our friends from Pacific Lutheran.

When we debate the resolution "The War in Iraq is Just," first an observation. Josh and I believe initially that we don't really need definitions, that we're talking about the war in Iraq currently going on, and we will seek to justify it.

Our first observation, then, is that of burdens. Josh and I believe that its important to realize that we do not have to prove that it is pragmatic, convenient or expedient. Remember that ethical issues seek to reach a higher standard, and let's talk about why that's important. Remember that when you ask yourself whether slavery is justified, you consider the ethical principles before you consider such pragmatic things as whether it helps the economy or not. We must first seek to justify the underlying ethical principles of our actions. Now, that does not mean that Josh and I will seek to exclude the consequences of those actions, we think those are important, but the ethical principles are the baseline.

Having said that, the criteria that we will offer you is that of ethics. Josh and I believe that it is open-ended enough to allow both sides to offer their own frameworks to evaluate the debate in terms of what our obligations are.

Our second observation then is Josh and I's ethical framework. We rely on the philosophy of Emmanuel Levinas, who tells us about the obligations that each of us is having to the other.

Our A point. Emmanuel Levinas says that our ethical obligation to the other is undying, it is always part of our lives. Levinas argues that our interaction with other people, that our knowledge of them, is what makes us who we are. We do not exist as individuals, we do not have identities, unless we first interact with other people in the world, that indeed they give us the very standpoint to say "we are different from you therefore we know who we are, but additionally that we are the same as you that we come from you," and therefore our ethical obligation is undying.

Our B point is what Levinas says this means in the real world. Levinas realizes that actions sometimes have bad consequences initially, but he says that inaction is always worse than action when considering the ethical obligation to the other. Specifically he talks about genocide committed by the Nazis. He believes that military action in that specific instance certainly caused casualties, and had problematic responses, but basically what he said is you can go to war in bad conscience, but you also not go to war in equally bad conscience or worse conscience. Your point.

Question: Now, if we have this obligation to the other, how does Levinas tell us to evaluate whether our obligation is to go to war, for example, or if our obligation might be to seek other ends, or means, rather. Means.

Answer: Certainly, Levinas would want you to consider all of your means. He would want you to consider every opportunity available. And that's our argument is not that you can't do that.

Our C point is that is why inaction, in general, is worse in the face of suffering of others. Our argument throughout the round will be that in the face of suffering of others, inaction always encourages that suffering and encourages the abuse of others. We will argue that it is always an incentive to those who will do evil in our world to know that we seek never to stop them, that as long as we can find some kind of reason for our own self-interest, or for our own pragmatic concerns, that those people will basically get the message that we will never stop them from what they do.

Josh and I have two substantive observations to tell you why Iraq fits this ethical criteria. So our third observation is that Iraq requires military intervention. The A point under this is that democracy is defensible and it is fair. Josh and I believe that such a system of government is always the only one that recognizes the basic equality of people.

The B point is that even the people in the anti-war crowd are really unable to deal with the idea of regime change in terms of the Iraqi people. They say "well, maybe the Iraqi people don't want it," but in an oppressive regime you never really know the opinions of people within that country. Its not like we had polls in the death camps in Nazi Germany that tell us whether the Jews wanted us to intervene there or not. Our argument is that when you don't live in an open and free society the opinions are always skewed.

But our next point is that additionally we think people have ignored this particular situation and Saddam's treatment of his own people, the gassing of Kurds, because the numbers are lower. Because its politically expedient for us to say that that argument is not as important as other appeals to international law, but your point.

Question: Thanks. Can you give me a historical example of when the United States, or really I think any other major world player, has been able to successfully implement the democratic reforms that you tell us are a necessary justification for war?

Answer: Well, I think the example I talked about with Germany comes to mind, right? I mean, I was just talking about that. They're a democracy now.

The next point is that arguments against the war are eternally self-focused and eternally delaying. First of all, most of the arguments you hear are "well, we have to preserve our international coalition," but again those concerns are always self-reflexive. They are always about our own power and about our own concern. No one really talks about why, because a leader killed his people, and because he has gassed thousands of people, that, that somehow our international concerns and our worries about whether we're in the long term going to be about a very powerful or well-liked nation are more important than our ethical obligations to the other.

Additionally, let's talk about why they are always eternal. If our moral intervention right now is not justified on an ethical basis, then that means it is never justified. If we can't intervene to save the Iraqi people now, we can't do it in ten years, and we can't do it in twenty years. Which means something very simple, that although civilians may die in this particular war, and you may think that is unfortunate, we think that is always outweighed by the fact that you eternally say people must suffer, must die, can live under an unjust regime without intervention, that you basically give that system of total mortal pacifism, which we prove is unjustified.

Our final observation, then, is that of the alternative of inspection. The A point is that Saddam has not been stopped by inspection. No one argues that this man does not want weapons of mass destruction. No one says that he does not have a hunger for them. And even when inspections have worked to curb that desire in the past, they have always failed once the international community turned its attention away from the problem, which it always does.

But our next subpoint under this is that inspections, again, don't really solve for the problem of Iraqi weapons, they didn't, and they won't. Saddam Hussein in this war has already used missiles that have a longer range than the international agreements he signed. Whether you agree with the Bush administration about the particulars of this war, it is critical to note that there is key, clear evidence that he has violated these prohibitions and that the weapons inspections did not work and have not worked.

Our next point under this is that the United States has a unique responsibility to stop Saddam. Now, often people say "well, the United States is at fault for Saddam, we propped up his regime, we paid him." That may or may not be true, but there is no denying that if the United States is responsible for an oppressive regime that does not allow democracy to function, that has committed types of genocide, then why the United States doesn't also bear a unique responsibility to stop it. If we started it, then certainly we have the opportunity and the obligation to stop the suffering and problems that exist within that country. Because we believe that the ethical concerns of the other side are always short-term, that they are always self-reflexive, and they would say to let people live in injustice forever, we ask you to side with the government.

FIRST OPPOSITION CONSTRUCTIVE SPEECH (8 MINUTES)

I hope and think that Pacific Lutheran University is going to win tonight's debate. However, regardless of what happens tonight, there is absolutely no thing, nothing that could happen, that would refute or negate the influence that the following people have had on my life. I want to start by thanking individuals specifically attached to the tournament, Jill Freeman and the entire [debate program at] Portland State University, Brian Shipley, Robert Trapp, and all the members of the topics committee.

I hope that's not as popular as I get. The next thing that I want to do is talk about a few people specifically important to me. Ed Inch, Amanda Feller, Julia Patriche, whose name I still can't pronounce, and the members of the PLU squad, have been people that are more than friends, but have been [of] significant importance to me, as far as the way that I think, the way that I act, and the way that I'll go upon my life, come upon my life, forever. I can't say that about very many people.

The other person I want to mention specifically, is Leah Sprain, you're great. And my parents, who have no idea what I do, but are remarkably supportive of it.

Congratulations.

The government team in today's debate tries to set up a very interesting dichotomy. They tell you, that the alternative to having this war in Iraq, is undying pacifism. I tell you, that's not an appropriate way to ask yourself whether or not the war in Iraq is justified, and that they have to accept that there are alternatives that existed to launching a full-scale invasion of Iraq, and that the comparison of inaction with war is the kind of thing that makes this standard exceptionally problematic. Let's go, start at the top of the case and move through to see why the war with Iraq is simply not just.

Let's start at the top, where they offer us a discussion of how you can't view something pragmatic, it has to be a higher standard, and they tell you that higher standard is whether or not you actually fulfill your commitment to other people. But the problem with this is that this assumes, that you necessarily improve the plight of those individuals, that you act to help. Now, unless they can actually justify that, you know, trying to help other people is the only standard that, well, okay, first, I want to explain why this kind of idea of just helping other people is not a legitimate justification for war, then I want to talk about the basic fact that this just simply has not been proven true, simply has not been justified in the case of the war with Iraq.

Now let's move on to start why this standard simply doesn't work. The first thing that I would tell you is that if you allow yourself to justify war, according to what other people might want, then you put yourself in the unnecessary condition of speaking on their behalf in every case, and the fact that a tremendous number of Iraqi civilians have been arming themselves and throwing themselves against the American army demonstrates the fact that we haven't been speaking to that, speaking on their behalf, all that well.

The next thing that we can really look to here is that if you accept that in the short run you can accept civilian casualties and other individuals dying, in the pursuit of their own good, then you can justify any action, any means, to get to your end. That means, that if you were to accept this standard, right, that if, combined with speaking on peoples' behalf, this means that if you were to accept this standard, that you could justify, you know, well, wiping out the Native Americans across North America, because we did it for them, even though they didn't want it. And the basic fact of the matter is, we didn't do anything good for them. I'm not saying they advocate that, I'm saying that's what the standard allows. Your question.

Question: I don't understand how the standard allows that, right, like who says that we did that for their good? I certainly don't.

Answer: We did. We said that.

Question: I didn't say that. You did.

Answer: We said that, and I think what we'll see when we move on to the rest of the case is that we are saying that we are doing it for the Iraqi people in this case as well, but we simply haven't seen any evidence that it's going to come out to their benefit.

Let's move on. When they go on to their first contention, the second observation, they tell you that we have an undying obligation to other individuals. My first important answer here is that this doesn't necessarily demonstrate that war is the option that we ought to be undertaking. We could, for example, use additional diplomatic actions. We could use a partial military action. We could actually, hey, send new aid instead of sanctions, and I would tell you that would weaken the Iraqi regime ten times more effectively than sanctions or war. Now that means that there are other options available, than simply expanding this aggressive action against the nation of Iraq. Whoa, microphone.

The next thing that we see here is that the Iraqi war simply has not been justified when it comes to the case for caring for the Iraqi people. In order to uphold this, and in order to use their Germany example, for example, for example, which I'm going to talk about in a minute, they would have to actually demonstrate that our motivations in this case are to help other people. But wait, right, that's only, that's only been part of the justification that George W. Bush and the rest of the administration have used. Really, I think, that's been the justification that they've used to placate world opinion, and that in the long run we aren't going to see the kind of dedication that's actually required to mediate these kinds of problems, right? Remember, at one time it was about regime change, and then it was about proliferation, and then it was about Al-Qaeda running across the top of northern Iraq. None of this demonstrates that the United States is acting in the interests of the Iraqi people. Your question.

Question: Do Josh and I have to rely on the justifications that the Bush administration made for the war, or can we rely on our own justifications?

Answer: Unfortunately, it is the Bush administration that is responsible for deciding whether or not these ends that you advocate get carried out. And I would tell you that the Bush administration is not going to do any of those things, right, they might say they do this for the Iraqi people, but they do it for all sorts of other reasons, like geopolitical strategy, for their own political gain, for economic interests, and all of those factors. Now, it's true that you could say that the war could be justified if we were doing it with a long-standing commitment to the Iraqi people. But you don't, that doesn't prove the resolution true, you have to prove that the war is justified to the degree that these things are actually going to take place, and they're simply not.

Let's go to the third observation. They tell you that fighting in defense of democracy is defensible and fair. My first answer here again, is that this assumes that we can effectively put democracy in place. Which simply isn't something that we've seen successfully done in the past. Well, let's talk about the most recent example, right, Afghanistan. Very, very democratic now, because we chose him.

The next thing that they tell us is that Germany is an excellent example of this taking place. Well, there's a number of significant differences between what happened in Germany and what's happening in Iraq. The first thing is that we utterly decimated the nation of Germany, and if they're going to accept that that's the kind of action that's going to necessarily have to take place, in order for this regime change to take place, I don't think that's such a great thing. The next thing I would tell you is that Germany and Iraq's industrial and economic structure is astoundingly different, right? This is a country that had all of the roads, all of the schools, that it needs, except for the ones that we destroyed. Iraq is not in that category, right? The next thing that we see, not at this time, is that following the war with Germany, we had what's called the Marshall Plan. You heard anyone talking about anything on the scope of the Marshall Plan for Iraq? You heard anyone, you know, actually, the answer to that question is "we'll figure it out when we get there," right? We simply haven't seen that kind of thing effectively justified when it comes to the American government action, and we haven't seen the kind of international coordination that will actually be required to effectively solve this problem. Which, actually, is the next real distinction with Germany, right? Not at this time. Is that in the war with Germany, oh, we have what's called the Allies. We don't have the United States and Great Britain that are going to be pseudo-dedicated to this action, we have half, or almost half the world, actually dedicated to rebuilding this country, and we don't have that in the current system. If anything, what we see is the kind of divisiveness brought upon by U.S. unilateral, sort of unilateral, action, the kind of divisiveness that's going to ensure that we can't effectively rebuild Iraq in the way that is necessary, and actually, in order to actually improve the plight of individuals within Iraq.

The comparison's not with Germany. It's with Afghanistan. In Afghanistan, we see coalition control in essentially one city, Kabul. Outside of that, you still have individual warlord-type individuals ruling in these regions. We haven't seen a dramatic increase in human rights. We certainly haven't seen a dramatic increase in the standard of living, and that these individuals are utterly forgotten, now that we've moved on to our next attack.

At the bottom, they tell us that Saddam Hussein cannot be stopped by inspections. Probably true. The first thing that you need to look to here is that this doesn't necessarily justify the war, and that it doesn't demonstrate that we would leave an improved condition upon the Iraqi people, in the event that we actually do this war.

The next thing that I would tell you, is again, this ignores that there are other options, other means, and that, in general, we simply see that aiding the people of Iraq is not our goal, and won't be the end of this conflict.

SECOND GOVERNMENT CONSTRUCTIVE SPEECH (8 MINUTES)

Before I begin, I'd like to extend some thank yous. First and foremost, I'd like to thank the entire organization at the University of Wyoming, for accepting me on their team, for giving me great coaching over these past two years, and all the support and friendships that we've made as a group together, specifically Matt Stannard, (. . .), Tracy Mahoney, who's unfortunately no longer with us, but still supports us in her outside activities.

Additionally, I owe a debt of gratitude to Mr. Ron Underwood at (. . .) High School, who actually got me involved in this activity. As well, Dr. (. . .) and Dr. Jim Solomon from Modesto Junior College for spurring me on in my career.

I'd also like to thank a warm thank you to both Bob Trapp and Brian Shipley for making this tournament run on time, of course our tournament hosts for putting on one of the best national tournaments I've ever attended, and of course, last, but certainly not least, our good friends from Pacific Lutheran University, congratulations for making it this far, and let's go ahead and get on to the debate.

The first thing I want to do is start off with the ethical framework that we talk about on the burdens. Now, the response coming out of the leader of opposition is that these ethical justifications only work when you assume that, in fact, we can improve the lives of the Iraqi people. It's unfortunate that he makes this argument and then doesn't argue the entire case because Michael gives you those justifications further on in case when we talk about removing a regime that will, for all perpetuity, in fact oppress its people, violate their human rights, and politically persecute them. That analysis doesn't go ignored. It shows you, in fact, that our actions, justified through an ethical framework, do improve the lives of the Iraqi people. Additionally, I say that we justify action over no action. To take no action whatsoever, in fact damns those people to a life where they are in fact oppressed, where their human rights are violated, and where they are under the constant iron fist of a dictator. Additionally, we also remove a threat that's been a source of instability within the Middle East, to its neighbors. Remember, this man hasn't just attacked his own people, he's also attacked people living in western Iran as well as Kuwait, and violated their human rights.

On to [the] criterion of ethics. The first thing he tells you, is that, in fact, that Levinas allows us to speak for others. In fact, he says that Iraqi civilians are fighting in the streets against the United States army. However, we say this is fundamentally untrue. Most news analysts, as well as international analysts, believe that those people dressed up in civilian clothing are A, Iraqi soldiers, or B, Saddam Hussein's Fadayeen, whose members aren't civilians, who are (?fighting for the Ba'athists?).

The next thing, the next argument that he makes, here, is that we can justify any action by adopting the framework that Levinas gives us. For instance, we could say that wiping out Native Americans was something for their own good. I think you all realize the ridiculousness of this claim. I also think that you have to have more than a high school LD understanding of Levinas to realize that Levinas in fact tells us . . . yeah, that went a little too far, I'm sorry. Regardless, Levinas also tells us that we have to act in the interests of others to minimize the amount of pain within their life. That means that we don't go in and kill people for their own good, it means that we work to remove the institutions, structures and behavioral patterns that are causing pain, death and destruction in their own lives. With that, your point.

Question: Thank you. You continue to use this rhetoric of action or no action. But is that really the comparison that necessarily justifies war? Isn't there some sort of third way in between doing nothing and wholly invading another nation?

Answer: You guys are talking about all these other options, yet in your LOC you never explain what any of them (. . .) are.

Next, they say that we don't demonstrate why the war is the right option, but Michael tells you extensively on case that we have exhausted all other options. That diplomacy has not worked, that the U.N. passing seventeen resolutions has not worked, that inspectors have not worked, that sanctions have not worked, all those things leave us with (. . .) option, that we have to go to war. The only option he gives you is giving aid to Iraq, well that's just great. Give aid to the guy who misuses money coming in from the Food-for-Oil program. (. . .) even more. Additionally, his next argument here is that war is not justified, yet he's not giving you very solid analysis as to why this war's not justified. He keeps telling you that there are other options, but due to the fact that he can't tell you what those other options are, and that the only one he has given you is an absolutely terrible idea, Michael and I say that war is in fact justified in this case.

The next thing he tells you is that the Bush administration is shifting its motives on Iraq. I've got a couple of responses. Number one. Michael and I don't have to justify the war in terms of the Bush administration's agenda. All we have to do is stand up here today and give you moral and ethical reasons as to why the war is justified. Not at this time. Additionally, I tell you that the shifting motives that he lists off, in fact, in some cases, such as terrorism, weapons of mass destruction, and the fact that this regime is brutal on its people, are all good justifications for us to go to war, and Mike explains that to you in the original Prime Minister's constructive.

Additionally, he says, on his next argument, that, in fact, that, once again, that we must demonstrate why the war is justified. However, we do this extensively on case. Remember, they're not talking about the last argument Mike gives you, about why the United States is uniquely morally culpable to go in and remove this regime, and that is because we helped create that regime. Your point.

Question: Thanks. You tell us that you don't need to justify the Bush administration's motivations for doing this action, only that this motivation could be justifiable. But isn't that only demonstrating that the war in Iraq could be justified, if it was done by a totally different individual, with totally different motivations, with, well, a totally different war?

Answer: Look, it's justified specifically in-case, when we give you solid ethical reasoning, as well as solid historical reasoning, as to why it's justified. The fact that we lay out those justifications and you guys don't do a good job disputing them only proves the fact that the war is just and that we make those arguments.

Now, let's go ahead and move on to observation two. This first thing he says is that we haven't rebuilt nations democratically in the past, well, I'm thinking about Germany and Japan, as historical answers to that argument. The next thing he says is that Afghanistan is not democratic. However, remember, the Afghanis chose their own government in a Loya Jirga held in a conference in Bonn, Germany. The self-determination there was, in fact, pertinent. Additionally, not at this time, he says that we absolutely decimated Germany, but I tell you that's outweighed by the fact that A, we stopped genocide, but two, we had a plan of action to rebuild Germany, and three, helped set up a good democracy in Germany. The next thing he tells you is that Germany and Iraq are different in terms of infrastructure, and that we don't have a Marshall Plan or any sort of rebuilding plan for Iraq. I've got a couple of responses to this. Number one, we don't have to justify a plan to rebuild Iraq, but secondly, there is a plan to rebuild Iraq, the Bush administration has laid out how we will use an oil trust fund to use oil profits from the oil industry as a way to rebuild (. . .). The next argument he gives you is, that, in fact, there are no Allies with us in the war against Iraq. That's funny, I hear there are about fifty countries that are on our side. Additionally, even if those fifty countries weren't present, simply because others take no action, is not a guilt-free card for the United States to get out of its moral responsibility, (. . .).

The next argument he makes is on the D point, when, in fact, he tells you that Afghanistan is worse now, but there is absolutely no evidence to support this claim. Our argument is that Afghanistan is absolutely better now. Not only is the Taliban on the run, but they also have a woman who is heading up their Civil Rights and Education Ministry, that is looking to integrate women into the schools, that is looking to get rid of the religious police, that is looking to finally come to some sort of equality. Our argument is that under the Taliban that never would have happened.

Observation four, the alternatives to inspection. Kyle says that, in fact, inspections probably wouldn't work, but the next argument he gives you is that that doesn't justify the war. However, I think that the failure of diplomacy, the failure of inspections, and the lack of good alternatives coming out of the opposition team only proves to justify the point Michael and I are making, that war is our only alternative in this case, and that only through military actions can we repeal and destroy this oppressive regime. The next argument he makes is that there are other means, again, this is the same tired argument he's been making throughout his entire speech, yet he doesn't tell you what those other means are. I say, until they do, they, in fact, don't have any sort of an argument with respect to other means.

The last thing that I want you to pay attention to comes on the moral level, and that's the C point to this position. That the United States has a unique responsibility to take care of the problem that we helped create in Iraq. Remember, Michael's analysis comes out quite clearly in the PMC, that if we don't act now, we condemn the Iraqi people to a life of persecution, to a life of human rights violations.

This war is morally justified now. The actor of the United States has moral reasons to do it now, and has to live up to its moral responsibility. Ladies and Gentlemen, for those reasons, the war in Iraq is just.

SECOND OPPOSITION CONSTRUCTIVE SPEECH (8 MINUTES)

I too would like to extend my thanks to some of those who have not been mentioned, specifically Tom Custer for serving as NPDA president, and the work that Brent Northrup and (. . .) and the other executives who maintain that this organization functions as an organization, and to give us the ability to have a large tournament where we all get together. So thank you.

Specifically, the other members of the PLU squad, I feel that Kyle and I being here is only a representation of all of the work that we do together, and I am indebted to you, and I hope that we, I know that we will keep in touch, and this is more than just an activity where we talk too much.

But finally, I would like to thank Kyle, and realizing that indeed you have been a fantastic partner, and it's been a great three years.

And, to my first debate coach, my father, who made the mistake of teaching his daughter how to argue better than he does, which he regrets every day.

Now, the government team in today's debate sets up a situation where they say that we're obligated to other people, and that we can justify our obligations by saying that any inaction is bad, and therefore any action is justified. I think in today's debate that that's not enough to justify war, and specifically, when Kyle and I say that we have to have a higher standard. At the point where we can't guarantee that we're going to look to the human rights violations, and actually make life better for the Iraqi people, we can't justify this action by simply saying that inaction isn't an option either, and that fundamentally, in today's debate, you won't see that they've upheld the warrant for the resolution.

Beginning up at the top of case, they begin by laying out burdens, and they say that all they have to do is say that the current situation is unjust, and that they violate rights. But, no, I think they have to do more than that, right, they actually have to provide you a framework in the real world that says that these types of things are going to be resolved.

It's one nice thing to say that we want to act ethically and morally, but how are we going to guarantee, given the real framework we exist in, the Bush government, for better or worse, that any of these human rights abuses that they talk about are actually going to be resolved, after this war? I don't think they've provided you any warrant or justification why any of these things fundamentally change. And at that point, simply because they've attacked their neighbors in the past, isn't a justification for us to go to war with them. In order . . . with that, I'll take your point.

Question: Okay, so does that mean, that, in fact, if you knew people were dying, and you went to try to save them but couldn't save them, then your actions wouldn't be morally justified?

Answer: No. What I'm saying, specifically, is one, you haven't articulated how people are dying, right now, you talk about historical examples, but you haven't proven this now, nor have you proven that the Bush administration and other people will actually be able to fundamentally resolve any of these issues, after the war. All you've done is created a situation where we justify killing them now, but we don't know what end that's actually going to get us to. Why can we justify this means when we don't know the end?

Moving on to (. . .). Kyle argues that we are assuming that we speak on behalf of these people, but we don't actually know this. They say it's untrue if we look at news analysis, one, I think that those are U.S. analysts, but more importantly, how can we begin to know these things? How can we know what our obligations to these other people is, and, more importantly, they've never shown you how we actually resolve these within the real world framework that we talk about. We see that this type of action only justifies any means to get to this type of utopic end, a utopic end that they never show you that the Bush administration will actually get us to. Now, they later say that this isn't important, that they're not confined to the Bush administration, or their rhetoric. I think that this is fundamentally inaccurate, at the point where we're justifying war, we're justifying the actual killing of individuals, but without knowing the end that they talk about. It's really great, they talk about inaction is bad, action is good. But if we don't know what the action actually gets us, we have to look pragmatically at the fact that we're killing people, and we don't know what it gets. We don't know what the end is for, and at that point, this type of idea that any action is justified only promotes things like the end justifies the means. This justifies things like genocide, as Kyle points out, at the point where we can say "well, we think it would be better for them, and therefore we're going to act in this manner." I'm sorry, not at this point.

Moving on to the first point, we then talk about how war is not the only option, and indeed there are others. And, for example, Kyle talks about how we could lift the sanctions and we could have aid. Now, he says why would we do this if we have a dictator who's misused the Oil-for-Food program? Well, one, I think that this is a viable option, when you realize we could lift sanctions, meaning we're no longer hurting the individuals within this country, and then we could set up a framework where not only are we getting rid of some of the human rights abuses, but actually having people who can stay alive, because they've asked for things like food, but that we also set up a framework where maybe we could have better diplomatic situations, that we can have diplomacy, that we can have inspections that actually get rid of those types of weapons of mass destruction, rather than providing a justification for them to be used. With that, I'll take your question.

Question: Okay, in 1988, we had no sanctions, and we were giving that government aid. Saddam then gassed a whole bunch of Kurds. Like, why has the empirics of that situation not proven that aid and a lack of sanctions still just don't stop an evil man?

Answer: After 1988, we had a war, and we didn't prove that that stopped an evil man either.

Kyle goes on to say that we need to demonstrate more than a motivation, we have to, they would have to legitimize a motivation to help that would actually justify the types of ends and create the utopic situation they talk about. They say, well, they're not tied to the Bush administration, but they are, we're in the real world, this war is occurring on the terms of the international community, they have to support that those actions are justified. They don't ever do that, they say that, you know, some action might be good, but they don't show us what means that gets us.

Which brings me on to the next contention about the war in Iraq. They talk about how democracy is good, but I don't think that they ever get us to a point where we can assume effective democracy is put into place. They talk about a situation like Germany or Japan, but Kyle does a good job of showing you that this isn't Germany, right, we decimated their entire country, that this would be the type of action that they would be justifying, and most specifically, that it be more likely that we have a situation like in Afghanistan, where we see that the warlords are making the decisions in that Jirga, that's it's not a situation where we have people actually making their own democratically elected decisions, and we haven't stopped any of the human rights violations that they indict. This is where, on the pragmatic level, that we shouldn't be justifying a war, because we don't know what ends might actually happen, and, indeed, that decimation becomes a reason that we wouldn't want to have war, that we might want to explore other options that don't require us to kill a whole lot of people in the name of "well, we don't know exactly what we're getting," and specifically, when we look at the coalition, they say yes, we admit that the coalition (. . .), but no one has come forward to say exactly what they're going to do about it. An oil trust fund? That doesn't guarantee democracy. That isn't an international commitment. What, in the end of today's debate, can we justify killing these people over? I don't think we have any guarantees that, indeed, one, nobody said that there isn't going to be Saddam Hussein, two, there isn't going to be racism against the Kurds, or three, that any of the bigger issues are fundamentally going to be resolved. I don't think they can justify that, and at that point, an ethical consideration that there might be a justification isn't enough. They need to prove that we actually increase and actually can act upon in these peoples' interests. I think that becomes pretty clear.

Moving on to the inspections. They say that there's been a failure of alternatives. I think that Kyle and I say that there are still alternatives, that, for example, we haven't tried lifting the sanctions, that we haven't tried more diplomatic measures, and indeed, the fact that, at one point, we justified this war in order to get more weapons inspectors into the country, and then, actually, later had the war and made the weapons inspectors leave, only justifies this idea that we don't know what we're fundamentally stopping in today's debate.

Now finally, they say that the United States has a unique responsibility because we helped create it. I think, in today's debate, this is what you have to remember, that, yes, we created this, and I don't think they've fundamentally shown us the United States has said that we're going to take an active role to overcome it, and that we're not simply going to recreate another problem, right? I think that this is at the level where we haven't seen that we're fundamentally going to get rid of this, these same human rights abuses, nor have we shown in today's debate what the real type of democracy, or lack of human rights, or the real results of what the situation in Iraq is, and without this type of justification, I don't think that you see, indeed, that the war in Iraq that is currently occurring is just.

Opposition Rebuttal Speech (4 minutes)

I think that these two debaters from the University of Wyoming are astoundingly talented, gifted individuals, who have contributed a lot to our community, and they deserve your congratulations.

It is a great pleasure to take part in this activity. I think I've forgotten like a million people to thank. I love you guys.

Oh, and one purely self-indulgent moment. My last name is "Mach." I don't blame you. I've never corrected anybody.

What we see pretty clearly is that the government intends for you to do two things when you evaluate this round. The first thing that they want you to do is naturally assume that the war will take place in the way in which they want the war to take place. The next thing that they want you to assume is that there are simply no other alternatives besides inaction and full-scale invasion of another nation. We, I think, have conclusively demonstrated that there are not only other options besides war, but that in addition to that, in the real world conditions that we see, the way that the war actually is, we just don't see the kind of commitments that they say are really needed in order to make the war a just action.

Let's start with the first real issue, and that is simply there are other options, there is a third way besides choosing inaction or war. They focus a lot on this idea of simply giving them aid, right, but we talk about stuff like, for example, lifting the sanctions, which is a little bit of a joke, right, because he killed the Kurds with the weapons we gave him, when we lifted the sanctions, but what we're telling you is that these options do exist, that in the case of Iraq, we simply have not pursued them to the degree that we ought to have, in order to actually justify the wholesale slaughter of individuals within another nation, and that before we can justify the war in Iraq, we need to be more convinced that these options have been effectively exhausted, and the basic fact, that we've sent weapons inspectors into the nation of Iraq, is not a sufficient justification to demonstrate the fact that other alternatives still do not exist, right, this is a difficult burden for us to outline what that policy should be, but it's a more difficult burden for them to demonstrate that war can be justified when you might even be able to consider that peace is a possibility instead.

The next thing that we see pretty clearly, in a second here, is that history simply does not tell us that we will be effective as a coalition, in actually doing any of the things that they say are necessary in order to actually justify a war. This is where we have this Afghanistan, Germany comparison, right? We tell you the war in Iraq is going to be fought like Afghanistan, and what do we see in Afghanistan? The first thing we see is elections. Yeah, by the warlords that still control eighty per cent of the country. The next thing that we see, very importantly, is that the United States' commitment to the rebuilding of Afghanistan, that the united commitment to rebuilding Afghanistan, is decreasing every day, that every day we decrease our long-term commitment to this nation. I mean, hey, now it's all about Iraq, right, that's what we're talking about. Afghanistan simply hasn't seen the long run focus that's actually necessary to rebuild this country. Now, they attempted to prove this by extending this idea about Germany, and how great it was that we were able to rebuild this country, but they ignore all the profound differences, right, this was a nation that had an amazing economic and industrial infrastructure before we actually destroyed this country, something Iraq doesn't have, except for oil. The next thing that they, of course, ignore, is that in order to rebuild Germany and Japan, we leveled them, we absolutely, utterly destroyed this nation, and I would tell you that you can't justify that action in order to get some kind of hypothetical end of democracy, which I don't think we'll see.

The last thing that we really see, is the final voting issue, and this is pretty important, is that they need to justify, and demonstrate, more than just that the war could be justified, but that it is, according to the terms on which it's being fought now. This is important. The first thing that we look to is that Bush has continually offered us different justifications for this war, so when they say, well, Bush has promised that we're going to rebuild Iraq, well, he's promised a lot of stuff, folks, right, we need to be convinced that this is actually going to take place in order for it to happen. The next thing we see is this oil example, that Bush has promised we're going to use the profits from oil to rebuild the country, only demonstrates that we aren't even making a commitment here, right? All we're saying is we're, you know, we're not going to take all of their oil away to rebuild their country. It's not the same thing as a broad, international coalition, coming together and saying "we are going to make a wholesale effort to make this country better than it is today." That's the Marshall Plan that we saw in Germany.

And finally, again, think about this in the long run. Do you think this commitment will last . . . how long? Not long enough. I urge you to vote for the opposition.

GOVERNMENT REBUTTAL SPEECH (5 MINUTES)

It's been a long eight years, so let me begin.

First, the opposition team in this round has no viable alternative. The mere fact that they list for you a couple of options that could work, possibly, maybe, is never going to be enough to beat back the analysis we give you in case. At the point where we're giving you legitimate reasons to believe that the removal of Saddam Hussein would work to stop his oppression of the Iraqis, and the fact that all that they can do is give you a couple of, "well, sanctions, maybe, or aid," is never going to beat back the analysis in case, and I'll show that when I get there. The next thing is that the opposition relies on the principle of uncertainty. They rely on the idea that we don't know for sure that we'll make things better. But let's talk about why we're always going to win that debate. First, every empirical example in this debate is on our side, and let's talk about the only one they even claim to win, which is Afghanistan. They drop Josh's arguments about how Afghanistan is not a utopia, it is not perfect, but it is better off now than it was before. That is not just the (. . .) of a democratically elected government, but for the work that Josh tells you that government is doing, in terms of women's rights and education, and at the point where they're not able to give you a single example of where U.S. intervention has made things worse, instead of not as good as it could be, doesn't mean that the current situation in Iraq is (. . .). The next thing, is that they tell you, I catch the phrase is Kyle's final speech, that we don't justify the "wholesale slaughter of Iraqi civilians," but I don't think that anywhere in this debate do they prove that that happens, or they show you any kind of quasi-problems that come from our intervention.

Having given that overview, let's go to the line-by-line. First, they tell you we can't guarantee that we will make life better. Even if Japan and Germany are different, we have made life better there, but in Afghanistan, they also drop our analysis. No, Afghanistan's not perfect, and Josh and I will never claim it is, but at the point that it's better, that certainly fulfills the moral obligation that we're giving you, and they don't address this. They tell you that Iraqi soldiers, or the Iraqi people are fighting against us, but first, this is always nonresponsive to my analysis in case, you don't really know the general sentiment of opinion in a repressed country. But secondly, they tell you "oh, this is just

U.S. analysts." That's not true, Josh tells you people all over the world are realizing that this is true. But additionally, the Iraqi opposition hasn't been huge people, rioting in the streets, it's been a couple of attacks on American soldiers. We tell you that those themselves are Iraqi soldiers.

Now, let's look at our obligation to the other. They tell you that it's better to lift the sanctions, that that probably would work, and in response to my question, Leah points out, well, we had a war and we didn't stop Saddam Hussein then, but let's talk about why we didn't stop him. Because the international coalition didn't want us to back then. The international coalition, especially Saudi Arabia, said "leave Saddam Hussein in power," another example of our following the wishes of others, instead of responding to our own ethical obligations.

They tell you that we have to be the Bush administration, but that is not true. Two people can agree on the same conclusion, and yet reach different reasons for why that conclusion is true. Yes, we have to defend this war. No, we do not have to defend the reasons that President Bush has given for it. We do defend Bush's actions, we do not have to defend his reasons for that. The resolution says that we must prove it is just, it does not say that we must prove the Bush administration is right, in everything it's ever said, and Josh and I are giving you a consistent story. We're showing you that intervention in terms of Saddam is always going to be better than inaction. Remember the arguments about perpetuity, that even if they were able to prove to you some kind of quantified number about how many civilians die in our initial action, they can't prove to you that that's not better than eternally letting Saddam stay there, because if their arguments are true today, they'll be true in ten years, and they'll be true in twenty.

Finally, let's go to our argument about how this requires military intervention. Their arguments are that warlords are still in Afghanistan. Yes, that's true. All this proves to you is that the United States is not perfect, is that military intervention won't always solve, but I tell you in my first speech that you can go to war in bad conscience. You can also stay out of war, you can also avoid your ethical obligation in worse conscience, and I don't think they give you a single example of how we make things worse. Germany and Japan might be different, but Afghanistan is very much the same. If it's true that every day our attention goes a little bit away from Afghanistan, that still isn't responsive to the argument that things in Afghanistan are better today than they were before the war. Warlords were there in Afghanistan before we intervened, it's not like we caused that problem to exist. What wasn't there was an education ministry, that was actually working to get women's right realized, to actually see them implemented. Additionally, they drop all of Josh's arguments about how the Bush administration has provided a plan to rebuild Iraq. That he has said he will set aside their oil. That that trust fund will be there. There's just not a response to this argument on your flow.

What I think this means to you in the end, is that uncertainty is never a justification to avoid ethical arguments. That our argument is they say do nothing. They give you a couple of brief ideas about what might work, but all the empirical analysis shows us that those things have failed in the past, and there's no reason to believe they would work in the future. Without development of those options, for the ethical reasons we give you, you vote for the University of Wyoming.

THE RESULTS

Seven judges evaluated the arguments presented by these debaters. On a vote of 4–3, the Government team represented by the University of Wyoming was declared the winner.

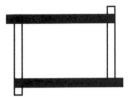

APPENDIX C
CASE STUDY FOR ANALYSIS

Kevin Cooper escaped from the California Institute for Men, a state prison in Chino, California, on June 2, 1983. He admitted that he hid for two days and two nights (part of the day on Thursday, Thursday night, Friday, and Friday night) in a vacant house (the Lease house) near the prison. On Saturday night four members of the Ryen family who lived next door to the Lease house were hacked to death and a fifth was left with serious injuries. Cooper was ultimately arrested and charged with four counts of first-degree murder and one count of attempted murder in the first degree, as well as with escape from state prison. On February 19, 1985, he was convicted of the crimes, and following a separate penalty hearing he was sentenced to death. On May 6, 1991, the California Supreme Court affirmed the convictions and the death sentence and the United States Supreme Court declined to hear the case. Cooper's attorneys continued to pursue additional and different appeals, however, alleging that there were serious errors made in the investigation of the case and in the presentation of evidence to the jury.

We have included an order filed by the United States Court of Appeals for the Ninth Circuit on February 8, 2004, for your analysis and study. This order provides a fascinating illustration of the intricacies and complexities of arguments in a legal forum. After reading the court's arguments, answer the following questions.

1. Identify the primary elements of the prosecution's narrative of the case. What was the motive attributed to the defendant? How did the prosecutor establish issues related to the defendant's means and opportunity to commit these crimes? What were the most compelling forms of evidence found to support a claim of guilt? How do you believe such evidence would likely influence jurors' perceptions of guilt or innocence? What elements of this evidence did you find less than fully convincing? Why?

2. Identify the primary elements of the defendant's narrative of the case. In what ways was the defendant's narrative incompatible with that offered by the prosecution? What evidence did the defendant offer to support his narrative? How effectively did the defendant's attorneys refute key elements of the prosecution's evidence? Why do you believe the jury failed to accept the defendant's position in the initial court proceedings? Why do these same claims find some support among the appellate justices?

3. What were the substantive questions of law and/or procedure advanced in this appeal? How did the different justices evaluate these arguments? What was the final court ruling? Do you agree or disagree with this ruling?

4. What arguments did you find to be missing from these transcripts? What additional arguments might you offer to support either the approval or the denial of a stay of execution?

5. How might your own personal political beliefs, ideology, experiences, or values influence your reading and evaluation of these arguments?

KEVIN COOPER, Petitioner, v. JEANNE WOODFORD, Warden, San Quentin State Prison, San Quentin, California, Respondent.*

Judges: Before: James R. Browning, Pamela Ann Rymer, and Ronald M. Gould, Circuit Judges. Order; Dissent by Judge Browning.

Order

Kevin Cooper, a California death row inmate whose execution is scheduled for Tuesday, February 10, 2004 at 12:01 a.m., has filed an application to file a successor petition for writ of habeas corpus under 28 U.S.C. § 2244(b)(3), and a request for stay of execution. His request for an order authorizing the district court to consider this petition—his third application [*2]† in the federal system following denial of his original habeas petition—is premised on the existence of evidence with respect to a blood spot, cigarette butts, and shoe print impressions that he asserts was manufactured by the state and which, if known to the jury, would have weakened the links in the state's chain of circumstantial evidence. He asks for another chance affirmatively to demonstrate his innocence through available mitochondrial DNA testing of hairs found in one of the victim's hands, and testing for the presence of a preservative agent EDTA on a T-shirt. However, with immaterial exceptions, this application turns on facts that have long since been known and that have already been presented and resolved adversely to Cooper in state court evidentiary hearings, proceedings before the California Supreme Court on direct and collateral review, in his original habeas petition in federal court, and in connection with his applications in this court to file second or successive petitions. To the extent that the claims are formulated differently in the petition he now asks to file, they are nevertheless based on facts that were available and could previously have been discovered [*3] with the exercise of due diligence. For this reason, Cooper fails to make the showing that the Anti-Terrorism and Effective Death Penalty Act of 1996 (AEDPA) requires for approval of his application. 28 U.S.C. § 2244(b)(3)(C).

---

* 357 F.3d 1019 (9th Cir. 2004) No. 04-70578; (February 8, 2004, Filed). Retrieved online 8/31/04 from LexisNexis.

† The starred numbers that appear in brackets represent itemized pieces of evidence introduced in the trial.

In addition, Cooper's petition does not set forth facts that are sufficient to show by clear and convincing evidence that, in light of the evidence as a whole, no reasonable factfinder would have found him guilty of the offenses charged. The few items of evidence upon which Cooper now relies that were not before the jury have little or no probative value and fall short of showing that it is more likely than not that no reasonable juror would have convicted him.

Cooper has made no showing of actual innocence, nor has he shown that it would be manifestly unjust for the courts to decline to revisit the same issues again. Accordingly, we deny the application to file this successive petition. Given this decision, there is no basis for granting a stay.

I.

On June 2, 1983, Cooper escaped from the California Institute for Men (CIM), a state prison.[1] He admitted that he stayed in a vacant house (the Lease house) next door to the Ryens' residence [*4] on Thursday night, all day Friday, and Friday night; he hid in the bathroom when one of the owners of the Lease house stopped by on Saturday morning. The murders happened Saturday night. Using a hatchet or axe and a knife, he hacked to death Douglas and Peggy Ryen (37 separate wounds for Douglas, 32 for Peggy), their ten-year-old-daughter Jessica (46 wounds), and eleven-year-old Christopher Hughes (26 wounds), who was spending the night at the Ryens' home. Cooper also inflicted chopping wounds to the head, and stabbing wounds to the throat, of eight-year-old Joshua Ryen, who survived.

At the Lease house, a blood-stained khaki green button identical to the buttons on field jackets issued at the state prison from which Cooper escaped was found on the rug. Tests revealed the presence of blood in the shower and bathroom sink of the Lease home, and hair found in the bathroom sink was consistent with that of Jessica and [*5] Doug Ryen. A bloodstained rope in the Lease house bedroom was similar to a bloodstained rope found on the Ryens' driveway. A hatchet covered with dried blood and human hair that was found near the Ryens' home was missing from the Lease house, and the sheath for the hatchet was found in the bedroom where Cooper stayed. Buck knives and at least one ice pick were also missing from the Lease home, though a strap from one buck knife was found on the floor.

Blood found in the Ryens' home was the victims', except for one drop on a wall near where the murders occurred. It belonged to an African-American male, which Cooper is. Two partial shoe prints and one nearly complete shoe print found in the Ryens' house were consistent both with Cooper's size and the Pro Keds shoes issued at CIM.

The Ryens' vehicle, which had been parked outside their house, was missing when the bodies were discovered but was later found in Long Beach. A hand-rolled cigarette butt and "Role-Rite" tobacco that is provided to inmates at CIM (but not sold at retail) was in the car. Similar loose leaf tobacco was found in the bedroom of the Lease house where Cooper had stayed. A witness testified that Cooper smoked hand-rolled [*6] cigarettes using Role-Rite tobacco. A hair fragment discovered in the car was consistent with Cooper's pubic hair and a spot of blood found in the car could have come from one of the victims but not from Cooper.

Cooper was charged with four counts of first degree murder and one count of attempted murder in the first degree, and with escape from state prison. He pled guilty to escaping from state prison. On February 19, 1985, a jury convicted Cooper of the first degree murders of Franklyn Douglas Ryen, Jessica Ryen, Peggy Ann Ryen and Christopher Hughes, and of attempted murder in the first degree of Joshua Ryen. The jury found true the special circumstance of multiple murders, which made Cooper death-eligible under California's sentencing scheme. The jury also found true the special circumstance that Cooper intentionally inflicted great bodily injury on Joshua Ryen. The jury then determined the penalty as death on the four murder counts. On May 6, 1991, the California Supreme Court affirmed the convictions and sentence. *See People v. Cooper,* 53 Cal. 3d 771, 281 Cal. Rptr. 90, 809 P.2d 865 (1991). The United States Supreme Court denied a petition for writ of certiorari on December 16, 1991. [*7] *Cooper v. California,* 502 U.S. 1016, 116 L. Ed. 2d 755, 112 S. Ct. 664 (1991).

On March 24, 1992 Cooper requested appointment of counsel and a stay of execution from the United States District Court for the Southern District of California. He then filed a petition for writ of habeas corpus in the district court on August 11, 1994, and an amended petition on April 12, 1996. Meanwhile, he returned to state court to exhaust a number of claims. On February 19, 1996, the California Supreme Court denied Cooper's state habeas petition. Cooper then filed a supplemental petition in district court on June 20, 1997. Following an evidentiary hearing, the petition was denied on August 25, 1997. We affirmed in *Cooper v. Calderon,* 255 F.3d 1104 (9th Cir. 2001), and Cooper's petition for a writ of certiorari was denied by the United States Supreme Court. 537 U.S. 861, 154 L. Ed. 2d 100, 123 S. Ct. 238 (2002). Cooper filed numerous additional papers in state court, and another federal petition for writ of habeas corpus on April 20, 1998. We treated his appeal from the district court's denial of that petition as an application for authorization to file a second or successive petition for writ of habeas [*8] corpus based on trial counsel's ineffective assistance with respect to the Koon confession, which we denied. *Cooper v. Calderon,* 274 F.3d 1270 (9th Cir. 2001). Cooper then filed a request to file another successor petition that involved DNA testing and tampering, which we also denied; *Cooper v. Calderon,* 2003 U.S. App. LEXIS 27035, No. 99-71430 (9th Cir. Feb. 14, 2003), 2003 U.S. App. LEXIS 27036 (Apr. 7, 2003) (orders).

Cooper has filed six writs of habeas corpus in the California Supreme Court, the most recent of which was filed on February 2, 2004 and denied February 5, 2004. The petition before the California Supreme Court raised similar claims to those asserted in this application (actual innocence, tampering with evidence, failure to disclose exculpatory evidence, offering unreliable eye witness testimony of Joshua Ryen, denying Cooper the effective assistance of counsel during post-conviction DNA proceedings, and refusal of the state superior court to accept his petition for filing). The supreme court denied all claims on the merits and also denied those having to do with evidence tampering, failure to disclose exculpatory evidence/submission of false testimony to the jury, and offering Ryen's unreliable testimony [*9] as untimely, *In re Robbins,* 18 Cal. 4th 770, 780, 77 Cal. Rptr. 2d 153, 959 P.2d 311 (1998).

II.

Cooper's application is governed by AEDPA. Under AEDPA, in order for us to grant Cooper's application to file a successive petition, he must present a claim that was not previously presented in a federal habeas petition, and that relies on either a new rule of constitutional law made retroactive to cases on collateral review by the Supreme Court, or a factual predicate which could not have been discovered through due diligence and that would be sufficient to establish by clear and convincing evidence that, but for constitutional error, no reasonable factfinder would have found him guilty of the offense. 28 U.S.C. § § 2244(b)(1), 2244(b)(2). We must decide whether his application makes a prima facie showing that satisfies these requirements. 28 U.S.C. § 2244(b)(3)(C).

Cooper argues that he has satisfied these prerequisites because evidence that he says is newly discovered through DNA proceedings, including evidence of false statements by the criminalist and continuing attempts to prevent Cooper from proving his innocence, provide factual predicates for compelling [*10] constitutional claims. As we will explain, findings by the state trial court after an evidentiary hearing are directly to the contrary. Cooper further contends that the evidence as a whole, including a confession by Kevin Koon, establishes by clear and convincing evidence that, but for the state's treachery, no reasonable factfinder would have been led to find Cooper guilty. As we will also explain, the district court found that the Koon confession would have had no effect on the outcome of the trial, and this court denied Cooper's request to file a second or successive petition on the same issue.

Further, Cooper submits that a claim is not subject to the requirements of § 2244(b) when the events that give rise to the claim occurred after resolution of the prior habeas petition. For this he relies on *Stewart v. Martinez-Villareal,* 523 U.S. 637, 644-45, 140 L. Ed. 2d 849, 118 S. Ct. 1618 (1998), and *Hill v. State of Alaska,* 297 F.3d 895, 898-99 (9th Cir. 2002). These cases are not helpful, however, because both involved issues such as competence to be executed that could not have been included in an earlier petition.

Finally, Cooper maintains that the requirements [*11] of § 2244(b)(2) need not be satisfied for a second or successive habeas corpus application to be considered by the district court because actual innocence is a constitutional safety valve. *See Schlup v. Delo,* 513 U.S. 298, 130 L. Ed. 2d 808, 115 S. Ct. 851 (1995); *Herrera v. Collins,* 506 U.S. 390, 122 L. Ed. 2d 203, 113 S. Ct. 853 (1993); *McCleskey v. Zant,* 499 U.S. 467, 113 L. Ed. 2d 517, 111 S. Ct. 1454 (1991). We do not decide in this case whether or not this is so, because as we shall explain, Cooper has neither affirmatively proven actual innocence nor shown that it is more likely than not that, in light of all the evidence, including reliable new evidence of actual innocence, no reasonable juror would have found him guilty beyond a reasonable doubt. *See Carriger v. Stewart,* 132 F.3d 463, 478 (9th Cir. 1997) (adopting this standard).

III.

The petition that Cooper asks for leave to file asserts nine claims. We consider them in turn.

Actual innocence (claim one). Cooper's application repeats his theory of defense—that he did not commit the murders and the prosecution provided no motive. He relies on evidence, or the lack of it, that he also relied [*12] upon at trial or presented in his first federal habeas petition and applications for second or successive petitions: that Joshua Ryen referred to several assailants and said he had never seen Cooper before; that three suspicious men were observed in the vicinity of the murders on the night they occurred; that the number of weapons used indicates multiple assailants were involved; that law enforcement ignored information about other possible suspects, in particular Diana Roper's that Lee Furrow (her boyfriend) may have participated in the murders and left "bloody" coveralls in her closet; that the police destroyed the coveralls; that the state ignored a purported confession by Kevin Koon; and that cigarette butts were tampered with. All of this, except perhaps for the cigarette butts (which we consider in connection with the second claim), has been known since the time of trial, but regardless, does not show that Cooper is probably innocent.

Evidence that Joshua Ryen said that three strangers had been at the house earlier looking for work and at one point said that he believed they may have been involved was before the jury. It lacks probative force given that he also testified that [*13] he only saw one person in the house when the murders occurred. Other people could have been at the house, too, yet Cooper's innocence would not be shown because his blood was on the wall and strong circumstantial evidence connected him with the house and the Ryens' car. Cooper's reliance on the Roper evidence is misplaced, because that evidence would show that Roper had a "vision" that the coveralls might have some importance to the

Ryen murders, and that the law enforcement official to whom the coveralls were given believed they looked stained but not *blood*-stained. That officer testified at an evidentiary hearing in state court that the coveralls had hair, sweat, dirt, and manure on them. He testified similarly at trial. Thus, the evidence *was* considered by the jury. In addition, both the state trial court after an evidentiary hearing, and the district court on Cooper's first habeas petition, determined that the coveralls had no exculpatory value at the time they were destroyed and that there was no factual basis for finding any bad faith on the part of the prosecutor or sheriff. The first federal petition likewise resolved that the Koon "confession" was not material. Another [*14] inmate (Anthony Wisely) told officers that Koon confessed, but Koon himself said that he had not. It is not more likely than not that no reasonable juror would have found Cooper guilty based on this.

Cooper points to one piece of evidence that is newly discovered, that an inmate at the Chino Institute for Men where Cooper was incarcerated before his escape recanted (on January 8, 2004) his trial testimony that he gave Cooper a pair of Pro Keds tennis shoes shortly before Cooper escaped. Even if the inmate's recantation could not have been discovered previously through the exercise of due diligence, this evidence alone lacks clear and convincing force and is not sufficient to show that no reasonable fact-finder would have found Cooper guilty if this fact had been known. The same applies to Cooper's claim that evidence exists that Pro Keds shoes were also available to the military and were not special-issue to CIM. The reason is that no matter what the source of the shoes, the same print impression was found outside the Ryen master bedroom, on a sheet on the Ryen bedroom waterbed, and in the game room of the Lease house. This connected Cooper, who stayed in the Lease house, to the scene [*15] of the crime. Considered in light of all the evidence, the newly discovered recantation would not be sufficient to establish that no reasonable juror would have found Cooper guilty.

Cooper's successive petition also alleges that his innocence would be manifest by mitochondrial DNA testing on blond hair clutched by one of the victims and EDTA testing on a bloody T-shirt, and would have been manifest but for mishandling of Exhibit A-41 (the blood spot found in the hallway of the Ryens' home), cigarette butts from the Ryen car and the Lease house, and a shoe impression. Information about how the exhibits were treated and tested is not newly discovered. Dr. Gregonis, the criminalist who analyzed the blood spot (Exhibit A-41), was extensively cross-examined at trial about his analysis and about the fact that he had changed his original analysis. The trial court found after an evidentiary hearing that all tests had been conducted in good faith. The post-conviction DNA testing claims were also before us, and resolved, in connection with Cooper's application for a second and successive petition. That application (in Case No. 99-71430) and Cooper's request for us to reconsider our denial of [*16] it, which we treated as if it were a new application, were based on DNA testing, asserted deficiencies in the testing process, and tampering. We concluded that there was no basis for a petition based on any of these claims. *Cooper v. Calderon*, 2003 U.S. App. LEXIS 27035, Case No. 99-71430 (9th Cir. Feb. 14, 2003) (noting that DNA tests to which the state and Cooper agreed are not exculpatory and denying motion to file a second habeas corpus petition as Cooper failed to present newly discovered facts establishing his innocence); *Cooper v. Calderon*, 2003 U.S. App. LEXIS 27036, Case No. 99-71430 (9th Cir. Apr. 7, 2003) (order denying Cooper's petition for rehearing that was based on asserted deficiencies in the testing and tampering). These issues may not be revisited. 28 U.S.C. § 2244(b)(1).

In addition, there was a three-day evidentiary hearing in June 2003 with respect to whether further mitochondrial testing was warranted on the hairs in the victims' hands, and whether law enforcement personnel tampered with or contaminated the evidence that was analyzed using nuclear DNA testing. The trial court found that Cooper had not shown that mtDNA testing of the hairs recovered from the victims' hands was material [*17] to the identity of the perpetrator, and that even if the results were favorable to him, it would not create a reasonable probability that a different verdict would have been returned by the jury. The trial court also found that Gregonis (and other San Bernardino officials) credibly testified as to the chain of custody of the evidence in question, that Gregonis did not contaminate or tamper with any piece of evidence, and that Cooper made no showing that law enforcement personnel tampered with or contaminated any evidence in his case. *Order Denying Motion For Mitochondrial DNA Testing, Claim of Evidence Tampering, and Request for Post-Conviction Discovery,* Case No. CR 72787 (Superior Court of the State of California in and for the County of San Diego, July 2, 2003). These findings are presumptively correct, 28 U.S.C. § 2254(e)(1), and no clear and convincing evidence alleged by Cooper rebuts them.[2]

[*18]

Evidence tampering, destruction, and withholding (claim two). Cooper argues that the heart of his claim is that the state at trial, and through today, continues a pattern of deception and manipulation of evidence, inept and corrupt practices, and concealing official misconduct. In particular, he faults the work of criminalist Daniel Gregonis about most of which, as his application notes, the courts are well aware. The application points to newer evidence that Gregonis and Department of Justice criminalist Myers mishandled and contaminated evidence in 1999 and thereafter in connection with DNA testing, that Gregonis tampered with Exhibit A-41, that the state failed to deal with other blood samples in the vicinity of Exhibit A-41, that cigarette butts were mishandled, that evidence (such as the footprint, and sheath) were planted, and that leads were not pursued. The application also asserts that some of the officials involved in the investigation of the Cooper case were themselves at some time the subject of criminal investigations, the most significant of which in his view was San Bernardino Sheriff's Department Crime Lab manager William Baird. The district court already considered [*19] Cooper's allegation that the prosecution should have informed him about Baird's termination from the Sheriff's Department in 1988 (three years after the trial and five years after the investigation occurred), and determined that there was no *Brady* or *Agurs* violation[3] and no reasonable probability that, had the evidence been disclosed, the result of the proceeding would have been different. That other officials have been investigated for matters unrelated to the Cooper case is largely irrelevant. Cooper suggests that the *Brady* duty extends through post-conviction proceedings, but even if so the duty would be to disclose information that was material to trial. Finally, so far as tampering with the DNA testing (which occurred during post-conviction proceedings) is concerned, the state trial court determined in its evidentiary hearing that Cooper's claims lacked merit, and we resolved in connection with Cooper's motion for a second habeas corpus petition that nothing claimed about the DNA testing satisfies the requirements for a second or successive application.

[*20]

Failure to disclose exculpatory evidence (claim three). Cooper's application asserts that the prosecution knew about, and suppressed, Baird's alleged heroin use, failed to disclose information that three Hispanic males who were in jail on other charges in the summer of 1984 discussed their participation in the Ryen murders, and that the warden did not think that the tennis shoes that left the prints were particularly unique. However, none of this information is newly discovered.

Unreliable or altered testimony of Joshua Ryen (claim four). Cooper claims that Joshua Ryen's perceptions and recollections changed and were unduly influenced by law enforcement. Cooper also claims that the state's interference deprived him of relevant testimony. However, this is not newly discovered.

Denial of access to the courts (claim five). Cooper claims that he was denied access to the courts because the state trial court refused on January 23, 2004 to accept his most recent petition for writ of habeas corpus and two discovery motions, and the California Supreme Court denied his petition without requesting informal briefing. We discern no constitutional violation cognizable on federal habeas [*21] review. There is nothing untoward about the superior court deferring to the supreme court, particularly given the time exigencies involved, and Cooper's claims were adjudicated by the supreme court on the merits. The superior court had already denied Cooper's request for additional, mitochondrial DNA testing and found that it would shed no light on the outcome of the trial.

Evidence about bloody coveralls (claim six). As Cooper acknowledges, the claim regarding the destruction of the bloody coveralls has been raised in every available forum, and has been denied in every forum.

Ineffective assistance of counsel (claims seven, eight and nine). Cooper raises three claims that he was denied effective assistance of counsel with respect to the Koon confession, the bloody coveralls together with Lee Furrow's possible participation in the murders, and evidence of brown and blond hairs in the victims' hands that could not have come from Cooper. Nothing averred about the Koon confession is newly discovered. We previously determined that an ineffective assistance claim based on it would be a second or successive petition and denied leave to proceed with respect to it. *Cooper v. Calderon*, 274 F.3d at 1275. [*22] In any event, as the district court determined, the Koon confession was not material so even if counsel were deficient, there would be no prejudice. Nor is there anything new about connecting the coveralls to Lee Furrow or the fact that the victims were clutching hairs or fibers differently colored from Cooper's.

Either because the claims were previously raised and are now barred, 28 U.S.C. § 2244(b)(1), or were previously known or discoverable, 28 U.S.C. § 2244(b)(2)(B)(i), and because the facts underlying the claims in light of the evidence as a whole do not show clearly and convincingly that no reasonable factfinder would have found Cooper guilty, 28 U.S.C. § 2244(b)(2)(B)(ii), Cooper's application fails to satisfy the requirements of AEDPA and must be dismissed.

IV.

Cooper argues that apart from AEDPA, he has shown actual innocence sufficient to preclude imposition of the death penalty, *Herrera*, 506 U.S. 390, 122 L. Ed. 2d 203, 113 S. Ct. 853, or that he has at least made a strong enough showing of innocence to permit consideration of procedurally barred claims under *Schlup*, 513 U.S. 298, 130 L. Ed. 2d 808, 115 S. Ct. 851. [*23] *Carriger*, 132 F.3d 463. We do not believe that the standard for either is met.

There are two types of actual innocence claims. A free-standing claim of actual innocence does not require due diligence, and protects the entirely innocent. The threshold for establishing actual innocence regardless of constitutional error at trial is "extraordinarily high." *Carriger*, 132 F.3d at 476 (quoting *Herrera*, 506 U.S. at 417 (O'Connor, J., concurring)). We have held that it is higher than the standard to invalidate a conviction because of insufficient evidence, which is that no rational finder of fact could convict beyond a reasonable doubt in light of all the presently available evidence. *Id.* Rather, a freestanding claim of innocence requires affirmative proof of innocence. *Id.* Put differently, a petitioner making a freestanding claim of actual innocence "must present evidence of innocence so strong that his execution would be 'constitutionally intolerable even if his conviction was the product of a fair trial.'" *Id.* at 478 (quoting *Schlup*, 513 U.S. at 316).

Cooper has not affirmatively proved his actual [*24] innocence by "'reliable evidence not presented at trial.'" *Calderon v. Thompson*, 523 U.S. 538, 559, 140 L. Ed. 2d

728, 118 S. Ct. 1489 (1998) (quoting *Schlup,* 513 U.S. at 324). At most he alleges the stuff of which cross-examination is made, not evidence that he did not do it. *See Carriger,* 132 F.3d at 477 ("Although the postconviction evidence he presents casts a vast shadow of doubt over the reliability of his conviction, nearly all of it serves only to undercut the evidence presented at trial, not affirmatively to prove Carriger's innocence.").

However, "while a petitioner making a *Herrera* claim must present evidence of innocence so strong that his execution would be 'constitutionally intolerable *even if* his conviction was the product of a fair trial,' a petitioner making a miscarriage of justice claim need only present evidence of innocence strong enough 'that a court cannot have confidence in the outcome of the trial *unless* the court is also satisfied that the trial was free of nonharmless constitutional error.'" *Carriger,* 132 F.3d at 478 (quoting *Herrera,* 506 U.S. at 442-44 (Blackmun, J., dissenting)) [*25] (italics in original) (internal quotation marks omitted). To permit consideration of a procedurally barred claim, a petitioner must show that "in light of all the evidence, including new evidence, 'it is more likely than not that no reasonable juror would have found petitioner guilty beyond a reasonable doubt.'" *Id.* (quoting *Schlup,* 513 U.S. at 327).

Other circuits have stated that the *Schlup* "gateway" has been codified in AEDPA and requires a petitioner to show a factual predicate which could not have been discovered through due diligence, and that would be sufficient to establish by clear and convincing evidence that, but for constitutional error, no reasonable factfinder would have found him guilty of the offense. *See, e.g., David v. Hall,* 318 F.3d 343, 347 n.5 (1st Cir. 2003) ("In AEDPA Congress adopted a form of actual innocence test as one component of its threshold requirements for allowing a second or successive habeas petition; but it also provided that this second petition is allowed only where the factual predicate for the claim of constitutional error could not have been discovered previously through the exercise of due diligence. [*26] ") (citing 28 U.S.C. § 2244(b)(2)(B)); *Flanders v. Graves,* 299 F.3d 974, 977 (8th Cir. 2002) (stating that the *Schlup* "gateway" to consider otherwise procedurally barred claims is "partially codified" in AEDPA at § 2244(b)(2)(B)(ii); *see also In re Minarik,* 166 F.3d 591, 600 (3rd Cir. 1999) (stating that AEDPA "significantly altered" the showing a petitioner is "required to make in order to proceed on new claims in a second petition," by requiring a petitioner to show actual innocence and that the factual predicate for the claim could not have been previously discovered through due diligence); *cf. United States v. Barrett,* 178 F.3d 34, 48 (1st Cir. 1999) (referring to the "actual innocence" exception to the bar on second or successive petitions as part of the pre-AEDPA test).

Were we to adopt this reasoning of other circuits, Cooper's lack of due diligence would foreclose his actual-innocence-as-a-gateway argument. But we do not need to resolve this question because Cooper cannot show actual innocence under either the "clear and convincing" AEDPA § 2244(b)(2)(B)(ii) requirement, or the "more likely than [*27] not" *Schlup* requirement. To the extent that AEDPA does not codify *Schlup,* we believe for the same reasons that no sufficient showing for a second or successive application is made, that none is made for purposes of *Schlup.*

In addition to what we have already explained, even if Cooper were entirely correct that the post-conviction DNA testing to which he agreed was deficient, and even if Dan Gregonis, the San Bernardino County criminalist who Cooper claims contaminated evidence to incriminate him did contaminate evidence to which he had access, the *other* items of evidence to which the criminalist did *not* have access also inculpate Cooper. That would include a hand-rolled cigarette butt recovered from the Ryen station wagon, a hatchet (one of the murder weapons) with blood and hair evidence, that part of the blood-stained T-shirt which matched Cooper's DNA, and a blood-stained button found in the Lease house. Of course, the jury convicted Cooper without the benefit of DNA evidence, and a reasonable jury could find him guilty even without the incriminating results and even if cross-examination of the criminalist would show that he was negligent or corrupt or both [*28] in connection with it. In any event, the state trial court explicitly found that no such conduct occurred. Finally, there is no reasonable likelihood that mitochondrial DNA testing would be probative of innocence, for any number of people could have come and gone through the Ryen house leaving hairs.

In sum, neither singly nor in combination do these items establish Cooper's innocence, or show that it is more likely than not that no reasonable juror would have convicted him in light of the new evidence. To the contrary, there was clear and compelling evidence that linked Cooper to the crime. After escaping from prison, he stayed at the Lease house that was next door to the Ryens' home; his blood was found on the hallway wall opposite the master bedroom door of the Ryen house; shoe print impressions in the Lease house matched the pattern of prison-issued shoes and one of them was bloody; cigarette butts and tobacco in the Lease house and Ryens' station wagon were prison-issued; a blood-stained khaki green button identical to buttons on field jackets worn by inmates at Chino Institute for Men was found on the rug in the bedroom that Cooper used in the Lease house after the murders; [*29] a hatchet was missing from the Lease house and its sheath was found in the bedroom that Cooper used; and that bedroom and its bathroom, which had been cleaned earlier that day, showed signs of blood after the murders. *See People v. Cooper,* 53 Cal.3d at 795-800 (detailing the evidence of guilt).

As we deny Cooper's application for authorization to file this successor petition, and no other ground appears for issuing a stay, we also deny his request for a stay of execution.

APPLICATION DENIED.

DISSENT: James R. Browning, Senior Circuit Judge

Kevin Cooper is scheduled to be executed at one minute after midnight on Tuesday, February 10, 2004. He seeks two things.

First, Cooper wants to test two pieces of blood evidence for the presence of a preservative. Recent DNA tests of a blood spot and a bloody t-shirt have produced a positive DNA match for Cooper. Cooper contends there has been tampering and that his blood was placed on the evidence after it was collected. A simple and inexpensive test for a preservative in the blood will determine whether he is correct. The test would show whether the blood on the spot and on the t-shirt had [*30] a chemical used by crime laboratories to preserve blood samples in their possession.

Second, Cooper wants to test strands of long blond or light brown hair found clutched in the hand of Jessica Ryen, one of the murder victims. We already know the hair did not come from Cooper, an African-American. Cooper contends Jessica pulled the hair from one of her killers. Photographs in the record clearly show that the amount of hair is substantial, and it is clutched in Jessica's hand. The test could rule out the hair having come from one of the victims. There is evidence in the record to indicate that the crime was committed by three Caucasian men. Thus the test could also corroborate that evidence.

The State has been asked to permit these two tests, but refuses. As justification for its refusal, it states that Cooper had a fair trial, that the evidence of Cooper's guilt is overwhelming, and that it needs to proceed with Cooper's execution.

Contrary to the State's assurances, Cooper did not have a fair trial. Cooper has presented a sworn declaration of a state prison warden that, if believed, suggests that the State fabricated crucial evidence linking Cooper to the murders for which he has [*31] been convicted. Nor is the evidence of Cooper's guilt overwhelming. Indeed, as the evidence mounts that the State used unreliable and fabricated evidence to convict Cooper, the evidence of his guilt correspondingly diminishes.

There should be no hurry to execute Cooper. If he is truly guilty, these simple tests will resolve the matter. If he is truly innocent, those same tests will tell us that. When the stakes are so high, when the evidence against Cooper is so weak, and when the newly discovered evidence of the State's malfeasance and misfeasance is so compelling, there is no reason to hurry and every reason to find out the truth.

I. Nature of the Current Proceedings

Cooper has applied for authorization to file a second or successive petition for habeas corpus under 28 U.S.C. § 2244(b)(3)(A). We must grant authorization if we find that Cooper has made a *prima facie* case for relief under a second or successive petition. "By '*prima facie* showing' we understand simply a sufficient showing of *possible* merit to warrant a fuller exploration by the district court." *Woratzeck v. Stewart,* 118 F.3d 648, 650 (9th Cir. 1997) (quoting *Bennett v. United States,* 119 F.3d 468, 469 (7th Cir. 1997)) [*32] (emphasis added).

There are two possible standards that Cooper must satisfy.

First, if Cooper's claims are entirely governed by 28 U.S.C. § 2244 because he is seeking to file a second or successive petition, he must show that

> (B)(i) the factual predicate for the claim could not have been discovered previously through the exercise of due diligence; and

> (ii) the facts underlying the claim, if proven and viewed in light of the evidence as a whole, would be sufficient to establish by clear and convincing evidence that, but for constitutional error, no reasonable factfinder would have found the applicant guilty of the underlying offense.

28 U.S.C. §§ 2244(b)(2)(B)(i) and (ii).

Cooper has presented newly discovered evidence, including evidence of a constitutional violation in the form of a significant violation of *Brady v. Maryland,* 373 U.S. 83, 10 L. Ed. 2d 215, 83 S. Ct. 1194 (1963). Based on the record before us, there is a *prima facie* case that Cooper could not previously have discovered this evidence through the exercise of due diligence. In addition, Cooper has presented previously known evidence that is newly relevant [*33] because of intervening events since he last sought authorization to file a second or successive petition. Cooper's new evidence constitutes a "factual predicate" for the claims he seeks to present in his petition for habeas corpus. If Cooper's new evidence is believed and "viewed in light of the evidence as a whole," he has made out a *prima facie* case that such evidence would be "sufficient to establish by clear and convincing evidence that, but for constitutional error, no reasonable factfinder would have found him guilty of the underlying offense." 28 U.S.C. § 2244(b)(2)(B)(ii).

Second, if Cooper's claims are governed by the more lenient standard of *Schlup v. Delo,* 513 U.S. 298, 130 L. Ed. 2d 808, 115 S. Ct. 851 (1995), he need not satisfy the "clear and convincing evidence" requirement of § 2244(b)(2)(B)(ii). As long as he has satisfied the requirement of § 2244(b)(2)(B)(i) that the factual predicate of his claim "could not have been discovered previously through the exercise of due diligence," *Schlup* would require only that he "show that it is more likely than not that no reasonable juror would have convicted him in the light of the new evidence." [*34] 513 U.S. at 327. If Cooper's new evidence is believed, and considered in light of the record as a whole, Cooper has made out a *prima facie* case that would entitle him to relief under the "more likely than not" standard of *Schlup.*

We do not need to decide whether the "clear and convincing evidence" standard of § 2244(b)(2)(B)(ii) or the "more likely than not standard" of *Schlup* applies. Cooper has made out a *prima facie* case under either standard.

II. Background

On June 2, 1983, Cooper escaped from the minimum security area of the California Institute for Men ("CIM") where he was incarcerated. He broke into and hid in an empty house in Chino Hills, about two miles away, in San Bernardino County, southeast of Los Angeles. The house was owned by a man named "Lease." Cooper made telephone calls from the Lease house to his girlfriend asking for money, but she refused to help him. Cooper's last call from the house was at about 8:00 pm on June 4.

The Ryens lived next door, about 125 yards away from the Lease house. During the night of June 4, 1983, the members of the Ryen household were viciously attacked. Doug and Peggy Ryen, the father and mother, were [*35] killed, as were their ten-year-old daughter, Jessica, and an eleven-year-old house-guest, Chris Hughes. Doug and Peggy's eight-year-old son, Josh, was left for dead but survived. The bodies of Doug, Peggy, Jessica, and Chris, as well as the still-living Josh, were discovered the next day by Chris's father. All of the murder victims were killed by multiple chopping, cutting, and puncture wounds. Josh suffered the same type of wounds. Jessica was found clutching a substantial amount of long blond or light brown hair in her hand, some of which had roots attached.

Cooper was apprehended at the end of July 1983, and he was tried for capital murder in late 1984 and early 1985. Cooper took the stand and testified that he was innocent. He has consistently maintained his innocence. Cooper testified at trial that he never went to the Ryen house. He testified that he left the Lease house after that last phone call at 8:00 pm on June 4 and hitchhiked to Mexico. Uncontradicted evidence at trial indicated that Cooper checked into a hotel in Tijuana at about 4:30 pm the next day, June 5. After seven days of deliberation, the jury found Cooper guilty of death-eligible first degree murder. After four [*36] additional days of deliberation, the jury sentenced Cooper to death.

III. Newly Discovered Evidence

Cooper seeks authorization to file a second or successive habeas application based on newly discovered evidence. Cooper attaches two new sworn declarations, both signed in January 2004, which, if believed, would indicate that crucial evidence may have been fabricated. Evidence presented at trial showed that Cooper left a bloody shoe print on a sheet in the Ryens' bedroom. A newly presented declaration by the then-Warden of CIM at Chino, if believed, demonstrates both that the State committed a clear violation of *Brady v. Maryland*, and that the State likely fabricated the evidence of the shoe print.

Cooper also presents new evidence, as well as pre-existing but newly relevant evidence, pertaining to recent DNA testing by the State. In 2001, the State tested three items of evidence for the presence of Cooper's DNA: a blood spot in the hallway of the Ryen house; blood on a t-shirt found beside the road three days after the murders; and saliva on two hand-rolled cigarettes the State claims to have found in the Ryens' abandoned station wagon. Cooper seeks additional testing of the [*37] blood to determine if a preservative is present. The presence of a preservative would show that Cooper's blood was planted. If believed, Cooper's evidence—both new and newly relevant—would suggest evidence tampering.

Finally, Cooper presents a declaration of Christine Slonaker, who states that she was in a Chino Hills bar on the night of the murders. She says she encountered two blond Caucasian men—one in a light colored t-shirt and jeans, the other in overalls, and both wearing tennis shoes—who were inebriated and spotted with blood. The declaration is new evidence, dated February 7, 2004, and if believed, would further corroborate pre-existing but newly relevant evidence that Cooper was not the man who committed the Ryen/Hughes murders.

A. The Bloody Shoe Print

Only two pieces of evidence at trial directly connected Cooper to the Ryen house. One was a bloody tennis shoe print found on a sheet in Doug and Peggy's bedroom. The other was a single spot of blood found on a wall in the hallway.

Several people testified at trial about the shoe print found on the Ryens' bedsheet. Several testified that Cooper had a new or close-to-new pair of "Pro-Ked Dude" tennis shoes. One [*38] key witness testified that prints from a "Pro-Ked Dude" shoe were found on the sheet in the Ryen house, on the shower sill in the Lease house, and in the game room in the Lease house. "Pro-Ked Dude" tennis shoes are manufactured by Stride Rite solely for distribution in prisons and other institutions. They are not distributed to the general public.

The testimony of two witnesses, William Baird and James Taylor, was particularly important on this point. The California Supreme Court specifically discussed and relied on their testimony in sustaining Cooper's conviction on direct appeal. *People v. Cooper*, 53 Cal. 3d. 771, 797-98, 281 Cal. Rptr. 90, 809 P.2d 865 (1991).

William Baird was the Crime Laboratory Manager, in charge of collecting and analyzing evidence connected to the Ryen/Hughes murders. The sheet from the Ryens' bedroom was not initially thought to have any footprints. A bloody footprint was discovered on the sheet after it was taken to the lab. Baird's assistant, David Stockwell, testified that the foot-print could be seen when the sheet was folded the same way it had been folded when in the Ryens' bedroom (thereby bringing together two parts of the footprint that [*39] were separated when the sheet was flat). (Exhibit 191.)[4] Baird testified that the shoe print on the sheet matched two prints found in the Lease house, and that the prints had been made by a close-to-new "Pro-Ked Dude" shoe, made for and distributed only to prisons. (Exhs. 99, 210). Baird further testified that he had a close-to-new "Pro Ked Dude" shoe of approximately the same size in his lab, previously obtained from another prison. He testified that this shoe allowed him to analyze the print on the sheet and determine that it came from a prison-issued "Pro-Ked Dude" shoe. (Exh. 210.)

James Taylor was an inmate at the CIM during the time Cooper was incarcerated there. Taylor was a recreation attendant at the prison. As part of that job, he issued tennis shoes to inmates. Taylor testified at trial that he initially gave Cooper a pair of "P.F. Flyer" tennis shoes. He testified that Cooper, then imprisoned [*40] under the false name of David Trautman, exchanged his "P.F. Flyers" for a pair of black "Pro-Ked Dudes" a few days before he was transferred to the minimum security area. (Exh. 103.) Cooper escaped from the prison soon after he was transferred to the minimum security area.

Cooper attaches two recent declarations as exhibits to the habeas petition he seeks to file. The first is a handwritten sworn declaration of James Taylor, dated January 8, 2004, which states:

> 1. I was an inmate at the Reception Center West (RC-W) at the California Institute for Men in Chino California in May and June of 1983.

> 2. During that period of time, I met David Trautman, whose real name I understand to be Kevin Cooper. I met Kevin when he tried out for the basketball team. My job at the prison was recreation attendant. I was responsible for issuing basketball shoes to men in our unit who played on the team.

> 3. I issued only one pair of shoes to Kevin Cooper. I issued him a pair of P.F. Flyers. This brand was the best brand of shoe for basketball that the prison stocked. Kevin did not trade these shoes in to me for a pair of Keds, nor did he trade these shoes in to me for any other pair. (Exh. [*41] 100.)

Second, and more important, Cooper attaches a sworn declaration of Midge Carroll, who was Warden of CIM at Chino while Cooper was incarcerated there. Warden Carroll's declaration, dated January 30, 2004, states:

> 1. I was the Superintendent, or Warden, of the California Institution for Men at Chino, California, from 1982 through 1985. As Warden of this state penal facility, I had extensive contact with members of the San Bernardino Sheriff's Department who were responsible for the investigation of Kevin Cooper as a suspect in what became known as the Chino Hills Murders.
>
> 2. I was employed by the California Department of Corrections from 1966 until I permanently retired in 1999. . . .
>
> 3. As the Warden of the California Institute for Men at Chino, my contact with San Bernardino County deputy sheriffs about aspects of the investigation in the Kevin Cooper case included conversations with one of the lead detectives about shoeprint evidence found at the crime scene. I communicated to one of the lead investigators that the notion that the shoeprints in question likely came only from a prison-issue tennis shoe was inaccurate. I came to this conclusion after conducting a personal [*42] inquiry of the appropriate staff, including the deputy warden, the business manager responsible for procurement, and the personnel responsible for warehousing. I learned that the shoes we carried were not prison-manufactured or specially designed prison-issue shoes. I learned that the shoes were common tennis shoes available to the general public through Sears and Roebuck and other such retail stores. I passed this information along to the detective. Had I been contacted, I would have testified to this on behalf of either the prosecution or defense, and I would have provided supporting documentation.

(Exh. 101.)

Both the Taylor and the Carroll declarations are newly discovered evidence. The Taylor declaration, by itself, is not particularly helpful to Cooper. It is, of course, a recantation of extremely important evidence introduced at trial, but a mere recantation by a non-governmental agent, absent an accompanying constitutional violation, is not a sufficient ground for habeas relief.

The Carroll declaration, on the other hand, discloses a clear *Brady* violation. Under *Brady v. Maryland,* 373 U.S. 83, 10 L. Ed. 2d 215, 83 S. Ct. 1194 (1963), the prosecution has a constitutional [*43] obligation to turn material exculpatory evidence over to the defendant. This obligation is independent of any specific request by the defendant for such information. *United States v. Agurs,* 427 U.S. 97, 107, 49 L. Ed. 2d 342, 96 S. Ct. 2392 (1976). The duty extends to impeachment as well as exculpatory evidence. Evidence is material "if there is a reasonable probability that, had the evidence been disclosed to the defense, the result of the proceeding would have been different." *United States v. Bagley,* 473 U.S. 667, 676, 87 L. Ed. 2d 481, 105 S. Ct. 3375 (1985); *see also Strickler v. Greene,* 527 U.S. 263, 280, 144 L. Ed. 2d 286, 119 S. Ct. 1936 (1999); *Kyles v. Whitley,* 514 U.S. 419, 433-34, 131 L. Ed. 2d 490, 115 S. Ct. 1555 (1995).

The significance of Warden Carroll's communication must have been clear to the San Bernardino Sheriff's Department investigators. They knew they had little or no direct evidence connecting Cooper to the Ryen house. The "Pro-Ked Dude" tennis shoe print provided that evidence. Because of the testimony of Baird and Taylor, the State was able to tell a damaging story about the presence of a bloody "Pro-Ked Dude" footprint in the bedroom of the murder victims, [*44] a footprint only Cooper, an escaped prisoner, could have left. But if Warden Carroll had been put on the stand and had been believed by the jury, the State's story would have been shown to be untrue.

The failure of the State to provide Cooper with the information that Warden Carroll gave to the San Bernardino Sheriff's Department, and that she now provides in her declaration, was unquestionably a *Brady* violation. Such a *Brady* violation meets the threshold requirement in 28 U.S.C. § 2244(b)(2)(B)(i) that "the factual predicate for the claim could not have been discovered previously through the exercise of due diligence."

It is the State's withholding of the Warden's evidence, rather than any lack of diligence, that explains why Cooper's attorneys have not presented this evidence before. *See Jaramillo v. Stewart*, 340 F.3d 877, 882 (9th Cir. 2003) (explaining in the context of cause for procedural default that failure to discovery a *Brady* claim lies with the state if the petitioner had no reason to know of state's withholding); *cf. Strickler*, 527 U.S. at 287-88 ("[A] defendant cannot conduct the 'reasonable and [*45] diligent investigation' . . . to preclude a finding of procedural default when the evidence is in the hands of the state."); *Julius v. Jones*, 875 F.2d 1520, 1525 (11th Cir.), *cert. denied*, 493 U.S. 900, 107 L. Ed. 2d 207, 110 S. Ct. 258 (1989) (*Brady* claim not procedurally barred because defendant may "rely on a belief that prosecutors will comply with the Constitution and will produce *Brady* material on request"). If the Warden's declaration is believed, the State misled Cooper's attorneys by asserting that the prison issued "Pro-Ked Dude" shoes. We should not penalize Cooper by transforming the State's constitutional violation into Cooper's lack of diligence.

B. DNA Testing

As soon as DNA testing became technologically possible, Cooper asked that it be done on the evidence in his case. The State finally consented to DNA testing on three items: a spot of blood found in the hall of the Ryen house; a t-shirt found beside the road three days after the murders; and two hand-rolled cigarette butts the State purportedly found in the Ryens' abandoned station wagon in Long Beach, California.

The DNA testing was performed by a laboratory of the California Department [*46] of Justice in Berkeley, California in 2001. The result was a positive match for Cooper for all three items. Cooper seeks to present newly discovered evidence surrounding the DNA testing. Cooper also seeks to present previously known but newly relevant evidence—evidence that takes on a new meaning in light of the DNA testing.

1. The Blood Spot from the Hall

A blood spot, marked in evidence as A-41, was taken from the hall in the Ryen house. Daniel Gregonis, the criminologist for the San Bernardino Sheriff's Department, testified at trial that this blood was consistent with Cooper's. Gregonis was impeached at trial based on deficiencies in his testing of the physical evidence, particularly including the A-41 spot.

Cooper presents newly discovered evidence of tampering with A-41 prior to DNA testing. When it came time for the DNA testing, Cooper's defense team noticed that Gregonis had simultaneously checked out A-41, as well as samples of Cooper's blood and saliva, for a 24-hour period on August 13 and 14, 1999. (Exh. 146.) According to Gregonis, this was done at the direction of the District Attorney in order to determine whether A-41 still existed. (Exh. 105.) Although [*47] Gregonis claims that he did not open the glass bindle that contained the pillbox that contained the A-41 sample when it arrived for testing at the DNA lab in 2001, Gregonis's initials were present on the tape that seals the package. (Exhs. 36, 38, 94.) In common laboratory practice, a seal with an individual's initials on it indicates that the individual opened a bag, and constitutes the only record of the evidence bag being opened. (Exh. 106.) The presence of Gregonis's initials suggests that, contrary to his sworn testimony, Gregonis opened the bag containing A-41. Further, the seal protecting A-41 from contamination was different when counsel viewed it in 2001, compared to when it was viewed in 1998. (Exhs. 36, 38.)

Cooper also presents evidence, not available at trial, that the sample has changed physical form since the trial. In 1995, A-41 consisted of plaster chips in a metal pillbox. In 1998, however, it consisted of a capped vial that contained white chips and the metal pillbox, inside of which was a smaller vial containing more white chips. In 2001, A-41 consisted of a vial with white chips and a metal pillbox with an empty vial inside.

The evidence of tampering with A-41 was [*48] not available to the defense at the time of trial. Moreover, Cooper presented this evidence to the California courts as soon as they learned of it, when DNA testing occurred in 2001. Cooper's counsel could not have reasonably been expected spontaneously and repeatedly to check all of the evidence logs when there was no reason for the State to have checked out the evidence. Rather, they discovered that Gregonis had accessed the evidence when the sample was taken to be tested in 2001. They raised the issue before the state courts soon thereafter.

This newly discovered evidence suggests the possibility that A-41 was contaminated with Cooper's blood or saliva, both of which he had also checked out at the same time. Such contamination would, of course, invalidate the results of the DNA testing. The newly discovered evidence of tampering is particularly important when considered in light of other mishandling of evidence adduced at trial. Gregonis testified that he had conducted a blind study of A-41, in which he tested the sample without knowing that Cooper was a suspect. (Ex. 147.) However, his own notes belie that fact. He knew Cooper was a suspect and had a sample of his semen by which [*49] he would have known which enzymes in the blood in A-41 would tie Cooper to the sample.

This was not the only time Gregonis may have used an improper scientific technique or contradicted himself at trial. When Gregonis conducted further testing, he did so by placing A-41 and Cooper's blood side-by-side for comparison. Although he initially denied doing so, he changed testimony when given his own laboratory notes that indicated otherwise. (Exh. 151.) Reflecting the problems of not having performed a blind study, Gregonis apparently changed his initial results of tests on A-41 so that Mr. Cooper's enzyme profile would match that of the donor of the A-41 sample, admitting that he had changed his notes after the fact only when confronted by counsel at trial. (Exhs. 152, 12.)

2. The Bloody T-Shirt

Cooper presents no newly discovered evidence directly relevant to the bloody t-shirt. As already recounted, however, Cooper has presented newly discovered evidence suggesting that the "Pro-Ked Dude" shoe print on the sheet from the Ryens' bedroom may have been fabricated. Cooper has also presented evidence from which one may draw a conclusion of possible tampering with the A-41 sample. The inference [*50] of tampering with that sample is, of course, made stronger if it is shown that the same was done with other evidence.

As detailed below, there is also already-known evidence linking the t-shirt to a potential suspect, Eugene Leland ("Lee") Furrow. Furrow's girlfriend, Diana Roper, and Roper's sister, Karee Kellison, have provided declarations stating that Furrow came home early in the morning on the night of the murders, driven in a brown station wagon containing several people. Previously that evening, Furrow had been wearing a Fruit-of-the-Loom t-shirt that Roper described as identical to the bloody t-shirt found beside the road and introduced into evidence. Furrow was no longer wearing the t-shirt. Instead, he was wearing coveralls that were spattered with blood. Furrow took off the coveralls, put them in the closet, and departed quickly. Roper strongly suspected that Furrow was involved in the Ryen/Hughes murders and turned the coveralls in to the police. As will be recounted below, these coveralls were never turned over to the defense, but were, instead, thrown away by the police into a dumpster.

Cooper has not been able to determine the precise mechanism by which his blood [*51] might have been placed after the fact on the t-shirt. However, he has provided enough evidence, both newly discovered and already known, to raise a reasonable suspicion that there has been tampering with the t-shirt.

3. The Hand-Rolled Cigarettes

Cooper presents newly discovered evidence that the hand-rolled cigarette butts tested for the presence of his DNA were not those introduced as evidence at trial in 1984. One of the butts, designated V-12, had measured 4 mm long when it was introduced at trial. (Exh. 95.) However, when it was tested in 2001 for the presence of Cooper's DNA, that same butt measured 7 mm in length. (Exh. 98.) This suggests either mishandling or tampering, and calls into question the DNA test linking Cooper to the Ryens' station wagon in which the butts were supposedly found. As with the A-41 sample, Cooper had no reason to check the length of the cigarette butt until the DNA testing occurred.

The import of this new evidence becomes clear in light of evidence available at trial that the origin of the cigarette butts was questionable, and that the butts, like other evidence, changed in form between trial and DNA testing. The circumstances of how the cigarette [*52] butts were found is somewhat suspicious. Although police found in the Lease house several cigarette butts of the type ultimately found in the Ryen car in Long Beach, only one of those cigarette butts was logged into evidence. (Exhs. 33, 18.) During an initial investigation of the station wagon, Detective Hall made no mention of any hand-rolled cigarette butts of the type smoked by Cooper. He did, however, find and inventory other small pieces of evidence in the area in which the cigarette butts were ultimately found. (Exh. 17.) Further, Detective Hall found other cigarettes in the car, although these cigarettes were subsequently lost. Only during a second search of the car, conducted by other criminologists, was one cigarette butt of a type issued in prisons found. (Exh. 22.) This is the butt (V-12) on which the DNA testing was done.

V-12 appears to have been mishandled before and during trial. During a pre-trial hearing on July 12, 1984, Gregonis testified that V-12 appeared to have been Cooper's. However, he said that independent verification of this fact would be impossible due to the fact that he "exhausted the sample." (Exh. 169.) However, V-12 appeared at trial, albeit not in [*53] cigarette form but rather in a metal container containing tobacco and the tobacco paper. (Exh. 97.) This disappearance and reappearance of V-12 is similar to the disappearance and reappearance of A-41, the blood spot which was also supposedly exhausted, only to reappear when further testing was needed. (Exhs. 12, 153.)

Given this evidence of mishandling, it is a permissible inference that the cigarette butt tested for DNA was not actually the butt introduced at trial; that the tested butt had not been found in the Ryens' car in Long Beach; or that, in any event, the cigarette butt evidence had been so mishandled as to render any DNA test, at the very least, unreliable.

C. Slonaker Declaration

In a declaration dated February 7, 2004, Christine Slonaker provides new information about the night of the Ryen/Hughes murders. (Exh. 212.) Slonaker recounts that on that night, she was with two friends at the Canyon Corral Bar in Chino Hills, and two men came into the bar. "Both men were Caucasian and had blond hair. One of them was wearing a light colored t-shirt and jeans. The other man was wearing overalls. Both men were wearing tennis shoes . . . they appeared to be under the influence of [*54] drugs." From afar, she thought that they were covered in mud, but they approached her and her friends, and while they were engaged in conversation, Slonaker realized that it was not mud. "The spots on them were blood. Most of the blood was on their shoes and the front portion of their clothes. They also had blood splatters on their face and arms." Slonaker recalls asking them: "Do you realized you are covered in blood?" One of Slonaker's friends also told one of the men: "Get off of me. You're covered in blood."

Slonaker recounts that the men were refused service, and escorted out of the bar. Shortly thereafter, a police officer arrived at the bar. The following morning, Slonaker heard about the Ryen/Hughes murders, but did not report what she had seen because she assumed that the police had been aware of the two strange men after seeing an officer that night at the bar.

The Slonaker declaration is a new piece of evidence suggesting that someone other than Cooper committed the Ryen/ Hughes murders. It corroborates and reinforces evidence discussed below.

IV. Other Evidence

The newly discovered evidence, particularly the *Brady* evidence introduced by the Carroll declaration, substantially [*55] changes the State's case against Cooper. Under either 28 U.S.C. § 2244(b)(2)(B)(ii) or *Schlup*, our task is to evaluate the newly discovered evidence in light of all the other evidence in the record. In the material that follows, I summarize both evidence that was presented at trial and evidence that has been unearthed since then. Viewing the totality of this evidence in light of the Carroll declaration, I conclude that Cooper has made out a *prima facie* case that entitles him to file his second or successive petition for habeas corpus.

Warden Carroll's declaration casts doubt on the authenticity of the shoe print on the sheet taken from the Ryens' bedroom. The State knew from Warden Carroll that the prison did not have special prison-issue shoes. Nevertheless, the State put on witnesses testifying to precisely the contrary. William Baird, the Crime Laboratory Manager, testified that he had a "Pro-Ked Dude" shoe in his lab, to which he matched the "Pro-Ked Dude" print on the Ryens' sheet. But we now know from Warden Carroll that it was highly unlikely for there to have been a "Pro-Ked Dude" print on the sheet, because "Pro-Ked Shoes" are special-issue [*56] prison shoes. We also know from Warden Carroll that Cooper could not have had such shoes, and we know that there is no reasonable possibility that anyone else would have had such shoes. Failing to turn over this information was a clear *Brady* violation, and the reliability of the "Pro-Ked Dude" evidence was undermined.

The following is the evidentiary picture into which we must fit this new knowledge. We know that during the night of June 4, 1983, the members of the Ryen household were viciously attacked, and that four out of the five members of the household were killed. Josh, the Ryens' eight-year-old son, survived. Josh had been cut in the throat and was unable to speak when he was first taken to the hospital. But he was able to communicate by pointing to letters and numbers. He told his interviewers that three or four men had done the killings. (Exhs. 53, 54, and 55.) He was separately asked if any of the men were black or had dark skin. He said no. (Exh. 53.) While still in the hospital, he saw a picture of Cooper on television. He said that Cooper had not done it. (Exh. 60.) Detective Hector O'Campo took notes of the interviews. He left out of his notes Josh's statements about [*57] multiple killers. (Exh. 68.) Several other people in the hospital (including a nurse, a doctor, and his grandmother) heard Josh say that there were multiple killers, and that he had never seen Cooper before. (Exhs. 57, 59, 61.)

A year and a half later, Josh testified by videotape that Cooper had done the killing. At trial, he recounted seeing a man with a "puff of hair." At the time of his arrest, a month and a half after the murders, Cooper wore his hair in an Afro; Cooper was seen on television at the time of his arrest in his Afro. However, at the time he escaped from prison, Cooper wore his hair in braids. (Exh. 73.) There were no recovered hairs from a black person in the Lease house, indicating that Cooper had not combed out his braids in the house. (Exh. 167.)

The pathologist who performed autopsies on the victims initially believed that multiple people had done the killings, given the number and varied nature of the wounds. (Exh. 63.) He later testified that the killings could have been done by a single person, and testified that he only considered this after it was suggested to him by investigating officers. (Exh. 63.)

A blood-stained hatchet was found beside the road some [*58] distance from the house. A beige Fruit-of-the-Loom t-shirt was also found beside the road (at a different location) about 3 days after the killings. Cooper did not have such a t-shirt when he left prison, and the owner/occupants of the Lease house had no such t-shirt. (Exh. 29.) There was also no evidence that the t-shirt came from the Ryen house.

The Ryens kept a truck and a brown station wagon in their driveway. They left their keys in the ignitions of both vehicles. (Exh. 78.) After the murders, the brown station wagon was missing. It was found several days later (different witnesses testify to different dates) in a church parking lot in Long Beach. (Exh. 17.) Long Beach is on the coast, just south of Los Angeles. It is almost 50 miles due west of Chino Hills. Tijuana, where Cooper checked into a hotel at 4:30 pm on June 5, is just across the border into Mexico, slightly over 100 miles south of Chino Hills.

Nothing appears to have been taken from the Ryen house. Money left exposed on the counter remained. (Exh. 79.) Peggy Ryen's purse, containing money and numerous credit cards, was left undisturbed. (Exh. 78.)

The police testified that the following things were found in the [*59] Lease house: hand-rolled cigarettes butts with a type of tobacco issued in California prisons; a blood-stained button consistent with those found on jackets issued by California prisons; a blood-stained hatchet sheath; and evidence that there might have been some washed-away blood (visible through the use of "Luminol") in the shower and sink, and in spots in the hall that could have been footprints.

Although Cooper smoked many hand-rolled cigarettes while he was in the Lease house, only one was logged into evidence. (Exhs. 33, 167.) As discussed above, the State's handling of the cigarette butt evidence was dubious. The hatchet sheath was found in plain sight on a bedroom floor during a second search of the Lease house, but that was after it had been searched previously and the sheath was not detected. The police officer who had previously searched the bedroom denied that he had been in it; however, his finger-prints were found on a closet in the bedroom.

The evidence presented by the State of washed-away blood is also weak. Luminol reacts to blood, but also to certain metals, vegetable matter, and cleaning agents. It is impossible to tell without follow-up testing which of the possible [*60] reactants is causing the reaction. Furthermore, Luminol is extremely sensitive, detecting at a sensitivity level of between 1 part per million and 1 part per ten million. It can detect reactants that have existed unnoticed for years and after many washings. The fact that Luminol reacted with the sink and shower does not even establish clearly that there was any blood in them, let alone when it had been deposited.

Cooper's blood was not found in the Ryen house, except (perhaps) on the disputed spot on the wall in the hallway, A-41. That spot was tested and mishandled by state criminalist, Daniel Gregonis, as described above.

Not only is the evidence that was presented by the State at trial weak, there is also considerable evidence that the Ryen/ Hughes murders were committed by three other men. In a declaration dated November 21, 1998, Diana Roper told the following story which was never presented at trial: during the early morning hours on the night of the murders, her then-boyfriend, Lee Furrow, came home, in a car driven by others. "Lee and Debbie walked through the front door. They were in a hurry. I heard the car depart. Lee was wearing long sleeve coveralls with a zipper in the [*61] front. The coveralls were splattered with blood. . . . He did not have the beige T-shirt or Levis on that he was wearing earlier in the day." (Exh. 82.) Furrow left the coveralls and quickly departed with Debbie on a motorcycle. (*Id.*)

Roper recounted that the bloody t-shirt introduced into evidence was similar to the t-shirt Furrow had worn the day of the murders: "The T-shirt in this photograph looks exactly like the T-shirt Lee was wearing on June 4, 1983 including the manufacturer, the size, the color and the pocket. I am absolutely positive the photograph of this T-shirt matches the T-shirt that Lee was wearing at our house the afternoon of June 4, 1983." (*Id.*) According to Roper, this was the same t-shirt she had previously bought for Furrow.

It is unclear, by contrast, how Cooper would have obtained a t-shirt like the one later found bloodied. No Fruit-of-the-Loom t-shirts were distributed at the prison. The occupants of the Lease house have provided evidence that none of them had such a t-shirt. And there was no such t-shirt in the Ryen house.

Roper also thought that she recognized the hatchet: "[A] few days after the murders I heard on the news that a hatchet was [*62] found near the crime scene in Chino. I immediately walked to the washer area of our house. Lee's hatchet was missing. . . . The hatchet [introduced into evidence at the trial] looks like the hatchet . . . , which I found missing after the Ryen/Hughes murders. I cannot say for sure if it is the same hatchet that Lee owned but the curvature of the handle is the same. Even more striking in similarity than the curvature of the handle is the style of the handle, which has a sort of an American Indian pattern to it." (*Id.*)

In the same declaration, Roper recounted: "Prior to meeting me, Lee was convicted of the murder of Mary Sue Kitts. Lee confided in me that he not only killed Mary Sue Kitts, but he also dismembered her body and threw the body parts in the Kern River." (*Id.*) Furrow strangled Mary Sue Kitts at the direction of Clarence Ray Allen. *People v. Allen,* 42 Cal. 3d. 1222, 1237-38, 232 Cal. Rptr. 849, 729 P.2d 115 (1986). Allen is currently held under sentence of death in a California prison.

Roper's sister Karee Kellison was in the house with Roper that night. In a declaration dated November 15, 1998, Kellison recounted the same story about the arrival and departure of [*63] Lee and Debbie. "Lee was wearing long sleeve coveralls, which were spattered with blood." (Exh. 197.) She also recounted, "I saw Lee and Debbie get out of a car. There was not sufficient light to identify who the other occupants in the car were. However, there was enough light to see that it was a station wagon, kind of brown in color." (*Id.*)

Christine Slonaker's February 7, 2004 declaration, (Exh. 212.), corroborates Roper's and Kellison's accounts of the night of the Ryen/Hughes murders. Slonaker encountered two Caucasian men—one wearing a light-colored t-shirt—at the Canyon Corral Bar in Chino Hills on the night of the murders, both of whom were covered in blood. Slonaker's account is supported by pre-existing evidence from Canyon Corral Bar employees. The bartender and manager testified that Caucasian men, whom they described as being extremely inebriated, had been in the bar on the night of the murders, one wearing a light-colored or beige t-shirt. (Exhs. 30, 31.) The bartender testified that the men were refused service and asked to leave the bar, corroborating Slonaker's account.

After Roper heard about the murders, Roper called her father to ask him to come to her [*64] house to confirm her opinion that they were spattered with blood. He agreed with her that they were. Five days after the murders, Roper gave the coveralls to Detective Eckley and told him that she thought they were connected to the Ryen/Hughes murders. Eckley then contacted Detective Benge, who instructed him to write a report and forward it to Sergeant Arthur, the chief investigating officer in the homicide division. (Exh. 194.) On June 10, 1983, Sergeant Stodelle told Arthur about the contents of Eckley's report about the coveralls. (Exh. 200.) Eckley's report clearly recounts Roper's story that Furrow had come home with the bloody coveralls on the night of the murder; that he had left them in the closet at her house; that he had been paroled three years before from his sentence for killing Mary Sue Kitts; and that she believed that the coveralls were connected to the Ryen/Hughes murders. (Exh. 194.)

Arthur made no attempt to recover the coveralls from Eckley. (Exh. 83.) Eckley made several attempts to contact the homicide division in June and July 1983, but his telephone calls were not returned. (Exh. 185.) The preliminary hearing in Cooper's case began on November 9, 1983. On [*65] December 1, the day the defense began its presentation, Eckley threw away the coveralls in a dumpster. (Exh. 185.) In May 1984, the Kellison-Roper family contacted Cooper's trial counsel about the coveralls. This was the first information he had received about them. It was not until December 1998 that an investigator for Cooper discovered a disposition report for the coveralls. It contained the initials "K.S.," which suggests that Eckley did not act independently in disposing of the coveralls.

Independent information given investigators in 1984 by Anthony Wisely, then an inmate at Vacaville, develops more fully the account provided by Roper and Kellison. Wisely told Detective Woods on December 19, 1984, that he had smoked marijuana with a certain Kenneth Koon while in prison. (Exh. 85.) He recounted to Woods that Koon had told him that he had participated in the Ryen/Hughes murders. (*Id.*) Roper was romantically involved with both Koon and Furrow around the time of the murders.

In his report, Woods wrote that Wisely told him that Koon told him the following. Koon was with two other men that were in the BRAND or the Aryan Brotherhood, and they had driven to a residence in Chino [*66] on the night of the Ryen/ Hughes murders. Two men got out of the car and were in the house for about ten or fifteen minutes. One of the men was carrying two axes or hatchets, and also was wearing gloves. When the men returned to the car, one of them stated that "the debt was officially collected." Wisely said that "Koon thinks they hit the wrong house[.]" Koon said that one of the men involved "was very upset because they apparently had left one kid alive." (Exh. 85.)

Roper stated in her declaration, "I heard Lee say many times there are three rules to follow anytime you do a crime. They are wear gloves, never wear your own shoes and never leave a witness alive." (Exh. 82.) Nikol Gilberson, in a declaration signed November 21, 1998, stated that she was Lee Furrow's girlfriend from late 1983 to late 1984. She recounted in her affidavit that Lee Furrow "on several occasions" told her these same three rules.

This evidence against Cooper, taken as a whole and viewed in the light of the State's *Brady* violation, is extremely weak. There is also a plausible story told by Roper, Kellison, Slonaker and Koon (told through Wisely) that the true murderers are Furrow, Koon and another person. [*67] Cooper has clearly made out a *prima facie* case that entitles him to file his second or successive petition for habeas corpus.

V. Conclusion

Based on the foregoing I would authorize Cooper to file his proposed petition for habeas corpus. I would also grant a stay of execution.

Notes

[1] These facts are taken from *Cooper v. Calderon,* 255 F.3d 1104 (9th Cir. 2001).

[2] On Saturday night, February 7, at 11:18 p.m. Cooper's counsel transmitted to the court a February 7, 2004, declaration of Christine M. Slonaker. It relates her experience at the Canyon Corral Bar on the night of June 4–5, 1983. Others who were at the bar at the same time testified at trial about the behavior of three strangers who came to the bar that evening. To the extent that Slonaker's account twenty-one years later differs from that of other percipient witnesses, it just "serves to undercut the evidence presented at trial, not affirmatively to prove [Cooper's] innocence." *Carriger,* 132 F.3d at 477. If, on the other hand, the new evidence places Cooper's claim in "a significantly different and stronger evidentiary posture," then the state courts have to be given an opportunity to consider it "in the first instance." *Aiken v. Spalding,* 841 F.2d 881, 883-84 & n.3 (9th Cir. 1988). In that case, the federal courts could not consider it because Cooper has failed to exhaust his state remedies.

[3] *Brady v. Maryland,* 373 U.S. 83, 10 L. Ed. 2d 215, 83 S. Ct. 1194 (1963); *United States v. Agurs,* 427 U.S. 97, 49 L. Ed. 2d 342, 96 S. Ct. 2392 (1976).

[4] I refer to the exhibits as they are numbered in the habeas petition that Cooper now seeks permission to file.

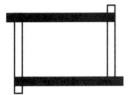

GLOSSARY

abstraction. The notion that as one's language becomes more general (less concrete) there is greater opportunity for confusion and obfuscation. For example, "writing implement" is more abstract than "pen."

ad hominem. A false attack on an advocate rather than on the advocate's argument. This is a fallacy of reasoning in which an individual offers criticism of an advocate as the grounds for rejecting the arguments of the advocate. It is considered a fallacy because the attacks on the advocate may have nothing to do with the wisdom of the arguments.

ad populum. A false appeal to the people. This is a fallacy of reasoning in which an advocate offers the agreement of most people as the grounds for a claim. It is considered a fallacy because the majority may be wrong.

adjacency pairs. Two statements that occur one right after the other and that are defined by their relationship to each other.

adversarial. A system of interactions that pits advocates against each other as opponents in order to test the quality and credibility of their claims.

affirmative. The side in an academic debate that advocates support for the resolution.

alternate use time. Time used by debaters to prepare for their next speech or cross-examination period.

ambiguity. The deliberate use of overly broad or unclear language to confuse or conceal an advocate's real thoughts or motives.

analysis. The separation of a claim into its constituent parts for individual study.

appeal to fear. A false appeal to the need for safety. This is a fallacy of reasoning in which an advocate offers a threat as the grounds for compliance with a demand. It is considered a fallacy because the threat of force denies the audience any real choice.

appeal to pity. A false appeal for sympathy. This is a fallacy of reasoning in which an advocate offers a request for sympathy as the grounds for a claim. It is considered a fallacy because the request for pity may have nothing to do with the wisdom of a claim.

appeal to tradition. A false appeal to the way things have historically been done. This is a fallacy of reasoning in which the advocate offers a history of behavior as the grounds for continuing to act in a particular manner. It is considered a fallacy because previous ways of doing things may not justify doing things the same way in the future.

arguing. The process of resolving differences of opinion through communication.

argument by analogy. A form of inference suggesting that if two things are alike in some respects they will also be alike in other respects.

argument by example. A claim that examines one or more specific cases and then generalizes to other like or similar cases.

argument from causal correlation. An argument that examines specific cases to identify a pattern of relationships between them that will permit a more general inference to be drawn.

argument from causal generalization. A claim that reasons deductively from a general claim that is presumed to be true to a specific case that is unknown.

argument from sign. A claim that identifies a substance and attribute relationship between a generalization and a specific case.

argument style. The manner in which one conducts himself or herself in an argument. Some arguers are passive and some are active.

argumentative metaphor. The epistemic function of metaphor. A linguistic device in which an advocate contends that phenomenon "A" should be seen as phenomenon "B."

arguments. The claims that people make when they are asserting their opinions and/or supporting their beliefs.

artistic proof. Support or grounds for a claim that originates with the advocate.

audience. The readers, listeners, or viewers reached by a speaker, a book, a broadcast, or some other form of communication.

backing. The support for an argumentative warrant.

begging the question. A fallacy of reasoning in which the advocate offers a restatement of the claim as the grounds for the claim. It is considered a fallacy because the advocate has not offered new information that constitutes support for the claim.

better definition standard. A means used in academic debate to determine which definition, when there are competing definitions, should be used to interpret the resolution.

blame. The reason or cause for the existence of an ill; sometimes referred to as the inherent need.

breadth standard. An argument in academic debate concerning the means used to determine the better definition of terms in the resolution. For example, debaters may argue that broader resolutions are preferable and thus, the better definition is the one that provides the broadest interpretation.

brink. An element of a disadvantage. The argument that the present system is on a precipice and that the proposed action will push the system over the edge and thus result in some undesirable consequence.

burden of proof. The understanding that whoever advances an argumentative claim has the responsibility to provide evidentiary support for it. In academic debate, this refers to the expectation that the affirmative has the obligation to prove the resolution true.

burden of rejoinder. The obligation of the negative in an academic debate to disagree with or refute the affirmative position.

case flow. That part of the systematic note-taking process in academic debate in which the arguments dealing with the affirmative case are recorded.

character. The ethical integrity and personal qualities of a speaker or an actor in a story.

character type. The function and/or role the actor plays in an argument, for example, hero, villain, or victim.

characterological coherence. The ability of an actor in a story to act out his or her role in accordance with the audience's expectations for that role.

circumvention. An argument claiming that a proposal will not work because there exists a motive and a means for individuals to get around the intent of the proposal.

civil. Pertains to the rights of individuals and to legal proceedings concerning those rights.

claim. A conclusion of an argument.

clash. A sharply focused disagreement between rival positions.

coalitions. Alliances of factions.

comparative advantage case. A set of arguments through which an advocate demonstrates that there is an advantage to the adoption of the advocated policy when that policy is compared to the present system.

competence. A component of credibility. An audience's assessment of the capability and/or ability of a source or a witness to either make a specific observation to support a claim or to render a judgment.

competitiveness. A standard in academic debate for whether or not a counterplan should be accepted instead of the affirmative plan, whether or not the counterplan constitutes a reason to reject the resolution.

compromise. A settlement of differences. An accommodation reached between competing interests.

conclusion. The claim advanced in a syllogism.

conflict resolution. Tactics or strategies introduced to resolve problems and reduce tensions.

connotative meaning. The unique meaning given a symbol or word by an individual. The emotional or attitudinal meaning or meanings evoked in an individual by a particular symbol or word.

constructive speech. The speeches in an academic debate in which the debaters present the major arguments they will pursue in the debate.

context. An argument standard used in academic debate to determine the better definition of terms in the resolution. The view that such a standard should consider all of the other words in the resolution.

cost. The burdens or disadvantages that will be incurred if the proposed cure is enacted.

countercriteria. Criteria presented in an academic debate by the negative that are arguably better than the criteria selected by the affirmative.

counterplan. A plan advanced in academic debate by the negative as a replacement for the plan offered by the affirmative. It must be competitive and nontopical.

credibility. The audience's assessment of the competence and trustworthiness of a source.

criminal. Pertains to the administration of penal law as distinct from civil law.

criteria. The method in a value debate for determining the value judgment contained in the value resolution.

criteria case. A set of arguments through which an advocate demonstrates that the advocated policy is superior to alternatives because it better achieves a specified standard or standards.

cross-examination. Close questioning in order to compare the answers given to previous answers. Used to refute or discredit an adversary's case in the courtroom and to resolve questions and clarify information in academic debates.

Cross-Examination Debate Association (CEDA). Created in 1971 as an alternative to NDT debate and uses a more persuasive and communicative delivery style.

cultural knowledge. Those things we know to be true because we have been taught they are true by our culture. The shared values and truths codified in the rules, principles, laws, or practices adhered to by a culture. The values and truths contained in the stories shared by the members of a culture.

cure. The proposed solution for resolving an ill or harm.

debate format. The nature of speeches. The speaking order and the time limits permitted for each speech in the specialized argumentative field of academic debate.

decision calculus. The process that applies the cost involved in mitigating an ill to arrive at the benefits attained.

deductive reasoning. Claims that entail moving from the general to the specific.

denotative meaning. The explicitly shared understanding of a symbol or word such as that found in a dictionary.

descriptive statistics. Numeric representations that describe an entire population.

descriptive testimony. Grounds for a claim that relate the observation of supposedly factual (verifiable) information.

direct examination. Close questioning in order to solicit answers that will be helpful to support the development of one's own case.

disadvantage. An argument advanced in an academic debate in which the advocate claims that undesirable consequences will result from a particular course of action.

discovery. That part of the investigation of a legal case that focuses on finding the "facts" that are relevant to the claim being advanced.

doublespeak. A pernicious use of euphemistic language to confuse or conceal an advocate's views.

empathic listening. The capacity for listening sympathetically. Trying to understand or experience by relating to the problems of others.

epistemic function of language. The concept that the language we learn and employ shapes and constrains our understanding of what constitutes reality.

equivocation. The use of language with multiple meanings to conceal an advocate's actual views; or when an arguer declines to take a clear position.

ethics. A set of moral principles or values. The moral dimensions and quality of conduct and discourse.

euphemism. The use of mild or inoffensive language in the place of language that might offend or suggest something that is unpleasant.

events. The actions engaged in by the characters in a story.

examples. Specific instances or occurrences of a given phenomenon used as the grounds for a claim.

external consistency. A test of the grounds for a claim. Is the testimony offered in support of a claim in agreement with the testimony of others?

fallacy of composition. A fallacy of reasoning in which an advocate argues that what is true of a part is true of the whole. It is considered a fallacy because a whole may or may not possess the qualities of the individual parts.

fallacy of division. A fallacy of reasoning in which an advocate argues that what is true of the whole is true of the component parts. It is considered a fallacy because a component may or may not possess the qualities of the whole.

fallacy of false dichotomy. A fallacy of reasoning in which an advocate falsely divides the situation into only two alternatives. It is considered a fallacy because there may be other alternatives in addition to the two indicated by the advocate.

false reasoning by analogy. A fallacy of reasoning in which an advocate implies that one thing is like another. It is considered a fallacy because the compared things may not be alike in a meaningful way or their attributes are not similar enough.

false reasoning by causal generalization. A fallacy of reasoning in which an advocate falsely applies general principles to a specific case. It is considered a fallacy because the general principles might not apply in the specific case cited.

false reasoning by sign. A fallacy of reasoning in which an advocate too quickly draws a conclusion from a limited number of signs. It is considered a fallacy because the signs cited may be too few from which to draw a conclusion.

fiat. The assumption in academic debate that an affirmative need only demonstrate that a proposal ought to be adopted, not that it would be adopted. The assumption that the plan in an academic debate would be adopted by normal means if it is proven desirable and that, therefore, the focus of the debate should be on the desirability of the proposal, not on whether the proposal would actually be adopted.

field definitions. An argument in academic debate concerning the means used to determine the better definition of terms in the resolution. The view that the better definition for a term or for multiple terms in a resolution is one that might typically be used by members of an appropriate discipline or field of inquiry that might consider similar issues or problems.

field-dependent. Arguments that meet the requirements for argumentative proof in one field.

field-invariant. Arguments that meet the requirements for argumentative proof in all fields.

fields. Areas of human activity or interest. This might also include disciplines and/or topics or specializations of study.

flowing. The systematic process of note taking in academic debate.

future narratives. Scenarios, hopes, dreams, or expectations for tomorrow.

general sources. References that provide a broad understanding of a controversy. Such references may require little prior knowledge of a controversy.

generative capability of metaphor. The ability of an audience to infer additional similarities between the two phenomena linked in an argumentative metaphor.

goals case. A set of arguments through which an advocate demonstrates that the advocated policy has a better chance of achieving the policy goals that the advocate desires to achieve than do the policies of the present system.

grounds. The foundation or basis for a claim.

hasty generalization. A fallacy of reasoning in which the advocate moves too quickly from examples to a generalization without sufficient rationale. It is considered a fallacy because the number of examples cited may not be sufficient to support the claim or be typical of the claim to which the advocate is generalizing.

historical narratives. Scenarios, plot-lines, and accounts of events that have already occurred.

ill. The harm or problems identified in the present system.

image. A concept or mental picture of someone that is held by the public.

impact. The consequence of any given argument on the resolution of the dispute. In academic debate, the overall effect of an argument on the outcome of the debate.

inartistic proof. Support or grounds for a claim that originates with someone other than the advocate.

inductive reasoning. Claims that entail moving from a specific case to more general conclusions.

inferential statistics. Numeric representations that describe a sample of a population and infer that what is true of the sample is true of the population.

inherency. A type of ill identified by an advocate when addressing stock issues in a policy argument. Inherency suggests the ill or problem will repeat itself unless there is a change in policy.

internal consistency. A test of the grounds for a claim. Is the testimony offered as grounds for a claim free from self-contradiction?

interpretive testimony. Grounds for a claim that relate the judgments of the advocate or a source provided by the advocate.

interval sampling. A technique used by researchers to ensure that each member of a population has an equal and independent probability of being selected. The selection of members of a population based upon their specific place in space or time.

intrinsicness. An argument in academic debate that the value object possesses inherent qualities that are causally related to the value judgment.

jargon. The specialized or technical language of a profession, trade, or class.

language. A shared symbol system.

limiting definition. An argument standard used in academic debate concerning the means used to determine the better definition of terms in the resolution. The view that the better definition for terms in a debate is the one provided by an advocate that best narrows and clarifies the focus of the resolution.

Lincoln-Douglas (L-D) debate. A debate format in which two individuals debate each other.

linear. A claim for a process of reasoning that refers to how one action or event might impact another. In a disadvantage argument, for example, the claim that the proposed action will move the present system some distance down a path and that each step in that direction is undesirable.

link. An element of a disadvantage. The claim offered by an advocate that there must be a causal relationship between the proposed action and any resulting disadvantageous consequence that may arguably be likely to occur.

loaded question. A question that indicates to a witness how he or she should answer the question.

major premise. The first statement provided in a syllogism. Typically, the major premise asserts a generalization that prescribes the category.

margin of error. The acknowledgment by opinion poll researchers that their statistics are not precise but occur within a range of plus or minus the specified error from the indicated statistic.

minor premise. The second statement that is asserted in a syllogism. Typically, the minor premise relates a specific case or class.

modality. The degree of certainty that an advocate has for a claim.

mutual exclusivity. One of the two tests of counterplan competitiveness in academic debate. To be a reason to reject the resolution, the counterplan must be unable to coexist with the plan.

myths. Real or fictional stories that appeal to the consciousness of a people by appealing to their cultural ideals.

narrative. Having the characteristics of a story. Accounts used by advocates that may contain the essential elements of a well-rounded plot-line. These may include, for example a statement about history and/or a vision of the future.

narrative fidelity. The degree to which a story "rings true" with experiences or with other stories that are believed or known to be true.

narrative probability. How believable a story is; how coherent it seems to be.

National Debate Tournament (NDT). The national championship tournament sponsored by the oldest intercollegiate debate association, created in 1947 at the U.S. Military Academy at West Point.

needs case. A set of arguments through which an advocate demonstrates there is a problem in the present system that justifies the adoption of the advocated policy.

negative. The side in an academic debate that advocates rejection of the resolution.

net benefits standard. One of the two tests of counterplan competitiveness in academic debate. To be a reason to reject the resolution, the counterplan must be more advantageous than the affirmative plan or than both the affirmative plan and the counterplan.

non sequitur. Any claim that "does not follow" from the grounds offered in support of the claim.

obfuscation. A deliberate attempt by an advocate to conceal his or her real argument.

objective facts. Facts that are knowable and uncontested.

obvious truths. Generalizations that are commonly shared and understood.

off-case flow. That part of the systematic note-taking process in academic debate in which the procedural arguments and the disadvantages are recorded.

operational definitions. Methods of defining terms in academic debate in which terms are not explicitly defined but can be derived from the totality of the arguments advanced.

organizational culture. The values, norms, and practices that characterize an institution.

ornamental metaphor. A figure of speech in which the advocate asks an audience to see that phenomenon "A" has some characteristic of phenomenon "B."

overreporting. A problem in the statistical description of a phenomenon that may be caused by incentives to identify and report the specific instances of the phenomenon.

parametrics. An aspect of procedural arguments in academic debate. The argument claims that an affirmative case does not need to prove the whole resolution is true; rather, the resolution merely serves to set the boundaries for what is or is not topical.

parliamentary debate. A debate format that is modeled after debate in the British Houses of Parliament.

permutation. A tactic in academic debate used by an affirmative to show that a counterplan is only artificially competitive.

personal knowledge. That which we know to be true because we have had firsthand experience with it.

plan spikes. Elements in an academic debate of an affirmative plan that are incorporated to preclude disadvantages of counterplans.

point of information. The moment in a parliamentary debate when one speaker interrupts another speaker either to ask a question or to seek clarification of an argument that has been presented.

point of order. The moment in a parliamentary debate when one speaker interrupts another speaker and alleges that a violation of established rules has occurred.

point of personal privilege. A moment in a parliamentary debate that occurs when one speaker interrupts another speaker and asks for the right either to interject a comment or perhaps to momentarily suspend the contest rules.

policy debate. A type of academic debate in which the resolution calls for a plan of action that changes the present system.

power. The ability or capacity to act. The degree of influence or control that one may assert over others in any given situation.

precedent. A judicial decision that may be used as a standard in deciding other similar cases.

precision standard. An argument in academic debate concerning the means used to determine the better definition of terms in the resolution. The view that the better definition is one that is arguably more specific or concrete.

premise. Grounds for a claim that makes use of points of agreement between advocates and audiences.

preponderance of evidence. The standard for ascertaining culpability in a civil dispute.

presence. The strategy of making an argument or a claim seem especially noteworthy or important so that it is clearly understood and deemed significant by the audience.

presumption. The belief that most people, most of the time, are comfortable with the way things are. The belief that current positions and/or policies should continue until a good reason is presented for change.

prima facie case. The obligation in academic debate of the advocate affirming the resolution to present a story that, on its first hearing, would meet the burdens necessary to persuade a reasonable audience that the resolution is true. A set of arguments that may be considered sufficient to overcome the presumptions that are held by a community composed of reasonable people.

procedural arguments. The arguments in an academic debate that must be resolved by the judge prior to consideration of the substantive issues. These are the arguments that determine the process by which the truth of the resolution will be determined.

proposition. A statement that expresses the subject and defines the grounds for dispute.

proposition of fact. A statement that asserts a claim known as a certainty.

proposition of policy. A statement that outlines a specific course of action.

proposition of value. A statement that asserts a principle, standard, or moral claim.

random sample. A subset of a population where each member of the population has an equal and independent probability of being selected.

reasonable doubt. Rational uncertainty.

rebuttal. The exceptions that might be offered to a claim; the opportunity to speak so as to be able to refute the arguments that have been offered by one's opponent in a debate.

recency. A test of the grounds for a claim. Has anything happened between the date of the testimony and the time the testimony is used by an advocate that would make the testimony invalid?

reducing to absurdity. One of the strategies of refutation by additional consideration in which the reasoning behind the argument to be refuted is taken to its logical and undesirable conclusion. This type of refutation is also known by its Latin name *reductio ad absurdum*.

refutation by additional consideration. The strategy of refutation in which the advocate argues that the arguments of another do not take into consideration the complete picture; the process in which an argument is rebutted by a demonstration that the outcome of accepting that argument is not desirable.

refutation by denial. The strategy of refutation in which the advocate attempts to prove that the claims offered by another are erroneous. This is a process in which an argument is rebutted by denying the validity of the argument.

refutation by mitigation. The strategy of refutation in which the advocate attempts to minimize the importance of another's arguments. In this form of argumentation the strength of an argument is reduced by counterarguments.

refutation process. A series of actions that culminate in the denial of the arguments advanced by another advocate.

reluctant testimony. Observations or judgments given grudgingly by a source because the testimony is contrary to the best interests of the source.

research. The supplementation of one's own knowledge with the facts and opinions of others.

research plan. A strategy for determining what additional information is needed and the best way to obtain it.

resistance. That force exerted to oppose or retard movement or change.

resolution. Another name for the proposition used in academic debate.

reverse voting issue. An argument presented by an affirmative in response to a topicality argument, claiming that the issue of topicality should be a voting issue for the negative as well as the affirmative in order to discourage frivolous topicality arguments.

rituals. Behaviors that have been repeated so often that the participants come to know and expect the performance of these behaviors.

role. A set of assumptions about how individuals or characters should act based on perceptions of an individual's position, occupation, behavior, and/or status.

scene. The images constructed by an advocate that describe the context in which the characters act.

self-esteem. One's sense of self, self-concept, and sense of personal worth.

shifting the burden of proof. A fallacy of reasoning in which the advocate challenges another to refute his or her argument rather than offer grounds in support of the claim. It is considered a fallacy because each advocate has the burden of proving his or her own claim.

should/would argument. To dispute in an academic debate whether the plan would be adopted, rather than whether it should be adopted. This is considered an illegitimate argument in academic debate because of fiat power.

simple random sampling. A technique used by researchers to ensure each member of a population has an equal and independent probability of being selected. This type of sampling may, for example, make use of a random numbers table to generate a statistical sample.

slippery slope. A false appeal to the inevitability of an undesirable outcome if a first step is taken. This is a fallacy of reasoning in which the advocate argues that an action should not be taken because it will eventually lead to some unwanted end. It is considered a fallacy because one action does not necessarily lead to subsequent actions.

solvency. The affirmative burden in academic debate to demonstrate that the proposed course of action will actually accrue the advantages claimed. This is also known as the stock issue of cure.

specialized sources. References that give a detailed understanding of an aspect of, or a particular side of, a controversy. These types of references are especially useful for convincing an audience that may already possess background information or knowledge on a controversy.

standards. The method to be used in academic debate for determining how an issue should be evaluated. This type of argument is often used in debates concerning whether or not a particular case falls within the topic of the resolution.

stasis. The issue or point where one chooses to clash with or challenge a claim.

statistics. Grounds for a claim in which descriptions are expressed in numeric terms.

status quo. Refers to the way things currently are.

stock issues. Arguments that naturally recur in disputes over propositions of policy. Topicality, ill, blame, cure, and cost are stock issues.

stories. Accounts of events; the plot; an allegation of the facts.

storytelling. The process of sharing accounts or stories.

stratified sampling. A technique used by researchers to generate a sample in which the researchers divide the population into groups or strata that they want to sample. A random sample is then generated for each stratum.

straw man fallacy. A fallacy of reasoning in which an advocate presents a weak argument of an opponent and, in refuting it, characterizes all of the opposing arguments as equally spurious. It is considered a fallacy because the advocate may perniciously select a particularly inadequate argument to refute.

substantive arguments. The arguments in an academic debate that deal with the truth of the resolution.

syllogism. A form of deductive reasoning that consists of a major premise, a minor premise, and a conclusion.

symbols. Special types of signs that represent something by association; the building blocks of a language system.

systems analysis. The evaluation of a group of interacting, interrelated and interdependent elements and the consideration of how these elements function together to achieve an outcome.

take out. An argument of refutation in academic debate that breaks, or takes out, a link in the chain of reasoning.

testimony. Grounds for a claim that makes use of the observations and/or judgments made by the advocate or a source cited by the advocate.

theory of the case. A view of the dispute that accounts for the evidence and offers an explanation for the events that occurred.

time frame. A test of statistics that considers the time period described by the statistics. An element of a disadvantage concerning when the adverse consequences of a course of action will occur.

topicality argument. An obligation in an academic debate that the affirmative's arguments prove the specific resolution true. A negative debater who believed the affirmative was proving a different resolution true would challenge the affirmative's topicality.

Toulmin model. A tool to diagram and break down an argument developed by Stephen Toulmin, this model dissects an argument into its constituent parts to reveal the reasoning process.

trustworthiness. A component of credibility, and an audience's assessment of the integrity of a source.

tu quoque. Literally "you're another." The fallacy of reasoning in which an advocate defends his or her actions by pointing out that others acted in a similar fashion. It is considered a fallacy because the actions of others are frequently irrelevant to whether or not one's actions are responsible.

turnaround. An argument in academic debate in which a debater argues that a disadvantage is actually an advantage, or vice versa. This refutation technique is also known in nondebate contexts as turning the tables.

turning the tables. One of the strategies of refutation by additional consideration in which the advocate argues that the undesirable consequences identified by another advocate are actually desirable.

underreporting. A problem in the statistical description of a phenomenon caused by disincentives to report, identify, or announce the specific instances of the phenomenon.

unique. An element of a disadvantage. This argument claims that for a disadvantage to be proven true the proposed policy action must be demonstrated to be the sole cause of the identified disadvantageous consequence.

unique meaning standard. An argument in academic debate concerning the means used to determine the better definition of terms in the resolution. The view that the better definition is the one that does not render a word in the resolution meaningless.

universal audience. An abstract audience created by an arguer as a reference point for testing one's argumentative claims. Arguments appealing to a universal audience would be compelling, self-evident, timeless, and independent of local or historical contingencies.

value debate. A type of academic debate in which the resolution calls for a change in the value structure of the status quo.

value objection. An argument in a value debate claiming that the value or value hierarchy presented should be rejected because it is an undesirable value or value hierarchy.

values. Principles, standards, or qualities that are considered to be important.

verbal aggression. The tendency to attack one's opponent in an argument by using very confrontational and personal arguments.

verifiability. A test of grounds for a claim. Is the source offered as the grounds for a claim properly identified and available to all?

violation. A component of a topicality argument. This argument identifies the specific term in the resolution that the negative believes the affirmative has misinterpreted.

visual aids. Charts, graphs, photos, and other material that help to pictorially communicate information.

warrant. The reasoning that authorizes the inferential leap from the grounds to the claim.

whole resolution. An argument in academic debate that the affirmative must prove the truth of the entire resolution, not just an example or examples of the resolution.

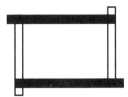

INDEX